CW00665427

Reliable four-by-four at 25°30N, 05°40'E.
Informed, reliable driving applies wherever you are.

Published by Desert Winds

Four-by-four driving

Third edition

Tom Sheppard

Author's note for the third edition

I hadn't expected the last edition to sell out in little over a year. I hadn't expected there to be anything significant to revise either. Wrong again.

Much, of course, remains unchanged. The basics, the need to understand, the mechanical sympathy and the off-road principles, for instance, are pretty much as they have always been and will stay so. Having said that, the increasing provision of 'traction control' drivelines that reduce or stop single-wheel spin across an axle is certainly making life easier if one wheel is off-loaded or on a low-grip surface. With differing degrees of effectiveness, it's becoming a standard feature in both 'soft-roaders' and what may be called 'the real thing'.

The marketplace – both sides of it, the sellers and the buyers – is at last recognising the benefits of four-wheel drive.

So there are more 4x4s out there. And ('ITDS' – see back cover) driveline technology is getting spread thinner, and with more tiny variations, over more models. Sadly it's often accompanied by – how can I put it? – 'somewhat oblique' PR output and dumbed-down product presentation by the brochure writers: usually an impenetrable fog of generalities and toy-worship that needs dissection and a little more down-to-earth analysis.

Technicalities and drivelines matter: see Section 2.

For overlanders the necessary and laudable advances in emissions control can bring fuel compatability problems in their wake if your vehicle complies with the latest Euro-regulations. Section 7 explains most of it.

As ever, hats off to the engineers; the people who actually design and make this stuff. I hope you find the book useful.

TS

Third edition, published 2013

ISBN 978-0-9532324-9-9

Contents:

KINGS ARMS

SECTION 3. 4x4 DRIVING – PRELIMINARIES

SECTION 4. OFF-ROAD TECHNIQUES

SECTION 5. RECOVERY

SECTION 6. ADVANCED DRIVING

This book ...

First-timers, macho men, busy mums. This book is aimed at first-time four-by-four drivers and fleet users alike – a wide span of folk who have a surprising amount in common. Whether you are tip-toeing into the water or working hard at the deep end, it helps in both cases to know, or be reminded of, the principles of swimming. Since the standard licence test doesn't cover much off-road driving, there's quite a bit on that here but the book also has much to make on-roaders nod , smile and feel newly enlightened.

Know what you are buying. The aim of the book is to distil the essence of what makes 'four-by-fours' different from normal cars and how to take best advantage of it – there's more to it than just the height and weight of the vehicle. With the Catherine-wheel of fancy trade names, bloated styling, side-rails, extravagant wheels, ridiculous tyres and electronic tinsel, those restless marketing people have to maintain the illusion of something new – and, naturally, more complicated. This book keeps a steady eye on the fundamentals all the time and points out in the friendliest way what isn't particularly new, explains what it is really all about and distinguishes between essentials and confectionery.

Wide, blurred market. The 4x4 market now covers a wide span of application. Increasingly manufacturers recognise the benefits of sharing the power between all four wheels, even on small, decidedly on-road cars. Nor, despite the band-wagonners pointing accusing fingers at 'non-politically correct 4x4s', does it take much to differentiate between what is needlessly heavy and thirsty for the job it does and a modest, fuel-efficient vehicle that just happens to benefit from four-wheel drive. But there are, of course, people who do need a highly capable off-road performer for which four-wheel drive is just the first weapon in the armoury.

4x4 systems. Is your 4x4 actually in four-wheel drive all the time? If not, why not and how is it engaged? (Yes, it does help to know even if you just go to the supermarket.) Can you use 4x4 anywhere? Do you actually need it on the highway? What about the 'little gear lever' or the twisty knob? Amazingly, many motoring magazine 'road tests' ignore these points – as do some manufacturers' presentations. Droning media comment about the plastics, the cup holders, the iPod dock or the stitching on the upholstery often leave no space for the fundamentals.

But I never go off-road ... ! Does the 4x4 system actually matter? Do I need to know? Yes; it really does help. Despite all the fancy trade names like Supa-Tork or Megga-Grip and parroted clichés about 'directing torque to the wheel that most needs it ... ' there are only three basic types of 4x4 and, as Sec 2.3 shows, the concepts are very simple.

... and I do (go off-road)! The off-road techniques outlined in this book will help you realise the fullest potential of your off-roader. They'll make your driving as safe and relaxed as possible, ensure that in difficult conditions you get stuck as infrequently as possible, hazard your vehicle as little as possible and that you damage it not at all.

Using the book. You will not carry all of this book in your head. Reading it, you will not only get to know the strengths and limitations of your vehicle but you will learn how to read the ground and apply the variations of technique you will encounter. Soon it will be instinctive; you will have written your own book.

Manual and automatic transmission. Because manual transmissions require more detailed description, the emphasis in this book should not be interpreted as favouring that technology. Automatic transmission has enormous advantages. Used on- or off-road, it is very driver- and vehicle-friendly. A well-

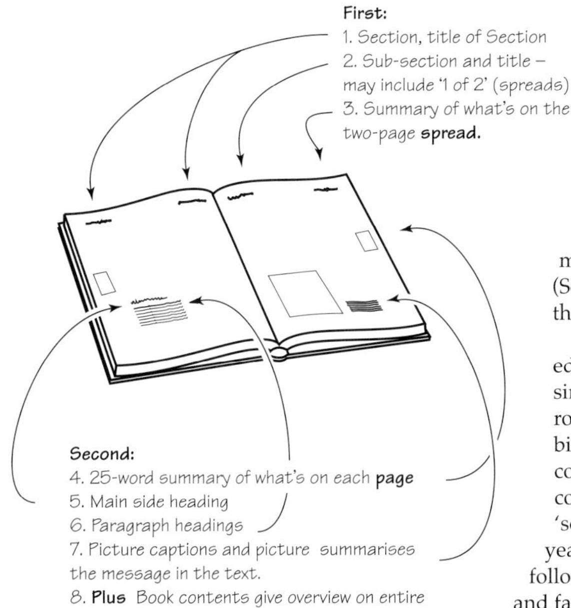

matched engine and gearbox driveline is a dream to use, especially off-road.

Additive experience. Many readers will already have experience in off-road operation and have developed their own techniques of doing things differing slightly from advice here. In the preparation of this book it was found that such inputs were usually suited to subtly different conditions, and were not conflicts of method. Experience was nearly always additive rather than reflecting opposite views. Given common aims of safety and care of the vehicle the best course was usually self-evident.

Signposting. Not many will read this book from cover to cover; or even from the front. If you do you will maybe notice some repetition; this is because most will plunge into individual Sections – or even dart about within Sections – and the book is designed to accommodate that. If it bugs you, apologies.

But easy access and signposting has been one of the aims. Open at any page and you will know where you are and what is under discussion.

The book is broken down into Sections and sub-sections. Coverage of the section – eg Section 2.3 – is also indicated on the title page of that section.

The diagram (left) summarises the signposting. Some terms used in the book may be new to you and a glossary (Sec 9.1) gives some insight into how things work.

Soft-roaders arise! The first edition of this book followed four similar titles. The tenets of off-roading, like learning to ride a bicycle, do not change but this new compact edition addresses the considerable strides that so-called 'soft-roaders' have made in recent years. Whilst most, regrettably, have followed the bloat-trend and got bigger and fatter, the main progress has been in the drivelines. In the beginning 'auto-engage' 4x4 often amounted to no more than a viscous coupling between front and rear propeller shafts. Now it's a whole lot smarter. But, as we shall see, still has limitations.

Skoda's Yeti is a 'soft-roader', and not full-time four-wheel drive. But the Haldex system (p.2.16) – widely used in other soft-roaders – engages 4x4 at start-off. Ideal for snow.

Fundamentals

Different approaches. The Jeep Wrangler's pared-down, focused off-road functionality (right) and (below left) the Mercedes-Benz M-Class – on the surface a luxury 4x4 that'll get you to the ski-slopes in supreme comfort with no complications. But M-Class offers an optional low-range gearbox, hi-rise suspension and diff locks centre and rear to yield impressive off-road performance.

Philosophy

Progress. Things have all moved on a bit in recent years, haven't they. 'Four-wheel drives' – four-by-fours – no longer conjure up visions of square-rigged, mud-splattered, off-roaders. The motor industry and the general public have at last taken on board the fact that powering all four wheels instead of just two is an advantage for quite ordinary on-

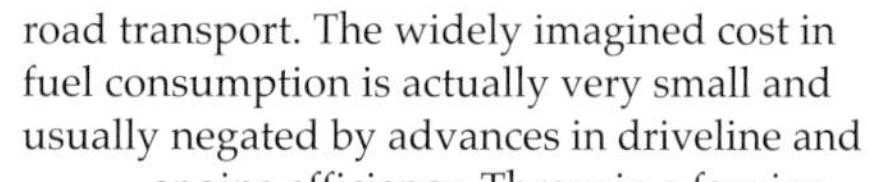

road transport. The widely imagined cost in fuel consumption is actually very small and usually negated by advances in driveline and engine efficiency. Throw in a few icy winters plus technology that has got a great deal smarter and 'suddenly', as media persons are fond of saying, four-wheel drive is a pretty straightforward, sensible way to go.

Of course powering all four wheels demands more shafts and gears and is thus more expensive to make and buy. But even that aspect changes day by day, with the advent of hybrids and electric motors driving the back wheels to help out engine-driven front wheels. And, bottom line, it has to be admitted that much of the technological innovation is aimed at

getting the advantages of 4x4 without the added manufacturing cost. Accountants, market analysts and PR persons sit (as perceived by four-wheel drive purists!), hook-beaked atop their perches scotching elegant engineering concepts in favour of something 'tailored to the market', ie cheaper but flash enough to pull the punters.

The hard stuff. Quite a lot of this book is devoted to off-road driving techniques – but almost as much, in this edition, deals with the ever-expanding field of 'soft-roaders' and 'crossovers'. Even 20 years ago it was clear that the archetypal on/off-road vehicle is here to stay. Industry, civil engineering, the emergency services, the overseas relief agencies, agriculture and the defence Services would in some cases be totally incapacitated without them. In many overseas regions such vehicles are often the only means of maintaining point-to-point land communications and transport.

'Be certain not to damage the ground we drive on - especially vulnerable when wet.'

New usage. And in the developed countries these vehicles have found (irrespective of the fact that all four wheels are driven) a niche in the automotive marketplace among those warming to their capabilities as the most practical of family hold-alls – the kind of car that can tow a canoe-trailer to a mountain lake or do the school run and return with four children, a wet dog, a lawn mower and four sacks of compost picked up en route. As a bonus, they have a high-level

Idyllic setting for off-roader use. Well-drained chalk track with dry grass obviate any environmental damage here. Nissan's robust Patrol is one of a select group of 4x4s that combine leading off-road capability with sensible levels of practicality and comfort without going to extremes.

driver eyeline and are also enormous fun to drive off-road.

Special responsibilities. The very popularity and versatility of the larger, off-road-capable vehicles confers on us a special responsibility towards the environment when they are driven off the highway. And, wherever, the engineers and legislators continue their work in the pursuit of clean air; the latest diesels with particulate filters and catalyst-equipped petrol engines minimise atmospheric pollution.

The legislators, particularly, have a hard time and do a difficult and unpopular job. To cries of horror from industry they must assess what is achievable and level the playing field so that all manufacturers meet the same standards – from which we all benefit.

Tread lightly. As users, we must be certain not lastingly to damage the ground we drive on when off-road – especially vulnerable when wet. In so far as many of them will be new to the capabilities of their vehicles, recreational users must be especially aware of their responsibilities. In recent years ever-growing numbers of off-road enthusiasts have increased the potential for damage to vegetation, soil, water, wildlife and the solitude afforded by these areas.

All users of vehicles with an off-road capability will wish to familiarise themselves with environmental principles.

The Americans, who have a way with words, coined the phrase 'Tread lightly' to encapsulate a sensitive approach to the use of off-roaders on fragile landscapes that are prone to damage or erosion.

Torque gently. 'Torque gently', more specifically, conveys both an exhortation to drive with a gentle right foot on the throttle (or brake) – to develop 'mechanical sympathy' as well as sympathy for the ground we drive over off-road. It also suggests 'talk gently' and not indulge in inappropriately 'macho' antics.

Following the dual meaning will preserve both our vehicles and our environment for the future enjoyment of ourselves and others. Few could disagree with such a philosophy.

'Caring for the environment is far more important than the current fashion it may seem.'

Practicalities

And few, applying little more than common sense and good manners, would not come up with the following list of practical points to remember when operating away from tarmac roads.

People and wildlife. Especially in densely populated countries such as in Europe, remember:

- Allow wildlife priority over your own progress.
- Domestic animals too, especially horses and ponies, may be unused to the presence of vehicles in remote areas. Accommodate their nervousness; switch off and wait if necessary.
- Sheep that have strayed onto a track often run ahead of a vehicle rather than leaving the roadway. Be patient. Stop and let them disperse or pull over to let them pass by.
- Gamebirds and other wildlife often soak up the warmth of tarmac by sitting in the middle of country lanes or other clearings.

Your vehicle may panic them into running across your path rather than away from you – their rationale is to return to where they were before the danger appeared. Be prepared for this – and for the last minute appearance of a second or third bird from the hedgerow. In Africa it's 'the third goat syndrome'.

Recreational practise areas, such as the challenging Devil's Pit in Bedfordshire, afford owners the opportunity to examine the performance envelope of more capable off-roaders.

• Animals are often dazzled by headlights and may be unable to get away from the danger. Be aware of this; drive with extra care on unfenced lanes or open tracks. And that really does mean driving slowly.

• Be especially considerate towards walkers, cyclists (yes, cyclists; they aren't all red-light jumpers) or riders – especially in remote areas. Like it or not, you have an ambassadorial role to play and inevitably, arriving in a comfortable off-road vehicle whilst others are progressing 'the hard way', you will, to a degree, be perceived in the idle villain's role!

'Litter ... wherever you are, leave *nothing*.'

• Always respect the privacy of other people; not always easy to assess, but many go to remote areas to savour the peace and solitude.

Access. See p.7.4 for an overview of UK access rights (late 2011). In general, however:

• Be certain of your right of access to tracks and wild areas. (The good news is the growth of off-road driving schools and recreational practise areas.)

• A road marked on a map does not automatically confer a right of way. If in any doubt at all, ask or refer to a highly detailed map such as, in the UK, one of the OS 1:25,000 series.

• Access rights to land for vehicles varies from country to country. Make yourself aware of the appropriate regulations for the country in which you are driving. Developed, highly populated or densely legislated countries usually have complex regulations.

Erosion. Four-wheel drive vehicles can contribute enormously to erosion when

Ideal for the parachutes, parkas and packed-lunches, the long-established Mitsubishi L200, despite recently morphing into more extravagant bodywork, has taken a large slice of the UK pickup market. 'Super select' 4x4 system – for once an appropriate marketing moniker – offers a very wide range of driveline controls.

carelessly used off-road. Guidelines to minimise damage:

- New ruts form rain channels which cause erosion – especially where surface vegetation such as grass has been scraped away by spinning wheels. So keep off soft ground if possible – sinkage causes ruts.
- Do not spin your wheels on grass.
- In general, where a track exists, stick to it. Your wheel tracks away from it can tempt others to do the same and a another swathe of land can be spoiled.
- On the other hand, when travelling over open meadows with two or more vehicles, do not follow in each others' tracks. This precludes the forming of damaging ruts.
- Be doubly cautious when using mud tyres. Ideally they should be used only when deep mud is envisaged; they can quickly damage other ground.
- Use designated areas for training.

Litter. The world-wide golden rules apply wherever you are:

- Never leave litter under any circumstances – matchsticks, teabags, food wrapping, tins, bottles, anything plastic. Wherever you are, leave nothing.
- Take back what you brought with you.

Polishing your halo

Observing all the recommendations above will seem impossibly onerous the first time you read them. The second time you read them you will see just how much common sense and simple courtesy is involved. The third time (and this may be a little later), you will start realising that this is what you actually do and will feel good about it.

Caring for the environment is far more important than the current fashion it may seem. We all share humankind's newly realised responsibility. Enjoy your driving!

If you've momentarily forgotten the obvious ones, there are one or two quite compelling other reasons to avoid leaving litter!

It doesn't just go away.

Section 1

The ingredients

1.1 The appeal

Why buy – the appeal

The chicken and the egg. If you already have your 4x4 – this could be preaching to the converted. Or it could be providing a welcome rationale for one of those heart-versus-the-head situations that plague you when trying to decide on – or justify – a purchase that you just want to make (or have made) anyway. Why do people buy 4x4s? The American flair for the neat phrase has dubbed them SUVs – sport-utility vehicles – which sums up their appeal and uses very well. It may be, however, that you are trying to take a cool look at the reasons people buy these vehicles that so many seem to want and, possibly on a quite different list, also look at what they do actually offer.

Buy-appeal lies in high-up driving position, the feeling of security and carry-all capability. This would apply in two-wheel drive. In a 4x4 there's a lot more.

The appeal. Lets be honest, part of it undoubtedly is the 'Tonka-toy syndrome'. Driving a big truck, flying a large aircraft, driving a 4x4 – if you have been to your dealership and just driven round the block you will recognise the instant subjective appeal of even a small 4x4. To this you can add further, more practical, advantages to come up with your initial, day-to-day, benefits list that starts to look like this:

- High-up, 'command' driving position.
- View over all other traffic.
- Feeling of security and strength.
- At last the ability to take all the kids on the school run and their bags and the shopping, both dogs and leave the mower at the place who'll fix it.

There's more – a lot more. The list above is what you could use every day, be it a four-wheel drive or a large two-wheel drive estate. But in most 4x4s there is more than this. The 'four-wheel drive-ness' of the vehicle – putting power through all four wheels instead of just two – has benefits on-road and, together with other attributes we'll examine later, unique benefits off-road. An incidental advantage of the high-up driving position is that, unless the 'stylists' get carried away (which some already have), it is usually associated with a low waist-line and feeling of spaciousness.

'Soft-roaders' – blurring the edges. But there is now a well-established sub-class of 4x4s, one that is maturing and addresses those with few off-road aspirations in butch all-terrain vehicles. These medium or small 4x4s – a class sitting in the same territory as a modest estate or medium sized MPV – are for those seeking a capacious, taller vehicle with easy access, a high driving position and, above all, the ability of a 4x4 to cope with traction-hungry surfaces like packed snow, ice or wet grass. These are the 'soft-roaders', technically far more sophisticated than they were even five years ago, usually with 'auto-engage' four-wheel drive (see p.2.11) but without low-range gears (see p.2.13).

Soft-roaders – the detail. Choosing one is something of a minefield and picking your way between the brochure-writers' bland generalities, the apparent technophobia of the motoring magazines and widespread dealership ignorance about drivelines is important. Both from the viewpoint of knowing what you're buying and also the nuances of what to expect, you really should be aware of the driveline set-up and this is dealt with in Section 2.3. It really isn't complicated.

On-road benefits

What you get with 4x4. You'll get some of the points mentioned on the left with some large estate cars – the feeling of security and large carrying capacity. But putting the engine power through all four wheels – either:

- all the time,
- when selected, or
- 'automatically' (ie when sensors decide you need it) –

will also give you grip when you wouldn't otherwise have it. (The different generic types of four-wheel drive are dealt with a few pages on in Section 2.3. It does help to know what they are: simple again.)

Getting a grip. Subliminally you already know what the next list is going to contain – those situations that take you a little by surprise and make you uneasy at the wheel regarding road grip. You'll nod seeing:

- Wet, 'greasy' corners.
- Wet autumn leaves on corners.
- Tree-shaded, north-facing corners where the frost hangs on.
- Blind corners onto which a hidden gate has just discharged a muddy tractor.

And of course:

- Packed snow.
- Snow or ice in the gutters or verges that allow one wheel to spin.

Having all four wheels handling the power in these situations – with individual wheel-spin inhibited too – is going to make things a lot easier and safer.

Off-road benefits

No contest. In the context of off-road operations the rationale for 4x4 provides its own answer and opens huge vistas of capability, and enjoyment, for professional and recreational use. The needs of public utilities, armed forces, farmers, civil engineers and, in recent years, the horizon-widening enjoyment that 4x4 abilities can bring, ensure full application of designers' ingenuity in achieving off-road performance.

Horses for courses. However, as with most other commodities, you will find vehicles built for specific sectors of the market – built down to a price, up to a capability target, to this or that level of comfort and interior luxury. Know about this. Look beyond the shallow brochures lovingly depicting the bottle-holders and upholstery pattern. Look first, and carefully, at the basics of the concept and the vehicle's designed-in capabilities. You will know, already, of the irrational, paradoxical, arguably crazy, specifications where the ultimate in luxury has been combined with the ultimate in off-road mud-plugging performance. It sells but it may not be for you.

In permanent 4x4, take-you-by-surprise traction situations are dealt with at any time. But a vehicle's design purpose can lean either toward on- or off-road use. *See Section 1.3.*

Within the limits. Because you may need most guidance on this, utilising this off-road aspect of off-roaders' performance safely and keeping within their limits forms a significant part of this book.

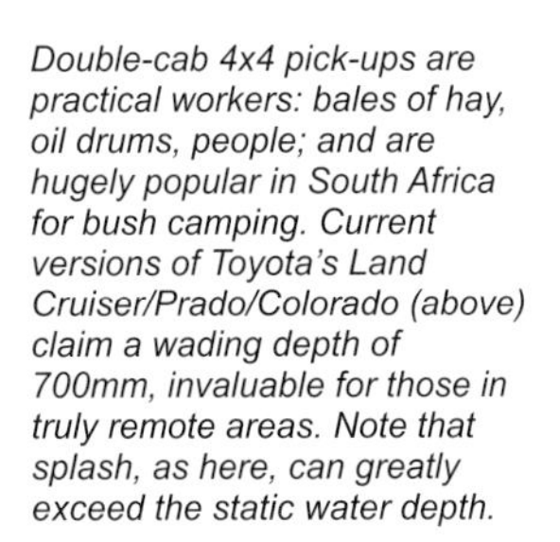

Double-cab 4x4 pick-ups are practical workers: bales of hay, oil drums, people; and are hugely popular in South Africa for bush camping. Current versions of Toyota's Land Cruiser/Prado/Colorado (above) claim a wading depth of 700mm, invaluable for those in truly remote areas. Note that splash, as here, can greatly exceed the static water depth.

1.2 Why four-wheel drive

Halving the load

Terminology. It is worth an initial thought about what four-wheel drive or 4x4 really does do. Incidentally, '4x4' ('four-by-four') means there are four wheels, of which four are driven by the engine. So a normal car, be it front wheel drive or rear wheel drive, is a 4x2 'four-by-two' – four wheels in total, of which the car is driven by two. Some types of truck are referred to as a 6x4 – six (wheels driven) by four.

What it does – and doesn't, do. A 4x4 does not double the power on the road; it takes the power you already have and spreads it between four wheels instead of only two. If a vehicle needs a certain amount of push (tractive effort or traction) to make it go at a given speed or traverse a certain type of terrain, a true 4x4, by having twice as many driven wheels as a 4x2, will actually *halve* the tractive load on a given piece of ground *(so long as it has a 50/50 front/rear drive split – Type 1 and Type 3, see p.2.11)* and thus greatly reduce the chance of spinning wheels under power. Four-wheel drive is thus a considerable benefit to effective operation and to safety all the time.

4x4 doesn't double the power on the road but it does halve the ground stress compared with 4x2 – less risk of wheelspin. Braking, of course, is no different.

Off-road ingredients. If 4x4 is now combined with large wheels and large amounts of wheel movement on supple, well-damped springs, the ingredients of an effective off-road vehicle, capable of operating on rough uneven ground, are also starting to take shape.

Why 4x4? Here's why

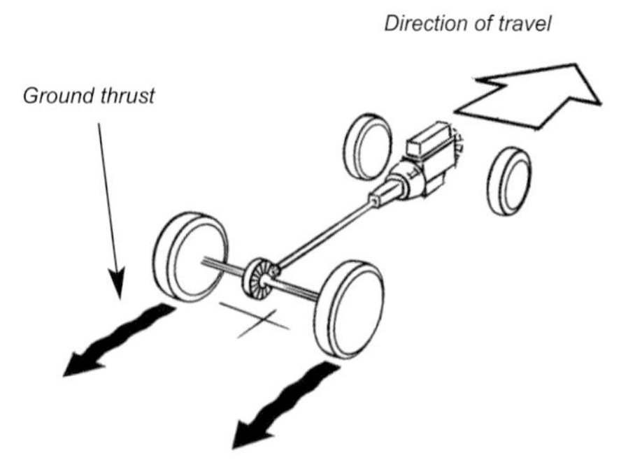

4x2 – all the power is going to just two wheels. High ground stress. Wheels may slip or spin

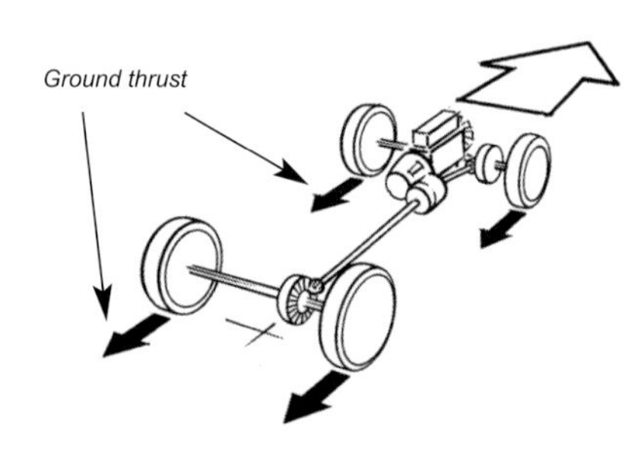

4x4 – same power spread between four wheels. Half the ground stress. Traction evenly distributed.

Doubling the effect

Maintaining traction. Thus if conditions are such that an ordinary 4x2 car driving only one pair of wheels could spin those wheels and lose traction, a 4x4 will actually be twice as effective in using the power of the engine: half the tractive load per wheel will probably kill wheelspin altogether.

More from four. The diagrams above sum this up. All over the world there are bits of ground – oily tarmac, icy roads, glazed snow, wet grassy fields – that will not accommodate the tractive effort needed under certain conditions when power is put through one pair of wheels. Put that power through two axles – four wheels – thus halving the traction required of each wheel, and your 4x4 is likely to get you through, securely and under complete control. This, of course, is irrespective of the size of the vehicle.

Even 4x4s have limits. Of course conditions may be so bad or the traction required so high that even a 4x4 spins its wheels or needs lower gears. These occasions – usually off-road – are addressed later in the book but in general four-wheel drive enhances safety and effectiveness on- and off-road at all times. As we shall see, if you are driving any vehicle with *permanent* four-wheel drive then you are at a further advantage – always ready for the unexpected rather than having to assess the conditions and then select 4x4 with a separate control lever or wait for some 'automatic' selector to do it for you – after sensing incipient wheel-spin.

Traction from all four wheels is the overriding advantage of 4x4 when conditions are demanding. Such vehicles as Discovery (left) and Toyota's Amazon (above) have permanent four-wheel drive – unlike most 'soft-roaders' as we shall see. Sand is notoriously unpredictable when it comes to load-bearing strength and spreading the tractive effort between all four wheels is of enormous benefit.

1.3 The compromises

Compromises?

Real life. There are potential compromises involved in making an off-roader also suitable for on-road use. The requirements and machinery are different. Designers get better and better at reducing the conflict. Where cost is less of an issue, remarkably high standards of on-road and off-road performance can be achieved. Elsewhere, the mix of vehicle characteristics can be optimised for on- or off-road but, with the new soft-roaders, less capable off-road, the compromises are far less noticeable.

Off-roaders are a battleground for conflicting design criteria – mostly concerning suspension movement. Off-road you need lots, which can cause cornering roll on-road.

Handling

The off-roader problem. By definition, off-road obstacles tend to be big and uneven so an off-roader needs ground clearance, big wheels, lots of up-and-down axle movement and long-travel road springs. It is not too difficult to accommodate this on your drawing board but the vehicle gets to be tall, leans on corners and may handle oddly.

Narrowing the gap between on- and off-road optimisation. Nissan's Patrol had a disconnectable rear anti-roll bar to allow awesome wheel movement off-road. Re-connected on-road, it minimises body roll.

Body roll and unsprung weight. Body roll is common with tall 4x4s. Anti-roll bars (p.9.3) help limit roll but also limit axle movement relative to the body; bad news off-road. Four-by-fours' large wheels on the end of beam axles give good ground clearance but also amount to high 'unsprung weight' – ie the bit of the vehicle below the springs.

(Unsprung weight? If you think about it, there is a vehicle attached to the top of the road springs – that's the engine and the bit with the passengers in it – and there is a part of the vehicle attached to the bottom of the springs – the wheels and most of the axle too. That bottom bit is the unsprung weight and rides directly on the ground.)

The higher this unsprung weight the more difficult it is to get a smooth ride for the body and passengers. If the springs are multi-leaf leaf-springs (unkindly but appositely referred to as 'cart springs') then they are less responsive than coils to small road irregularities and the ride is even worse.

The best saloon cars have coil springs and lightweight unsprung components so they can follow the contour of the road with least inertia, staying more constantly in contact with the road and thus, as well as giving a smooth ride, also yielding the best grip, braking and road-holding.

Independent suspension. Many current off-roaders have independent front (and rear) suspension with coil springs instead of a one-piece beam-axle but it costs them under-axle obstacle clearance off-road – see p.3.9.

Make allowances. So an off-roader will not always handle, ride or corner like a top-flight luxury saloon. Handling, ride and cornering are where you must expect compromises when you buy an off-roader or SUV ... but advances in design mean the situation keeps getting better.

Performance

Weight, power-weight ratio. The size and toughness of an off-road vehicle means it is usually a lot heavier than an on-road car – despite (as in the latest Range Rover, aluminium monocoque build). This takes its toll in road performance, fuel consumption

The usual trade-offs – handling, drivability

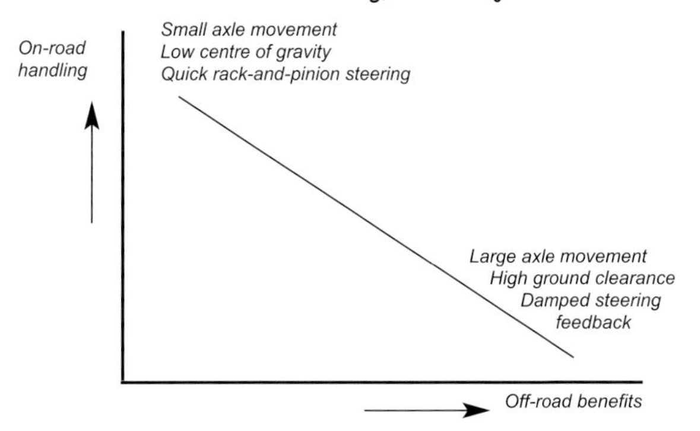

and, since power-weight ratio is involved, acceleration too. Designers put large engines in off-roaders to raise the power-weight ratio and recover lost road performance but fuel consumption is often the price paid – albeit previously unheard-of mpg is now almost becoming the norm with modern diesels.

Happy medium. Road-burning performance, especially with today's traffic densities, is rarely useable and a mid-range diesel gives quite enough punch for most users. More important, it is more economical and flexible (torquey) than a petrol engine.

Concept – luxury vs workhorse

Overview. Few salesmen are likely to admit, even-handedly, where their product lies in the grand scale of a luxury vs work-horse concept – ie where the compromises lie and to what extent. All will portray comfort levels as luxurious, space as huge, off-road capability as Godzilla-like and on-road performance as lithe, smooth, crisp and rapid. Some of these values are a matter of personal priorities but, if you want an off-road workhorse, then additional to the all-important driveline spec, keep an eye on:

- Total payload additional to driver
- Payload as a proportion of gross vehicle weight
- Power-weight ratio – BHP per tonne of gross weight
- Is there a low-range transfer gearbox?

These are some of the attributes that tend to suffer as a vehicle is biased toward the luxury end of the scale.

Clever design. Advances have been made in reconciling on- and off-road design demands but:

- Be aware there really are difficulties to be overcome – luxury vs workhorse
- Know what you want of your vehicle
- Know where you want it to sit (or where your current vehicle sits), on the either/or see-saws highlighted on the diagrams here.

Unsprung weight – beam axles etc – give off-roaders a less silky on-road ride but those same axles provide the good ground clearance needed in the rough.

Soft-roaders – new kids on the block. But if you will go off-road only at county shows, camp sites or fetching winter hay for your four-legged dependents, today's 'soft-roaders' offer a very sensible solution.

The more the luxury (below), the fewer the workhorse attributes. The better the on-road handling (above), the less the off-road benefits – usually. No brochure will admit to where its product lies on diagrams like these or admit to any compromises but the diagrams do show what the designer is up against and how ingenious some of them are in conquering both ends of the scale at the same time. Complexity is usually the price paid when edging off-road workhorses up and to the left.

The compromises – function

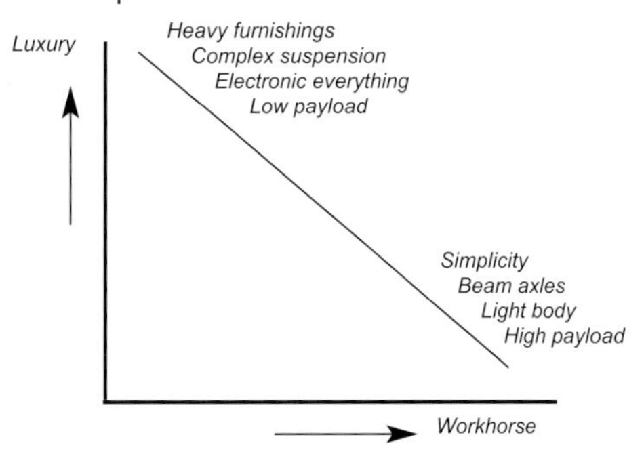

Section 2

Four-wheel drive systems

2.1 Driveline basics

Drivelines matter

Drivelines matter – how the power of the engine gets to the wheels. They determine how, when, and to what extent, you get four-wheel drive: especially in a 'soft-roader' where the need for weight and cost savings influence performance and the vehicle is in two-wheel drive most of the time.

The design and software engineers' ingenuity has overcome most of the compromises, but drivelines can have a significant effect on performance on slippery surfaces and off-road.

If you are driving, or thinking of buying, any 4x4 – but particularly a new-generation 'soft-roader' – you should know the detail of how your driveline works.

The Royal Air Force desert rescue team based near Tobruk was equipped with some of the 13000-odd Series 1 Land Rovers supplied to the British armed forces. Toyota's 1955 Series 20 Land Cruiser (inset) succeeded it's basic Jeep-lookalike BJ. It had selectable four-wheel drive but, unlike the Series 1, no low range gears.

Four-wheel drive used to be pretty basic: a select-when-required facility to get you out of trouble off road. Its wider application and benefits are now being appreciated.

In the beginning ...

Way back. Few will be unaware that the era in which the utility of four-wheel drive became recognised was during the Second World War. When it was over, the legacy of the immortal Willys Jeep soon spawned similar vehicles. Land Rover was one of the early ones in 1948 – born of inspiration, expediency and the availability of aluminium after the war. Toyota, following the BJ that could have been mistaken for a Jeep on a dark night, quietly joined the trend.

4x4 – only when required. These were essentially normal two-wheel drive vehicles but used selectable four-wheel drive (and low range gears) as an emergency facility for difficult off-road operation. 4x4 was regarded this way for a long time.

Permanent four-wheel drive and its concomitant cost, complexity and side-effects was not seriously considered for normal road vehicles until much later, notably pioneered by the early Range Rovers.

The perfect driveline. A whimsical look at the evolution of the 'Perfect 4x4 Driveline' is shown opposite. It highlights how a simple idea encountered problems and how they were solved by the now ubiquitous differential gear. (Actually patented by Englishman Richard Roberts in 1832 who – see opposite again – is not, after all, thought to have been a friend of Leonardo da Vinci. Or of Mr DiCaprio).

Required reading! Do follow this through in the treatment on the following few pages. It provides a bedrock understanding of four-wheel drive systems, is essential to the validity of your choice of vehicle and very relevant to your most efficient use of it in everyday operation. Don't believe it when you hear yourself saying 'Ah, that's too technical for me.' Relax. You'll see it's all remarkably simple.

Do start here – please! Genesis of a perfect 4x4 driveline

Take a look at this first. The next sections – indeed, the whole of the book – will make more sense if you do. Correction ... will probably ONLY make sense if you do. Let's divulge Leonardo da Vinci's perfect 4x4 system. (Maybe it wasn't him but it was someone with similarly bright ideas – possibly Leonardo DiCaprio?)

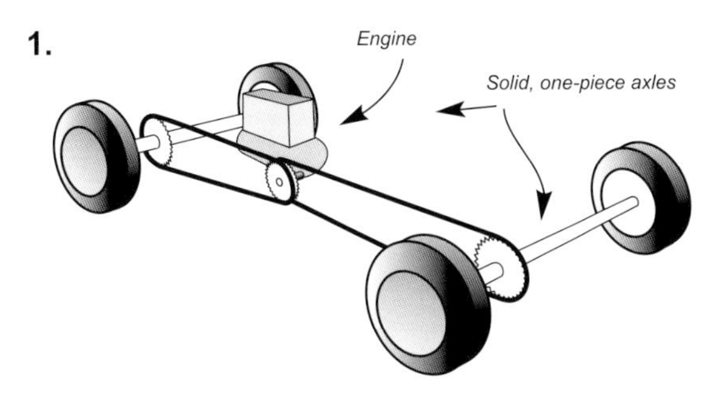

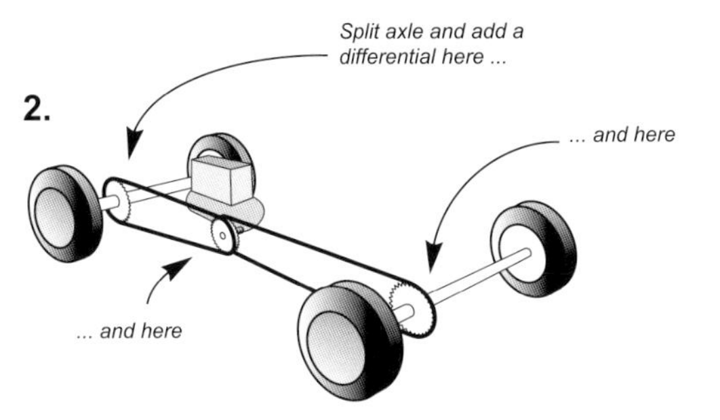

... and make them lockable (see photo 2.7)

Phase 1. The perfect four-wheel drive system. Four-wheel drive equals all wheels geared to each other (or chained – it's easier to show here). Yes? If one, two or even three wheels go over icy patches or slippery clay there's no problem or wheel spin; the remaining wheel(s) will continue to give traction – since all the wheels are geared together and go round at the same speed. Even the ones on the ice or mud won't be dead or braked; they'll be turning at the right speed. Eureka – the perfect system for four-wheel drive!

Phase 2. The compromised perfect system. Phase 1's perfect system got shot down in flames. They found it wouldn't go round corners properly – the outside wheel travels further than the inside wheel so there was skidding and tyre-scuffing. (They also found that on a winding road – or even doing a 180 in a car park – the front wheels travel farther than the back wheels - see photo next page.)

Leonardo's friend had already invented differential gears. So get three sets. **You don't do differentials? Check the next spread for the full elegant exposition – it's all very logical.** But – this will do you for now – consider an axle being driven to rotate at 100 rpm. Split the axle, put a diff between the 'half-shafts'. Now the wheel on the outside will be able to go (say) 10% faster whilst the other goes 10% slower – or any other split of rpm resulting from the different needs of each wheel. So fit a diff to both axles. And because, additionally, the front wheels travel farther than the rears on bends, (that picture overleaf again) do it also where the drive from the engine divides to go to the front and rear prop shafts. This means the front prop shaft (or chain) can go a little bit faster than the rear shaft or chain.

That's three differentials – one each in the front and rear axles and one in the middle.

Now you can go round corners OK. Eureka Mk 2!

Phase 3. The modified, de-compromised, perfect system. Ah; small problem for perfectionists. The system now allows for the natural speed variations between left and right wheels depending on the distance travelled by each wheel. It also allows the front wheels to travel farther than the rears. But differentials permitting these variations can also allow (in extremis) one rear wheel (say) on a patch of ice to spin away to its heart's content while the other wheel stays still. The same thing can happen at the front and centre diffs. **This random wheel spinning is a fact of life and its elimination or avoidance is fundamental to the functioning of an effective 4x4 on- or off-road.** So these diffs must be 'limited slip' or manually lockable such that excess spin will not immobilise the vehicle. That should do it. And it does! (As we shall see – pp.2.6-2.9 – it can be done)

Phase 4. Bean-counters' modified, re-compromised, perfect system. It had to happen of course. Diffs are expensive, especially with 'locking' systems that may be subject to misuse and (horrors!) subsequent warranty or liability claims. Cue cheaper variations, some eliminating front/rear 'hard gearing' altogether, others using 'soft' diff-locks like viscous couplings. So began the era of 'soft-roaders' – with 'auto-engage' 4x4 systems; a sort of non-permanent 4x4. They used to be pretty feeble but they're a good bit smarter now. Check out the post-Leonardo big picture – **see (after 'Differentials') Section 2.3 'Types of four-wheel drive' and Section 2.5 'soft-roaders'.**

2.2 Differentials

We all know about differentials

Check your DNA helix. You have to suspect it's part of the human genome by now, a subtle mutation resulting from subliminally watching cars turning corners. It's been passed on from generation to generation. So everybody knows, more or less, what a differential *does*. But few really know how it *works*. Yes, it matters!

First check the diagram opposite. Differentials are exceptionally ingenious yet very logical. Do remember that when driving straight ahead, the little cluster of bevel gears – the whole bunch in the middle that does the actual 'differentiating' – go round with the crown wheel, inert and with no relative motion to one another. *No comprendo?* Follow the diagram and you will.

Yes, the front wheels really do travel further than the back wheels in a turn. And of course the outer wheel travels further than the inner wheel. Both situations could cause severe problems with a 'Phase 1 Leonardo perfect 4x4 system' as shown on the previous spread. Use of differentials fixes that. Note that here we have pretty much the same grip on all four wheels. When all that changes ... see next spread.

Luckily nearly everyone knows what differentials DO. Knowing how they actually WORK and how they are controlled is essential for making an informed choice when buying a 4x4. And operating it.

Genesis of a differential. No; read it!

1. It's best to know about this. The engine – the fist on the lever – is just turning the axle with a wheel at each end. As we've seen, the wheel on the outside of the turn has farther to go than the wheel on the inside. So in a turn, skidding, scuffed tyres and poor grip will result.

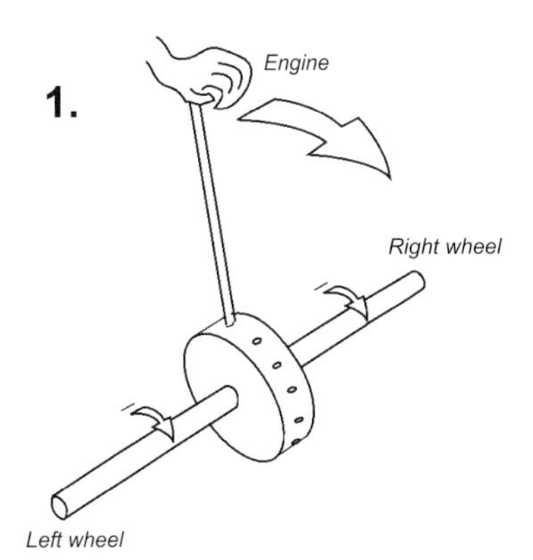

2. Now let's think about it. First, split the axle into two 'half-shafts'. With this arrangement the engine is still turning the axle but the pivoted linkage to each half enables a degree of freedom for each half-shaft to follow a slightly different path – here turning right. As shown here, this isn't enough, of course. So change the two 'peg-wheels' for bevel gears. And instead of the pivoted link, substitute another (meshing) bevel gear (pinion) between them. See diagram 3.

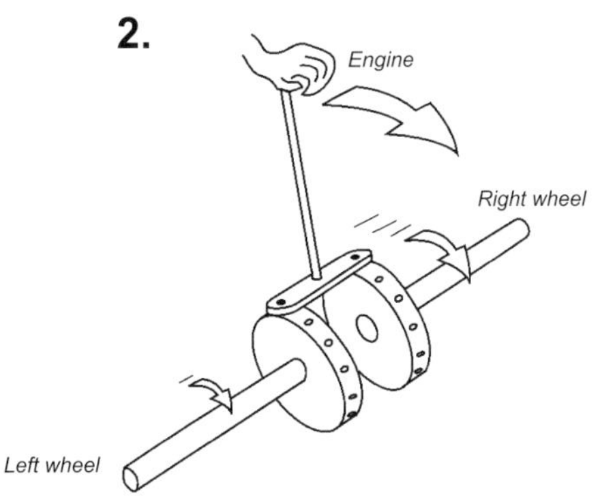

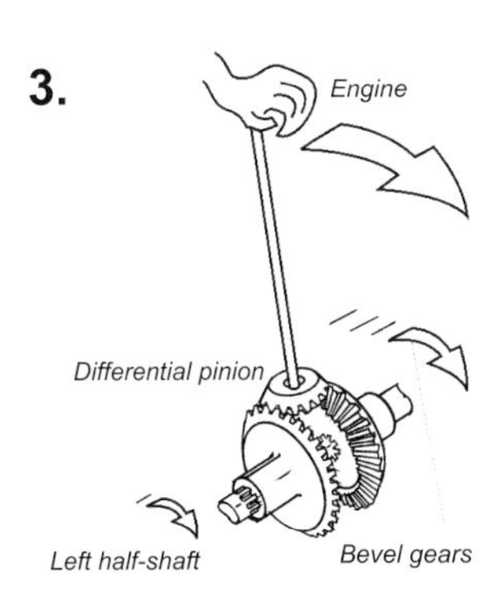

3. Despite the bevel gears shown here the basic set-up is as the above sketches – the engine is still 'pushing' both halves of the axle round so that both rear wheels are rotated under power. The only difference now is that the 'half-shafts' have the freedom to fully accommodate the need (in the right turn here) for the outside wheel to travel further than the inside wheel. Note, however, that the differential – for that is what it now is – apportions the drive 'fairly', ie if the left wheel goes 15% faster, then the pinion wheel ensures the right wheel goes 15% slower. (And as we'll see, that can extend to the extremes, off-road (or on ice), of one wheel or axle speeding up by 100% and other one standing still – see photo next page.)

4. Now substitute a large 'crown-wheel' (sometimes also called a 'ring gear') for the lever and fist in the other diagrams and (thanks to *'Popular Science'* magazine's beautiful 1941 artwork here) you can see the final picture. **Just to re-emphasise it, note that the entire 'differential' gear cluster (above) is bolted to the crown wheel and revolves with it. Its cluster of smaller bevel gears are inert, with no relative movement to one another, until a corner** or – as we shall see – until there are significant differences in traction between the left and right wheels on the axle, eg: dry concrete vs packed snow – or, see photo next page, one wheel in the air. Brilliant concept! Poetry!

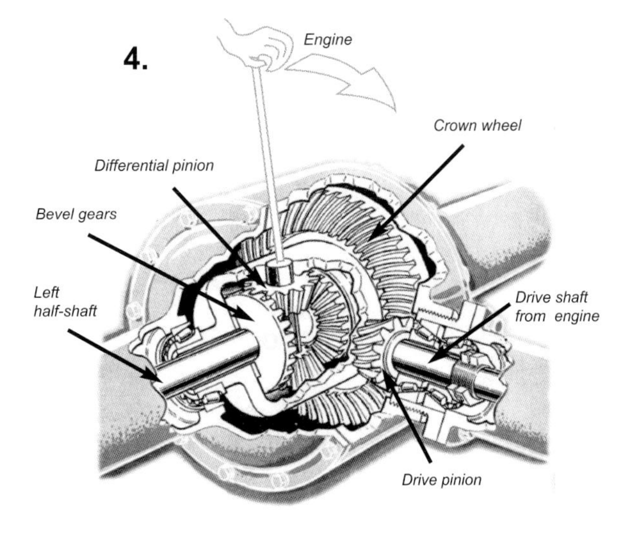

Controlling differentials – the need

The Morris Oxford scenario. Most ordinary cars – 4x2s as we can now loftily call them – have been working quite happily with a simple, 'open' differential between the driving-axle half-shafts, like that on the previous page, for more than a century.

But they occasionally had problems when icy patches gave one wheel a lot less grip than the other. When this happened, the diff, allowing the power to take the line of least resistance, permitted the least-grippy wheel to spin a bit; or even quite a lot. Few of us will not have seen the results in icy weather or when packed snow can turn a minuscule incline into a source of deep embarrassment for surprised drivers.

Differentials are brilliant. But in difficult or extreme conditions – which we are thinking about in a book with this title – there can be problems with excessive wheelspin.

Is four-wheel drive the answer? Yes; partly. Certainly driving four wheels is better than driving only two but if it's not your day exactly the same problem can leave an early 4x4 spinning a wheel at opposite corners of the car and getting nowhere.

Wheelspin. Something must be done. When a 4x4 is called on to perform more demanding duties – in a day to day industrial situation or seriously off-road – something must be done about wheelspin. The classic, brutalist, all-or-nothing solution is to fit a diff lock: a simple set of manually-engaged interlocking spigots that slide together to lock one half-shaft to the other, 100%. We're back to Leonardo's Mark 1 soap-box device (see p.2.3). The Mercedes Type 461 G-Wagen (see pictures pp 2.4 and 2.9) is thus equipped and it works like a charm – better than anything else before or since.

Drivers are human. It's only disadvantage is that the driver has to remember to disengage the diff lock when it is not required lest the skidding and tyre scuffing mentioned on p.2.3 cause loss of grip when cornering. Also a diff-locked front axle (forgotten) can leave the driver with the impression the front wheels are set in concrete. The steering feels immovable.

Do pay attention, Hoskins! When a proportion of the public doesn't know – amazing but true – whether their car is front-wheel drive or rear-wheel drive, it is arguably best to make forgetting to disengage a diff-lock a fail-safe event. Hence 'limited slip' diffs.

'Limited slip' diffs. A spigot-type 100% diff lock should only be engaged when stationary or when both wheels on that axle are going the same speed. To preclude damage most have a 'hold-off' until the spigots align. A clutch-type diff-lock engages more softly with less shock-loading; it can also can be programmed to off-load in sharp turns to preclude the 'set-in-concrete' steering feel.

The usual way of doing this is to put a pack of clutch plates between the two halves of the diff instead of the conceptual spigots. Something electronic sniffs out the difference in speed between the two shafts and engages the clutch in proportion.. The clutch pack, in effect, binds the two shafts to one another.

Forget the media cliché. And that's what diff locks are about – binding one shaft to the other – rather than the cliché so favoured by brochure writers and the media about 'transferring the torque to the wheel that most needs it'. It locks the shafts together.

'EDL' - electronic diff lock. May be called an 'ELD' too, the so-called 'electronic diff lock' (or ' ... locking diff') is simply a programmed, electrically-activated clutch pack across the two halves of the diff. No wheelspin? No speed difference, no pressure on the clutch plates. Lots of spin? Speed difference sensed, pressure applied, shafts locked together – gently. And it gets smarter still. Nowadays there's a 'pre-emptive mode' where (like the Haldex – see p 2.17) electronics apply diff lock at start-off for the 'icy gutter' scenario. There's then the 'reactive mode' as described above where diff lock engages if slip or spin is sensed. These phases can overlap elegantly on slippery climbs – see picture on p.2.19.

Fanfare. Enter the bean-counters. It always happens. EDLs are a bit pricey and 'Maybe everyone doesn't need one, eh, JB?' The man has a point on both counts as there are other ways of addressing the problem of wheelspin – almost (but not quite) as good, but less expensive. Traction control.

ABS to the rescue. ABS? Yes, the anti-lock braking system. That's the one with speed sensors on each wheel. If the wheel is about to lock it releases brake on just that wheel for a tiny instant. Those speed sensors are very sensitive – and very useful.

We have ways of making you torque. ABS wheel-speed sensors can be used in a different mode: to detect when, in a difficult traction situation, one wheel is spinning frantically while the other one is stationary – see picture left. With speed-difference data available, a black box can be programmed to trigger braking to the spinning wheel. This is generically 'traction control' and makes or 'transfers' torque to the stationary wheel.

Oh, really? If your reaction to this is surprise, think again about the diff allocating drive to the line of least resistance. If a touch of brake is applied to the spinning wheel, then that ceases to be the line of least resistance and some torque will be diverted to the stationary wheel. That's about to happen in the picture opposite. The offside wheel is spinning fast, the ABS sensors pick this up, and via the control unit, apply a touch of brake. When that happens, the wheel on the ground (the one that will get you moving again) is empowered to do so. (If this doesn't gel for you, see box on p.2.19.)

So what's the problem? You don't want this cross-axle braking to chime in too early. Going round a sharp corner, for example, there's a speed difference between left and right front wheels. So there's a torque threshold – usually seen as a time delay – built in; that's what you're seeing in the photo opposite. So the system can seem – and be – slow to operate. The braking is based on the degree of 'slip', finely programmed to avoid excessive torque transfer which might precipitate a stall or the stationary wheel digging-in.

Diff-locks – manual or automatic can still the frenzy of a spinning wheel.

Let's call a spade a spade. The brutal truth is that ABS-sensed, brake-activated 'traction control' is a cheap substitute for a locking or limited-slip differential but is a lot better than nothing. It works after a second or two (sometimes with tyre smoke). But .....

This (left) is a Freelander under severe and unfeeling provocation. Why is the nearside front wheel stationary and the offside spinning? It's the differential. The differential for the front wheels is uncontrolled and with the off-loaded wheel will spin (that's not the whole story here: see above 'ABS to the rescue'). This early Discovery (right) has permanent four-wheel drive – front and rear prop shafts with a differential sitting between them, permitting one shaft to go a little faster than the other. The power in such a setup – as ever – will take the line of least resistance, Here, with weight transference to the rear wheels and the fronts off-loaded and on very loose ground, the centre diff allows the front wheels to spin. In fact the Discovery centre diff is manually lockable. Here it's been deliberately left unlocked ('open') to show what happens if you don't – as you should – lock it off-road.

Controlling differentials - definitions summary

*Let's recap the diff definitions clearly: a few PR folks and brochure-writers appear to need some help on this too. A **'locking diff'** is what it sounds like – one axle half-shaft locked immovably to the other; left shaft connected to right shaft: think G-Wagen, Jeep Wrangler Rubicon. A **'limited-slip diff'** attempts this but usually does it via clutch plates – a gentler set-up that cushions an engagement which can be modulated, but/and thus allows a controllable degree of slip between left and right half shaft: Discovery, Range Rover.*

*Then there is '**traction control'** which mimics a limited-slip diff by braking a single spinning wheel: Freelander, Evoque, Tiguan, Yeti. Because you are killing energy by braking a wheel (plus heating and wearing brake discs) this is conceptually inefficient, needs very careful control and requires a healthy supply of spare torque from the engine. However, as it uses componentry from a standard ESP (electronic stability programme) or ABS, and is dependent only on software, it is virtually zero-cost. Attractive.*

Moreover that software and some smart algorithms can establish dual- or multi-level traction control – typically a button-selected sharpening of reaction times (eg. via Haldex on Tiguan, Yeti; Terrain Response on Freelander, Evoque; and, independently on Panda 4x4. Another approach: two-level, sharper, braked-wheel traction control is also achieved when low-range is engaged on the non-Rubicon Jeep Wrangler.)

King of the castle. Land Rover's impressive Discovery 4 makes a diagonal climb of the company's demonstration 'Toblerone' ridge with centre and rear axle diff-locks (EDLs) automatically engaged to preclude the 'diagonal suspension' problem (see text, right). Front off-side wheel spins little because low-range gears keep throttle light.

Controlling differentials (contd)

Differentials: roundabouts and swings. Magic within certain limits but they can need controlling

Realism rules. Don't let talk of 'cheap alternatives' on the last page put you off too much; a little maybe, but not much. Calling a spade a spade includes being realistic. Being realistic means addressing: – usage and cost.

Realism – usage. Most of the vehicles equipped solely with brake-activated traction control are the so-called 'soft-roaders' that are designed for improved road performance on ice and snow and the occasional traverse of a muddy meadow at a horse-show or campsite. Where a 4x2 might wheelspin itself into total immobility, a soft-roader will likely get through, albeit maybe after a second or two's hesitation in some cases. Soft-roaders are dealt with in more detail at Section 2.5 but for now remember they must meet two usage criteria. One is providing four-wheel drive. This is cleverly and rapidly dealt with by current methods of engaging drive to the rear wheels of a basically front-drive car. The other is additionally requiring 'traction control' to counter left/right wheelspin.

Realism – cost. To equip such a vehicle with advanced off-road transmission would inevitably price it out of its market sector. And no prospective owner wants to be forced out of his budget range or pay extra for features that will seldom if ever be used.

Off-road, off tracks, wild country. Where a 4x4 will operate regularly in demanding off-road – or 'no-road' – conditions, the design-engineers apply appropriate solutions, some of which have been covered on the previous spread. As we shall see later (p.4.14), 'diagonal suspension' is the classic stopper where, without control of the differential, wheels at opposite 'corners' of the vehicle will lose any usable traction and spin. Locking the two halves of the axle drive-shafting together with a diff lock is the solid, no-nonsense solution. Do it (like the Mercedes G-Wagen – right – does) and the vehicle will continue on its way.

Land Rover's (and others') approach to this problem (picture left) is to make such 'locking' automatic. Electronics sense axle half-shaft speed differences, pass the information to a control unit which then electrically engages a clutch between the shafts, binding (but not locking) them together.

Start-off lock. In this and some 'soft-roader' systems, the diff is locked briefly on start-off ('pre-emptive mode') and also when significant half-shaft speed differences are detected ('reactive mode'). Unlocking occurs automatically – gradually and exponentially over a variable period when normal conditions prevail. The same principle applies to the center differential. The aim is effortless, fool-proof off-road performance over just about any reasonable obstacle. Many will be (rightly) suspicious of electronics but, invoking reality, with a modern buying public mostly unable to do their own servicing due to the complexity of current vehicle systems, technical awareness these days is low. And awareness of the finesse of engaging (and the all-important disengaging) of manual diff locks is also rare. Getting it wrong can lead to accidents. And of course, in this day and age, that also leads to litigation – from which accountants and legal departments understandably recoil in horror. So manual diff locks and the risk of litigation are best avoided. Hence EDLs.

Free-diff wheelspin can be controlled by the braked-wheel approach or by diff locks. Diff locks or EDLs are best but more costly.

Check this if you ever doubted the value of all-round diff-locks. Three of the G-Wagen's four wheels sank into the soft sand and were heading for a no-traction situation. The fourth one (front right, here), on firmer sand, had what it needed. With diff-locks and reverse that one wheel enabled back off. No wheelspin, no digging-in, no drama – and in this case, no electronics either. Classic. And classic simplicity. Any questions?

2.3 Types of four-wheel drive

Selectable, auto-engaged or permanent

Got differentials? OK, now drivelines. This is one of the most important sections of the book – so long as you're happy with differentials! Sweep away the blizzard of trade names – ActiveTrak, Control Trac, Selectrac, Super Select, Torque-on-Demand, All-Mode, 4-Matic, xDrive and who knows how many more. There are only three generic types of 4x4 system and the next few pages are going to distil it all, plus all the twiddly bits. Whatever else you don't know about your 4x4 and driving it – you can ditch all the off-road driving stuff in this book if you want – do be clear about your 4x4 driveline.

All 4x4s are not the same. Technophobic PR and sales persons, under-briefed brochure writers, too-busy engineers and gloss-over magazine 'experts' often combine to leave you confused about what really is going on.

And media persons are all too ready to dismiss explanations as 'too technical' or 'unnecessary'. Wrong on both counts. Life is about detail. And it's surprisingly simple anyway. You've likely already got the gist of it from the diagrams opposite.

Beware The Emperor's New Clothes. These are still the basic three generic types of four-wheel drive, though auto-engage systems are proliferating and getting smarter.

Different approaches. Driving all four wheels all the time but in a way that accommodates the slight differences in distance travelled by left and right wheels, front axle and rear axle (desert picture, p.2.4), is the ideal. We saw this (p.2.3) with Leonardo's 'modified, de-compromised perfect system'. From the design-engineering point of view this is easy to achieve. The differentials (sketches, p.2.5) that allow the left wheel to go faster or slower than the right wheel have sat in the middle of a normal car's driven back axle for over a hundred years enabling the outside wheel to go further when it turns a corner. They can just as easily be installed between the front and rear prop shafts of a 4x4 vehicle.

A centre differential adds cost, weight and bulk so if you make 4x4 selectable – for use only when needed – then you can usually do away with it. Some argue, shakily, that 4x4 uses more fuel than 4x2 so the facility should be used only when needed. The result is a bunch of different design philosophies which we'll call, for convenience here (these are not EU- or UN-sanctioned categories!) :

- Type 1. Selectable 4x4
- Type 2. Auto-engaged 4x4
- Type 3. Permanent 4x4

Re-check the basics. Peek back again to page 2.3 which covers the whole 'Leonardo' progression from soap-box to 'bean-counter's modified, re-compromised, perfect 4x4 system'. Keep that in mind (and tongue in cheek) and all this modern stuff clunks into perspective. The trade-name disguises and TLAs (three letter acronyms), like the Emperor's New Clothes, fall away.

Don't forget low range. We're just looking at types of four-wheel drive at the moment so remember all the above types (like the 2012 Mercedes ML) may or may not be combined with a two-speed transfer gearbox. As we'll see on the next spread, this gears the final drive ratio down by a factor of around two – in effect giving you a 'second set' of extra low gears for heavy duty towing or sustained off-pavement operation such as undertaken by many civil engineers.

'Soft-roaders'? This is a general usage term but briefly, such vehicles – with their unofficial and purely colloquial category – are designed to give owners the benefits of four-wheel drive traction and safety on snow, ice, wet grass and the like, but without the extra set of low range gears that would be required for demanding off-road conditions.

Their 4x4 system is usually Type 2 (see opposite) achieved in various ways (Sec 2.6). This is a 'soft', automatically-engaged, connection between front and rear prop shafts usually using clutches to give four-wheel drive when needed – and reverting to 4x2 when not. It's not a 'hard' connection. Demographics being what they are, 'soft-roader' buyers are often not mechanical enthusiasts and manufacturers make the auto-engage systems as simple as possible – as well as (see Sec 2.5) taking the opportunity to include some quite smart nannying too.

4x4 systems – the three generic types and applications

NB. Low range gearbox omitted for clarity. (See next spread.)

Type 1. Selectable 4x4

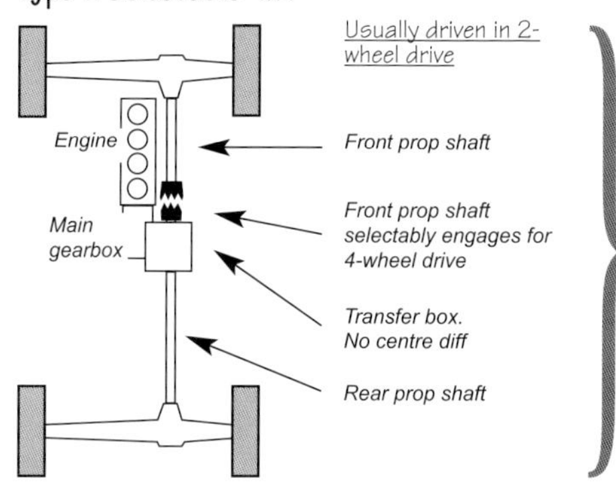

Typically used on working pickups. 4x4 selected only when needed. With no centre diff this produces a 'locked centre diff' effect, benefitting traction in severe off-road conditions. But 4x4 must be disengaged on hard surfaces or when not needed; steering forces are higher in 4x4.

Type 2. Auto-engaged 4x4

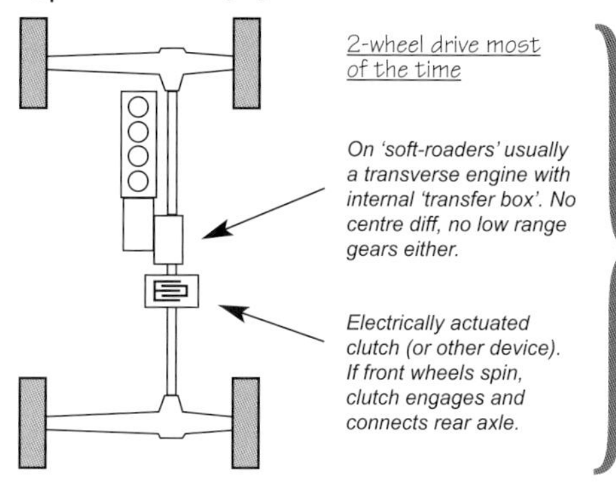

Virtually the standard format for soft-roaders. Usually, a transverse engine with front half-shafts emerging direct from the integral gearbox (centre diagram p.2.39) and no need for the transfer box shown left. There are many iterations of this concept – many use a Haldex electro-hydraulically actuated clutch (p.2.17).

Type 3. Permanent 4x4

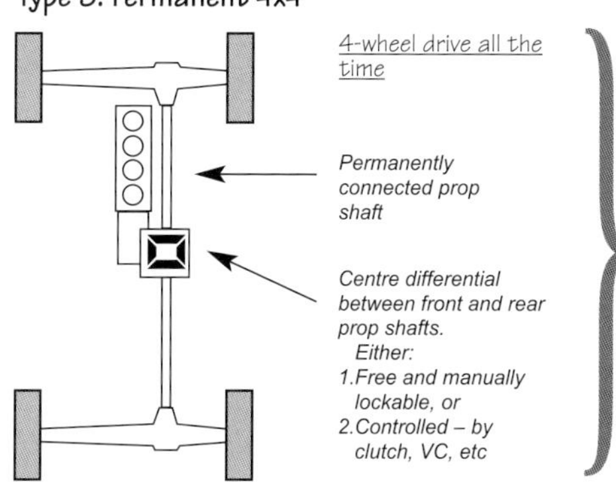

The norm for serious off-roaders (and, strangely, for luxury 4x4s such as Cayenne, Range Rover, Touareg, etc). One or more diff locks provided.

2.4 Traction – 4x4 and low range

Typical 4x4 transmission

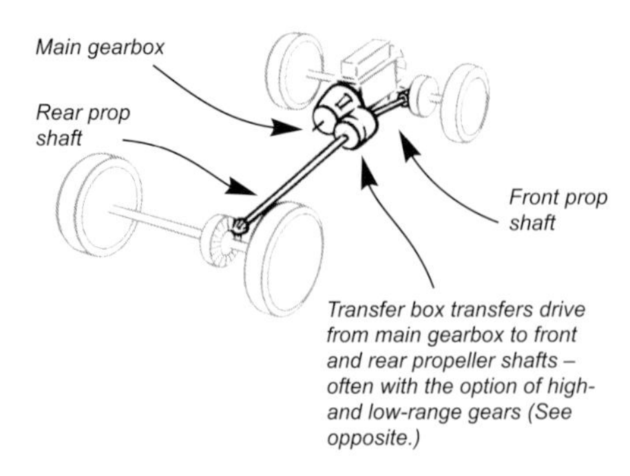

Ingredients of traction

Traction is enhanced by four-wheel drive on all surfaces, but the other half of the equation, off-road, is flotation – big wheels, big tyres and, when needed, low tyre pressures.

Pushing backwards and downwards. With all this talk about traction, a quick look at its real meaning would be timely – especially in the context of 4x4 and the 'little gear lever' (or rotary switch or button ...) for low range. You'll have scanned the Leonardo system on page 2.3 so will know roughly what's coming.

Traction tends to be thought of as pull – farm tractors pulling wagons. It's easier to regard it as push – the bottom of the wheel pushing against the surface of the ground to move a vehicle forward.

In perfect conditions of smooth roads and infinite grip one-wheel drive would suffice. But if roads are wet and slippery and where no-road conditions are muddy, four-wheel drive means three wheels can still push if one gets on a slippery patch (especially, as we've seen, if there are diff locks available).

Off-road – push with float. Away from the perfect conditions of one-wheel drive, the real world, off-road particularly, is often soft as well as slippery. Spreading the weight over a bigger 'footprint' helps prevent sinkage. Big wheels have a bigger ground footprint than small ones and this footprint can be enlarged still further in emergency conditions by letting tyres down a little. (There are important speed and safety implications to this – see Sections 4.7 and 8.2) Big wheels also give a smoother ride over rough ground.

Big wheels? Watch the tyres. A word of caution. To retain design-spec gear ratios, big diameter 'styled' wheels (18-22in rims) must have the same overall diameter (including tyre) as a 16 inch rim on standard tyres. They are usually therefore fitted with low profile tyres which are unsuitable for off-road use as well as giving a harsher ride on-road – see picture p.8.9. Unless you're desperate to be labelled a 'cool dude' steer clear of large diameter rims with low-profile tyres!

Ground clearance. Large overall tyre diameters also ensure greater ground clearance over obstacles. Beam axles keep this ground clearance (p.3.9) constant – unlike most independently sprung front ends – and keep the tyres' tread always flat on the ground. If your usage is biased to off-road, beam axles are usually best. Having said that, some designers have addressed the problem with 'cross linking' (Range Rover *et al*) through which an independent suspension does not suffer loss of clearance.

Grip and gradient – enemies of traction. If poor grip can be overcome by driving all four wheels and also benefit from bigger wheels, the other enemy of traction is gradient – uneven surfaces, steep hills (or heavy loads up not-so-steep hills). The extra traction you need for this – 'power', or more accurately, torque – can come from additional low gears: the other half of the traction equation – see below.

The ingredients. So the ingredients of traction, especially off-road, are:

- Drive to all four wheels
- Big footprint wheels
- Under-axle, under-belly clearance
- Extra 'power' (torque) – see next.

Extra gears – low range

Lower gearing. Extra-low gears are available on most 4x4s – but these days not

Two-speed transfer gearbox – high and low range

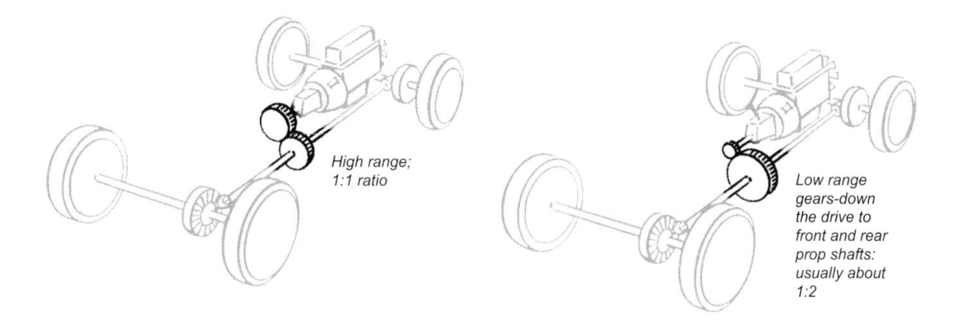

all, such as 'soft-roaders'. These gears are not all in the same gearbox.

The transfer box on a 4x4 is what transfers power from the normal gearbox to the rear and front axles thus making it a 4x4. But this extra transfer gearbox is what is on the other end of 'the little gear lever' on many 4x4s. As well as 'transferring' power to rear and front axles, is also a two-speed affair with high and low ratio gears. The small manual lever is the best way of controlling the transfer gearbox but often – cost and easier cab design – manufacturers replace it (accepting the poor ergonomics) by a rotating switch or button with electrical selection.

Doubling the number of gears. Not all 4x4s have a two-speed transfer box but, in those that do, it is a simple solution to providing extra torque through extra gears. It is 'downstream' of the main gearbox and by selecting low ratio it gears-down *all* the gears in the normal gearbox by a ratio of about 1:2 depending on manufacturer.

In 'high' range the gears are unaffected. So your 4x4 has a transfer box to effect the four-wheel drive function and, additionally in serious off-roaders, to provide what amounts to a complete set of very low gears so that a 5-speed box yields 10 gears. Making a single gearbox with ten forward speeds which could be successively selected would result in an expensive, heavy, complex item.

Low ratio for heavy jobs. The 'low box' is selected for specific heavy duty tasks as we shall see (Section 3.2).

Low ratio gears are available when the vehicle has a two-speed transfer box – invaluable off-road – and for towing boats out of the water.

Classic application of the low-range of gears afforded by a two-speed transfer box. Using low range drops the gear ratios of all gears in the main gearbox by around 1:2. Trying to move even this lightweight boat on soft ground in a vehicle lacking a low range would likely result in much clutch slipping, revs and sweaty palms. The low-ratio approach is calm and controlled; see Section 3.2.

2.5 Soft-roaders – generic

Block the sales-talk; get real

Soft-roaders have cheaper, less effective drivelines but still do well within their more limited performance envelope.

As ever, horses-for-courses. First take a sample of, for instance, the product line-up from Land Rover and Toyota four-by-fours at the time of writing:

- Land Rover make Freelanders costing £19k to £34k. They also make Range Rovers priced £66k to close on £90k.
- Toyota produce RAV4s at £23k-26k. And Land Cruisers at £30k-£46k.

All car interiors these days are pretty darn good. The high fliers might splurge a little more on the leather, woodwork and audio but by and large there is little to complain about in any of them.

So where does the price difference get accommodated? Certainly manufacturers' margins are bigger on the top models but, in general, cheaper 4x4s are a bit smaller and have a simpler technical specification than the top-of-the-range models. That technical specification almost invariably affects the

driveline – the way the 4x4 function is achieved and with what limitations.

Sensible purchasers, if they just want a moderate-sized vehicle that will accommodate kids, kit and clobber and – importantly – not get banjaxed by snow and ice in the winter, will see little point in crippling the budget by buying a leather-clad leviathan that will climb Mount Kilimanjaro in third gear.

Enter the soft-roader – usually an auto-engage 4x4 with clever little bits and pieces that will address wheelspin, 'split-mu' (ice in the gutter) and packed snow when the commuter rush has squashed the thin snowfall into a glazed skating rink before the gritters got round to your location. Soft-roaders have got pretty smart in recent years – in particular addressing the left/right wheel spin issue.

If a soft-roader is what best suits your purpose, this section goes on to examine what to look for within the genre, how front-rear and side-to-side wheelspin is controlled and how much the performance envelope is extended in the best. It's hard not to regard some of the current brochure-speak and PR as deliberately misleading. Either way, do pay attention to the driveline. 'ITDS' – see back cover!

Take a cold hard look at what you want of your 4x4. Soft-roaders are infinitely smarter than they used to be and will satisfy most non-expedition, non-extreme users.

Beguiling styling. The Range Rover Evoque (left), despite its starry looks, has a tweaked Freelander driveline also based around the well-known auto-engage 4x4 Haldex Gen-4 electro-hydraulic clutch unit (next spread). Skoda's well-respected Yeti (above) has it too; plus an 'Off-road' button to quicken traction-control response. Manufacturers write their own software to control the Haldex and brake-activated traction control.

Progress in auto-engaged 4x4

Soft-roaders get smart. If you're an experienced, old-school off-roader you may admit to having – now or in the past – a somewhat patronising attitude towards any 4x4 without low-range or a 'gears and shafts' connection between the front and rear axles. Such, indeed was a description that fitted what came to be known as 'soft-roaders'. In the main it still does and implied, correctly, a lesser order of off-road capability.

Passive and active systems. Today's 'soft-roaders' are not what they once were. It is important to distinguish between what may be termed 'passive' auto-engage 4x4 systems and 'active' systems. In the early days, auto-engage systems depended on the rotational speed difference between front and rear wheels (or prop shafts) to engage 4x4. In other words you had to have wheelspin at one end before you got drive to the other. Viscous couplings worked like that; so does the 2013 Fiat Panda 4x4, albeit chivvied-on by electronics.

Auto-engage 4x4 is ideal where there is an infrequent requirement, Systems that engage 4x4 for start-off and pull away are a real bonus.

'Active' systems like the Haldex explained opposite, provide hydraulic power all the time (electric pump and/or hydraulic accumulator) ready to respond instantly to ECU triggering of the 'need 4x4' command. Plus pre-emptive 4x4 on start-off.

Market-wise a policy of dumbing-down led to the acceptance – still prevalent and applicable to both passive and active systems – of this foolproof all-wheel drive system where drivers did not have to think about engaging and disengaging 4x4 manually. It's popular too with accountants and product-liability folks for shunning provision of a costly, possibly lockable, centre differential.

Grippy start. However, if a system – in principle – can automatically engage and disengage 4x4 when required and is also cheaper to make then it merits examination – especially – nay, vitally – if the requirements of the buying public are considered. As we've seen, it's what a lot of people want. Also, as a hangover from the days of selectable 4x4, four-by-two was perceived to be the way to go for normal driving (in order to lower fuel consumption fractionally) and 4x4 was saved for special occasions like front-wheel spin on ice. But then the thinkers (Haldex, BMW) lit upon some other 'special occasions' when going into 4x4 would be useful. Like starting off and accelerating when contributions from all four wheels are helpful.

ABS wheel-speed sensors at each wheel was already opening a huge opportunity to use such information to engineer smart stability-control systems. Could this output be fed into some all-knowing, smarty-pants algorithm to take care not only of front-rear wheelspin but left-right slip as well?

As ever, all these ideas meant it was electronics to the rescue. But put it all together and situations presented themselves where an acutely-sensed set of critical parameters – wheelspin front/rear, wheelspin left/right, stability situations, oversteer/understeer – could be brought to heel by engaging 4x4 and braking individual wheels to get the ship back on course.

The smart systems

Auto-engage plus. So now some clever kit lies within the typical soft-roader. Soft-roaders are still the smaller, lighter, versatile school-run carry-alls capable of moderate off-road performance. They are still front-wheel drive vehicles with an auto-engaged 4x4 system bringing in drive to the rear wheels by activating a multi-plate clutch on an otherwise 'freewheeling' rear prop shaft.

And they have no low range gears – an important point to remember if you're tempted to try steep gradients slowly or crawl over obstacles.

Smart? When? Typically today's best soft-roaders will probably also have a software programme that engages 4x4 when starting off and accelerating. This is sensible stuff because moving off and accelerating is when the engine is working hard to move a tonne or more of metalwork up to 30 or 40 mph. So that's when the vehicle is asking for the most traction it can get – preferably without wheelspin on icy roads. As we've seen, spreading the push between four instead of two wheels provides exactly that.

Typical, real-world soft-roader Haldex driveline schematic

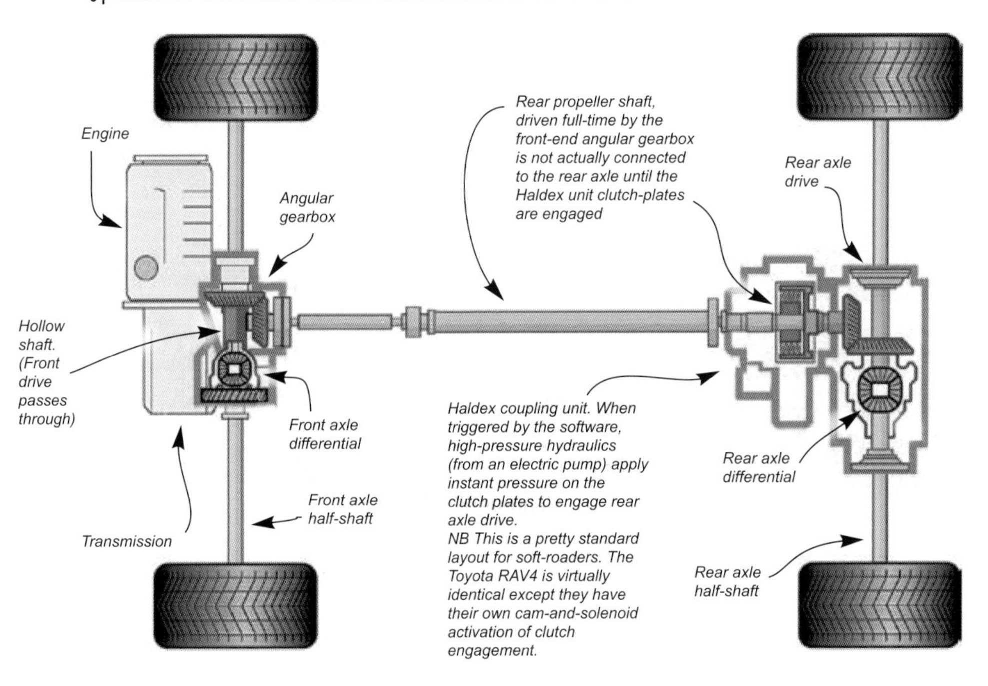

The front-rear connection

Similar approach. There's a broad similarity in auto-engaged four-wheel drive systems. Usually the vehicle is in two-wheel (front) drive with a propeller shaft to the rear axle 'freewheeling' and not connected. The connection-in-waiting between the two is usually a multi-plate 'wet' clutch, similar to that on a motorcycle. Engagement of that clutch can be:

- Automatic, triggered by a speed difference between front and rear axles caused by front-wheel slip. This, (see opposite) can be 'passive' or 'active' with a separate hydraulic power source.
- Plus manual selection – useful as in Nissan's XTrail' selectable '4x4 lock'.
- Other triggers determined by the software such as (see above) starting off and accelerating to cruising speed after which disengagement takes place.

Clutch activation. Physical activation of that clutch engagement and the controlling software vary from one manufacturer to another, though. Toyota's RAV4 in-house system uses a purely electric cam-actuation of the rear clutch pack. The widely-used Swedish Haldex system (Tiguan, Audi Q3, Freelander, Evoque, Yeti, Volvo XC series etc) uses an electrically-driven hydraulic pump to fill a (pressure) accumulator to 30 bar (or a constantly running pump).

When triggered by the software, this can instantly engage the clutch pack when bidden to do so and that clutch can deliver considerable torque to the back axle. Haldex provide the unit; programming it for the ECU (electronic control unit) is left to individual manufacturers. Such a programme can be fully automatic or 'controllable automatics' such as Land Rover's 'Terrain Response' or Skoda's 'Off-road' button.

When buying a soft-roader look carefully at how the front/rear drive connection works and check if there is a manual override. That can be very useful.

Braked-wheel traction control – the articulation case

Wheelspin on off-loaded wheels: left/right wheelspin due to 'diagonal suspension'. (Not enough articulation – see pp.3.10 and 4.14.) Taken gently, the vehicle failed here with wheelspin front-left and rear-right. These off-loaded wheels were then allowed to spin for about three, gritted-teeth, smoky, seconds; then the vehicle pulled away. OK but far too slow a reaction. Traction control braking on the off-loaded wheels had eventually transferred torque to the gripping wheels; hot brake discs front-left and rear-right confirmed it. A neat demo of braked traction control – OK for snow and 'split-mu', but, compared with a 100% diff lock, or EDL, pathetic. (*'mu' – the Greek letter μ, in case your keyboard won't do it – indicates friction, grip, traction. 'Split-μ' means the left wheel, say, is on good traction like dry tarmac and the other is on ice - see image facing page.)*

Car body datum

Front wheels ground contact plane

Rear wheels ground contact plane

'Diagonal suspension' *off-loads left-front and right-rear wheels resulting in cross-axle wheelspin at both ends.*

The benefits of cross-axle wheelspin control apply as much to all-weather school-run commuters as to lantern-jawed explorers.

Variations on a theme. Few soft-roaders nowadays (Terios, Forester, Grand Vitara ... ?) have permanent 4x4 with a centre diff. One or two, such as the Nissan XTrail, allow useful bypassing of the auto-4x4 stage and the driver can select 4x4 when required rather than wait for the auto-engage. This will remain selected until road speed reaches around 20mph; it will then disengage but resume 4x4 if the speed drops below the disengage speed; a typically Nissan common sense approach.

The left-right connection

Battling wheelspin – two cases. With the front-rear connection sorted out, attention must now be paid to eliminating a left or right wheel spinning on its own. Soft-roaders never used to have such a facility. But adequate winter-driving performance demanded cross-axle wheelspin be addressed and significantly reduced. Such wheelspin is normally due to a low-grip patch on one side of the vehicle – the so-called 'split-mu' case – see picture opposite. But in uneven off-road conditions, individual wheels can become sufficiently off-loaded (or even clear of the ground) to allow spinning. This (picture facing page) could be called the 'articulation case' – needing traction control.

Those ABS speed-sensors. The same set of sensors utilised by the ABS (anti-skid braking system) to monitor individual wheel-speeds are used to establish traction control. (Additionally, these sensors, plus lateral and longitudinal solid-state accelerometers use a central ECU to give stability control, hill-start assist, downhill control – and brew the tea?)

Traction control. Many 4x4s, including soft-roaders, have left/right wheelspin control effected by auto-application of individual-wheel braking on the spinning wheel (rather than the superior but much more expensive limited-slip or locking differential) – something covered in some detail on pp.2.6, 2.7. The ABS wheel-speed sensors deliver the information to an ECU which then activates selective, individual-wheel braking. Such brake application has to be very precise – (see box below)* – enough, no more, and allocated according to the prevailing situation. The best systems will

***Traction control brake application**

That bit above with an asterisk about '...Such brake application has to be very precise ... '? Remember on page 2.3: '... the differential ...apportions the drive 'fairly', ie if the left wheel goes 15% faster, then the pinion wheel ensures the right wheel goes 15% slower. (...or ...) one wheel ... speeding up by 100% and other one standing still'?

Ever jacked your car up, both rear wheels off the ground? Engine idling, in gear, both back wheels go round lazily at the same speed. If (don't actually do this, please!) you grabbed (ie braked) one rear wheel and stopped it, the other wheel – thanks to the differential – would go round twice as fast.

So with braked-wheel traction control you can't just slam on brake – that could snap a half-shaft or kangaroo the vehicle forward, The braking has to be feathered so that the stationary wheel accepts torque proportional to the apparent slip – the difference in wheel speeds.

In a locking diff you're simply binding one half-shaft to the other which is exactly what you want (See Leonardo's 4x4, p.2.3) With traction control, in horribly crude terms, you already have wheelspin and then have to stop it.

Braked-wheel traction control – the 'split-μ' case

Impressive demonstration of what can be achieved (Evoque on test). A very steep slope, standing start, left wheels on cleared tarmac, right wheels on packed snow: about two seconds wheel spin then off up the hill. With a Discovery or Range Rover and EDL (electronic diff lock – see p.2.6) there'd be no spin. There, the 'pre-emptive phase' (see p.2.9) engages short-period diff-lock from standstill anyway, immediately overlapped here by the 'reactive phase' – reacting to incipient wheelspin. With no front-axle EDL, those vehicles would rely on braked front-right wheel for front-end traction.

base this brake application on sensing slip but generally design-engineers err on the side of less rather than more so reaction times can be slow – agonisingly slow if your expensive tyres are smokingly still in contact with the ground (see picture opposite).

A poor substitute but ... . Again facing realities, such traction control, with its time delay, brake wear and energy inefficiencies, is a poor substitute for a locking or limited-slip diff but it keeps costs down and can deal effectively with most of those awkward, usually transient, situations on packed snow – see below (and upper pic overleaf!).

Combat footage! Video still of prototype Freelander 2 test. No axle articulation could match this track. The vehicle paused briefly, raised wheel spun for about 1-2 seconds before being braked and steady progress was resumed, Full marks to Haldex and traction control software algorithm. Time delay has been reduced on Evoque (but would be zero on a 3-diff-locked G-Wagen.)

Sadly no longer a UK-import, the Daihatsu Terios, small as it is, has permanent 4x4 with a centre differential. Excellent; but though this is lockable manually, there is no cross-axle wheelspin control.

The overall picture

Soft-roaders, even with the current driveline technology are not dedicated off-road vehicles and should not be regarded as such. Whilst most of the drivelines are conceived to avoid the weight, packaging problems and, principally the cost, of permanent four-wheel drive with a controllable centre differential, they will nevertheless overcome most of the on-road traction problems likely to be encountered in a bad winter or on untreated roads – most especially so if winter tyres are fitted.

Unpaved tracks of moderate quality, wet meadowland such as sports fields and horse-show venues, campsites – even some wild camping – should not present any problems. The off-pavement performance of the latest soft-roaders has improved out of all recognition in recent years.

The usual absence of low range gears in soft-roaders can to some degree, and for brief periods, be offset by automatic transmission's ability, non-damagingly, to take the transmission to a given max-torque figure through torque-converter slip. Slipping a dry manual clutch to that degree would be very bad for the vehicle (pics p.2.18).

With a soft-roader avoid undue articulation (see pp.3.10 and 9.3), avoid steep / rough gradients and obstacles that need to be taken very slowly. Rough gradients and slow obstacles can precipitate undue wheelspin which, though temporary, can be hard on tyres and extremely hard on clutches of manual-transmission vehicles.

The snapshot. So which vehicles have got what? Light-bulbs over heads and Eureka moments of comprehension will (hopefully!) have resulted from the foregoing pages in Section 2 but an indication of who does what and with what kind of driveline might be useful. The rate of proliferation of new 4x4s, soft-roaders – or those badged as 'crossovers' to further blur the distinctions – would demand an almost weekly update. So the following 'Section 2.6 – Snapshot' is just that, to give you a feel for the situation at the time of writing and with luck may help prospective buyers make their decisions.

2.6 Drivelines – snapshot

What to look for

Beware! Technophobic sales persons. The trials and travails of the automotive salesman will be many. His aim is to boost turnover, his loyalty will be to his employer, his knowledge-base must encompass the contents of Glass's Guide to second-hand (and part-exchange) car prices, his gaze must be steady despite the knowledge that a new model is coming out shortly to displace the one he is trying to move, his grasp of finance must be sure. His shirt must be crisp and his manner appealing.

In the face of all this there seems, all too frequently, little room left for in-depth product knowledge or technical detail – a syndrome often apparent with those staffing the stands at motor shows too. The cool styling, the heated seats, the cup-holders, the Bluetooth, the iPod connectivity, the unimaginable surfeit of audio wattage and loudspeakers will often define the limits of the staffer's technical expertise as well as filling the first 15 pages of the embarrassingly shallow brochure, out-sourced to a minimally-briefed Glossover and Fudge.com.

Don't be taken in by slippery generalities and vague answers to specific questions. Relish, with warmth, a salesman who is honest enough to say 'I don't know – but I'll find out!' But still, be persistent. And copy p.2.38 for your clipboard before you buy.

And incidentally, auto-engaged 4x4 with a residual 2% drive to the rear axle on dry road is NOT 'permanent 4x4' though brochures, salesmen and PR writers routinely try to kid you that it is. Similarly, braked-wheel traction control is NOT a locking diff or EDL.

ITDS – It's The Driveline, Stupid! Not as memorable an acronym as KISS (Keep It Simple, Stupid), but it serves as a clumsy reminder of the main reason for picking up this book. Never mind the leather-topped gearstick, the overhead video, the gold-plated iPod dock and the warmed water-bed for the Weimaraner – the driveline is the most important part of what you are buying or have bought. By-pass the fancy ® and ™ items and three-letter acronyms that clutter up the brochure. Ask about the driveline; know about it, be sure of what it does for you and the way you'll be using your vehicle.

Priorities? The questions. What to ask:
- Permanent 4x4, selectable or auto-engage?
- Really 'permanent', around 50/50 front/rear split with centre diff?
- Diffs lockable? Manually or auto?
- Real locking diff or braked-wheel traction control?
- If auto-lock, how? When? What %?
- Auto-4x4: active or passive? (p.2.16)
- Any modifying control such as Terrain Response or an Off-Road button?
- What does that do – *exactly, in detail?* (Don't accept 'Transfers the torque to the wheel that most needs it'.)
- How (and how quickly) is front/rear wheelspin taken care of?
- How (and how quickly) is left/right wheelspin taken care of?
- Manual or auto transmission? (opt for auto if possible).

Not all soft-roaders are yet the same in what they offer. Be clear on your requirements and pursue them. Beware smooth-talking salesmen who don't know what they don't know.

Not often thought of as soft-roaders, Volvo's XC-series (the XC60 here) are nevertheless auto-engage 4x4s utilising the Haldex system (p.2.17) to bring rear-axle drive into play. Volvo is careful not to tout serious off-road capability. Here, and on winter tyres (see p.8.9), you'll be OK.

Tech sales flair:
'So what's the little W-button?'
'Winter.'
'Ah! Smart. Snow. Avoids wheelspin. Start off in second, then? Re-maps the throttle?'
'Er ... . Coffee, anyone?'

When trying to understand a modern 4x4 driveline first take on board what is connected to what and how. Only then talk about 'torque transfer'.

Our wonderful media. If the smooth-talking, detail-averse technophobes of the showroom floor sadly leave more of an impression than the down-to-earth minority who really know their stuff, the same cannot be said for our beloved media. There the technical shut-off seems to be consistent, early and widespread. One glossy UK magazine, which it is tempting to label 'The Yahoo's Weekly', can invariably 'review' a new-model 4x4 without referring to the driveline at all. The feel of the plastics, depth of the cupholders, sat-nav accuracy and the handling at suicidal degrees of oversteer on an Alpine pass all get earnest assessment but the bits that really matter, the fundamentals, somehow get left out.

Many may remember the days when magazines had technical editors and skilled artists produced diagrams and drawings to explain how everything worked. Now, an amazingly detailed cutaway commissioned by the manufacturer for mega-bucks is reproduced postage-stamp size in the magazine with no caption or explanation.

So do not turn to the run-of-the-mill automotive journals for guidance on the real-life criteria governing choice and usage of a 4x4 – be it soft-roader or hard-core off-road performer. At the time of writing possibly the most sensible UK motoring 'magazine' is, (not that there's much of it), *The Daily Telegraph* week-end motoring supplement.

Common-sense rules. The points on the previous page are a start. Nothing is so complex it cannot be explained simply. But the gap between the engineers and the customer seems to be ever widening, bridged only by superficial, under-briefed brochure-writers and PR persons. The engineer communicator is a rare breed. Seek them out.

Don't talk torque. Though part of the cool media jargon, it really can be confusing to talk about torque when trying to understand 4x4 drivelines. Far better to think about shafts clamped to other shafts; what's driving what. Remember: torque is a *reactive* concept. It depends on the resistance the wheel is experiencing at any given moment.

Mechanical connections. Relevance? If a solid, all-diffs-locked, everything-clamped-together, 4x4 setup (Leonardo, Phase 1, p.2.3) is on a dry track the 'torque split' is said to be 50/50 front/rear. The jargon (accurately enough, but confusingly) has it that if one end is on ice, this setup has a 'torque-split' of 0/100%. And if the grip changes a bit it could be 15/85%. Yet the driveline and what's clamped to what is the same. So what matters are the *mechanical connections* in the driveline; the clichéd 'torque split' could be anything.

With braked-wheel traction control it actually is valid to talk about 'torque transfer'. Instead of spinning free, the precisely-braked wheel-in-the-air (or on ice) will transfer its rotational energy back over the differential to the stationary wheel (see pic p.2.6) and make it revolve. It is, to borrow the imagery Mercedes use in trying to explain 4Matic (see next spread), simulating a grippy surface for the hung wheel so that the diff can split the power more or less equally again between the two wheels on the axle.

BMW xDrive driveline schematic – essentially rear-wheel drive (BMW X1, X3, X5)

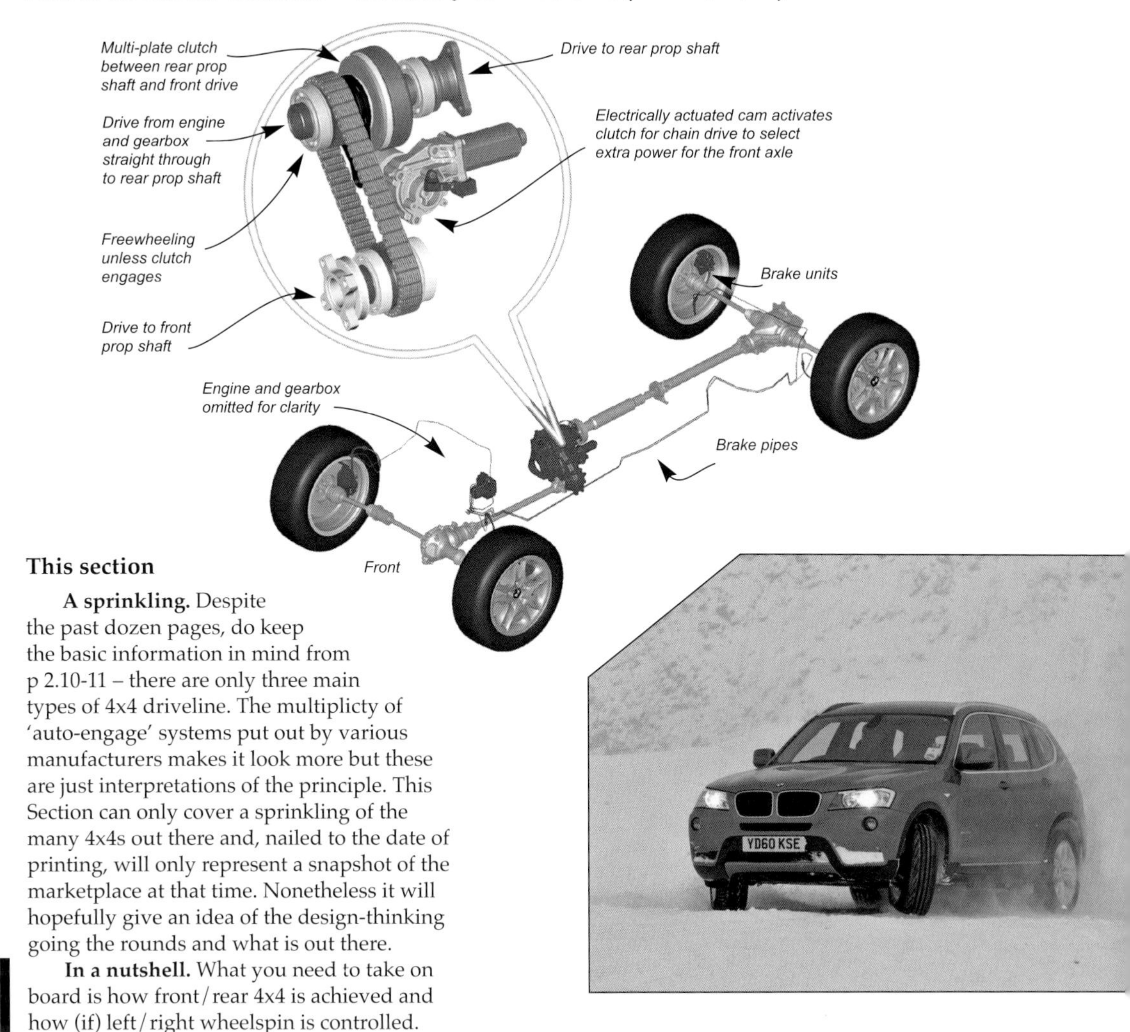

This section

A sprinkling. Despite the past dozen pages, do keep the basic information in mind from p 2.10-11 – there are only three main types of 4x4 driveline. The multiplicty of 'auto-engage' systems put out by various manufacturers makes it look more but these are just interpretations of the principle. This Section can only cover a sprinkling of the many 4x4s out there and, nailed to the date of printing, will only represent a snapshot of the marketplace at that time. Nonetheless it will hopefully give an idea of the design-thinking going the rounds and what is out there.

In a nutshell. What you need to take on board is how front/rear 4x4 is achieved and how (if) left/right wheelspin is controlled.

BMW xDrive

Soft-roader. BMW's X-Series 4x4s – currently the X1, X3 and X5 – do not aspire to rock-crawling off-road capability and have no low-range gears. Their 'xDrive' system is there mainly to cope with winter conditions and enhance on-road grip. BMW have followed their rear-wheel drive credo by biasing the power to the rear axle in the ratio 40/60 front/rear. Thinking in terms of shafts and gears, this is done, not with a torque-splitting epicyclic centre-diff but by first taking a simple drive from the engine and gearbox direct to the back axle (diagram above). To this shaft is attached a 'wet' multiplate clutch (like a motorcycle's) which connects to the front axle. Clutch plate pressure (and slip) is such that it will

Despite the bulk and presence of a BMW X5, it (like the other 'X' models) is a soft-roader with a slipping clutch delivering variable power to the front axle. On full steering lock even that is cut.

transmit only 40% of the available torque to the front. If the ABS wheel speed sensors signal the rear wheels are spinning (on ice, say), the clutch plates will clamp harder, lock up and all the drive goes to the front wheels – the so-called '100% torque transfer' – in reality this just means front and rear prop shafts are clamped together.

Note that xDrive (lacking a centre diff) can be regarded, in effect, as another version of the simple 'Type 2 auto-engage' 4x4 system seen on p.2.11. In BMW's version the drive to 'the other axle' is partly 'engaged' all the time and the 'auto' function can take it from partly- to fully-engaged when required.

Lacking a centre diff, the clutch pack is programmed to disengage completely if a sharp steering angle (tight turn) is sensed.

If max front drive is required an electric actuator, responding to wheelspin messages from the ABS sensors, moves a lever and cam to quickly bring extra pressure on the clutch pack that engages full front axle drive. (At which pont, if the lock were 100%, there is no front/rear differential action. BMW is careful to claim 'almost 100%' torque transfer!)

The very first Freelanders, front and rear axles joined only by a viscous coupling (and nothing else), claimed 'permanent 4x4'. In fact, cruise no-spin conditions allocated only 10% of power to the rear axle (due to different ratios in the front and rear diffs that stirred and 'pre-loaded' the viscous coupling). Like the BMW X-series, a better description would have been 'auto-engage'.

Like most soft-roaders nowadays, the BMWs deal with left/right wheelspin by using ABS-sourced wheel speed data to apply selective braking to individual wheels.

Fiat – Panda 4x4

Simplicity rules. At last, a small 4x4. Simple, light, unpretentious, with a 1.3 litre diesel option, the 2013 Panda 4x4 driveline has nevertheless changed as the years have gone by. Once only a viscous coupling – automatic, but slow to react – an all-new auto-engaged 4x4 driveline has been introduced, albeit 'passive' (p.2.16) and dependent on a degree of front-wheel spin to

Panda 4x4. Despite the snow, it's difficult not to warm to this small, light, effective little auto-engaged 4x4 from Fiat. Though dependent on a degree of front wheel spin to engage the rear drive, electronic control contributes. Interestingly, and using trickle-down technology from the 4x4, Fiat's 4x2 version, called Trekker, equipped with ESP (stability control), provides button-selectable traction control to mimic a diff-lock and inhibit cross-axle spin in icy conditions. Bravissimo!

initiate bringing rear-axle drive into play.

The rotor and stator of a hydraulic pump are attached respectively to the front and rear halves of the prop shaft to the rear axle. Rotational movement between the two (ie when front wheel spin is experienced) generates hydraulic pressure to compress clutch plates and couple drive to the rear axle

Misleadingly referred to by Fiat as an electronic locking differential (ELD, and see box p.2.8), braked-wheel traction control is among the functions that (via a solenoid valve and electronic coupling-control unit intervention) ingeniously combine auto-engage 4x4, stability control and traction control. A selectable button (inappropriately marked 'ELD') sharpens the traction control reaction time. Neat.

Suzuki's Grand Vitara (left: 3- and 5-door options) has permanent four-wheel drive, manually lockable centre diff, and locked-diff low-range gears. Braked-wheel traction control too. Transmission mode selection is electric but via a common-sense rotary control – 4H, 4H.lock, 4L.lock. Jimny (below) has push-button selectable 4x4, low range and optional automatic gearbox.

Suzuki Grand Vitara – and Jimny

All the kit. It is tempting to regard the Grand Vitara and Jimny duo as soft-roaders because they are small but in fact both have low-range gears. Early Grand Vitaras (*Grands Vitarae?*) had an unconventional and rare APTRAC type cam-plate centre diff that actually split torque 47/53 front rear but it had the disadvantage of permitting an off-loaded wheel to spin once it sensed no feedback of torque through ground-contact. It was also noisy.

Type 4 and 5 Grand Vitaras have a conventional centre diff (see p.2.5), selectably lockable. When selecting low range the diff lock engages as part of the selection process (see selector inset). These models, now equipped with stability control and utilising the ABS wheel speed sensors, have braked-wheel traction control to take care of left/right cross-axle wheel spin.

The long-established Jimny, (right), another small 4x4 – with impressive off-road credentials – once an ardent supporter of the Series 1 Land Rover approach to driveline controls, is still part-time, selectable four-wheel drive (Type 1 on p.2.11) with high and low range gears, but now 4x4 selection is achieved by pressing a button – with the clutch dipped. Being selectable 4x4 predicates no centre differential and the front/rear prop shafts are thus 'locked' any time 4x4 is selected. There are no cross-axle anti-wheelspin arrangements.

The Jimny has a 1.3 litre petrol engine, Euro 5 compatible (p.7.24), and now offers a four-speed automatic gearbox option.

Panda and Jimny spurn the annual bloat factor affecting other makes. The Grand Vitara, also moderate dimensionally, has real permanent 4x4 and low range gears.

Mercedes-Benz G-Wagen 463 driveline – simplicity, function: the off-road benchmark

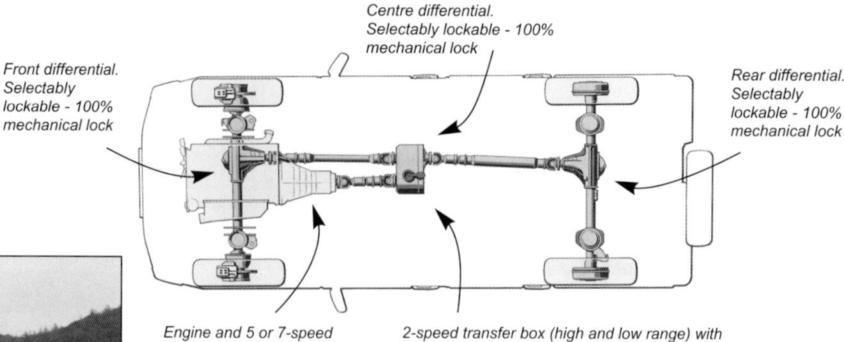

Mercedes G-Wagen 463. Minimal automatics, minimal electronics, 100% mechanical diff locks (no slippage), manually selected. And de-selected. Arguably the best.

Mercedes' G-Wagen, has the thinking driver's, no-nonsense, benchmark 4x4 system. 21st century interior bling on some models, as with Range Rover, is an incongruous distraction.

Mercedes-Benz 4x4 systems

Wide range of systems. Mercedes-Benz has been making all-wheel drive vehicles since 1926 and, with its current wide range of products from lively hatchbacks to large trucks, has covered a correspondingly wide range of systems.

G-Wagen. The first versions of the G-class, popularly known worldwide as the G-Wagen (from the German Geländewagen), were made in 1979 and both the vehicle and its driveline, still produced close to their original concepts, could be described as classics for their robust functional simplicity and fitness for purpose. This is as close as it gets to the ideals covered on p.2.3.

The diagram above shows a real permanent-4x4 system – 'shafts and gears', no 'apportioned torque', slipping clutches, braked wheels disguised as diff locks or electronic intervention. (Currently, for ABS and stability control, there is, of course, electronic control.) The diff locks – rear axle, centre between front and rear prop shafts, and front axle – are manually selectable; and must be de-selected when not required.

But ... . Whilst this system equips a vehicle with virtually unstoppable off-road capabilities there are real and potential problems, as touched on elsewhere. Firstly (see photo and caption on p.2.9 – a mute testimony to the excellence of the concept), the system must be massively engineered since a situation could arise when one wheel and one axle half-shaft is taking all the torque the engine and gearboxes can produce. Such engineering is heavy and expensive.

Secondly, novice drivers forgetting to unlock the differentials can experience handling problems. A locked rear axle in a sharp turn can, through scuffing, lose grip and allow skidding. A locked-diff front axle in an attempted sharp turn can leave the impression that the steering has jammed.

Mercedes, nevertheless, treating G-Wagen operators as thinking professionals, have held to the principles of ultimate off-road traction. Other manufacturers address the potential issues here by inserting clutch systems in the differentials also controlled by electronic sensors programmed to take account of steering commands.

Mercedes have now addressed transient wheel-spin by adding 4ETS (see opposite) to the G-Wagen which is a braked-wheel traction control system like that described on pp.2.18 and 2.19.

Despite the appearance of just another luxury 4x4, the 2012 M-class (left) tackles serious off-road operation head on. The Off-Road Pro option includes low range gears, selectable diff-locks centre and rear, and suspension lift. (Right) The no-cursor, rotating-knob transmission mode selectors' tiny LEDs will be hard to see in bright sunlight. (See also Evoque, p.2.36).

Twenty year heritage – 4Matic, 4ETS. This system has appeared in four different versions since 1987, including changes as radical as exclusion and re-inclusion of centre and rear locking-differentials. Now (2013) a fifth iteration has appeared bearing the same name - see p.2.28. ('4Matic-soft' or '4-matic-lite' could – see over – be a better name.)

4Matic is common to nine Mercedes-Benz models as original equipment or as an option but one of its most recent applications is to the 2012 model ML (above). 4Matic and its partner system 4ETS are fair examples of fuzzy brand names – attracting the usual panacea accolade in the brochures.

Basically a permanent four-wheel drive system, the 4Matic/4ETS (Electronic Traction System) mix provide comprehensive front/rear and left/right wheel slip control usually using centre (and rear) clutch-controlled limited-slip differentials together with individual wheel braking. Despite the smart acronyms, a fairly standard recipe.

Though easily and usefully adapted to off-road applications, the original aim of 4Matic/4ETS was traction and handling stability in winter conditions for ordinary cars. Detailed analysis of the longitudinal and lateral components of tyre grip in acceleration and cornering situations was carried out – all against the backdrop at production level of cost, weight, packaging and overall effectiveness.

At one point diff-locks were ditched in favour of (only) 4ETS wheel-braking traction control but later reinstated. (See next page!.)

Though arguably just another luxury 4x4, the ML, after a somewhat flaccid start driveline-wise in the early years, now has a more robust and responsive system. It is, sensibly, now also optionally available with (at surprisingly moderate cost) the full inventory of off-road equipment – the so-called 'Off-Road Pro Engineering' package (OK we get the picture!) – that includes low-range gears, manually selectable diff-locks centre and rear, 'Airmatic' air-suspension that raises under-belly ground-clearance by a dizzy 110mm (and oxygen?), with auto speed limit, off-road configured ABS brakes, start-off assist and the currently obligatory steep downhill automatic speed regulation.

4Matic gained an early reputation for impenetrable complexity, addressing every conceivable issue in the vehicle dynamics lexicon but after two decades, many applications and three previous versions, is now settling down as a mature high-end system (doing pretty much the same as Land Rover's driveline on the Discovery 4 and Range Rover does). Both, bottom line, are – see p.2.11 – just Type 3 permanent-4x4 with ABS and stability control add-ons.

Like 'Terrain Response' (Land Rover) driveline settings, the ML has a similar selector (above,right) to set up 'Trailer', 'Winter' 'Sport'. 'Auto', 'Off-road 1' and 'Off-road 2' mode (for ultra-steep gradients). Auto box gear change points, throttle map and 4ETS are tweaked accordingly.

Mercedes' 4Matic has gone through a number of iterations over the years. Basically permanent 4x4, now (overleaf) stepping confusingly into auto-engage.

New-variant 4Matic. Announced early 2013, confusingly bearing the same 4Matic name, the 'new' system appears to be a routine Type 2 (see p.2.11) auto-engaged 4x4 system – basically front-wheel drive – with an electronically-controlled hydraulic clutch pack to summon varying amounts of rear-axle input as required. (Press releases incorrectly term it 'permanent all-wheel drive' implying a centre-diff 50/50 split.)

As usual such a system includes a tie-in with stability control, ABS and (4ETS) braked-wheel traction control. The presence of a clutch pack allows elimination of a centre differential between front and rear axles. (Here we go again – see previous page!)

This, in effect, is the Mercedes-Benz version of Haldex (p.2.17) – except, significantly, it is essentially 'passive' (p.2.16) in that the hydraulic rotor pump for clutch activation is dependent, first, on a difference between front and rear prop shaft speed.

'New variant' 4Matic should be re-named. The Sprinter manages to be both Type 1 and Type 2 4x4 (p.2.11) at the same time!. 4x4 is selectable – to enable an auto-engage system.

There is nothing globally 'new' about the concept, only the hardware components that effect its implementation, variations of which will apply to a number of new models in the future. Integration with new dual-clutch automatic gearboxes, improved efficency and low weight are the main characteristics and benefits.

Rate and degree of rear-drive engagement are further controllable according to programming, stability criteria and selectable options such as 'Sport' mode in road cars. No mention is made of pre-emptive 4x4 engagement on set-off.

Commercial cousin – Sprinter 4x4 *et al.* Four-wheel drive vans are a slightly special breed of vehicle. Often out-sourced by manufacturers, they finish up as slightly odd mutants of split parentage.

Mercedes-Benz Sprinters are one of those background vans that you hardly notice, delivering parcels, groceries or anonymous boxes all over the place, all the time.

Slightly more noticeable for its (110mm) raised body is the 4x4 version – designed and built in-house by Mercedes and a natural for a huge range of commercial applications as well as the basis of a camper van for exploring wilder places.

Rear-wheel drive as a 4x2, the 4x4 has push-button selection for the rear axle but, in a kind of hairy-armed version of the 'new-variant' 4Matic yet to come, final drive to the back-end is via a clutch – as usual to avoid the weight and cost of a differential in the middle of the vehicle.

There are no mechanical diff locks but ETS traction control – inevitably integrated with a stability system (ESP: electronic stability programme) and ABS – takes care of cross-axle wheel-spin. (The ESP is sensitive to body movements so detects load and centre of gravity to ensure ESP commands are appropriate.) ETS braked-wheel traction control, which could overheat in prolonged off-road operation, has an overheat warning.

A considerable benefit, low range gears are an option but gearing-down is only a 1.42% drop so it's also useful for just normal driving in confined spaces.

An interesting vehicle – factory-designed and built, not out-sourced. 3.5 tonnes GVW (5t option), over 600mm fording, manual gearbox (6 speeds) or auto (5).

Mercedes Sprinter 4x4 is, in effect a 'selectable soft-roader', not pretending to be a G-Wagen but it balances demanding on-road and track performance with the preservation of the torque-limited rear drive.

Skoda

Yeti. Skoda's reputation for soundly engineered cars is enhanced by their resistance to the current trend to ever-bigger 4x4s. The Yeti's moderate dimensions, lack of bloat and versatile interior with removable back seats are a positive selling point. As an auto-engage 4x4 soft-roader with a Gen-4 Haldex coupling (see p.2.17) ready to engage the rear axle when needed (and at start-off), plus cross-axle, braked-wheel traction control, the Yeti driveline is almost identical to that of the VW Tiguan (p.2.30). It even has an Off-Road button fulfilling the same functions. Automatic versions of the Yeti have a dual-clutch (DSG) gearbox – quick but less tolerant of low-speed off-road control than a torque-converter 'slush-pump' auto.

Moment of truth. The camera has caught the front right wheel just starting to spin on the slippery mud before the traction-control cuts in.

Subaru

Forester. Subaru PR makes much of being 'unlike others' and this is true of their driveline which, unusually for a soft-roader with no low range, is permanent four-wheel drive with a centre differential *controlled* by a viscous coupling to prevent excessive front/rear prop-shaft spin. So drive to all four wheels is there all the time – real permanent 4x4 – with none of the engage/disengage sequence or small time-delays inherent with auto-engage 4x4.

Quenching cross-axle wheelspin, however, is still by ABS speed-difference sensing and ECU-triggered single-wheel brake application (see photos p.2.18).

Sadly, at the time of writing Subaru don't have a (rough-terrain friendly) automatic transmission to take the new diesel engine's high torque output so optimum application of this manual-gearbox vehicle is in slippery snow, ice and surface mud conditions rather than rocky off-road (see p.2.18).

Skoda's Yeti has a classic Haldex Gen-4 auto-engage 4x4 set-up plus an 'Off-road' button to tweak the software control parameters. The Forester is permanent 4x4 with centre diff.

Tyres are part of the driveline and winter tyres, virtually standard equipment in Europe, are only just catching on in the UK. Some experts aver a grip increment equivalent to 4x4 after 2WD.

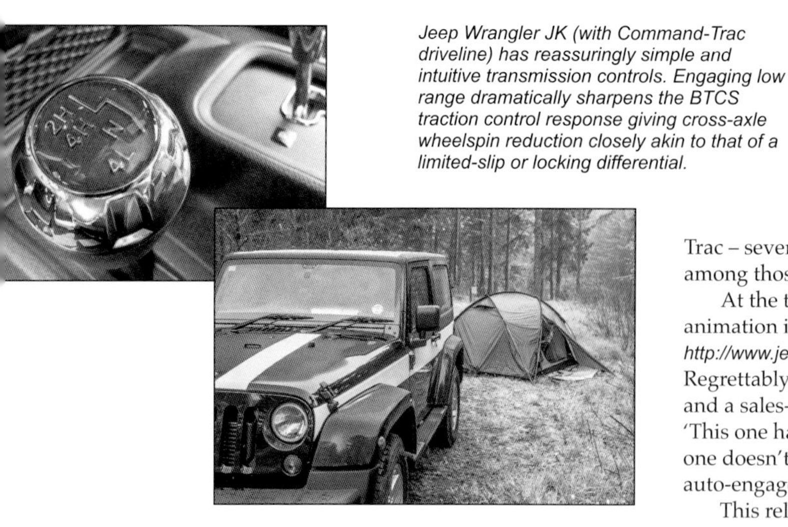

Jeep Wrangler JK (with Command-Trac driveline) has reassuringly simple and intuitive transmission controls. Engaging low range dramatically sharpens the BTCS traction control response giving cross-axle wheelspin reduction closely akin to that of a limited-slip or locking differential.

Jeep – 70 years plus

Graded options. Who needs what and who wants what – plus the ever-present realities of production cost and pricing, have resulted in no less than *nine* 4x4 driveline options for vehicles within the Jeep range of products. Easier if they'd been labelled 1-9, Jeep's addiction to fancy, non-intuitive trade-names makes for early brochure-glaze onset and checking option-costs as the first-try method of establishing which direction the functionality is heading.

The name game – ®™etc. Selec-Trac, Command-Trac, Quadra-Trac, Quadra-Drive, Freedom-Drive and Rock-Trac – several with 'I' and 'II' sub-species are among those to be boggled at.

At the time of writing, some excellent animation is a good primer at: *http://www.jeep.com/en/4x4/how_systems_work/* Regrettably there is 'torque' talk (see p.2.22) and a sales-oriented refusal to say clearly 'This one has a centre diff, lockable and that one doesn't have a centre diff at all so is auto-engage and therefore cheaper'.

This reluctance (industry-wide, to be fair) manages, as ever, to defeat a visualisation of what you're buying and what is connected to what. A pity, since provision of such a wide range of product, if clearly displayed, can help those – if not wishing to ascend the Himalayan foothills in third gear – to choose a vehicle more oriented to their needs. And those that do can be similarly informed.

A summary in mechanical-connection terms, appears opposite.

2011 Grand Cherokee was available with Quadra-Trac I or Quadra-Trac II (see opposite). Q-T II gives it high-end off-road performance: low range, multi-sensor-controlled centre diff, and centre-diff lock on start-off. The system works well, with its well-matched automatic transmission. Alas, on-the-move range-change at higher road speeds (low-to-high, see Section 6) is not catered for but a selectable neutral permits towing in auto. On 2012 Overland models, Quadra-Trac II is replaced by Quadra-DRIVE II (adds limited slip rear diff). All Jeep models have BTCS (see opposite).

Jeep – main driveline formats, 2012

Command-Trac I

(Type 1 4x4 – see p.2.11)
For: All Wranglers except Rubicons which have deep 4:1 low range (vs standard 2.72:1)

Manually selectable 4x4 with 100% front-rear connection. Braked cross-axle spin control.

Quadra-Trac I

(Type 3 4x4 – see p.2.11)
For: Grand Cherokee SRT8, and Grand Cherokee Laredo and LaredoX

As Quadra-Trac II but no low range gears: 'free' centre diff (no spin control). Braked cross-axle spin control.

Quadra-Trac II

(Type 3 4x4 – see p.2.11)
For: Standard on 2011 Grand Cherokee Limited and Overland (UK)

As Quadra-Trac I plus 2-speed transfer box, clutch-controlled centre diff. Clutch locks on start-off and in 4-low range.

Quadra-Drive II

(Type 3 4x4 – see p.2.11)
For: Option on some 2011 Grand Cherokee. Standard on 2012 Overland model

As Quadra-Trac II with addition of rear-axle limited slip diff.

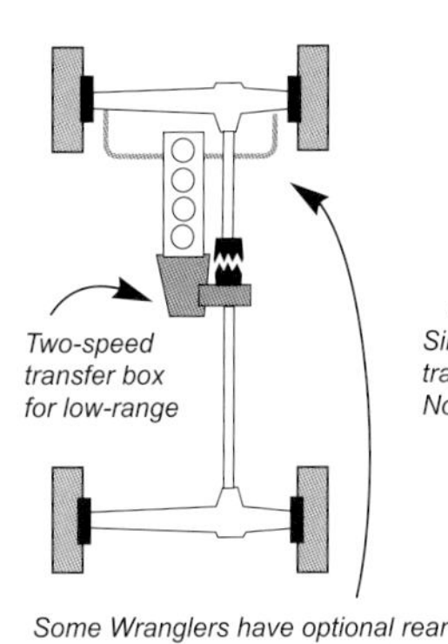

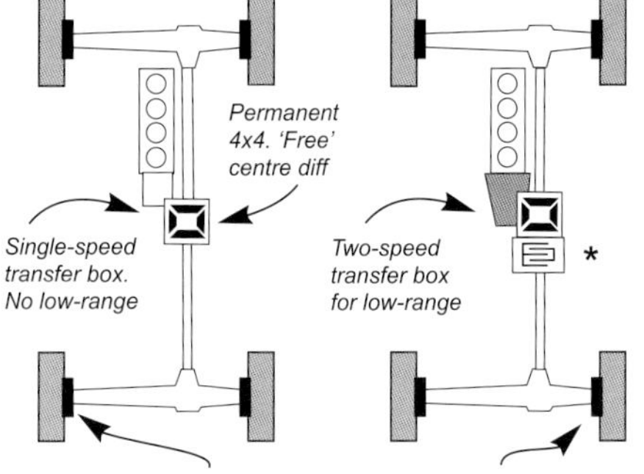

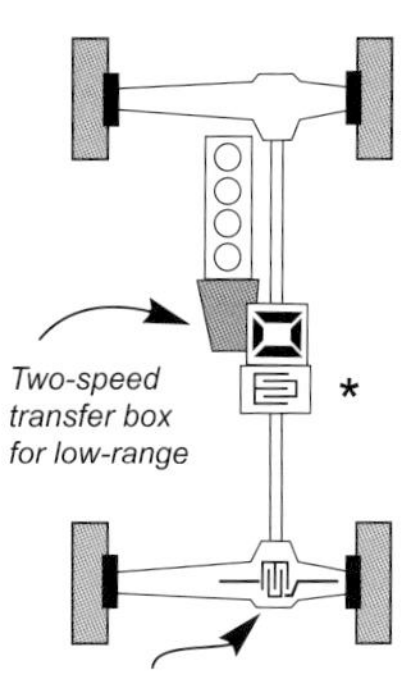

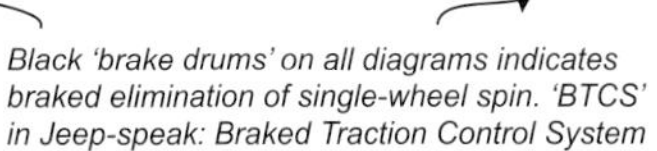

Notes 1. * Clutch-pack variably locks front / rear prop shafts together. In sharp turns clutch eases off to preclude binding transmission.
2. Command-Trac II is the same as Command -Trac I but with button-select low range.
3. 'Freedom-Drive' I and II is basically front 2WD with auto-engage 4x4 and selectable 4-lock. Freedom Drive II has low range.

Jeep Grand Cherokee, Overland model, has air suspension, controllable to add 104mm to normal underbelly clearance. Main transmission selector is familiar gated lever, easy to use without looking. Low range is button-selected (top left). Fine-tuned suite of parameters – throttle response, gear-change points, braking etc is activated by no-cursor rotary knob with LED indicators. Such mode options and downhill speed control, pioneered by Land Rover's Terrain Response, seem to be de riguer in up-market 4x4s but (many feel) hinder development of appropriate driver skills and sensitivity.

Volkswagen

Tiguan. Apart from two 4x2 models, all Tiguans – what VW calls a compact SUV despite its size – are 4x4s: classic, straightforward Haldex-enabled auto-engage drivelines (p.2.17) with ESP and a left-right cross-axle braked-wheel traction control set-up for that wheel-in-the-icy gutter situation. Like Skoda's Yeti, the Escape version has an 'Off Road' button to enhance off-pavement performance: it de-sensitises the throttle, increases cross-axle anti-wheelspin control sensitivity, enables Hill Climb Assistance and steep descent control and sets the ABS up for loose surfaces. Both versions start off in 4x4.

VW's Touareg has a permanent 4x4 driveline of exemplary functionality with a straightforward and foolproof way of controlling it.

Tiguan Escape's 'Off road' button rearranges the deck chairs for what's to come.

Beware the brochures. Alas, at the time of writing the Tiguan brochure, like many, displays enthusiasm at the expense of accuracy. It claims 'permanent four-wheel drive' when in fact prior to auto-engage, drive to the rear is only 10%. And that 'Electronic Diff Lock (EDL) further enhances capability' when in fact braked-wheel traction control is the system (p.2.19 bottom left). Although simulating such an item to a degree, there is no Electronic Diff Lock fitted.

Touareg. Here the brochure errs the other way, omitting to make clear that VW, sensibly, have produced two versions of the Touareg. The first is a simple permanent 4x4 with a Torsen limited-slip centre diff, no low range and an 'Off Road' button similar in function to that of the Tiguan above. The other is something of a wolf in sheep's clothing, the Escape model with (4XMotion) claiming a 1-in-1 (that's 45°!) climb ability. To achieve this a fully lockable centre diff is fitted between the front and rear prop shafts, the rear diff is also fully lockable and there is a low-range gear set too.

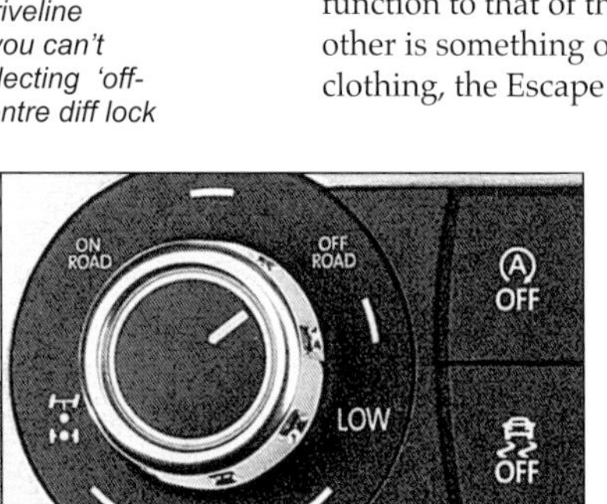

Touareg Escape - wolf in sheep's clothing. The driveline control is a model of clarity, logic and ergonomics. Rotary driveline selector (with cursor!) ensures you can't select low-range without first selecting 'off-road' set-up. You can't select centre diff lock without first selecting low range and you can't select rear diff lock without first selecting centre diff lock. Nice! Just as it should be.

The Touareg Escape has probably one of the clearest and most intuitively fool-proof transmission mode selectors available – see left. It also makes sure things are done in the right order. An important point for the most demanding (deep sand) off-road conditions, low-to-high range change on the move is OK to 25mph.

The Touareg's controllable air suspension can selectably raise the underbody clearance by 70mm for off-road driving.

Mitsubishi

Shogun. One of the originals and a veteran of many a gruelling Sahara rally, albeit usually in a highly modified form, the Shogun (or Pajero as it called in other parts of the world) has understated pedigree.

The Shogun's 'Super Select' driveline offers every conceivable option a driver is likely to want. The basic mechanics comprise a centre differential between the front and rear prop shafts with a viscous coupling to control front/rear spin (like the Subaru Forester). Plus stability and traction control.

Starting in 2WD high range, you can select 4H which is 4x4, but OK for on-road use due to the centre differential and viscous coupling control. If things get tough you can lock the centre diff by selecting 4HLc: best not to use this on road except maybe in snow and ice conditions. If things get really tough you can select low range by pushing through to 4 low and then 4LLc which gives 4x4 low range with centre diff locked. If you're still in trouble call out the JCB! Changing from low to high or *vice-versa* can, alas, only be done with the vehicle stationary, the makers say.

L200 pickup. A vehicle with an equally long history, the L200 is available in a number of different versions, the upper echelons of which, like the Shogun, provide automatic transmission and Super Select control of the driveline options.

The '4Work' and '4Life' L200 models offer 'Easy Select' instead of Super Select driveline control. This is essentially selectable 4x4 (Type 1, p.2.11) with no centre differential and thus is unsuitable for use on hard roads in 4x4 – unless they are covered in snow and ice. Low range gears and rear diff lock are provided and the same (here acceptable) limitations apply.

Some may find the L200 body styling and 'chromorama' add-ons a little over the top but there is no doubting the hardware beneath – to which a lead position in the UK pickup sales tables attests. The fancy embossed leather transfer box control lever top (use your torch and spectacles) would be clearer in white plastic.

Un-flashy, almost matronly in appearance, the Shogun is a solid, down-to-earth 4x4 with pedigree and a driveline able to tackle most obstacles on and off the road.

Nissan

Captain sensible. Nissan's 4x4s: common-sense, straightforward, down to earth – in overall conception, execution and drivelines. Test driving competitive 4x4s in the Gulf, only Nissan's top-model Patrol stood out against the idiocy of other brands' leather seats in such a hot, humid, steam-bath climate.

Nissan's common-sense approach to design engineering extends to its drivelines – auto-engage with manual override on the X-Trail and selectable 4x4 on Navara.

Thus their drivelines, though in the UK limited to selectable and auto-engage 4x4 (Types 1 and 2, p.2.11), are similarly simple and intuitive to use. The Navara pickup has selectable 4x4 giving a 100% front/rear bind, low range gears, plus ESP and left/right traction control.

The auto-engage (Type 2) X-Trail is default front 2WD with 'auto' or, usefully, driver-override selectable 4WD. Both 4WD modes revert to 2WD above 20mph. In common with similar systems, start-off on the X-Trail is in 4WD even if 2WD is selected so, with left/right traction control, elegantly covers the icy-gutter situation.

The 4WD version Qashqai is, effectively the same system as X-Trail including driver-selectable 4WD – plus traction control.

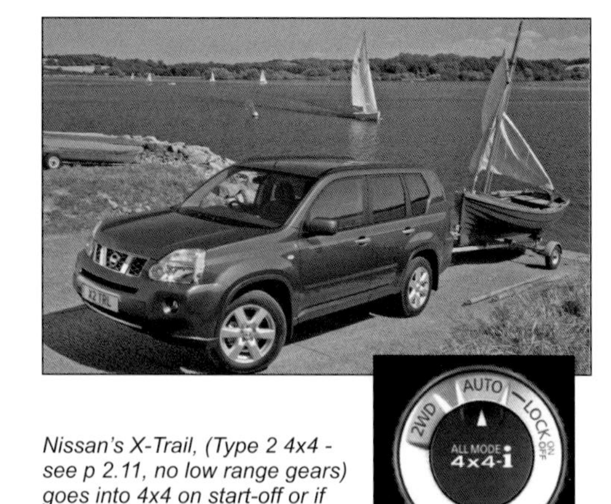

Nissan's X-Trail, (Type 2 4x4 - see p 2.11, no low range gears) goes into 4x4 on start-off or if wheel-slip detected but can be manually selected at 'Lock'.

Juke. Beneath the glitz: brave, special. Despite it's perky looks and a pretty launch brochure that seems to indicate it can only be driven by cool city-cats at night, the Juke 4WD version has a uniquely smart driveline.

The Juke design engineers at Nissan have made a courageous decision and dispensed with a conventional differential at

Navara, default 2WD, has selectable 4x4. Its 4H and 4LO gives 100% lock between front and rear prop shafts so not for use on grippy surfaces. Limited slip rear diff on V6 Outlaw.

An Evoque-ative shape and some fancy underpinnings in the 4WD version. A frame from an excellent US promotional video (right) shows the marketing folks don't always overstate the clever stuff. 'Torque vectoring' really is torque (power) vectoring. Here (an underneath rear view looking up) slippery conditions have put the Juke in 4WD. The left turn, sensed by steering angle, accelerator and G-sensors has released some clutch-pack grip on the inside rear wheel to increase torque on the outside rear wheel to 40 of the 50% allocated to the back end. Helps it into the turn when conditions are tricky and the driver is going (too?) hard.

the back axle with its associated need, ideally, for control of excessive left-right spin. Instead they have a simple bevel-gear drive and an electrically controlled clutch pack on each rear half shaft.

In 'straight and level flight', as it were, both clutch packs are controlled to allow equal power to each rear wheel.

The controllability of each clutch pack, monitored, sensed and dictated by inputs of steering angle, lateral-G and accelerator demand (in general, summarising the speed, sharpness and urgency of the turn), allows the ECU to vary the individual clutch 'grip' on each half shaft.

Thus in a left turn (see diagram above), where the ECU reckons that of the 50% front-rear power allocation, the left/right split at the back end should be 10% left wheel and 40% right wheel, the left clutch eases up and the right clutch clamps down so that more power goes to the right wheel than the left. (Note the beauty of this as opposed to the braked-wheel approach with its heat, wear and energy-loss)

As mentioned above (p.2.22), to understand the ingenious logic of this more easily do try to think of what's connected to what rather than 'torque allocation'. That term is alright in a way but as already pointed out, torque is essentially a *reactive* concept, dependent on external factors such as surface grip etc, so does not fully or accurately define what is going on in terms of mechanical connection and the direction of power from the engine.

The Juke's rear-axle engagement and lateral power-split is unique and innovative among soft-roaders. It will be worth watching in the future for development and imitators.

Here, and in the perfect 4x4 system, the ideal is to match power to the ability of the ground to take it. So while in broad terms 'torque vectoring' is a nice shorthand expression for what is going on, what the ECU is busily trying to do is match what it allocates to the requirements of the particular manoeuvre being undertaken.

System-design-wise it is, compared to transmission design 30 years ago, a jaw-dropping undertaking. But sensors – not least the miracle of solid-state miniature accelerometers (lateral-G sensors) – and smart electronic software (so long as it works!) can produce the goods; even if you're not a cool city-cat driving at night.

Toyota

Three passenger-4x4s for UK. Though, alas for overlanders, the Land Cruiser 78 'Troopie' (p.7.16) is not available in UK, amongst the many Toyota products without which the world would surely stop rotating there are, of the 4x4s available in UK, three passenger vehicles (names keep changing):

- Biggest: Land Cruiser V8 (ex Amazon)
- Less big: Land Cruiser (ex – way back – Land Cruiser II, Colorado, Prado)
- Least big: RAV4 which is now an auto-engage soft-roader with no low range. (Was permanent 4x4 with locking diff.)

Toyota's Land Cruiser family has top class permanent 4x4 and an enviable reputation for reliability. Sadly, it lacks the facility to change from low range to high on the move.

Land Cruisers. The two Land Cruisers are real permanent 4x4s with a 40:60 torque-splitting Torsen centre diff (but also lockable, so 50/50 front/rear) and a two-speed transfer gearbox giving low range gears. Each is available in ascending specifications and the top model of each also has a lockable rear axle differential (see pic below). Both come with a standard five-speed automatic transmission (except the three-door version of the smaller Land Cruiser). A rotary selector enables high range or low range gears to be chosen, with centre diff free (ie normal Torsen control) or locked. It's unusual to be able to select low range with free centre diff – but invaluable, for example, if you you're asked to tow that monster trailer on full lock out of the hard-surface school playground.

The acronym fountain. Among the surfeit of TLAs (three letter acronyms!) plaguing the brochures is one (ATC) representing traction control – the usual format of ABS braking, stability control and single-wheel braking to control wheelspin on icy/muddy/slippery patches. There is also (on the Land Cruisers) Toyota's take on Land Rover's 'Terrain Response': MTS (Multi-Terrain Select) which tunes throttle response, auto-transmission change points and traction control to particular terrain type.

An astonishing degree of suspension control (yes, it does amount to part of the driveline) is available and the V8 claims it results in axle articulation ('single-wheel droop') sufficient to negotiate a 630mm step without lifting a wheel off ground-contact.

Range-change on-the-move is not Toyota-sanctioned (3mph hi-to-lo hardly counts) but with automatic gearbox you might get away with a sticky re-start in high range (see p.6.4).

The big Land Cruiser keeps armies, oil companies, and gendarmeries operating throughout the Middle East and Africa and has a bulletproof reputation.

Land Cruiser (top) and Land Cruiser V8 (left) have dial-selected low range, Centre-diff lock button (just out of shot to the left) enables low or high range to be selected with free centre diff – useful for heavy-duty manoeuvring on paved surfaces. Shown alongside the rotary selector is the rear axle diff-lock switch and suspension raising control.

Hilux pickup. Countless pickups world-wide bear the Hilux name which goes back two or three decades and its reputation continues to shine. The current 'Euro'-Hilux addresses the 'civilised' pickup market with a bewildering spread of features and options dependent on specification and build. The Hilux will normally be driven in 2WD but has lever-selectable 4x4 and low range (Type 1, p.2.11). According to (2.5 or 3 litre) engine and detail spec, the driveline also features ABS, stability control, traction control, and a lockable or limited-slip rear diff. Automatic transmission is available.

All Hilux models are blessed with the mystique of ADD – Auto Disconnect (front) Differential – another suitably obscure acronym, here denoting a sliding-sleeve disconnect of one of the front half-shafts when the vehicle is in 2WD. Inevitably, despite such enticing brochure-speak, the one item not disconnected is the differential; the crown-wheel and pinion and the front prop shaft, however, are. The putative fuel savings are said by some to be minimal.

RAV4 (2013 model left) is now an auto-engage soft-roader: no low range. Hilux specials have been shown at both poles. Tough, with selectable 4x4 and low range.

RAV4. Though, like Fiat's Panda 4x4, once sporting permanent 4x4 with selectably locking centre diff, Toyota's 'school run' RAV4 is now an auto-engage (Type 2, p.2.11) soft-roader. Conceptually matching Haldex's system (p.2.17) it uses Toyota's own electrically cam-engaged rear prop-shaft clutch-pack to bring in the back axle drive.

Toyota has a rock-solid reputation despite media fanning the flames of recent minor recalls. Ford has ambitions to take advantage of new interest in 4x4 world-wide.

The new-for-2013 Kuga is the mid-range occupant of what Ford promises will be a new suite of SUVs for Europe and world markets. This will include the US Escape and the yet to come EcoSport and Edge.

Ford

Kuga. Destined to be one of Ford's 'world cars' (and known in the US as the Escape), the 2013 Kuga succeeds its earlier Haldex-equipped antecedents with Ford's own soft-roader driveline. Essentially a normal Type 2 (p.2.11) auto-engaged 4x4 with electro-magnetically-triggered rear axle clutch engagement, Ford, like many manufacturers of such drivelines, utilise the feedback from ABS wheel speed sensors, steering-input sensors and lateral accelerometers (to measure yaw) to provide an advanced stability control system as well as a basically front-wheel-drive driveline calling upon rear axle input and braked directional control to enhance traction and stability. The entire system is automatic with no driver controls or off-road pretensions.

Land Rover's DC100 concept still keeps crystal-ball watchers guessing. Original PR mention of a 2 litre diesel and 8-speed auto-box on a 100" wheelbase frame is some cause for optimism but holding of the breath is not yet advisable.

Land Rover – 60 years plus

Icon. For once a media cliché applies. Though conceding seniority to Jeep, the term 'iconic' could surely be applied to Land Rover, known and – despite a few foibles – loved pretty much the world over.

Working vehicles. Little reliable detail has followed the 2011 announcement of the DC100 concept vehicle and in the meantime – and possibly into the future with overseas production – the Defender continues as Land Rover's bedrock working 4x4. Its hard-to-beat basic driveline – real permanent 4x4, selectably lockable centre diff, low range gears with a neutral position – still, after all these years, lacks factory axle diff-locks.

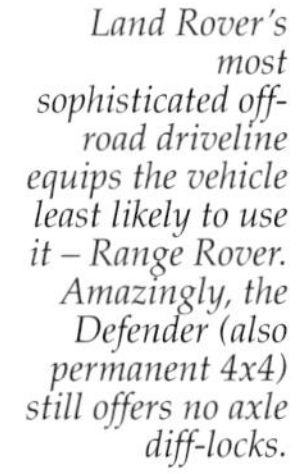

Land Rover's most sophisticated off-road driveline equips the vehicle least likely to use it – Range Rover. Amazingly, the Defender (also permanent 4x4) still offers no axle diff-locks.

Single-wheel spin is addressed by an optional, basic traction control system. There is no factory automatic transmission available for the Defender.

Despite its almost legendary charisma, the Defender will be out-performed on- and off-road by the Discovery and Range Rover.

Mid-sector sensible. Meanwhile the Freelander 2 uses the well-developed, auto-engage, Haldex-based (p.2.17) 4x4 system – now, for 2013, tweaked to the same standard as that on the shrewdly-conceived Evoque. This driveline will click with a very wide sector of the market and deal effectively with the demands of all-weather commuters, many campers and most country folk.

More up-market without going to Range Rover extremes of luxury, the current Discovery 4 offers one of the most capable (and semi-automated) off-road 4x4 systems available – a permanent 4x4 setup with electronic anti-spin control of a proper centre differential (EDL – electronic diff lock), low range gears, sophisticated traction control and (like Range Rover) the option of an EDL in the back axle too. When combined with its clever air suspension (including 125mm max lift) and clear cockpit readouts on the traction situation, the results – keeping the driver in the picture and producing first-class on- and off-road performance – are very impressive.

Top-end. Discovery driveline features apply equally to the Range Rover (opposite). As one of the most accomplished off-road vehicles and, quite separately, a top class luxury car espoused by heads of state and celebrities from all walks of life, the Range Rover's combination of qualities make it an illogical phenomenon – that is clearly here to stay and goes from strength to strength. Doubtless the accountants at Jaguar-Land Rover are crossing their fingers, whispering 'Well, if that's what they want!' – and holding their breath to see how long it all lasts.

Ergonomic sacrifice? Land Rover's 'Terrain Response' (TR), tunes driveline behaviour parameters to particular, driver selectable, off-road terrains – a feature that has caught on with other manufacturers, albeit

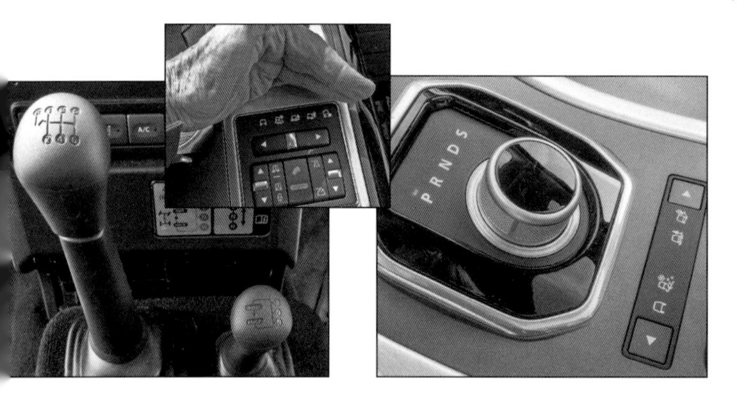

Evoque 'bottle-top' transmission mode selector (near left) and Range Rover TR selectors (above), shaded from the sun for readability (Note no raised guard-surround.) Current Defender's controls (far left) are simple, straightforward but could benefit from recessed white graphics.

Land Rover – main driveline formats, 2012

Defender – pre DC100-concepts

(Type 3 4x4 – see p.2.11) Permanent 4x4 with manually lockable centre differential. Manual transmission only. On-the-move range change – low to high – possible with special skills (see Section 6.2)!

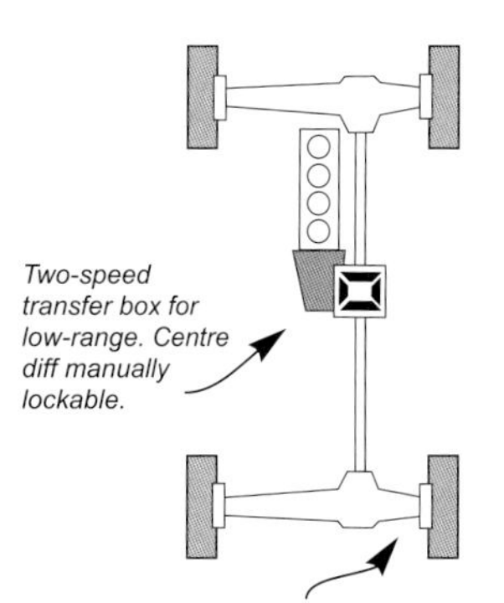

Stability/traction control is optional but standard on XS model. No in-house axle diff locks option.

Freelander, Evoque

(Type 2 4x4 – see p.2.11) Auto-engage 4x4 clutch-pack (Haldex Gen-4 coupling) engages rear axle on start-off and as required. (See diagram p.2.17) No low range. Auto transmission option. 2WD-only versions available.

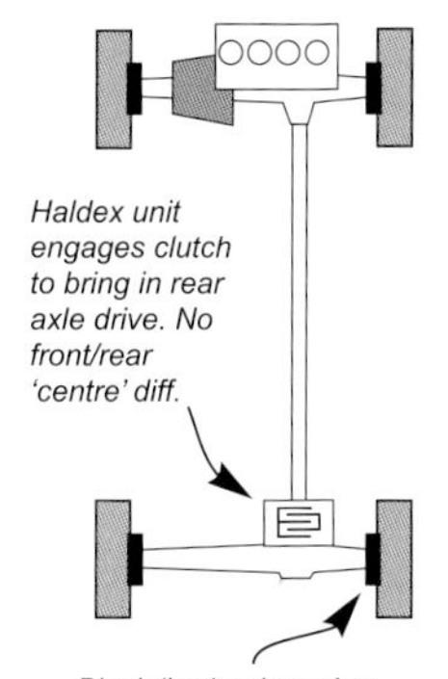

Black 'brake drums' on diagrams here equals braked elimination of single-wheel spin (traction control).

Discovery 4, Range Rover

(Type 3 4x4 – see p.2.11) Permanent 4x4 with electrically lockable centre diff – momentarily ('pre-emptively') locked on start-off. On-the-move range change – low to high – at up to 38mph. Automatic transmission standard (from 2011).

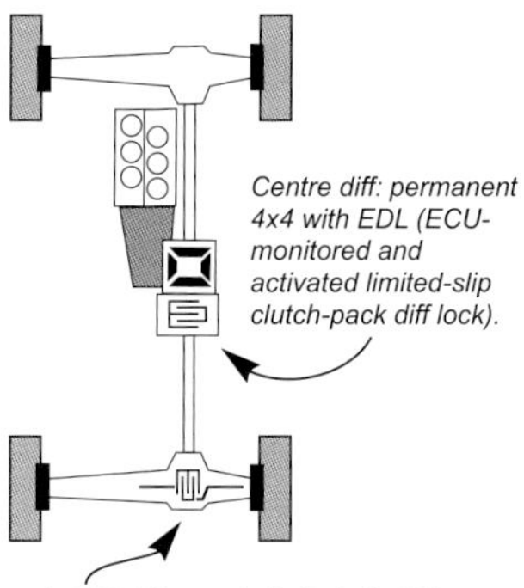

Rear axle EDL (Electronic limited-slip Diff Lock) optional. No front diff lock option but traction control and anti-weave trailer-control by individual wheel braking is standard.

compressed by some to a simpler optional 'Off-road' button (Yeti p.2.29, Tiguan p.2.32).

But now, like many manufacturers, Land Rover has jumped on its own bandwagon – the 'bottle-top' transmission main selector rising majestically out of the console, used by Jaguar and (some would say) pioneered as a better original by Volkswagen on the Touareg (p.2.32) only for off-road controls.

VW's 'bottle top' has a cursor too. Many, Land Rover included, don't – and to know what PRND auto-transmission or other mode you have selected you must look down and seek tiny LED indicators, necessarily shaded from bright sunlight (see pic opposite), and then cross-check in the instrument display. 'Bottle-tops' will be welcomed by style-freaks but there is much more to be said, ergonomically, for levers on the centre console – with selection-gates.

Simplicity benefits. A no-electronics 461 Mercedes G-Wagen with manual, 100% diff locks could probably equal or out-perform a Range Rover off-road but the Discovery and Range Rover driveline is more user-friendly, foolproof and beneficial on-road.

Range Rover, 2013: an almost bizarre combination of advanced engineering, off-road capability and exreme-luxury interior fit. Users in one demographic segment are unlikely to have any use for features beneficial to customers in the other. But it sells!

4x4 systems – pre-purchase checks: know what your getting*

Finally, do remember *if you're buying a 4x4 at all, it's the driveline you should be paying attention to. Do know about the front/rear axle connection and the cross-axle wheelspin control (traction control). Soft-roaders are vastly improved nowadays but still slower to react than permanent 4x4. For sustained challenging off-road operations always go for permanent or selectable 4x4 with diff locks.*

Fit for purpose? *++ boxes = demanding off-road spec. Look for checks in row 1, 2 or 3. Row 7, 8, then 10 makes you well-equipped for serious off-road operations.*

Fit for purpose? *+ boxes = significant benefit over 2WD on snow/ice, mild off-road terrain.*

Fit for purpose? *Traction control (+ box 11). Traction control – auto braking of a spinning wheel – is shown with a + box, ie as a soft-roader plus but, if you don't have a cross-axle diff lock it helps for limited serious off-road work too.*

		Row	Your choices: Option 1	Option 2	Option 3		Examples: Skoda Yeti	Discovery 4
1. Four-wheel drive system								
Front/rear axle connection								
'Hard drive' – shafts and gears (Types 1 and 3 on p.2.11)	*Selectable 4x4 [by lever (L) or button (B)], ie vehicle is usually in 4x2*	1				++		
	Permanent 4x4, with centre differential. Centre diff manually lockable, 100% (L)	2				++		
	Permanent 4x4, with centre diff lock, auto-controlled by clutch (C), or VC (V). Clutch locks briefly on start-off (CL)	3				++		✔CL
Auto-engaging 'Soft drive' – eg. Electro-hydraulically actuated clutch, No centre diff. (Type 2, p.2.11)	*2nd axle driven after front/rear speed difference sensed (and other criteria). Multi-disc clutch auto-engaged. Reverts to 4x2. Selectable 'Lock' 4x4 mode(L).*	4				+	✔	
	4x4 engages from start-off (pre-emptive) then releases at cruising speed	5				+	✔	
	Viscous coupling is sole connection (V)	6						
2. Two-speed transfer box (low range gears)								
	Standard or optional	7				++		✔S
	On-the-move range-change – cleared by manufacturer (eg. lo>hi at around 25 mph)	8				++		✔
	Range-change by: lever (L), button/knob (B)	9						✔B
3. Cross-axle wheelspin (traction) control								
	Axle diff-locks rear (R), front (F), limited slip, internal clutch (LS), Electronic diff lock (EDL)	10				++		R. EDL
	Traction control (auto braking of ABS-sensed spinning wheel): optional (O), standard (S)	11				+	✔S	✔S
4. Automatic transmission, special features								
	Auto box optional (O) or standard (S)	12				+	✔O	✔S
	Downhill cntrl (H), Off-road button or other mode selectors (M),	13					H.M	H.M

**See also p.7.17 – Expedition vehicle attributes*

Driveline 'snapshot' – the conclusions

Does it matter? *There will be some – the troubled, the poor in spirit, the weak, the halt, the lame, the sad of heart, the weary, the bewildered – who really do value the wheel cosmetics, the watch-strap tyres, the cup-holder count, the audio wattage, the stitching on the leather, the Bluetooth facility ... above the fundamentals of the driveline.*

But, when the last trumpet sounds, shall not the multitudes lift their faces to the sky and hear a Great Voice bidding them forsake their foolish ways and turn to page 2.21, for there shall they know "... the driveline is the most important part of what you are buying or have bought!"

Joking aside, however, ... and at the risk of undue repetition, our consumer media and brochure writers appear unable to separate the tinsel from the substance and are thus little help to anyone seriously considering the acquisition of a 4x4 of any type.

Check first the basic type differences on page 2.11, then the list on page 2.21. Then go slowly down the boxes on the facing page, before leafing through the snapshot section between pp 2.21 and 2.39 to see what, at the time of publication here, is on offer.

Remember that soft-roaders are pretty darn clever these days and that, standing back from it all, the vehicle makers are trying to reap the benefits of the Phase 1 Leonardo (p.2.3) whilst making the final result immune to the problems misuse of such a system could bring in its wake.

At the time of writing the Range Rover, Discovery, and Land Cruiser come pretty much at the top of the list of such a combination of function and being operationally foolproof for the ordinary user. Only a locking front diff has been omitted from these and other top-flight systems – a step too far for the product-liability vultures waiting for mis-use suits.

Comfort, convenience and utility are of course important but be clear first about the driveline you are buying or using.

(Watch out for the Nissan Juke rear-drive developments. Ford's Kuga – 'Curve Control' – is pecking at it by other means.)

None of this, of course, should eliminate the validity of considerations of utility, comfort – looks even – that influence a buy but getting a true perspective on feature values is essential before taking the plunge.

The basic 4x4 drivelines (see p.2.11):
Type 1: Selectable 4x4.
Type 2: Auto-engage 4x4.
Type 3: Permanent 4x4.
Each, here, has refinements to lift the performance. The Mercedes G-Wagen has manually selectable diff-locks front and rear. The Skoda Yeti has a smartly programmed Haldex Gen-4 coupling plus traction control and 'Off-road' button, And Discovery has programmed diff locks centre and rear.

2.7 Controls: buttons, levers, ergonomics – a reflection

What's to control?

A roundup, summary thing. You know about selectable four-wheel drive (page 2.10), and about two-speed transfer boxes (page 2.12). You know about the need for centre differentials between front and rear prop shaft when permanent 4x4 is fitted (Leonardo's Phase 2 design (page 2.3, also photo p.2.4). You noted that lockable diffs (picture, page 2.9) also do a mean traction job when you are badly off-road and three of your four wheels are having a problem.

Worthwhile overview. Your vehicle either has or has not a fancy 'automatic' electronic parking brake. (Dead battery? Well ... er ...?) And various toggle-button controls. Nonetheless, in the context of what you have or what you are thinking of buying, it is worth taking a steady back-seat view of today's controls ergonomics and protocols; the lever vs button debate. Big intuitive levers for important things where the lever's position indicates what's been selected; buttons where you don't know or are squinting for an LED somewhere.

Though there are seldom any customer options on the subject, an overview of controls and their ergonomics should be part of the pre-purchase assessment.

For production engineers buttons are a godsend: drill a convenient hole, snap it in and run some wires to it. LHD/RHD? No sweat, move the hole. Levers (manual) need more cost and parts to put in. Buttons? never mind the ergonomics, the punters will get used to it. Tell 'em it's cool or 'electronic'.

Three basic controls. A sepia-toned look into a WW2 Jeep or a Land Rover of Series 1, 2 or 3 vintage will have you noting three gear levers to control the transmission. Namely:

1. Selection of main gears
2. Selection of 4x4
3. Selection of low-ratio gears.

These days, though, according to what is fitted to your vehicle, there are controls for the selection of:

4. Centre diff lock (sometimes automatic)
5. Axle diff locks (sometimes automatic)
6. 'Other'(the favourite term for when the list gets too long) here includes traction control (if switchable), ditto ABS, various versions of steep-hill descent speed control, 'Terrain Response' – a means of 'tuning' responses of throttle, automatic transmission and diff locks according to the off-road conditions in which you are driving. And, to ward off litigation as much as directional problems, there is often a Stability Control programme of some kind which for off road operation may be switchable.

The little gear lever – et al. The transfer box lever, if there is one, usually looks after items 2, 3 and, if appropriate, 4 – the latter in both high and low range gears if it's a Defender (pic p.2.38). A manual lever is simple and totally unambiguous (also Wrangler p.2.30). But dash-mounted rotary electrical switches controlling actuators are a cheaper option and, if a push-before-you-twist inhibit is built-in on a sensible-sized unit (Land Cruiser p.2.36, Navara p.2.34, Grand Vitara p.2.25) then judging function-by-switch-position can be acceptable. Spring-back rocker-switches (Range Rover, p.2.36) don't offer this and need an LED repeater (hard to see in bright sun) *plus* an instrument pack alert. Not good.

Foolproof benefits? Such electrical selection, however, provided it is totally reliable, can be a boon for occasional users happy to be prevented from getting it wrong by inhibiting features which include ensuring the main gear selector is in neutral and/or the speed is very low – often 5-8 mph . If these conditions are not met, the selection is electrically blocked until they are. There is much to be said, however, for levers rather than buttons to control a major function, even if, as on aircraft, the lever just activates a switch. Its obvious visual position indicates what has been selected and it won't have been selected inadvertently; switches can be.

Ergonomics. No apology is made for here highlighting and, where appropriate, criticising, poor control ergonomics – how intuitive they are to use, how appropriate to their function, how easy (LEDs or LCDs) to see in bright sunlight, how proof they are against inadvertent or unsuitable selection, how self-evident in what has been selected. Read and reflect on the box at p.2.45 on the next spread about control protocols and, when buying, make intuitive simplicity your goal – or at least an influencing factor.

Taking this message on board will hone your own awareness and selectivity as a vehicle customer, get you a more suitable product – and with any luck the message might one day get through to the designers.

The glass soap-dish syndrome. Where 'Form follows function' should be the well-worn mantra, too often vehicle designers come up with the automotive equivalent of the oft-seen glass soap dish – loose on a chrome shower fitting, easily dislodged, no drain-hole, a veritable magnet to fumbling hands when you have slippery fingers and soap in your eyes. And lethal when smashed on the shower floor. Looks cute though.

Controls – what's to get wrong?

Preventing or accommodating? What is there to prevent? Low range selection can cause severe clonking in the transmission – and probably damage. In most cases the only way – lacking synchromesh – of eliminating this reliably and with no possibility of damage is to do it with the vehicle or shafts (or both) stationary – hence the inhibiting parameters mentioned above.

Preventing is cheaper. A similar situation applies to selecting 4x4 from 2WD. Usually this can be done safely on the move up to around 60mph – *provided the front and rear wheels are going round at the same speed.* However, if a driver, in 2WD gets into trouble with spinning rear wheels and engages 4x4 with them still spinning, severe damage will ensue. So de-clutch before selecting 4x4.

Except in 'working pickups', the majority manufacturer view on 'selectable 4x4' – cynical or pragmatic – is that since most driving is done on-road, cost can be kept down by providing Type 2 (auto-engage 4x4) so preventing drivers from crashing the gears and breaking things. As we have seen, soft-roaders with such a setup these days also incorporate significant other benefits as well into their drivelines. A lot of customers, happy to pay less, would support the auto-engage approach or just don't think about it.

Levers, not buttons, please. However, many off-road professionals like public utilities, farmers, civil engineers, and armed forces need permanent 4x4, prefer levers to switches and the ability to make undamaging selections easily when they want to. And if that means provision of a centre diff and a synchro transfer gearbox, then so be it.

So that's what's to get wrong. This rather long-winded rationale is important because it points out the sometimes conflicting commercial (price-driven) and user (function-driven) priorities that govern what appears in the market place – or more precisely, in the bowels of your off-roader's transmission system and thus in its transmission controls.

Know about it, define your preferences. We got there at last!

Transmission controls – conclusions

Choices – levers, switches, synchro. As with so many expositions, when you actually start at the beginning the conclusions are staring you in the face long before you actually spell them out. As we've seen, for their transmission controls, some vehicles have levers, some have switches.

Buttons and switches keep engineering and production costs down but levers are almost invariably more intuitive and ergonomically sound.

Type 461 G-Wagen's 'levers' policy leaves no doubt as to what has been selected. Organ-stop rear-diff lock pulls up full 15cm.

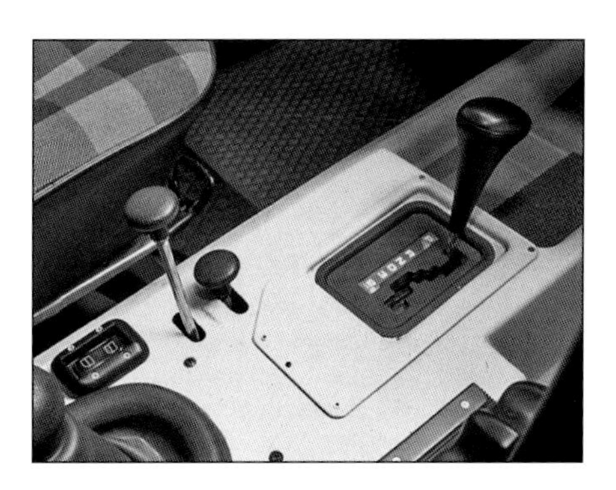

• Switches can be OK for low-cost, foolproofed operation where ultimate off-road performance is not needed – provided (not always so) you can clearly see what you have selected.
• Levers are best for total reliability and ergonomic position-related feedback.
• Synchro on the range change is necessary when you need all the off-road performance you can get.
• All levers are not the same and the facilities they offer can differ widely. Switches are often burdened with disastrous ergonomics. Praiseworthy exceptions: Touareg p.2.32, and Nissan's X-Trail/Navara p.2.34 (albeit there, in one case the scale goes round the cursor and in the other – preferable – the cursor goes round the scale.)

When using transmission controls be very aware of what's going on below. Don't select 4x4 or diff locks if one axle or wheel is spinning – unless you want a stripped diff or broken half-shaft.

Diff-locks. Many vehicles these days have an automatically locking centre, or even axle, differential. In other words, as we've seen, if the front/rear prop shaft (or axle half-shaft) speeds differ significantly a clutch of some kind will be brought into play to bind the shafts together. If there is no auto diff lock you may have a manual one (Defender, page 2.38) or no diff lock at all, the wheel/axle spin situation being taken care of by wheel-braking traction control – fairly effective but not the best for prolonged off-road use due to time-delay, heat generation and brake disc wear.

Wait for the lights. Where an axle diff-lock selection is manual, actual engagement of the diff-lock may or may not take place at once (eg Mercedes G-Wagen). There will usually be a reminder light associated with a control selection which will indicate, maybe a moment or two later, that the lock has actually taken place. (There are engagement spring inhibitors that will wait for conditions to be correct.)

Actually using the controls

• **Transfer gearbox lever – etc**. As a general rule or unless otherwise sanctioned in the driver's manual, stop the vehicle, select main gear neutral and de-clutch (or select N on the auto box) before selecting range change or diff locks – levers or buttons.
• **Synchro transfer box?** G-Wagen, Discovery, Range Rover (and a few other designs) have a synchro transfer box to allow range change on the move – low to high at up to 30 mph or more. (Invaluable in deep sand: you have to start in low range but would not dare stop to get into high range. High to low is an academic exercise since you'll have stopped by the time you want to change.)
• **4x2 to 4x4.** Nearly all selectable 4x4s (Type 1, p.2.11) can go from 4x2H to 4x4H 'on-the-fly', ie at any speed up to about 60 mph. *Always de-clutch* before doing so, to be sure the driven axle is not spinning.
• **The lights.** As already mentioned, watch for the warning light to confirm selection has actually taken place.
• **'Wind-up'; getting out of 4x4.** Vehicles with selectable 4x4 (Type 1, p.2.11) may, even on loose surfaces, occasionally suffer from a degree of transmission 'wind-up' due to the lack of a centre differential. When you try to deselect 4x4 you may find the lever virtually immovable. To relieve the wind-up (torsional conflict between the prop shafts), select reverse and go backwards for 10-20 metres, at the end of which dip the clutch and the lever will usually move freely – or respond to a sharp fist-thump back into 4x2. This phenomenon is more likely to occur on trucks (with, long, torsionally flexible propeller shafts).
• **Centre diff locks.** Centre diff-locks can usually be engaged while moving, *provided there is no front/rear wheel spin at the time of engagement*; so dip the clutch before doing so to cut off drive to the spinning axle and obviate clash.
• **Manual diff locks.** Disengage when no longer needed; especially the axle ones. This is essential. On the few vehicles where a manufacturer is brave enough to clear a front-axle diff lock (Mercedes G-Wagen), the steering becomes almost immovable with the front axle diff lock engaged.

CONTROL PROTOCOLS: A PLEA – DESIGNERS PLEASE READ

Position equals selected function. That's what they keep messing with isn't it – the way things are controlled. That's what we have to keep on re-learning. Remember light switches – old-style? A small lever a quarter to half an inch long. When it was up it was off. When it was down it was on. Its position gave you a visual indication of what had been selected. Then came progress. For switches, it was 'toggling': press once for 'On', press again for 'Off'. Momentarily distracted, which have you actually selected? You've come across it at home. Reading light doesn't work. Is it the bulb? Have I switched it on or off? Is it safe to touch that wire? You have to do a continuity check or rummage for your multimeter to be certain.

Toggling ... er ... . After toggling (simple stuff, that) came the time parameter. Press to change mode. Press and hold for two seconds and … . Hold, while pressing the other button … . Hold, press the other button, face north, sing two verses of Rule Britannia and … ! You get the picture. It is all too familiar. You could call it LOTI - loss of the intuitive. No problem if you are using the system every day and have first learned it but the invitation is out for complete confusion and possibly misuse if you are fresh to it. You, a mere customer.

350 page manual. From the viewpoint of the design engineer, immersed in the system eight hours a day, it is all terrific. Extraordinary control span from just one or two buttons. Far cheaper to produce, let the electronics do the work. For the customer, though, it's er … where's the handbook? (And the book is 25 mm thick – excluding the Serbo-Croat section.) Though such handbooks are often a thinly disguised umbrella against litigation, full of warnings ('We did tell you so you can't sue!'), one 4x4, recently released, has a 350 page English language handbook and add-on supplements. That's just to drive it. Your friend wants to nip down to the shops: do you throw him the keys and say 'Yeah, take the wagon!'?

Indicator by the switch? There are some mind-boggling examples. Something as fundamental – and hugely important – as whether a 4x4 is in low range or high range. Something that used to be selected by a great big lever, that firstly could never be selected by mistake and secondly gave unambiguous visual cues as to what had been selected. At least two 'premium 4x4s' have – amazingly – an unguarded toggle action switch to select low and high range. On one, to be sure which one you have selected you have to look, not at the switch, but at a caption on the instrument panel. (Worse, in some the passenger might have selected it when you were at the traffic lights and you didn't hear him say, 'Daddy, what's this for?') There isn't even an LED down by the switch. A later model at least has a two-position switch for this, plus an LED, so you can see (in bright sun?) what you have asked the electronics for.

'Bottle-top' gear selectors (left). *Current design fad is the rising round-knob selector with no cursor (Jeep, Land Rover). The knob is free-turning but you have to check another indicator – usually tiny LEDs, usually invisible in bright sunlight – to know what you have selected. Rotary selector is fine – but needs a cursor/pointer and captions (right) against which to position it. (Risers? What about five years' of grit, dust, spilled coffee and cake crumbs ingested as it goes up and down?)*

It *can* be done. Nor is this a mere Luddite tirade. ('Modern' is an old-fashioned word – the all-time classic oxymoron indicative of always looking back and long since replaced by 'cool' or 'hip' or 'New!!!' with at least two exclamation marks.) Nevertheless … modern control interfaces *can* be done properly and intuitively. The screens, modes, menus and settings for GPS equipment can pile high but US manufacturer Lowrance, for example, with screen prompts and basic controls have made it all easy and intuitive (pic p.7.5). Read the book once and throw it away. Likewise some DAB radios' 'scroll-and-push-to-select' protocol gives an ergonomics person a nice warm glow and is simple enough for anyone to grasp.

Learning for all. Certainly there is a subliminal learning process that we are all, necessarily, going through (or getting confused by). Is the control protocol time-dependent? If it's toggle, is there a remote indicator? Is it hold A and push B? Is it scroll and select? With the same knob or using an 'Enter' button? The folks in the white coats have got to do some learning too. As it says at the top: designers please read.

LOTI – loss of the intuitive – is all too common on control functions. Few customers get beyond feeling they are vaguely at fault for not understanding

2.8 Automatic transmission

Basic knowledge

Standard procedure. The tolerance and smoothness of an automatic transmission, makes it ideally suited to 4x4s – particularly off-roader applications. A suitably integrated automatic transmission will result in smoother progress at lower engine rpm than would be the case with a slightly tense driver operating with a manual gearbox.

For those new to automatics, standard procedure can be summed up briefly:

1. Though some stretch to seven or eight speeds, most automatic gearboxes are five- or six-speed units with automatic lock-up on at least the top ratio above a certain speed to minimise torque converter slippage.

Automatic transmission has definite advantages for off-road work as well as its obvious on-road benefits. Gentle changes preclude damage, enhance traction flow.

2. Most auto box selections are limited to P (park), N (neutral - ie no drive selected), R (reverse selected), D (drive - all forward speeds enabled). If there is a 3, or 2 below this it means that upward changes are limited to that ratio. Sometimes there will be an S (sport – lateral gear selector movement or button) to delay change-up under high power; usually a '+' and '–' beside it indicate manual ratio-changes are possible by use of the lever or steering-wheel 'paddles'.

3. Select 'N' on the main gear selector before making a transfer box selection. If the range change will not immediately engage, apply the brakes, engage 'D' briefly, go back to 'N' and try again. See p.6.6 for low box to high box on the move on some automatics.

4. If you are stopped for any length of time, engine running, select 'N'; it avoids overheating the transmission fluid.

5. If you are in 'P' or 'N' apply the footbrake before selecting a forward or reverse ratio to avoid creep or a jerk.

6. All automatics will respond to 'kick-down' (ie heavy sudden use of the throttle) to select a lower ratio and boost acceleration. Some respond more smartly than others!

Controlling the automatics

Automatic transmission off-road. Though traditionally most off-road operations are carried out by vehicles with manual transmission, this is no more than a statistical fact rather than validating any preferences. That there is considerable advantage in the use of automatic transmission off-road is attested by the fact that many military users specify it.

Advantages and disadvantages. The most obvious advantage of auto transmission is ease of operation for the driver. This is important for the military or public utilities user whose mind will be on the vital task in hand as well as driving. An auto is immeasurably beneficial for reducing fatigue in extended off-road operation such as expeditions, aid work or simple day-to-day use where poor tracks, rocks, pot-holes and the like demand frequent gear changes to negotiate difficult terrain.

There are significant benefits in terms of vehicle durability and protection from driver misuse and transmission shock loads. Off-road performance is considerably enhanced by an automatic's quick seamless changes of gear – most obvious in sharply deteriorating conditions such as soft sand or deepening mud where, with a well-matched engine/transmission pair, virtually undetectable down-shifts keep an unbroken tide of torque flowing to match the vehicle's need while the driver attends to – in these conditions – the all-important choice of route.

An automatic is particularly beneficial with a soft-roader where absence of low-range gears can sometimes be partly made up for by a degree of torque-converter slip – often enough to save the day – without clutch-burning or other mechanical horrors.

The only disadvantages of automatic transmissions are higher initial cost and slightly increased fuel consumption. As already indicated, however, major professional users with cost-effectiveness in mind compare this with the higher maintenance and repair costs of misused manual vehicles and still come down in favour of automatics.

Simple, but knowledge still needed. A 4x4 with auto transmission can be operated on a minimum-knowledge basis by, say, a fleet or pool operator with disparate drivers of differing experience. For these or the inexperienced a basic knowledge will suffice. On the other hand refinement of operating effectiveness and vehicle capability will result if time is taken learning to get the best from the system – see Sections 6.1, and 6.2.

Auto and low range

Auto – use low range. An auto will struggle manfully (using torque-converter slip) in high range off-road but do keep an eye on engine rpm and change to low in difficult off-road conditions. This is an easy trap to fall into if you have not much off-road time with a manual gearbox and cannot relate engine rpm to low-range speeds.

Poor engine braking. As indicated above, in comparison to a manual transmission, you will find an auto has surprising gradability in high range but, particularly off-road, engine braking is inherently poor even in low range. Engage '1' low range to obtain best engine braking on a descent but you will usually find cadence braking (see Sec 3.3), ABS or one of the hill descent programmes will be necessary also. Engage 1st gear low range early for if speed is too high this will not engage at all.

Steep up and down. A steep climb followed by a steep descent sums this situation up well. Whilst you will probably be able to climb a short steepish slope well enough in high range on 'D', you will need low range '1' for the descent.

To save doing a range change at the top of the incline the technique should thus be to engage low-range before the obstacle, and also go to manual-selection of gears if your system allows.

Select '3' (see below why), make the ascent and, at the top, with forward speed at a minimum, manually select '1' to get maximum retardation for the descent. See Section 6.3 for emergency procedure.

'Lift-off' elimination of wheelspin. The reason for selecting '3' before a slippery ascent or other potential wheel-spin situation is that as soon as the wheels begin to spin the automatic transmission sensors will recognise the reduced torque and change up. This will tend to eliminate wheelspin as soon as it occurs – in just the same way as you would lift off the throttle with a manual transmission to quench wheelspin near the top of a steep loose slope. A change up may not be what you want so selecting '3' rather than 'D' ensures change-up is not too high.

Muddy, 'forest floor' situations. The same applies for 'forest floor' slippery mud situations. Even though the main ratio actually in use may be 1st or 2nd, having the selector in '3' ensures that, as soon as wheelspin (reduced torque) is sensed, the gearbox will change up to 3rd to eliminate spin but not change into an inappropriately high gear.

An auto needs the help of low transfer gears just like a manual. Staying in high range in demanding off-road conditions will cause transmission oil to overheat.

Towing your auto

Beware! Do know the score. Danger of severe transmission damage lurks for an automatic 4x4 being towed if things are not done properly. Most 4x4s with auto require both the main gear selector and the transfer box selector to be selected to neutral before they can be towed with all wheels on the ground.

Not all auto-equipped 4x4s have a neutral position on the transfer box so must be put on a trailer. Some have a limited-speed-and-distance towing caveat usually indicating the lack of an available neutral in the transfer box and that the automatic gearbox will have damaging lubrication problems if these limits are exceeded.

Some, like the 'P38' Range Rover have a magic formula ('Put a 5 amp fuse in position 11.') in order for the transfer box to find neutral. Read the manual and remember these things.

Raised front wheels? Eek! Raised front-wheels towing can be harmful unless a prop shaft is removed; know your vehicle. Never mind if the recovery service truck has arrived and wants to get on with things. Just be absolutely sure your vehicle is being towed properly. Do your homework; write it down.

Section 3

4x4 driving – preliminaries

3.1 Mind-set

Mechanical sympathy

Be smooth and gentle with your vehicle. Using the power is not the same as being brutal. Avoid transmission clonks and let the clutch grip fully when it has to.

Preparing the ground. There are some important preliminaries, some nurturing of attitude, that you will find beneficial – either as a precursor to taking your new and seemingly large off-roader on the road for the first time, or before taking your now comfortably familiar 4x4 off the road for the first time. They may even benefit the experienced as a recap; the things you knew all along but could maybe brush up on. Not that you really need to of course ... !

Mechanical sympathy. All machinery responds well to being treated with respect and mechanical sympathy – even rugged off-roaders. There is more to this than just following maintenance schedules and keeping the oil topped up; that is vital but is not the whole user-interface picture. Smooth driving operation is the aim; no stabbing the brake or throttle, no forcing the gear levers, no thudding into holes or over bumps.

Be kind. Using the full capabilities of your 4x4 need not preclude your being kind to it. It is a tolerant vehicle but clunks in the transmission, prolonged wheel spinning, misuse of the clutch and harsh treatment of any of the controls, engine or suspension should be avoided. Specifically:

1. Transmission controls. (Gear lever and transfer box lever.) Moderate force and moderate speed is the best way to use these levers – firm and gentle. If it is difficult to engage low range, leave the transfer lever where it is, dip the clutch, engage first gear and let the clutch up slightly to reposition the gear wheels. Keep the clutch down and try again. Similarly, difficulty engaging first or reverse (or noise in doing so in some older vehicles) may be eased by dipping the clutch, quickly engaging a higher synchro gear (say, third) and then trying again.
If range-change (high/low ratio gears) is by buttons, of course, all you can do is ensure calm reigns before engaging – no high revs, no wheel-spinning.

2. Riding the clutch. Don't slip the clutch or 'use it as another gear'. Don't 'ride' the clutch either; by this is meant resting your foot on the pedal with slight pressure so as to be able quickly to disengage it. It is natural enough for a properly cautious or inexperienced

Smooth operation, making the vehicle flow over the ground (left) rather than jolt is an indication of the required mechanical sympathy. Work your vehicle well (right) but be kind and take the drama out of the driving.

driver negotiating a difficult piece of terrain to want to be able to use clutch and brake with the minimum delay but riding the clutch – in effect reducing the pressure of the clutch springs – will encourage clutch slip and cause premature wear. Have the clutch fully engaged and your foot clear of the pedal, even if its only a centimetre, whenever possible.

3. Wheelspin .... As we have seen and shall see in more detail, wheelspin is lost traction and prolonged wheelspin will scoop earth from under the wheels, digging a hole and worsening the situation. It is not good for the transmission either. A fast spinning wheel suddenly getting grip can cause shock loading on the transmission and the possibility of transmission damage.

3a .... but.. There are circumstances – certain types of mud with the best mud tyres – when controlled, short-period wheelspin will permit the tyre to cut through to drier ground and obtain traction where none existed before. The same approach in sand would be disastrous and cause bogging. So you must become wheelspin-aware, know how your tyre tread is faring and, as we shall see, make judgements. (Which, despite the arrival of Terrain Response *et al*, you will be the best person to do when you have experience.)

Pride – learn when to back off

Minimise the drama. Probably the most golden of the rules governing difficult off-road driving – and it applies to winter on-road driving too – is to admit defeat early and reverse out. Good off-road driving is achieved with the minimum of drama. Huge water splashes, spinning wheels and flying clods of earth are rarely necessary. Don't feel too bad, though; even the best drivers perpetrate these fireworks occasionally if they have misjudged the terrain – and usually feel a little sheepish afterwards.

Back off, try again. Often such drama stems from fear of failure and then trying too hard. You will learn from this book, and with practice, that part of the learning process is acquiring the procedures for initially getting it wrong – typically the failed steep slope scenario (Section 4.4). You will learn that getting it wrong first time usually does not matter; you will learn to relax. When a very steep slippery climb stops your vehicle and the wheels begin to spin, back off at once; try again, possibly with a little more speed and in a higher gear. Holding the vehicle with uncontrolled wheelspin will cause excessive damage to the ground, will usually worsen the vehicle's chances of making it up the slope and, in some cases, will cause a vehicle to slew sideways-on to the slope and possibly roll. See Section 4.4.

If it isn't going to go it's no big deal – reverse out while you can and try again. Getting through second time is better than having to be towed out on the first try.

Wheelspin alert! The same goes for stretches of deep mud or sand – though the two are quite different. If you do not make it through the patch first time and there is any sustained and ineffective wheelspin, stop before you bog deeper, reverse out and try again using a different route or different tactics. Do not be too proud to admit that you got it wrong.

3.2 Low range – when and how

Low range – 'power' and 'control'

Low range for power. There are two distinct applications for low range gears. Selecting low range on the transfer box is not just another gear but affects all the gears in the main gearbox (including reverse), gearing them down by around 2:1 or more in most cases. The obvious uses of the low range are thus occasions when you want a great deal of 'power' or tractive effort – towing a car out of a ditch, ascending a very steep slope, getting out of deep mud or sand or pulling a fallen tree trunk out of the way.

Low range for control. Less immediately obvious uses for the low ratio include the provision of *control* rather than high tractive effort. Examples of this might be steadying the vehicle on a very steep descent or, classically, allowing the vehicle to crawl over rocks slowly, steadily, without jarring – with your foot off the clutch pedal and without use of the brakes. Low box, first gear excels in this kind of exercise and can often be used with minimal throttle opening or even at idling revs. Rock crawling is a particularly appropriate application where there is otherwise the tendency to 'fall down the far side' of boulders and land with a thump.

Low-range gears have two distinct applications – power for extra steep inclines and control to restrain a vehicle on a steep descent or a crawl over rocks.

Low 1st – too low? Low range first, because of its enormous 'power' capability, is often too low for slippery surface conditions and it is easy to spin the wheels inadvertently through the application of more torque than the ground can take. So 1st-low should be used mainly when grip is very good, when momentum is not required and when there is little danger of spinning the wheels – usually when considerable tractive effort is needed. A common application is in affording engine braking down very steep slopes (see Section 4.5, 'Descending steep slopes'); though surprisingly (Section 4.8) some sand demands it.

First gear low box is ideal to control steep descents, occasionally 2nd. Always 1st with automatic transmission. If there's no hill descent control or equivalent be prepared to administer cadence braking – see next spread.

Top gear in the low box is a good gear for loping along tracks. Often about the same rpm as 3rd high but when difficult patches appear you're already in low range.

Saharan boulders epitomise the 'control' case where low range 1st gear gives steady rock-crawling capability with clutch fully engaged and engine not much above idle (centre diff unlocked). 1st gear start is sometimes appropriate to heavy towing but higher gears in the low box provide general off-road flexibility (below left). Avoid the temptation to 'use the clutch as another gear', ie don't slip the clutch.

What to start off in

Low 2nd – rule-of-thumb. Second is a good, rule-of-thumb, starting-off gear for most low range situations – muddy conditions, steep climbs and the like even with a heavy trailer. In snow you may even find using 3rd gear low range is the answer to preclude wheel spin on take-off. Because tractive effort available is then more closely matched to what the ground will take, there is less risk of wheel spin and the lost traction that results. As indicated in Section 2.8, with automatic transmission select '3' (to preclude too early a change into higher gears. This can sometimes also be the solution with manual transmission where conditions demand the delicate touch.

Gentle right foot! As momentum drops off be careful, in 2 or 3 low, not to spin the wheels.

Low 3rd, 4th, 5th – versatility. Third, fourth and fifth gears in the low range are good 'getting about' gears with manual transmission ('D' or '4' in auto) for the better parts of derelict mountain or desert tracks, for getting across the field or for forest tracks that are a bit awkward for high range. They bring out the vehicle's versatility and the ease with which it traverses cross-country terrain. You can make a respectable speed in low-box 5th or 'D', yet drop all the way down to 2nd without a range change when the going suddenly gets more difficult (see Section 4.2, 'Driving on tracks').

Lowest gear isn't always best. First low is often too low, over-torqueing the ground and generating wheel spin. 2nd-low is good rule of thumb start-off gear.

Driver still the key. We shall see in the ensuing Sections specific examples of what gears to use. And also that there is more to maintaining traction than just selecting a low gear. Driver sensitivity is more than half the battle – see next spread, 'Gentle right foot'. (Also p.6.4, 'High/low range overlap'.)

Thus there will also be times in slippery mud when a very gentle start in 3rd low will successfully drip-feed torque to the wheels when 2nd would have them spinning.

Max-power climbs often need sensitive throttle lift-off near the top to preclude wheelspin as momentum runs out.

3.3 Gentle right foot

Gentle throttle

Reading the ground. If your vehicle has low-range gears, realising the extraordinary potential of your vehicle depends a lot on your appreciation of how much traction the ground itself will take without allowing inappropriate wheelspin.

Wheelspin under power and lock-up when braking: two versions of the same thing – a discontinuity of rolling contact between the wheel and the ground.

Excessive throttle. As with a car on ice, too much throttle will 'over-torque' the driving wheels and make them spin rather than just grip. You could consider this as over-torqueing the ground, for the ground will only take so much push from the tyres before they slip. With such low gearing in the low range gears, this is especially the case in slippery conditions. As on ice and snow, a delicate throttle foot is the key to negotiating such off-road terrain and learning when the conditions are putting the vehicle on the verge of wheelspin.

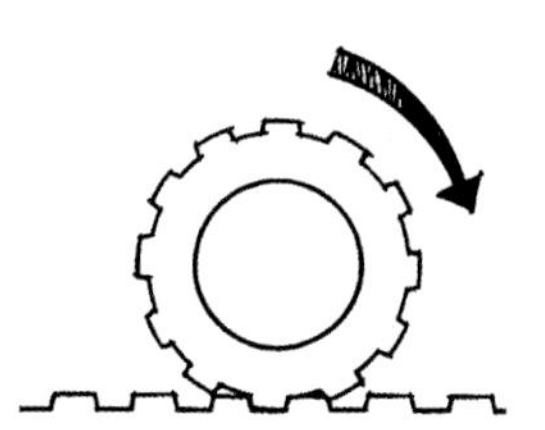

Continuous rolling contact. Conceptually, this is how your wheels and the ground should interact. Too much throttle (wheelspin) or too much brake (wheel slip) will break the relationship. Traction and accurate control will be lost.

Spinning wheels dig. Spinning wheels represent loss of traction, often a loss of directional control as well and, if you just let it go on happening, will result in ground being scooped by the spinning tyres from under the wheel and the vehicle becoming stuck. In a few cases (pp.4.26-27) this scooping will get through slippery mud onto drier ground – but not always. Alertness is the keyword. So there are good reasons for acquiring a sensitive throttle foot and not choosing too low a gear. Both will avoid wheelspin and help to maintain traction.

Traction control. As already introduced (pp.2.6, 2.19), braked-wheel traction control, if fitted, will monitor, and inhibit, inadvertent wheelspin and assist in maintaining traction under limiting conditions.

'Terrain Response'. Land Rover, Toyota, Jeep and others use a change to a less sensitive throttle response in the low range gears to make torque control easier for the driver. As we have seen, Land Rover – now widely copied – take it further on some models with 'Terrain Response', tuning a number of drivetrain parameters according to driver-selected terrain types.

Depending on your viewpoint this can be regarded as a useful driving aid or a nannying obstacle to your progression up the terrain-assessment learning curve through which you will develop your own sensitivity to on-the-ground conditions – your own, and prized, 'gentle (sensitive) right foot'.

Gentle brake

Excessive brake. Wheelspin represents a throttle-generated discontinuity of rolling contact with the ground – the ground and the periphery of the wheel are not in stationary contact with one another (diagram, left). Exactly the same situation arises in the case of excessive braking on slippery ground. One or more wheels lock up and slide over the ground resulting in a discontinuity of rolling contact – the periphery of the wheel and the ground are not going the same speed. In one case the wheel is slipping past the stationary ground; in the other the ground is (relatively) slipping past the stationary wheel.

All manner of clever automation takes care of situations like this now – Hill Descent Control and half a dozen similar programmes. If you don't have that you'll probably have ABS to stop the wheels locking when you brake. No ABS? Hard manual braking will lock the wheels. The back-stop is cadence braking – the driver's foot on/off the brake as fast as he can. It never fails. (NB Not all ABS systems work off-road. Some manufacturers, however, programme the slower repeat applications required for off-road use.)

Cadence braking

Same foot, same cure. Wheelspin and wheel slip respond to the same cures. Lifting your right foot off the throttle will stop wheelspin and lifting your right foot off the brake will stop wheel slide or skidding. In the case of braking, though, you applied the brakes because you wanted to stop. So re-apply them more gently.

Cadence braking – sheer magic. Best of all, employ 'cadence braking' technique – repeated jabbing of the brake pedal with your foot, quite gently, as fast as you can so that the wheel never gets a chance to lock. It's a kind of 'manual ABS'. Though it takes will-power to take your foot off the brakes to do this when you are trying to slow down, cadence braking is remarkably effective.

Cadence braking on-road too. Cadence braking, discovered and taught long before ABS was invented, works well on-road too – probably even more spectacularly. Off-road tyres often lack the on-road grip of tyres designed specifically for tarmac (see Section 8.2) and many is the case of a desert-tyred off-roader in rain on tarmac overseas being saved from certain collision by frantic cadence braking; frantic but controlled ... !

ABS – automated finesse. Anti-lock brakes (ABS) are now virtually standard equipment in all new vehicles. As many will know, ABS brakes employ a very fast form of automated cadence braking to obtain the maximum retardation on the most difficult surfaces without locking up any of the wheels. You will hear and feel, through pedal feedback, the brake relay working. So in the case of a vehicle fitted with this feature you will get maximum available braking and retain directional control – for given ground conditions. Beware, however; ABS will not reverse the laws of physics. If you are on ice, packed snow or slippery mud there is only so much any braking system can do. ABS and cadence braking will give the best possible braking for those conditions but, to repeat, neither can change the laws of physics.

Wheel slide on wet tarmac or slippery mud or ice? If you don't have ABS,back off the brakes and re-apply with rapidly repeated gentle jabs. That's cadence braking – sort of manual ABS.

Engine braking

Elegant, gentle. Engine braking, of course, is a very controlled and gentle way to achieve retardation as we shall see in the Sections to follow. But even that should not be regarded as an infallible solution to every problem, especially when it is very slippery. You can still finish up with sliding wheels – see Section 6.4. And, with selectable 4x4 (Type 1, p 2.11), remember that when you are in two-wheel drive your engine braking is only acting on two wheels, not four.

3.4 Geometric limitations

Clearance angles

Be aware of under-axle clearance and how it differs from belly clearance. Low-set towing hitch can cause tail end to dig in on steep ascents or crossing ditches.

Appreciating clearance. Common to negotiating all types of obstacle off-road is an appreciation of under-body clearance angles, clearance under the chassis and axle differentials and the amount by which the axles can articulate (move up on the nearside and down on the offside – and vice versa – see next spread).

Clearances, under-chassis angles. True off-roaders tend to be high and have lots of ground clearance, which is how they perform so well cross country. A few moments to study the accompanying diagrams, however, will help to refine your judgement on the kind of thing that can and cannot be done without touching bodywork or chassis on the ground. Under-axle clearance is relevant to the size of a single isolated rock or bump on the track between the wheels that can be driven over without fouling, but under-belly clearance relates to the (bigger) size of ridge undulations that can be crossed.

Clearance angles – what they are

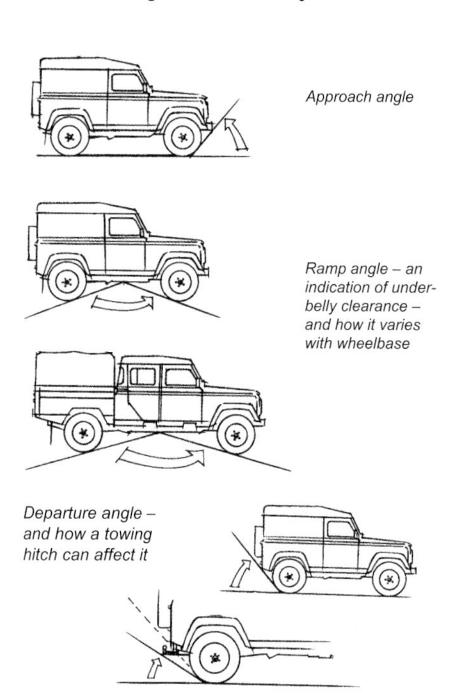

Ramp angle – belly clearance. The angle measured from the chassis at the centre of the wheelbase down to the periphery of front and rear wheels is the ramp breakover angle, usually called the ramp angle. Its significance is self-evident since it governs whether or not you will 'belly' (or 'high center' – US) the vehicle on a hump. Such a hump taken without thought of the ramp angle can result in getting bellied – stuck and immobile – with the wheels grappling for traction and the vehicle's weight taken directly on the chassis on the top of the hump (see p.5.4).

Underbelly damage. Depending on the design of the vehicle and provision or otherwise of skid plates, bellying can result in damage – usually to the exhaust system. If it bellies on the transfer gearbox the unit, as well as the gearbox mountings (not designed to take the weight of the vehicle or any ploughing operation) can be wrecked.

Variable suspension. As we have seen (and next spread), some upmarket 4x4s, in pursuit of improved ride (and to counter the inevitably high unsprung weight of their axle assemblies) are fitted with air suspension. This, for added cost and complexity, affords the opportunity to provide variable-height suspension for off-road use. This is now a fairly widespread option. Whilst early versions offered insignificant lift – 25mm or so – modern versions can effect a 50-125mm increase. This is at the cost of articulation – see next spread.

Axle clearance. Under-axle clearance is a more obvious limitation since it is always less than under-belly clearance. Do not be tempted to allow an axle diff casing to plough out its own path. Deep ruts, rocks submerged in soft mud or encountering hard or rocky going will cause the vehicle to come to a sudden damaging stop when the axle

Under-axle, under-belly clearance

Double-wishbone, independent suspension. Less ground clearance on bump than beam axle but is close with air suspension extended – sacrificing articulation

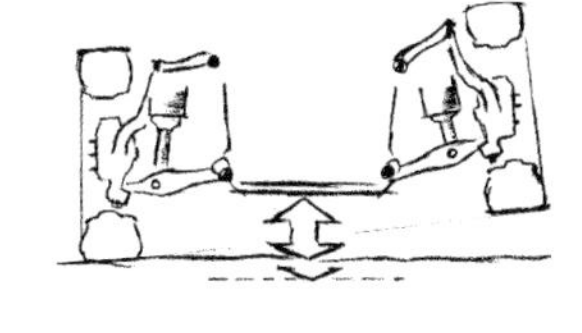

Beam axle. Constant ground clearance

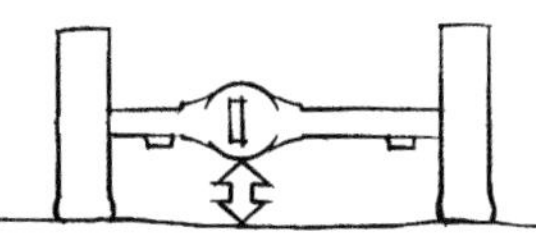

Underbelly clearance is almost invariably greater than under-axle clearance

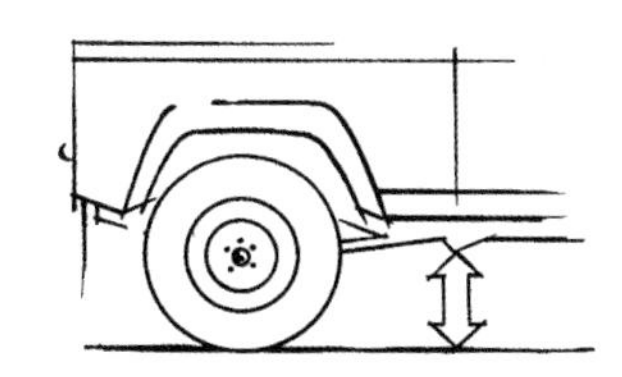

Know where parts of the vehicle may touch the ground. Tow hitch (top), is commonly forgotten and here leaves a rear wheel hanging. If a G-Wagen bellies, it will be on massive girder chassis, not on vulnerable exhaust or gearbox.

differential housing hits the obstacle. If in doubt, get out – see Section 3.5 on marshalling, sometimes also called 'spotting'.

Approach and departure angles. Approach angles (diagram, left) are large on most 4x4s but remember that tail overhang and departure angle is the one that will catch you out most often going up a very steep slope (see below). Regarding the common problem of 'hitting the tail', the departure angle is further reduced when a low-set towing hitch is fitted and it is not uncommon for an inattentive driver to dig the tow hitch into the ground while going forward up a very steep incline and then find that he cannot reverse back because the tow hitch prevents him doing so.

Big wheels, short wheelbase. The biggest wheels and the shortest wheelbase will give best under-chassis clearance angles – a Defender 90 or Wrangler on big tyres will do better than a pickup; their short rear overhangs also yield the best departure angles.

Long wheelbase and tail overhang call for more caution on rough ground – especially with aft-mounted fuel tanks.

Clearance angles – what they mean

The significance of – left to right – approach angle, departure angle and ramp angle.

Axle articulation

Axle articulation keeps wheels in contact with the ground and producing traction. A short wheelbase vehicle will be more agile than one with a long wheelbase.

Axle movement. 'Articulation' is not a self-explanatory term. Whilst it seems to imply an axle with a joint or two in the middle (which oddly enough the six-wheel-drive Pinzgauer at the foot of the page actually has) what the term actually refers to is the ability of the axles to 'rock', side-to-side, relative to one another. Articulation is the amount by which one axle can move, left wheel up, right wheel down or vice versa, in relation to the chassis and to its fellow axle – which is usually rocking the other way. The Discovery photo below illustrates it perfectly.

So it represents the degree to which your vehicle can keep its wheels on the ground on undulating 'twisty' terrain and thus retain traction under difficult conditions.

Articulation is thus a geometric limitation, albeit one of the less obvious ones. Extreme, unconstrained articulation also permits unacceptable degrees of body roll and is thus at odds with good on-road handling, normally kept in good order by anti-roll bars. (Some designers have a best-of-both-worlds solution with anti-roll bars that are disconnectable – eg Wrangler, Patrol.)

There is, of course, a limit to articulation. However extreme, there will come a point where the unevenness of the terrain results in one wheel being unable to follow the contour and that wheel will be left hanging in the air. Again, the Discovery shot shows this just about happening.

Generous axle articulation is an ingredient of good off-road performance.

Articulation – air suspension. 4x4s with air suspension instead of steel springs often have, as we have seen, the capability to extend the suspension units to afford more under-belly clearance off-road – VW Touareg, Discovery, Range Rover, Cayenne, Land Cruiser. This establishes a new 'static' suspension datum but wheel movement either side of this for bumps or dips after raising the suspension is more limited. So the real articulation with suspension raised is less than with it in the normal position.

What you are after is traction. One way of getting this is to be sure all four wheel remain on the ground all the time. This what the Discovery (left) is trying to do. The tall Pinzgauer (right) with 'swing axles' (ie hingeing in the middle) can't possibly achieve this amount of articulation so admits that the wheels will leave the ground and resorts to three-axle diff-locks to make sure the diffs don't spin the power away in thin air. (This means the axle half-shafts have to be beefy enough to take all the power on three or four of the six wheels. Heavy!

Turning, leaning, wading

Manoeuvrability, lateral lean. As with under-belly clearance, in terms of manoeuvrability, inevitably the shorter the wheelbase the tighter the turning circle.

Whether Darwinian evolution saw off-roaders coming is not clear but we all seem to be equipped with a well-developed and self-preservational fear of lateral lean in vehicles. The angle to which an off-roader can lean laterally without tipping is surprisingly high – sometimes as far as 45°. Comfortingly, we all chicken out before we reach it. Keep it that way! As covered in Section 4.6, 'Traversing slopes', the limit is in any case a static figure and should not be relied on when driving. Local bumpiness and the effect of even minor steering corrections make a considerable difference and a limit of half the figures given is recommended.

Wading depth. Maximum wading depth for most off-roaders is around 500-700cm – the limiting factors used to be water spray on the ignition harness of a petrol engined vehicle but is now more likely to be the height of the air intake and various breathers.

Turning circle is an important geometric limitation and is related to wheelbase. Despite a commendable steering angle, the Mercedes GL's 3075mm wheelbase give it a 560mm larger turning circle than Discovery.

Under no circumstances whatever, should water be allowed into the engine air intake. As shown at Section 4.10, there are preparations and precautions to be taken before wading to this depth.

Inspection first. When close to any of the above geometric limitations a preliminary survey on foot is what is required, preferably with someone to marshal you through or round the obstacle when you resume the driving seat. It is pointless to risk damage or getting stuck for the want of properly surveying the obstacle first. This is fully dealt with in the next spread.

If you are near to the limits, get out and take a closer look – see next spread. Traversing lateral slopes be sure small dips don't increase tip angle beyond prudent limits.

Side slopes always feel worse than they are – but don't press your luck! Recce a water crossing on foot first and then take it steady like this. Big splashes make good photos but not good driving.

Classic marshalling situation (left) where the marshaller alone can see all four wheels and position the vehicle correctly.

3.5 Look before you leap

On-foot survey

Inspect before you drive. It is invariably beneficial to do an on-foot survey of difficult obstacles before committing the vehicle. The aim of the survey is to pick the best route and ensure there are no previously unnoticed hazards such as rocks to foul the axles, deep ruts hidden in undergrowth or large obstacles under snow. A reconnaissance also gives you the chance to test the firmness of visible ground – soft mud or the strength of the sand crust on a dune.

Even if it's the 50th time that day, always make an on-foot inspection of difficult or unknown obstacles. Omitting it will risk getting your vehicle stuck or damaged.

Prod before you drive. An on-foot recce is especially important when fording streams and rivers where there is no established safe path. Nor will it be easy since you will have to establish not only the firmness of the river bed but also its evenness. Dropping into an underwater rock hole or suddenly descending to a depth that will drown the engine will require fundamental and major recovery procedures. Water deeper than about 35cm demands that wading plugs be fitted to the clutch housing and cam-belt drive housing in some early Land Rover vehicles. (See 'Wading', Section 4.10.)

Always worth it. An on-foot survey will delay you and is usually mucky or wet and cold. It is, however, far preferable to damaging the vehicle or finding you have a major recovery problem on your hands.

Marshalling (spotting)

External guidance – marshalling. If you are not alone, an invaluable adjunct to negotiating difficult ground with small clearances is to have your passenger marshal you through from outside the vehicle. Only someone outside the vehicle can properly see all four wheels and where they are going – and see the exact clearances under the axle casings (see photos p.4.33).

On a steep descent the driver can see far too little to be safe. The on-foot recce may be enough but, if in any doubt, a marshaller positioned some way off can give precision guidance. On rocky ground this can also avoid tyre sidewall damage on rocks.

Wading recce

On-foot recce especially important in rivers, where hazards are hidden

You've got to be 110% sure before you do this (above). Never mind the cold, without a recce and a prod, the vehicle could fall into an unseen swirl-hole like that in the diagram.

Overall view, take it steady. A marshaller should stand 5 to 15 metres ahead of the vehicle – facing it – where all the wheels can easily be seen. Guidance by the marshaller should be given unambiguously and entirely by hand and arm signals rather than by voice. At the risk of stating the obvious, be sure there is just one marshaller who is in total charge and make a conscious effort to take things one step at a time. Situations in which marshalling is required frequently spawn two or three people all shouting half-heard directions at one time; the general tension often generates a feeling that something decisive and effective must be done, immediately...! The calm and measured approach is to be preferred!

Marshaller in control. Obey the marshaller completely. Try not to take your eyes off him or her to make your own judgements on a situation you cannot assess as comprehensively as someone outside the vehicle. Stop if you are not happy but once moving, the marshaller is in control.

And for the marshaller, if there is something other than the signals shown below that you want to communicate, don't shout! Stop the vehicle and then walk over, calmly, and speak to the driver.

One marshaller only in control. Directions by signs, not voice. Stop if you're not happy; otherwise always obey the marshaller. He's the one who can see all four wheels.

Marshalling signals

Advance. Go back

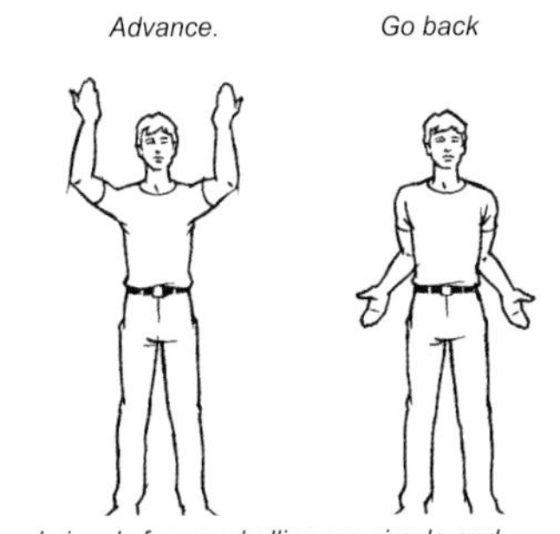

Stop

Steer in this direction

Hand signals for marshalling are simple and unambiguous, given close-up or at a distance.

Section 4

Off-road techniques

When trailer weight exceeds around 75% of tug weight, the laws of physics dictate you are entering a critical zone for stability.

4.1 Towing – *on*-road

Preliminaries – the theory

***On*-road?** Don't be too surprised that the first section about off-road techniques concerns *on*-road towing. Most 4x4 towing finishes up off-road anyway but is preceded by a long on-road section. So this is the holistic approach; hopefully all will be clear.

Theory matters? There will be many who, faced with pulling *that* trailer (no choice) with *this* vehicle (no choice) are of a mind to doubt the value of theory and just get on with it.

However hard-nosed and down to earth the job, knowing the theory will make operations safer.

An understandable view from a busy operator but airline pilots, similarly limited in choice of type or design of the aircraft they are paid to fly, do benefit a great deal – and safety is immeasurably enhanced – by knowing what is going on aerodynamically.

There is much folklore and many rules of thumb associated with towing and it is helpful and refreshing to know that what goes on really is quantifiable now and every parameter may be taken into account – from the spring rates of the towing vehicle (tug) to the types of bushes fitted to the suspension.

Famine and feast. A capable design analysis computer could produce enough information and study of variables to fill a book on this subject alone. The object of this section, in just eight pages, is to steer a middle course between the information famine of preceding years and the feast of data now available. The good news, for readers braced for another 'breakthrough' and overturning of received wisdom, is that virtually all the rules of thumb are valid. Knowing why, though – and their limitations – is absorbing and there are enough surprises to make it worthwhile reading further.

Trailer dynamics

Stability. Overriding priority will be given by all operators examining this subject to the question of stability and safety and brief treatment will be given therefore to:

- Straight line stability.
- Oscillation or weave.
- Steady turn stability.

Straight line stability. Consider a towing vehicle (tug) of infinite mass – the implication being that the towing pin moves in an undeviating straight line, uninfluenced by the trailer. The trailer behind it will tow straight for the same reason a dart or aircraft flies straight; as soon as the trailer deviates due to a gust or random side-load, the tyres will then be at an angle to the direction of motion and as a result a side-force will be generated by the tyres to push the trailer back in line behind the tug.

As the trailer approaches zero slip angle

Yaw angle and tyre slip angle – see also next spread

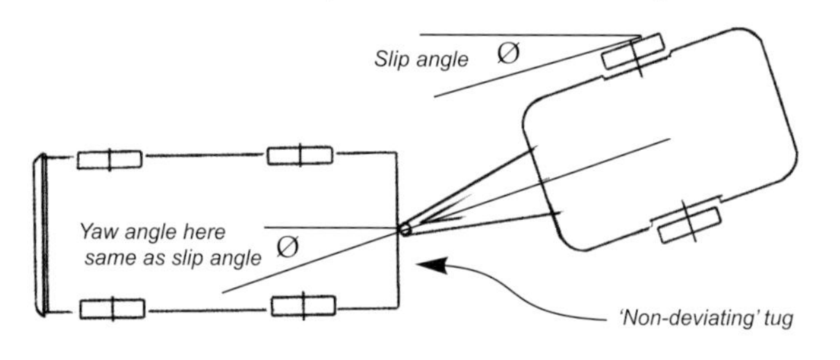

With an imaginary non-deviating tug, trailer displacement gives rise to tyre slip angle which in turn generates restoring side-force to put the trailer back on course in a single or decaying series of swings. If the trailer can influence the tug (see opposite, far right) complex swings can be self-sustaining.

the side-force also reduces until, when it is in line again, the side-force has disappeared. Fairly obvious stuff but it is important to consider this – the concept of slip angle and tyre side-force – before going on.

Right – an illustration not designed to scare but inserted (from a complete computer sequence) only to indicate that the result of a given combination of parameters and driving techniques can be predicted as a matter of routine. (50 mph, 2000 kg trailer, CG aft of axle, severe avoidance manoeuvre, .22 g braking.) How to avoid it in the absence of precise data is less easily predicted; knowledge of general theory, care and caution are best ingredients. Diagrams below – dynamics of tug/trailer interface with decaying or increasing oscillation can be analogous to swinging a school ruler on a pencil. See text.

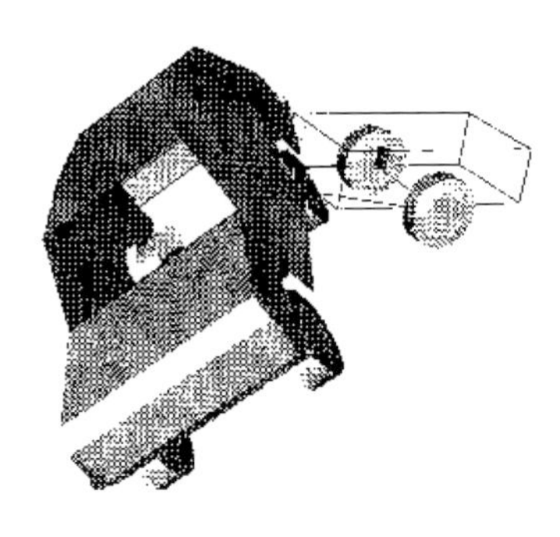

Oscillation, weave

Decaying or increasing oscillation. Few who have seen TV pictures of caravans 'mysteriously' turning over on motorways will need a definition of weave, yaw or snaking. However, do distinguish between decaying (convergent) and increasing (divergent) oscillation; the difference between what is mildly alarming and peters out and the ever-increasing swing that can result in an accident. Take an ordinary school ruler (the type with a hole in one end) and let it swing on a pencil held in your hand – diagrams below.

The middle diagram (the hand remains perfectly still) corresponds exactly to the tug of infinite mass mentioned opposite where the tug continues undisturbed on a perfectly straight course. The swing of the ruler gradually decays to nothing.

The third diagram corresponds to a tug that can move. As you know, moving your hand in a particular way can make the ruler swing with increasing amplitude. In moving your hand (with the pencil pivot) to make the ruler swing you are instinctively introducing an appropriate frequency and phasing of your movement to make the ruler swing as wide as possible. Try analysing exactly what you are doing and you will see how difficult it is to pinpoint the phase lead and frequency you are introducing. This is mentioned because although the computer, when given the tug/trailer dynamics to sort out, can apply the equations of motion and all the myriad modifying influences with tireless brilliance and accuracy, it reflects the number of variables and how critical they are when the overall stability result is considered.

Exact prediction of dynamics is possible. But the myriad criteria and their varying influence make it impractical to attempt in every case.

Decaying and increasing oscillations

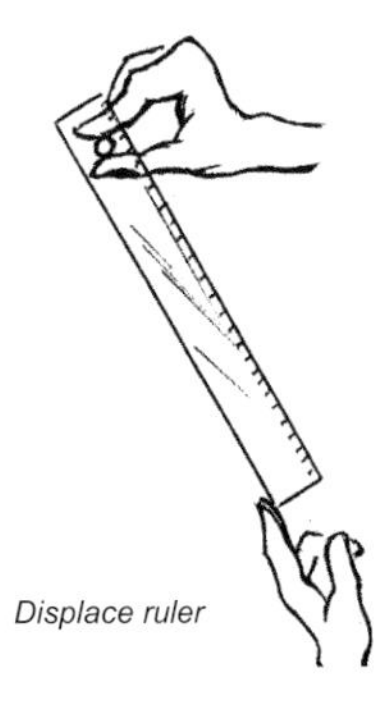

Displace ruler

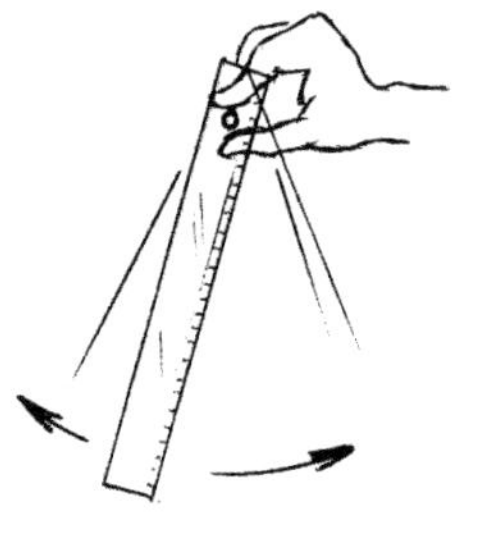

Static hand, decaying swing

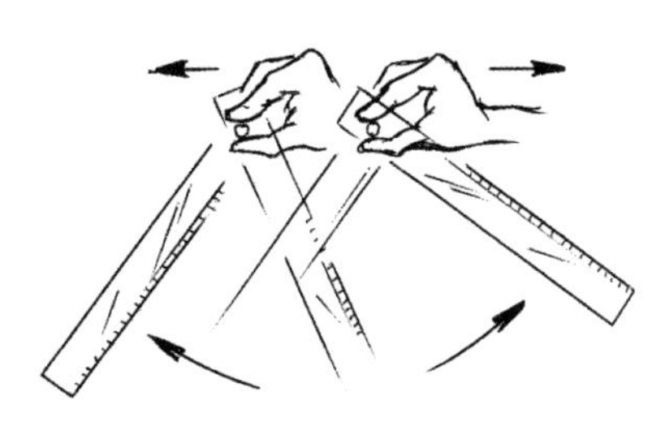

Moving hand, increasing swing

Whiplash effect. Let us therefore resort once more to an analogy, again using the school ruler. This time hold it in a horizontal plane, with your thumb and forefinger over the hole. Flick your wrist left and right and you will see as you do so that the ruler trails, moves and then overshoots the action of your wrist – what may be termed a whiplash effect. Get the combination of thumb-grip (damping) and wrist-speed wrong and nothing much happens; get it 'right' and a perfect 'whiplash' takes place; again you will note there is a particular combination of parameters that 'excite' the system and these are related to the weight of ruler, speed of motion, damping (thumb pressure), etc.

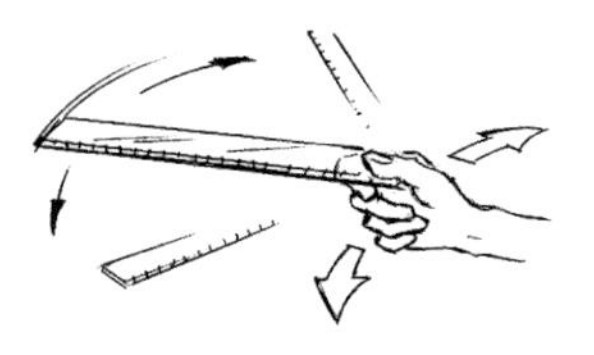

The parallels between these three 'ruler cases' and a tug and trailer will be seen at once:

- The decaying oscillation
- The increasing oscillation due to hand movement and
- The 'whiplash' effect – closely related to the above.

Forward trailer CG benefits stability in weaves but too far forward will exacerbate problems in sharp turn manoeuvres. Aim for trailer CG 10-20 cm ahead of axle.

With the ruler/pendulum the restoring 'side-force' is provided by gravity and inertia where in the case of the trailer the side-force is provided by the tyres.

Applying the analogy. It is clear so far that lateral motion of the tug, at given phase differences and amplitudes, is a fundamental influencing factor in the generation, sustaining and 'amplification' of lateral oscillation. Because it will affect what we can do about it, it is worth now probing just a little deeper into the actual situation with a tug and trailer.

We have considered the ruler (trailer) swinging about the pivot point (tow hitch) for convenience because that is what actually happens. But we must now grasp the fact that a trailer (or any other 'body'), given a turning motion, will naturally want to rotate about its own centre of gravity (CG).

Spin a Coke bottle on a table and it will spin about its CG. If you constrain one end while it is revolving (trailer nose hitched to a tow-hook) it will turn about that point but is still trying to rotate about is own CG so will exert a reactive lateral force on the hitch.

CG position. Remember the start point here is a conceptually displaced trailer to the right of the vehicle and the tyre side-force at the trailer then influencing its behaviour (diagram p.4.2). Look at where, in a typical tug/trailer pair, the tug and trailer CGs are located and how this affects the influence of trailer on tug – diagrams opposite (upper)

In a swing, a forward trailer CG (ie tyre side-force acting aft of the CG) tends to reduce yaw angle Ø; in effect reducing the angle between the tug and trailer (the pale grey lines). So this permits the oscillation to decay giving a result like the middle diagram on the last page (no hand movement).

The aft CG, on the other hand tends to increase Ø because tyre side-force is acting ahead of the CG. This encourages an increasing swing. Most readers will already know that a forward CG is best for trailers. When we look to the next sub-section and diagram, however, we will find that the CG should not be *too* far forward.

Steady-state cornering

Extreme forward trailer CG. You might perhaps have felt that the further forward the trailer CG the better would be its stability, but at extreme forward CGs in fast bends there is a *destabilising* effect of the trailer on the tug that actually increases with forward movement of trailer CG. The computer confirms that moving the CG even 30cm ahead of the axle in an accelerating steady turn can, in certain circumstances, cause breakaway of the tug towards the centre of the circle ('tuck-in') and subsequent rollover.

The lower diagram opposite makes clear what is happening. Although it is tyre side-force acting about the trailer CG, you may find it easier to think of it as 'centrifugal force' on the mass represented by the CG; either way, the trailer CG, being far forward, tends strongly to push the nose of the trailer (and the tail of the tug) towards the outside of the circle. There comes a time when the

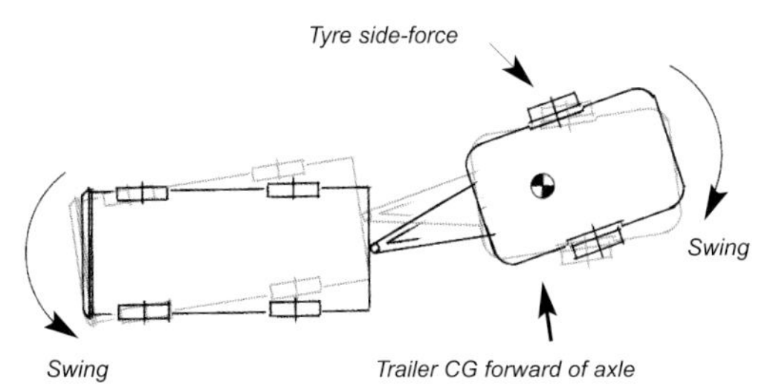

Assume trailer displaced to right, so tyre side-force is from right. Tyre side-force tends to turn trailer about its own CG, imparting motion to tail of tug that is stabilising (forward CG – left) or destabilising (aft CG – below)

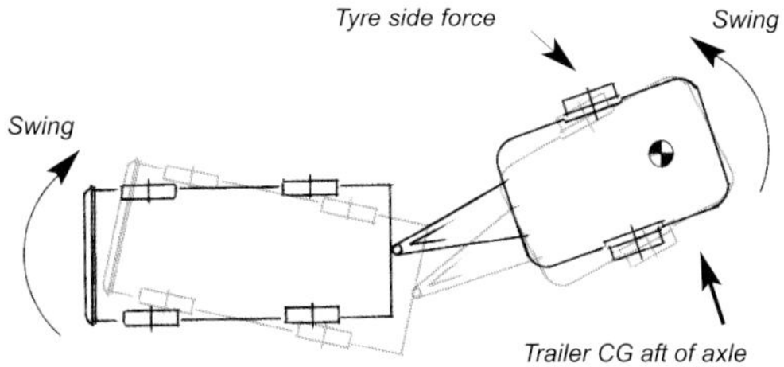

rear tyres of the tug can no longer hold on and the tail of the tug breaks away to the outside of the turn and the trailer, in hot pursuit, can provoke a rollover. The practical application of this information? Take corners slowly.

The compromise

Moderation in all things. In concept, therefore, we have a conflict. The weave-damping case demands a forward CG and the steady-state turn is sensitive to a too-far forward CG. Whilst all stability problems are more critical with a high trailer weight, your particular combination of variables and cornering methods will dictate your choice of CG position. On most of the initial computer runs a CG about 10-20cm ahead of the axle gave the best margin for stability. There are also, as we shall see, other practical factors that favour limiting the forward CG position such as keeping a moderate trailer nose load on the tug's towing hitch.

Evening–up the (side) loads. Clearly to minimise the effect of the trailer on the tug (where a trailer of comparative weight to the tug is used), we must aim to spread the cornering forces evenly between all the wheels involved – in an ideal world: same load, same tyres, same tyre pressures on all axles. The world is not ideal so we must instead be sure of the following:

- Don't overload the tug's rear axle.
- Tyre pressures appropriate to axle load; if in doubt err high.
- Trailer CG forward but not too far.

High trailer weight makes things worse – everything! Drive with extra care; you are fighting the laws of physics!

Fast or tightening steady turn with far-forward CG on heavy trailer can eventually cause the tug rear tyres to lose grip, permitting tail end to slide to outside of turn due to excess 'centrifugal force'. Long tug rear overhang makes things worse as trailer has more leverage.

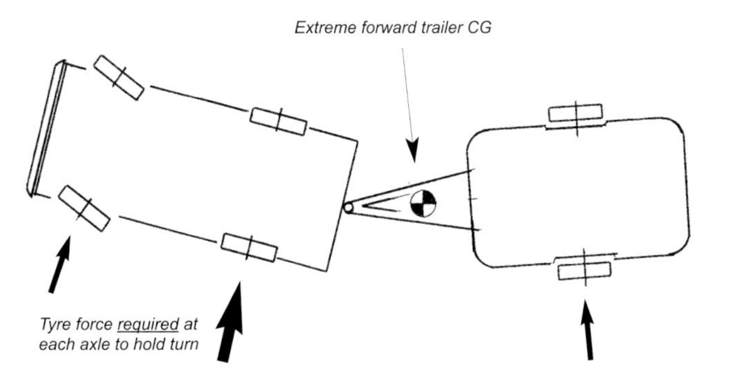

Practicalities

Safety first. No apology is made for the over-used cliché nor for the accent so far in this section on stability and safe operation. Provided the many relevant parameters are known, the behavioural characteristics of any tug / trailer combination can be predicted on computer models but in the real world they are not known and awareness of the theory of what is going on is doubly important.

Surprisingly, trailer operation is under-legislated with no periodic or age-related tests. Under-used trailers are prone to rusting-up or jamming of brakes.

In many parts of the world, and here the UK is included, legislation for trailer operational safety is skeletal and flimsy. Though complex, it extends to little more than construction and basic use and no regulations cover regular testing or functional checks to what are, in many cases, infrequently-used vehicles. Apart from catch-all 'roadworthy condition' rules, no periodic tests (brake function etc) are laid down.

Your responsibility. It thus behoves the user more than ever to ensure that trailers are in first-rate condition. Readers of this book will in some cases be those using heavy trailers up to and exceeding the weight of the towing vehicle. Be aware that, even using a large off-roader tug, *once you are past a trailer weight of around 75% of the weight of the towing vehicle the simple laws of physics dictate you are entering a critical zone in regard to stability, steering and braking; unrelenting care in operation is your responsibility.*

General towing considerations. The diagram opposite encapsulates all the criteria relevant to optimum load and stability in a trailer and should be studied carefully in relation to the trailer / tug combination you have. Nose load is critically important to towing stability when setting up a given trailer.

Two-bolt 3500 kg tow ball/jaw, variable height hitch – for twin-axle trailers (see Item 6, opposite). Four-bolt-fixing hitch OK for 3500 kg on ball, 5000 kg on pin. Robust 'NATO' pintle for use with round towing eye.

Some typical approved off-roader maximum gross trailer weights (consult current manuals)

Trailer/braking	*On/off road*	*Defender with 2.5D kg*	*Defender, any other engine kg*	*Discovery kg*	*Range Rover kg*	*2011 Range Rover kg*
1. Unbraked trailer	On road Off road	750 500	750 500*	750 500†	750 750	750 500
2. Trailer with overrun brakes	On road Off road	3500 1000	3500 1000	3500** 1000†	3500 1000	3500 1000
3. 4-wheel trailer with coupled brakes (see above).	On road Off road	3500 1000	4000 1000	4000† 1000†	4000 1000	3500 1000

** 750kg for 110 with self-levelled suspension. **Discovery Mpi 2750kg †Not Discovery Mpi*

Towing variables – seeking the optimum

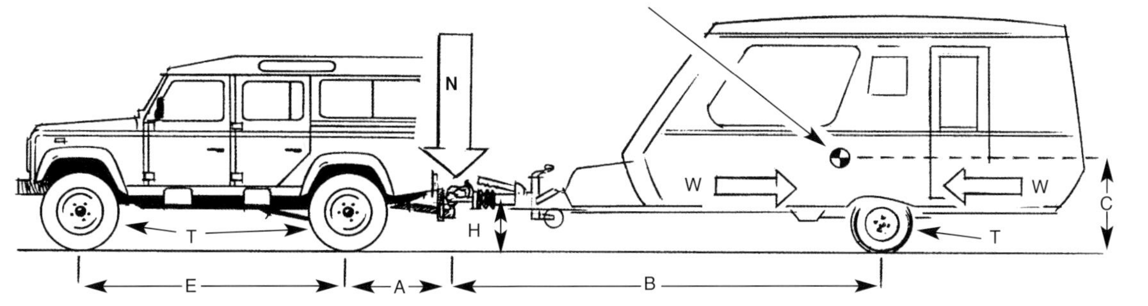

Go slowly through the variables:

1. A:E – minimise the ratio (small A, big E) when considering a towing vehicle.
2. A:B – minimise the ratio (small A, big B) when considering a trailer.
3. C:B – C not to exceed 40% of B, so keep CG low.
   C not to exceed 95% of trailer track (small C, wide track).
4. E:B – Small E, big B makes for easier reversing.
5. T – Tyre pressures – hard: use GVW settings (Sec 8.2) unless off road (Sec 6.4).
6. H – Same for trailer and towing vehicle. *Specially important with twin-axle trailer.*
7. **N** – Trailer nose weight. More nose weight equals more anti-weave stability but less cornering stability (lower diagram, previous spread and Note in Trouble Shooting table next spread) – 7% of trailer gross weight is a guide, BUT:
   1. Do not exceed limits of ball hitch or coupling head – usually 100–150kg.
   2. Remove twice this amount from towing vehicle payload – ie if N = 75kg, take 150 kg off listed max payload of vehicle when working out how much else you can carry in towing vehicle.
8. W – For a given nose weight, concentrate load close to trailer axle to reduce moment of inertia.

Note. CG position. To calculate CG position you need to know trailer gross weight (weighbridge), axle-to-hitch distance (drawbar length) and nose weight (bathroom scales or weighbridge). Then:
CG position (in cm, ahead of trailer axle) = Nose load in kg times drawbar length in cm divided by the trailer gross weight in kg.

Braking and weight. Braking method and capacity are especially important. Design and regulatory limitations applicable to some sample Land Rover products are shown opposite and give an indication of what to look for; note the large difference between on- and off-road cleared towing maxima. See also Section 6.4 Towing off-road.

Above 3500kg trailer gross weight coupled-brakes are mandatory but will be beneficial below this for their sensitivity. Single- or twin-line air or vacuum brakes with various reservoirs may be fitted. Fitment of such systems requires specialist knowledge and workmanship and should only be carried out by specialists.

Tow hitch, coupling-head strength. Remember that the widely used 50mm ball hitch is limited to a 3500kg trailer gross weight. Above this use one of the hitches shown opposite. Nose load must normally not exceed 150kg.

Rear axle load. The effect of trailer download on the rear axle of the tug has already been shown to be very relevant to stability – some, but not too much, is required. The download on the towing hitch is also like having additional payload far aft of the centre of the vehicle load bed – check the diagram at Sec 8.1 and you will see that the leverage of a 250kg on the tailgate actually increases the rear axle load by 341kg. The same applies to trailer nose load; see Note 2 under 'N' (Item 7) in diagram above.

Nose load is critical to stability. Remember too strength limits of the tow hitch. Nose-load is tug payload. Take double the nose-load off your residual tug payload.

A substantial tow car, even with auto-engage four-wheel drive, raises the important tug/trailer weight ratio as well as enhancing traction on wet sites. Mazda's CX7, voted towcar of its year, also has short rear overhang. A front-mounted hitch (above on a Land Rover Defender) is useful for precise manoeuvring.

Driving with a trailer

As soon as you are moving, check braking response. Always keep maximum space between yourself and vehicle ahead. Keep tug and trailer in line for braking.

Always check brakes. Although light, unbraked trailers will seem not to affect the vehicle very much it is wise to check overall braking action as soon as possible after starting off. Trailers with overrun brakes – especially if they have not been used for some time – can suffer from grabby, non-progressive, even asymmetric, brakes due to rusty brake drums and a test on a clear piece of road is essential before setting off with a newly loaded trailer.

Coupled brakes. Whilst coupled brakes should be more progressive, a test is still wise since the trailer may not be proportionally braked and still exert some residual push on the towing vehicle during braking.

Braking, general. Whatever the regulations permitting use of some trailers without brakes, braked trailers are more stable than unbraked. That said, any braking situation will exacerbate a marginal stability or safety problem. Keep this always in your mind together with the need to avoid braking except when the trailer and tug are in line. These considerations should lead to a conscious and consistent effort to drive with as much space between you the vehicle ahead as possible so that you are never called upon to brake suddenly or fiercely. Often your cargo (horses, say) will dictate this anyway.

Reversing. Reversing with a trailer is a well-known difficulty for drivers not used to it. In general, trailers which are long relative to the wheelbase of the towing vehicle (such as articulated trucks) are easier to reverse than those that are short.

Those that are shorter than the wheelbase of the tug are all but impossible to reverse any distance. As with all aspects of operating your off-roader, do not be afraid to admit you have got it wrong. If a trailer is that short, it will also be light; uncoupling to manoeuvre it by hand saves the difficulty – and embarrassment – of reversing it!

Auto-reverse brakes. Overrun trailer brakes work on the principle that a braking tug will cause the trailer to push against the hitch and in doing so apply its own brakes. Reversing such a trailer would ordinarily therefore cause the trailer brakes to come on and you must get out of the vehicle to apply an inhibiting catch before and after doing so.

Currently, all new trailers with overrun brakes have an auto-reverse fitment that senses the difference between overrun and reversing and no driver action is required. Be sure you are aware of which brake type you have.

Excessive braking. Harsh braking when towing causes the trailer to increase download on the towing vehicle hitch (hence need for centre of gravity constraints, diagram previous spread). This produces a rotating moment about the tug rear axle and a resulting offloading of the vehicle front wheels which can, in slippery conditions, produce front wheel lock-up. This will not happen with ABS brakes an, if your vehicle does not have ABS, the risk can be reduced by use of cadence braking (p.3.7).

Electrics. Lights, brake lights and direction indicators should be checked with the trailer and electrics connected.

Towing off-road – see Section 6.4.

The regulations

Details, details. *If there appears at the moment in UK to be a surprising lack of regulation regarding periodic inspection and serviceability of trailers, there is no shortage of legislation in other areas.*

Us. *On a practical note, first and most helpfully, NTTA (the National Trailer and Towing Association), a non-government group formed by manufacturers at:*

www.ntta.co.uk/law

They publish 'The NTTA Guide to Safe and Legal Towing'. Much of it is common sense but a great deal more is invaluable detail and well worth going through – including lights, brakes, servicing, loading, carrying horses and livestock, driving, reversing and (mechanical) stabilizers. (The document is dated year 2000 and pre-dates widespread use of computerised sway sensors and braking.)

Them. *As to Government regulations, the whole panoply is revealed at:*

www.gov.uk/towing-with-car

Important information includes:

1. Driving licence rules and what you can tow. (Licences issued pre- and post-1997 are subject to different rules. And fresh rules and tests apply to driving licenses issued after 19 January 2013.)

2. Car towing weight and width limits.

3. Towing equipment safety standards. (Rules regarding tow-bars, mirrors, brakes.)

4. Towing an American caravan or trailer.

5. The car and trailer practical test.

Does your trailer have auto-reverse brakes? Or must you operate a catch before and after reversing?

Towing – trouble-shooting summary

Symptom	What to do
1. Weaving	Move trailer CG forward, reduce trailer weight, reduce moment of inertia (concentrate weight closer to the trailer axle), increase trailer and tug tyre pressures, fit a hitch yaw damper, increase trailer drawbar length, reduce speed. **Auto-fix.** There is inevitably, now, a computer that comes to the rescue when needed. ESP yaw- and lateral 'g'-sensors sniff out symptoms of incipient trailer-weave and address the problem with a dab of brake on appropriate wheels. Such a system is fitted to Land Rover's upper echelon products and others.
2. 'Oversteer' cornering (tendency to 'tuck-in' when cornering)	Move trailer CG further *aft* (but not less than 10-20cm ahead of trailer axle), *reduce cornering speed,* increase tug rear tyre pressures. small reduction in tug front tyre pressures, reduce trailer weight, increase trailer drawbar length.

Note. You will see that, from the point of view of trailer CG position, the two conditions above are (literally) 'swings and roundabouts': improve the weave (swing) stability by moving the trailer CG forward and you could be in danger of encountering divergent oversteer on sharp/fast bends (such as roundabouts). Tendency to weave will in some cases be due to an inherent condition (in relation to your load) you can do nothing about – such as tug rear overhang, for instance. You may be compelled here to move trailer CG further forward than you would wish in order to quench tendency to weave. In these circumstances it may be the right decision so long as you ensure your cornering speeds are reduced, especially on roundabouts.

Typical unsurfaced tracks have moderately fast sections for which 5th low range may be ideal, enabling you to change down for the really rough bits without a range-change.

4.2 Driving on tracks

Aim to flow smoothly over rough terrain – don't let the vehicle jolt and jar. High gears in the low box very useful for rough tracks.

Sympathetic flow

Driving – smooth, calm. On tracks, even rough ones, your driving technique should aim to have the vehicle flow smoothly over it rather than jolt and jar. To state the unsurprising, if not the obvious, this will usually mean adjusting your speed downwards and varying it according to the unevenness immediately in front of the vehicle – typically slowing at the apex of a rise or the bottom of a dip, however small they may be, You'll likely find a speed that will cope with it all and yield a smooth ride.

If your vehicle has coil springs all round you will find it easier to achieve a jolt-free ride, albeit there are clever things that can be done with multi-leaf springs to give a pliant, stiction-free ride. Applying the mechanical sympathy mentioned in Section 3.1 will do much to foster an appropriately smooth driving technique for these conditions.

Taking a calm and unhurried approach will also help: correction – it is fundamental.

Which gears? High range 2WD in maybe 3rd gear is often quite adequate for driving on unsurfaced tracks, depending on the smoothness and frequency of rough patches but, as mentioned before (Section 3.2, 'Low range – when and how'), the high gears in the low range can be very useful on rough tracks. Such tracks usually have short, difficult sections for which the steady control of the low range gears will be required to preclude constant use of brake and clutch .

High gears, low range. Thus taking a track in, say, top gear low range will allow the driver to make a good pace without excessive revs yet change right down to 2nd or even 1st low when the ultimate low speed control and torque is required; this without the need to change transfer gear range.

There is, of course, quite an overlap between speeds in the high and low range gears – for example 4th or 5th low box being equivalent to 2nd or 3rd in high. To get a clear picture of the overlap between high and low range gears, see p.6.4.

Deep ruts with slippery sides (right) can mask normal steering feedback. You can be unaware your wheels are not pointing straight ahead. When grip is available, vehicle suddenly veers. Land Rover '4x4 info' display (above) is an invaluable aid in this respect, also showing the diff-lock status.

Automatics. As in many aspects of off-road driving, a well-matched auto gearbox is the ultimate aid to smooth driving – stress free for driver and vehicle.

Railway line effect

Slippery ruts. Driving along a deeply rutted track where the ruts are cut into slippery ground can be like driving along railway lines, albeit somewhat wobbly ones. Turning the steering wheel left or right does not have any effect since the tyres will not grip on the steep slippery sides of the ruts – see picture above, right.

The danger here is you can be driving with – unknowingly – some steering lock applied, which the vehicle is not responding to. When you reach level ground or a patch where traction permits it to respond to the steering lock, the vehicle will suddenly find grip and veer off the track.

Wheels straight ahead? Since this condition is not met every day it is doubly important to have the possibility in the back of your mind that the conditions may be of this type when you are in ruts. The way to preclude the occurrence is to monitor the self-centring of the steering. Periodically and very briefly reduce your grip on the steering wheel by keeping just a light frictional touch with the palms of your hands, letting it regain the straight ahead position, through castor action (see Glossary, Section 9.1). Also a visual check from the driver's window will establish which way the wheels are pointing. When using the window in this way beware of branches of shrubs or trees (always thorny overseas!) flicking in your face.

Traction

Existing wheel tracks. If there are already wheel tracks along the unsurfaced road you are travelling, this can affect the traction of your vehicle – for better or for worse. On wet or muddy tracks or in snow it is best to follow in the tracks of a previous vehicle since, in general terms, that vehicle will probably have cut through to the drier ground beneath and this will offer your vehicle more traction. See also Section 4.4, 'Climbing steep slopes', and Section 4.7, 'Weak ground' .

Beware driving with non-gripping steering lock on. Let self-centring castor-action periodically align your wheels in deep ruts.

Desert and bush. On routes over desert plains avoid the tracks of previous vehicle since they will have broken the stronger crust that normally forms on windblown sands – often you will have to divert from the track in order to do this. Beneath this crust is soft sand offering less flotation, likely to be badly churned which will make traction even worse. See 'Sand', Section 4.8. You may have to make similar diversions in bush country.

Fast relatively smooth tracks are one of the delights of 'off-road' driving but you should always be on your guard against sudden deterioration – typically a transverse gully or runnel – and the reduced braking the loose surface causes. Muddy tracks call for a delicate right foot.

Be on the lookout for ruts that have become gullies. They can quickly run you out of under-axle clearance.

Deep ruts, gullies

Under-axle clearance. Rough tracks will sometimes deteriorate into deep V-shaped gullies due to water erosion or extra deep ruts caused by the passage of trucks with larger wheels than yours. Keeping in such ruts can often lead to grounding the chassis or axle case of your vehicle and anticipation is needed to take appropriate advance action.

As the diagram opposite shows, you should aim to get out of the ruts early so as to straddle the gully. (In extreme cases you can use a hi-lift jack for this – see pp.5.4-5.) Care will be necessary to avoid steering up one or other of the gully walls which could lead to the vehicle being trapped with its side against the gully.

Steering feel. As indicated in the previous spread, because of the depth or slipperiness of the rut or gully, you may well lose the natural feel of the steering and find it hard to know exactly which way your wheels are pointing.

Worse, the combination of the wheel's natural castor angle, its offset (see below) and the terrain under it can cause the wheel to want to turn towards a steep upslope – ie the side of the rut or gully.

For this reason keep a firm grip on the steering wheel and check the wheels are pointing where they should be. To ensure front and back wheels are surveyed all the time when driving over gullies, use a marshaller ahead of the vehicle. If you're solo then lower the driver's window and observe the front wheel yourself – being careful, as ever, not to let your concentration blind you to the hazard of tree branches passing close to the vehicle.

Steering offset

Design nicety. As explained in the Glossary, steering offset is the distance between the centre point of tyre contact on the ground and the point where the extension of the wheel steering pivot (the notional

Rain or flood erosion can cause deep ruts to become gullies and there is the danger of the vehicle slipping down one side. Careful guidance by a marshaller who can see all the wheels is the only way to negotiate this kind of obstacle. The Range Rover has small steering offset making steering feedback more reliable here.

'king-pin') also touches the ground. The smaller this distance the more reliable will be the feel of the steering on off-road obstacles where left and right wheels may be subject to differing forces. Design-wise, it is not easy to achieve small steering offset with 4x4s and has only in recent years been acknowledged as desirable but it will lessen the feedback of one-wheel obstacles. Interestingly, the designers of Jeep's 2007 iteration of their hallowed icon took the opportunity to reduce the steering offset of the Wrangler JK from 50mm down to 14mm to reduce this one-wheel-in-cold-treacle effect when tackling variably rough ground off-road. Lest these gentlemen should crick their backs taking bows, early Suzuki Vitaras had a steering offset of only 8mm!

You will lose – or get false – steering feel driving gully sides. Get guidance and/or look out of the window.

Ruts that become deep gullies

1.

2.

Do not stay in badly eroded deteriorating ruts (1). Get out of ruts and (2) straddle the gully. Vehicle must be carefully guided in gully to sit evenly across it. If necessary, cut steps with a shovel to give tyres a positive footing without sliding down the gully side – and use a marshaller.

Without traction control or diff-locks to nail wheelspin (front left wheel), 'landscaping' – digging under the hung-up wheels – will lower the vehicle so that all four wheels are in contact with the ground and traction is regained.

4.3 Ridges and ditches

Diagonal suspension

Diagonal approach usually best but wheelspin is the main hazard. Know vehicle's articulation limits. Methods of crossing vary according to size of the obstacle.

Ridge – a mirror-image ditch. Ridges and ditches have particular significance in the context of suspension travel and wheelspin as shown on page 2.8. They can be encountered both on tracks and across open country. Though one is a mirror image of the other, ridges and ditches can introduce the same problems for the vehicle – grounding the chassis or hanging diagonally-opposite wheels in the air and losing traction by reaching the limits of articulation (see page 3.10).

The method of crossing these obstacles will require judgement according to their size since the recommended method of crossing a small ridge – diagonally – will lead to trouble if applied to a big (or abrupt) one.

Articulation – again. Articulation is also covered elsewhere (eg Section 3.4) but is a fundamental factor in the performance of a 4x4 off-road and – especially in one lacking effective cross-axle wheelspin control (traction control or locking diff) – is a basic cause of probably 90% of all failed traction situations – the inability to put four wheels on the ground and get each wheel to contribute to forward motion of the vehicle.

Long ignored, manufacturers, happily, are waking up to this and now offering axle diff locks or braked-wheel traction control. (See also relevant boxes pp.2.18 and 2.19.)

Size determines technique

Potential hazards. The sketch (left) shows the potential hazards; one wheel on each axle on the bump stops and the other hanging in mid air – and spinning. The best general advice is to take ridges and ditches diagonally with as much momentum as you judge to be prudent. If that seems like the ultimate escape clause, remember that some obstacles are better taken at right angles (if you can) to avoid risk of diagonal hang-up; others are best taken diagonally (if you can) to avoid jarring or hitting the tail as you exit – check the table below. Consider these obstacles in three sizes:

1. Small ridges and ditches. These may be taken at right angles within the limits dictated by vehicle under-belly clearance and rear overhang (departure angle). However this does mean that the respective front and rear axles will hit the obstacle square-on and probably impart a severe jolt. By taking the obstacles diagonally the vehicle will hit the bump or dip one wheel at a time and flow over

Ridges and ditches: diagonal approach vs right angles

Approach	*Advantage*	*Disadvantage*
Right angles	Precludes diagonal hang-up	May jolt, belly vehicle or hit tail
Diagonal	Avoids jarring	May cause diagonal hang-up

Two approaches. 'Diagonal suspension' encapsulates the ridges and ditches problem. Defender's simple approach – lots of articulation – keeps wheels on the ground in ditches and over ridges. Early ML Mercedes' arthritic suspension movement demonstrated on this notional 'ridge', enhances on-road handling but would need diff-locks or traction control to curb wheelspin off-road. Ultimate ridge-crossing capability shown on p.2.8.

the obstacle with a rolling motion but without any shock loading. Indeed if, when driving quickly over a plain, you encounter a shallow ditch which you had not seen earlier, alter direction immediately to take it diagonally. Don't hit it square-on. (Axle cases can bend!)

2. Medium-sized ridges and ditches. These may be classified as those that will give problems of under-belly or departure angle clearance and therefore cannot be taken at right angles. With these ones you thus have no option but to take them diagonally. The technique outlined above should be used.

3. Tall ridges and deep ditches. On-foot inspection and the assistance of a marshaller will almost certainly be necessary. These are obstacles that definitely cannot be taken at right angles and also, if taken slowly diagonally, may result in diagonally-opposite wheels lifting to allow (if you don't have axle diff locks) wheelspin and loss of traction. In these cases you have two options:

a. Provided the going is smooth enough, take the obstacle diagonally but fast enough for momentum to carry the vehicle past the momentary lifting of corner wheels.

b. Provided it is permitted, 'landscape' the ground with a shovel to remove the top of the ridge or edge of the ditch that will cause grounding of the chassis or tail end or suspension of the wheels. Then proceed as at 1 above.

Judgement required: speed and diagonal approach can help. Digging under hung-up wheels may be needed.

Learning gently. As with so many skills it takes longer to write and read this advice than to apply it. You will quickly learn to judge which situation you are in and how it relates to your vehicle's articulation and the presence or otherwise of diff locks. As ever, so long as you do not jolt the vehicle badly or ground the chassis it does not matter if you do not get this right first time – at least on small and medium obstacles. Do not be afraid to take it gently at first or admit you got it wrong; back off and try again – no damage has been done. (See also 'Self recovery', Section 5.1.)

4.4 Climbing steep slopes

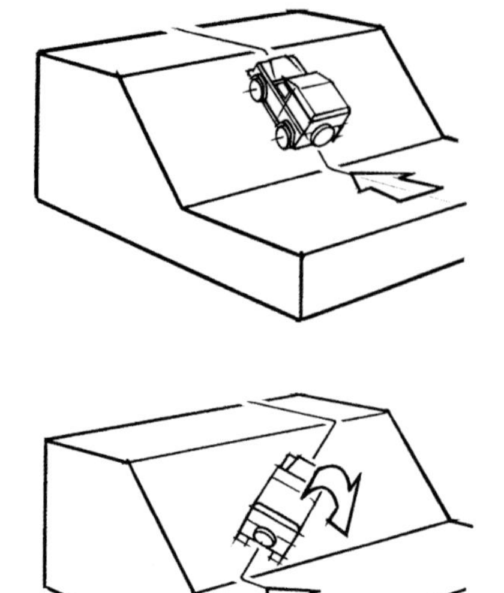

Going up a slope at right angles to the lip of the ridge is safe; a diagonal approach can provoke a rollover down the slope. The risk is made worse by any wheelspin.

Grip is invariably the limiting factor on steep slopes. The right gear (usually 2nd or 3rd low) and a sensitive throttle foot is the answer (see p.3.6). Keep at right angles to the slope.

Grip, gradient, momentum

Grip and gradient. The twin problems with steep slopes – gradient and grip – usually reduce themselves to one in cases where a 4x4 has a two-speed transfer box with a set of low range gears (see page 2.12 and diagrams page 2.13). Such a vehicle will usually have the power and appropriate gearing to climb a continuous slope of not far short of 1-in-1 or 45° – if the grip is there.

That gentle right foot. Grip is far more likely to be the limiting factor and we have seen in Section 3.3, 'Gentle right foot', how use of the right gear (not necessarily the lowest one) allied to a sensitive right foot can eliminate the wheelspin that can result from insufficient grip.

Climbing steep slopes is the classic application of sensing grip and being gentle with the throttle – and, see next spread, admitting defeat early in cases of wheelspin. Don't floor the throttle when you get wheelspin in the vain hope of getting up the slope; the vehicle could slide sideways off course and may tip – see diagram, left.

Go straight at the slope. Whilst a walker would take diagonal tacks up a steep hill to reduce the gradient, you should take the fall line direct in a vehicle, ie take the slope at right angles, head-on. The diagonal approach can be for ridges and ditches, not for steep slopes. This is to ensure the vehicle is laterally level – your walker can stand up straight when traversing a steep hill; a vehicle leans over (see 'Traversing slopes', Section 4.6) and is in danger of tipping down the slope in extreme cases, especially if you have been too brutal with the throttle and invoked wheelspin.

Momentum, traction, throttle control. Common sense steep slopes need no more than common sense tactics. If it is reasonably smooth and not excessively steep take a bit of a run at it in the right gear and do not over-torque the wheels to provoke wheelspin. Select the right gear *before* the slope and stay in it. Only an automatic will do a smooth enough and quick enough change if one is needed on the way up.

But on really difficult slopes, as ever, an on-foot recce will be needed. Such slopes are unlikely to be smooth. Tramping out the chosen route to locate any local bumps, tree stumps or rabbit holes that might cause a wheel to lift and spin will be useful.

Extra grip – from the steering wheel. If the track is rutted – and this can apply on level ground too, including churned sand – limiting grip can be enhanced by moving the steering wheel from side to side (11 o'clock to 1 o'clock) and cause the tyre sidewalls to contribute grip. (NB This will not work with BMW's xDrive. There, because there is no centre differential, the auto-engage drive to the front axle disengages when pronounced steering angle is sensed. Remember this if you are scrabbling for grip in deep snow!)

Classic example (below) of a 2nd gear low range slope needing a bit of momentum at the bottom and a readiness to lift off the throttle towards the top. One of the rare slopes (right, dry concrete!) where grip permits full use of the vehicle's ultimate climbing ability – 1st gear, low range.

Don't over-torque the ground

Use a higher gear ... . Unless you are tackling an unusual and exceptional climb such as 40° on rough dry concrete, 1st gear low box will be too low and will provoke wheelspin. Most 'normal severe' climbs will be best tackled in low box 2nd gear, or, if there is any amount of run-up available, a higher gear. Use the most run-up momentum you can, having established the ground is smooth enough to permit it, since the more you can utilise this, the less will be the demand for grip from the ground actually on the slope.

... or throttle lift-off. As you near the top of the slope your momentum may be running out and the vehicle will become more reliant on grip and traction. This is the point, quite near to the top, where the wheels are most likely to start slipping or spinning – usually (unless diff-locked) one of the front wheels due to weight transfer to the back of the vehicle. So it is thus, paradoxically, the point where you may find that lifting off the throttle helps keep that 'continuous rolling contact' (diagram page 3.6) without spinning the wheels.

Automatic applications. The equivalent of lift-off to de-stress the ground where traction is marginal will occur on an auto transmission vehicle if a selectable ratio is chosen – say 3rd – before a steep climb. The gearbox will change to 3rd as the throttle is lifted and reduce the risk of wheelspin. Selecting 3rd (ie ensuring no up-change beyond 3rd) will make sure the transmission does not change up too far when you lift off the throttle.

Take a run at it – as far as the terrain will allow – and be prepared to lift off the throttle near the top to preclude final-effort wheelspin as your momentum runs out.

Other side of the shot on the previous page: reversing lights on, backing down off earlier attempt. Nothing to fear getting it wrong even on slopes like this (left). But remember to keep both hands firmly on the steering wheel and back STRAIGHT down the hill.

Failed climb, recovery

First-time scare. If you are losing grip on a steep climb don't boot the throttle; it will accentuate the wheelspin. De-clutch and apply the footbrake. Your first failure on a very steep climb – nose of the vehicle pointing at the sky, brake leg trembling, maybe a dead engine and a plan view of the world in your rear view mirror – can be mildly scary. It can sometimes also be mechanically traumatic for the vehicle if a driver tries to bluff it out or attempt impossibly quick sequences of control selections during the 'recovery' descent. Remember 'Mind-set' on page 3.3; admit defeat early. Pause awhile, (there's plenty of time), back off and try again.

After failing, come down at right angles to the gradient. Going backwards, steering castor action is also reversed. Grip the wheel firmly to prevent 'runaway'.

Slowing the adrenaline. Observing – and practising – the following procedures makes a fail-and-try-again climb so matter-of fact that both driver and vehicle have a far easier time. Knowing this means you do not cane the vehicle unnecessarily hard in a white-knuckle attempt to get up first time. Climbs can fail with or without a dead engine:

1. Forward motion ceases, engine running, wheels spinning – grip problem.
2. Forward motion ceases, engine stalled – gradient problem.

Practise it – yes you can. Using the following procedures you will come back down the hill with both hands on the steering wheel (important, that), feet off the pedals – ie not on clutch, or footbrake but (engine idling) covering the throttle. Engine braking controls your speed of descent and no frantic use of gear lever or handbrake is needed. It looks complex first time you read it but, you can practise it, book in hand, if need be. There is no rush. (Procedure for manual transmission shown; Auto procedure is shown in brackets.)

Case 1: Failed climb, engine running. If you have failed the climb through wheelspin and loss of grip:

1. Clutch pedal down, hold the vehicle firmly on the footbrake, engine idling. (**1-Auto**: allow engine revs to die, brake, engage 'R' low box, gently release brake, jump to step 4.)
2. Engage reverse gear low range.
3. With both hands on the steering wheel and leading with the clutch, release the clutch and footbrake. The vehicle (engine still idling) will start back down the slope fully controlled by engine braking. At this stage your feet can be off all three pedals – ie you are in reverse, clutch fully engaged and engine idling. Remember that in reverse, steering castor action is also reversed and there is a tendency for the steering wheel to 'run away' to full lock if you do not *hold it firmly.*
4. Keeping both hands on the steering wheel, go straight back down, at right angles to the slope, to less steep ground.
5. Note. The admit-defeat-early credo is very important in a traction failure on a hill – ie with wheels starting to spin. If you do not quit the moment it is clear you are not going to make it, it is very likely the vehicle, wheels spinning on a

slippery surface, will slew sideways-on to the slope and there is a risk of it capsizing down the hill – diagram previous page. Even if it does not do this, the spinning wheels – usually one front wheel with its diagonally opposite back wheel – will scoop depressions in the ground to make your next attempt a lot more difficult.

Case 2: Failed climb, stalled engine. If you have failed the climb and stalled the engine in the process (see also diagram sequence right):

1. Engine is dead. Hold the vehicle on the footbrake, clutch position immaterial. (**Auto** transmission: go to step 5-auto.)
2. Engage reverse gear low range and remove left foot from clutch.
3. With both hands on the steering wheel, slowly lessen the pressure on the footbrake until your foot is off it. The vehicle is now held by the engine.
4. The vehicle may begin to move backwards on its own and in so doing 'bump'-start the engine. In which case let it continue back down the slope, under full control of engine braking, keeping both hands firmly on the steering wheel.
5. If the engine has not started under gravity, take one hand off the wheel to operate the starter motor briefly – with the vehicle still in reverse gear and clutch fully engaged (photo above right). This will invariably kick the engine into life and you are, as in 4 above, slowly descending back down the slope in full control, in gear, clutch fully engaged, left foot on the floor, both hands on steering wheel to resist any steering 'runaway', right foot hovering over throttle.
(5-Auto: Stall unlikely but .. foot still on brake, select 'N' or 'P', start engine, engage 'R', both hands on wheel, slowly release footbrake.)
6. Just as you would climb the slope at right angles to the gradient, make sure you go straight back down the slope – still at right angles to the gradient. When you reach less steep ground, use the controls in the normal way.

Failed-climb, dead-engine – engage reverse, feet off all the pedals (but throttle-ready), touch starter. So straightforward and calm it is worth shutting off the engine to use this procedure even if it has not stalled. Stalling engine puts very high stresses on it. Try to de-clutch before it actually stalls.

Back-down sequence, stalled engine

1,2

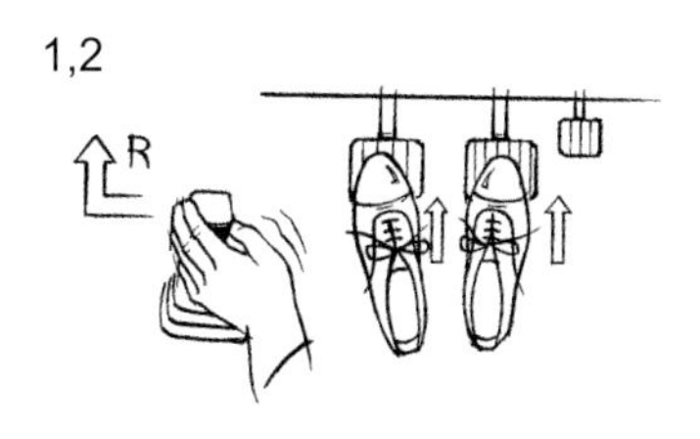

3,4

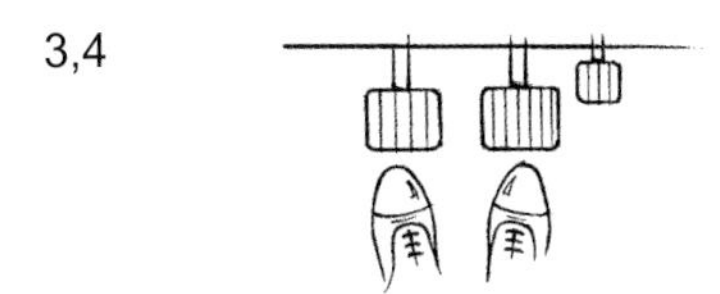

5

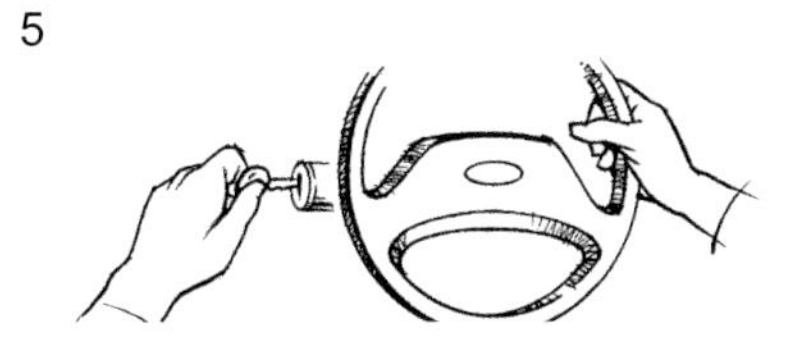

See list, adjacent column. 1, 2. Clutch, footbrake, into reverse. 3, 4. Feet off all pedals – but throttle foot ready. 5. Touch the starter briefly; both hands on steering wheel. 6. Reverse back on mirrors.

These procedures take far longer to read about than to do. They are really very simple. Practise on gentle slopes, then steeper ones.

4.5 Descending steep slopes

The view over the nose comes only when you are committed to the slope; so stop well short of the edge and recce on foot first. At the point of commitment you can often only see sky or the far side of the dip.

Gear to use

Remove the drama. The extraordinary agility of a 4x4 may make your first really steep descent an intimidating experience. A 45° downslope itself is unusual enough but to this angle you add the fact that you are looking even further downward over the bonnet; the result can seem vertical, especially when you are hanging forward in your seat harness. But this is an experience that you get used to remarkably quickly – usually after just one steep descent. As with climbs, the aim is to take the drama out of the situation and utilise the vehicle's facility for keeping you calmly in control.

Stop two metres from the edge (engine off, 1st gear, handbrake) and inspect on foot. Plan to use engine braking in low range.

Get out and look. A 45° slope is extreme but there are many lesser slopes that can still seem very steep and, as with the climb, an on-foot inspection is advisable to ensure that your planned route is safe. This is doubly important since when you come to the edge of a steep descent you can sometimes see nothing over the nose of the vehicle except the other side of the dip; only when you are actually pointing down the slope can you see the ground immediately in front of you – too late, if you didn't recce and got it wrong!

For this reason, among others, stop the vehicle for the on-foot inspection at least two metres before the edge of the slope – engine off, in gear, handbrake on. This will give you time, when you do start the descent, to get the vehicle fully in gear and with your foot off the clutch for the descent.

Rule of thumb, 1st gear low range. Using 1st gear low range will in nearly every case result in a perfectly controlled, feet-off-all-pedals descent. Actual retardation will depend on whether you have a diesel or petrol engine, whether or not it has a manual transmission and the condition of the slope but the rule is a good one and a safe one. It is important to remember that due to its higher gearing and the way it functions, automatic transmission offers very poor engine braking down steep slopes

The rationale. Your aim is to obtain maximum retardation without resorting to (and possibly overheating) the brakes which might also result in wheel locking and sliding. As always your aim is to preclude any possibility of discontinuity of rolling contact (see p.3.6) – ie no wheelspinning or, in this case, sliding.

Does sliding matter? Surely, say some, a locked wheel gives more retardation than a merely braked one. Not so. You will dimly remember from school, the coefficient of sliding friction is less than the coefficient of static friction. This is the *raison d'etre* for ABS brakes and applies on nearly all off-road surfaces and certainly on mud.

Ready for throttle. If the ground is too slippery even to provide the grip for the retardation of the throttle-off engine and you begin to slide, be ready to use the accelerator to help the wheels 'catch up' with the vehicle and eliminate any wheel slide.

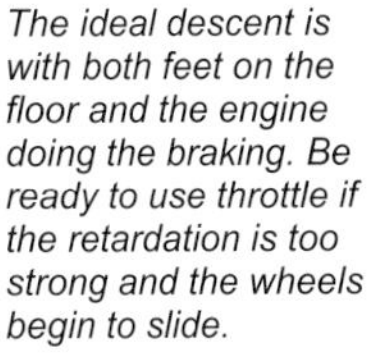

The ideal descent is with both feet on the floor and the engine doing the braking. Be ready to use throttle if the retardation is too strong and the wheels begin to slide.

Ready for exceptions. There may be occasions – long descents of loose ground or extremely slippery clay – where low range 2nd gear will be better than 1st in order to preclude an initial sliding-wheel glissade. One or two exceptions are covered at Section 6.4. Some descents – see photo page 6.9 – will actually demand 3rd low range and quite a lot of throttle to prevent nosing-in on a soft surface. As before, it is best to select the gear for the whole descent and stay in it.

Brakes

Brakes? Never say never ... An easy generalisation – and for good reasons – is to counsel against ever using brakes on a steep slippery descent. Braking on wet, muddy or loose-surface slopes – even with the excellent sensitivity of some 4x4's discs – can easily cause one or more wheels to lock and the loss of directional control in the resulting slide could be dangerous. The use of engine braking down steep slopes makes, in general, for a very safe, controlled way of keeping the vehicle from gaining speed and there is no danger of overheating the brakes. Often you are able to take both feet off the pedals and rest them flat on the floor while the vehicle trundles gently down the slope with the engine idling.

But... There are times when engine braking is not the infallible solution. That too can result in sliding with soaring engine throttle-off revs plus sensitive use of brakes. Time (see Section 6.4) for cautious de-clutching with cadence braking (p.3.7).

If your vehicle is fitted with ABS brakes – and they are one of the systems that can cope on- *and* off-road (many can't) – then brakes may be used on a slippery downslope. But try engine braking first.

Rule of thumb – 1st low and do not use the brakes. But... see Section 3.2 for cadence braking and ABS is magic in reserve. Accelerate if necessary.

Hill Descent Control. The proliferation of variously branded iterations of Land Rover's initial Hill Descent Control system (HDC) enables a driver to leave an automated mix of ABS and engine braking to the black boxes. Beware, however, some such systems default to an absurdly slow descent which invites a glissading slide with skidding wheels on slippery mud. So learn the common-sense procedures above. It's been said, by some cynic, that if you can recognise situations requiring HDC then you likely don't need it. It's hard not to agree!

Even the high-rollers can lean (above and opposite). The on-foot inspection is important (left). Look for bumps, dips or soft patches that affect lateral lean. Digging away the hillside ahead of the up-slope wheels can lower the actual tilt angle.

4.6 Traversing slopes

Assessing the ground

Side slopes don't feel right. Trust your unease and treat them with great caution. Inspect on foot looking for bumps or hollows that can affect vehicle's lateral stance.

Side slopes are different. From the last two sections – 'Climbing steep slopes' and 'Descending steep slopes' – the doctrine of always taking such obstacles at right angles to the slopes implies that traversing a slope is dangerous. And so it can be when the angle of gradient is severe. There will be times, however, when, on less severe slopes, you do need to traverse a slope laterally. Like your first steep climb and descent, your first traverse will be unnerving. Unlike climbs and descents, however, you will not quickly get used to it. And that is a good thing since the consequences of getting it wrong on a traverse are a great deal more serious than getting it wrong on a climb or descent.

Trust your instincts. There appears to be a built-in safety feature of human perception that makes a traverse feel a lot more dangerous than it is in relation to a vehicle's absolute tipping limits. Your vehicle will actually tilt to quite high angles *on perfectly smooth ground* without rolling over but to the driver, a traverse along a slope even one third of the maximum permissible can feel alarming. Follow your instinct and do not traverse slopes that feel dangerous. As ever, carry out an on-foot reconnaissance first and be on the alert for:

1. Slippery surface. Assess the surface to be sure it is not so slippery that the vehicle will slide sideways down the slope.

2. Bumps and dips. Look out for dips that the down-hill wheels may encounter and bumps that the up-hill wheels may roll over – rabbit holes and sawn-off tree stumps in particular. If you are not aware of them both will suddenly and alarmingly increase the tilt of the vehicle and further the risk of it tipping over.

3. Secure load. Any load in the back of your vehicle should be secure and as low as possible. Be particularly wary of roof-rack loads. Passengers should sit on the up-hill side – or dismount.

4. Marshalling. If there are any doubts about the effect of the terrain or if there are obstacles to avoid, then use a marshaller (see p.3.13) to see you forward and make sure he or she keeps an eye on all four wheels.

This one's OK but lateral slopes that are also slippery – see opposite, with a pool at the bottom! – demand special caution.

Escape manoeuvre, restraint

Be ready. The recognised escape manoeuvre is to steer down the hill if the vehicle slips or seems too close to the maximum tip angle. Think about this in your on-foot recce. Is it actually *feasible* to steer down the slope, what are the consequences? Is there a gully at the bottom?

As with normal steep descents, the nearer you can get the vehicle pointing directly down the slope the less the danger of lateral tipping. If you feel the machine getting laterally unstable turn down the hill quickly and give a little burst of throttle. The centrifugal force of the quick turn, further enhanced by the blip of throttle, will help keep the vehicle upright.

Restraint. Some means of restraining the vehicle may be practical such as passengers hanging on to the up-slope side – about the only time add-on running boards and steps really come into their own in off-road conditions! Or a rope can be used, attached to a roof rack. It goes without saying that using people pushing on the vehicle flanks from the down-hill side is not an acceptable risk!

'Escape' by steering down the hill, with a touch of throttle.. But plan the contingency in advance.

Side-slope escape manoeuvre

4.7 Weak ground

Ground stress – horizontal, vertical

Reading the ground. Soft ground is weak ground – vertically and laterally as well. The vertical context is well known – the tendency for a vehicle to sink in it – and the lateral connotations mean it will not take much thrust or braking from wheels without degenerating into slippery wheelspin or slide; the gentle right foot on brakes and throttle (Section 3.3) comes into its own in such conditions.

Soft ground is weak laterally and vertically – so it's gentle right foot again. Lock the centre diff (and any others), read the ground, judge what it will take without spinning the wheels.

Read the surface and adjust your throttle foot accordingly – getting the traction where you can, backing off where you can afford to do so in order not to lose the traction you do have. And occasionally (on the right tyres) applying a carefully judged burst of wheelspin to get through surface slime onto drier grippy ground (see photo upper left, next spread). Read the ground.

'Fifth-wheel' traction. On the limits in rutted ground, turning the steering wheel from side to side, 11 o'clock to 1 o'clock, is can help (also p.4.16 with caveats) get that little extra traction from the tyre sidewalls – especially with bold-tread mud tyres. It can work in sand as well where it has been churned by previous vehicles (p.4.29).

'Green lanes' are classic examples of low vertical and low horizontal ground strength – a mixture of the soft and the slippery.

Ground stress components

A 4x4 under power. Decreasing weight or tyre pressure (weight per unit area) and exercising care with throttle and brakes reduces both components of ground stress.

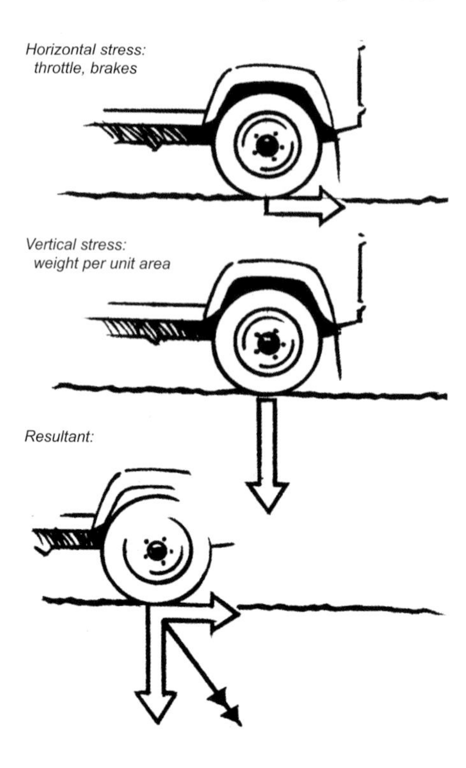

Horizontal load – throttle, brakes. The most immediate control you have when encountering weak ground is from within the vehicle – the horizontal stress on the ground created by the vehicle's linear motion – forward, back or braking. You should be in four-wheel drive if it is selectable – and the centre differential on a permanent 4x4 should be locked so as to preclude the possibility of one axle spinning any faster than the other. No hard and fast rule can be laid down as to the 'best' action then to take. Some situations will demand you accelerate on the good

Examples of ground that is vertically weak (soft, left), horizontally weak (slippery, below left) and close to the limit on both (right).

going to take you through the soft and slippery patch using momentum, others will demand you slow down to take it gently because it is uneven or of extended length. The only invariable rule is to gain momentum where you can without hazarding the vehicle by crashing over bumps or potholes and to also heighten your awareness of the risk of wheelspin. To minimise this, choose the highest gear you judge will get you through without over-stressing the engine – this will often be 2nd or 3rd low range. As for brakes, remember they stress the ground in the same way as driving torque at the wheels and insensitivity will result in sliding and less of that all-important rolling contact shown in the diagram on page 3.6.

Low range 2nd or 3rd will usually be the best gears for soft ground.

Tyres and tyre pressures

Tyres. Section 8.2 deals with tyres in more detail but the subject is inseparable from weak ground operation so some coverage is given here. Differentiating between vertical and horizontal stress in weak ground is important. As already mentioned, some weak ground needs cutting into to get to the firmer ground beneath: an aggressive, probably quite narrow, very open tyre tread for mud. Mud is slippery and thus horizontally weak but in a few cases can be relatively shallow so may be less weak vertically.

Soft-shoe approach. Other types of weak ground need the 'soft-shoe' approach – more tyre width to give flotation on bog or peat or moorland. Be very careful there; keep off unless you are very certain of bearing strength; it is notable for being vertically weak – to the extent, sometimes, of being virtually bottomless. Salt marsh, or sebkha, as it is called in desert regions, is a classic and very dangerous example (see next spread).

Tyres can effect a 'cutting' or 'floating' role. Reduced tyre pressures increase flotation and ride comfort but MUST be accompanied by reduced speed to avoid dangerous overheating

Sand is a special case (next Section) but is also classifiable as vertically weak and thus needing maximum flotation; for special reasons it also requires a very mild and particular tread type. As Section 8.2 makes clear, tyres can only be 'best' in one set of conditions and 'compromise' or all-purpose tyres are exactly that – a compromise. As you see opposite – a fairly thin layer of slippery mud on a reasonably firm base ground – the fattest tyres are not always the best.

Vertical load – per square inch. Once you have your chosen tyres and are on your chosen terrain, vertical load per unit area – the tyre pressures, rather than total vertical load – is the factor of which you will have easiest control. You may not think tyre pressures would make much difference since the total weight of the vehicle will usually remain the same, sitting on the same four tyres.

But bear in mind that 'emergency flotation' pressures (Section 8.2) can be two thirds of road pressures or less. This means the tyre footprint size increases (see diagrams p.8.13). The weight of the vehicle is spread over a correspondingly larger area so that – as in recognising the benefits of 4x4 which spreads the thrust over four instead of two wheels – you are asking less of the ground that is already having difficulty in supporting the vehicle's weight.

Weak-ground tyres for 'cutting' and 'floating'. Michelin XCL (right), excellent in mud/clay – open, bold, self-cleaning tread but noisy, L-rated (75 mph max, see Section 8.2),not very grippy on wet roads and subject to tread-block ;heel-and-toe' wear. High flotation version (265/75 x 16) of Goodrich All Terrain (left) is S-rated, quieter and grippier on-road but tread pattern is not as ultimately effective as BFG Mud Terrain on mud/clay. No one tyre can be good at everything but the BFG All Terrain is exceptionally versatile – and notably versatile in deserts.

Horizontally weak (slippery – left) and vertically weak (soft – below) ground need appropriate tyres and techniques. Note (left) how narrow a good mud tyre really is – here being used with controlled wheelspin to cut through to better traction. Flotation (below) is absolutely on the limits; left tyre has broken the crust, right tyre just holding on. See next Section and photo on page 4.31.

Low tyre pressures – when, how much. Reduce pressures only when needed – then re-inflate (see p.4.13, 'Rock, stones, corrugations'). The golden rule is: do not run with low tyre pressures without reducing your speed. With inappropriately low tyre pressures the steering and handling of the vehicle will be adversely affected. More importantly, however, if you don't slow down sidewall flexing can cause serious overheating of the tyre leading to tyre delamination or blow-out. Tyre pressures for particular conditions will vary according to:

- the vehicle,
- the axle load and
- construction of the tyres.

Typical axle loads and off-road tyre pressures for Land Rover vehicles are given in Section 8.2, 'Tyres'. Rule-of-thumb guidance figures are shown below:

1. ***Tracks and poor roads*** – 80% of road pressures, maximum speed 65 kph (40 mph).
2. ***Emergency flotation pressures*** – about 60% of road pressures, maximum speed 20 kph (12 mph).

Vertical load – reducing the total. It is common sense that reducing the overall load will give the vehicle a better chance on weak ground also enabling a greater reduction in tyre pressures to be used. In practical terms few will be able to dispose of payload to suit the going but the principle – and correct load distribution (p.8.4) – is worth remembering for the case of recovering a bogged vehicle - see Section 5.1, 'Self-recovery'.

Tyres MUST be re-inflated before exceeding the low pressure speed limits. Choice of tyres is important for frequent soft-ground operation – see Section 8.2.

Previous wheel tracks

Where others have been. As already mentioned, if the weak ground is wet or muddy, it will usually pay to follow the wheel tracks of a previous vehicle since that vehicle will have cut through to firmer ground and you may be able to take advantage of that. If the weak ground is sandy see next section.

4.8 Sand

With open salt water in the distance, this innocuous-looking track over the sebkha (salt marsh) can be very treacherous. Here one vehicle has strayed less than a metre off the track and sunk into the salty mush. (Note how near the surface the water-table is.) Going right off the track can lead to a major recovery problem – if you are lucky,

Initial rules

Different types. It is said that Eskimos have 50 different words for snow. There are probably at least as many different types – and conditions – of sand. Be clear what 'condition' means: churned, virgin, untrodden, crusted, wind blown, coarse, aggregate, fine rounded, superfine ... and more.

Wet sand, damp sand and a dozen types and conditions of dry sand each lead to different expectations of vertical and horizontal strength (flotation and surface shear strength) as well as behaving differently as far as compaction strength is concerned. Each thus demands, first, recognition and then different driving techniques.

There are many types of sand – all with characteristic bearing strengths. If the going has been churned up, break out onto unbroken sand. It will be stronger.

You will cover many miles on sand without difficulty but, when the bearing strength starts to get marginal, being instantly ready with throttle (and the right gear) to get you through a short soft patch is critical. (As ever, automatics are best.) And, in conditions of worsening flotation, avoiding wheelspin is vital since soft sand can be very deep. *Stop at once before serious wheelspin develops; reverse out while you can.*

There will be times when the terrain will demand on-foot inspection of tricky sections and 'stamping out' to ascertain firmness – approaching dune edges is a classic example (provided you have been able to stop on a firm enough patch to do a recce). Again, in limiting conditions or following a bogging, the vehicle will have a far better chance if tyre pressures are reduced – see diagrams and pressure/speed tables at Section 8.2.

Broad-brush guide. Some general rules first, if you are to get through the sand rather than trying to learn all the types at once.

1. *Dry sand.* If you are running out of traction or flotation, keep off previously churned or broken sand. Make your own new tracks.

2. *Damp sand.* Follow previous tracks which will have compacted the sand and made it firmer.

3. *Wet sand.* Keep off altogether. It can contain areas of 'floating' sand, or quicksand – bottomless with virtually no vertical strength.

4. *Sebkha (salt flat).* Very dangerous – unpredictably soft and bottomless. If a well-used track goes over a sebkha it will have compacted (paradoxically from beneath) into a smooth, relatively strong route. *Do not stray off the hardened track by even a tyre's width – see pic above.*

Sand types – the detail

Dry sand. Being an aggregate of small grains and large grains, nature's windblown sand, helped by night dews and diurnal heating and contracting, forms a surface crust which has more strength than the sand beneath; it is stronger in the cool of the morning than in the heat of the day. Use

Previously churned by large trucks (above), tracks can become very heavy going for smaller ones; there is then a case for diverting onto untrodden sand which, in cases like this (right) can be remarkably firm – usually an aggregate of large and small sand grains with an unbroken crust.

these characteristics to your advantage and be very careful not to break through into the soft sand beneath by excessive use of brakes; use the analogy of driving on a pie-crust.

Sandy tracks. Sandy tracks, by reason of the previous passage of vehicles, have no pie crust. Difficulty is likely where there has been a lot of previous truck traffic, even on sand sheet in open desert. Three things will happen here – the ruts will get deeper, the depth of churned sand will increase and the width between the ruts will increase. This is simply a function of the size of the previous vehicles, their wheel diameter and the width of their axles.

As ever, be ready to admit defeat early before getting into real trouble, and steer out of the track onto virgin ground if you can. The higher gears – 3rd, 4th and 5th – in the low range (centre and rear diff locked where applicable) will probably be best for tracks of this kind. The advantage of being in low range is that it will enable you to accelerate through suddenly worsening conditions without the risk of being unable to restart, having stopped to change from high to low box. For this reason do not stop except on firm going – or if you do have to stop be gentle with the brakes.

As the going gets heavier, more churned and more demanding. you will find you have to be firm with the throttle and use a lot of the torque at your disposal; this is different from the technique used on virgin sand.

Virgin sand. Some previously untrodden desert sand is remarkably firm and strong. But if you are close to the limits of flotation when on virgin, unbroken sand in the open desert (or once out of the ruts on the track) you have to be more delicate with the throttle in order not to break the crust of clean sand supporting you. The same goes for brakes and steering.

Previously unbroken sand, particularly, has a 'pie crust' that can be surprisingly strong. But be careful with throttle and brakes or you'll break through to the soft stuff.

On some dune surfaces it is best to let the vehicle come to a rolling stop without brakes at all. Similarly, when stopping your vehicle on sand remember that re-starting when facing up a slope is asking for trouble and you should therefore stop on level ground, or, if possible swoop round the dune surface so that you *always stop with the vehicle pointing slightly downhill.*

Dune formations will have firm areas dependent on position relative to crest, valley and wind direction. Salt flat is inherently dangerous. Keep off, except on tracks.

Sand dunes. Keep away from small, closely-packed dunes (photo opposite, far right). Lines of dunes larger than 6–8 metres high are usually sufficiently spaced-out to permit driving between them and taking a run crossing a saddle. Expect the firm bits to be the valley floor or half way up the dunes remote from the last sand-fall.

Cross dunes at the low saddles if you can (photo previous page). No vehicle will ever get up a sand-fall but if your dune crossing must involve a sand-fall descent, recce to ensure you'll not go over the edge into a wind-formed and inescapable bowl. Gain all the momentum you can in the valley floor and the firm part of the ascent, slowing as you hit the softer bit near the crest and come to a stop/pause at, and at right angles to, the crest. At this point you can still go back. If OK, 2nd low over the edge (sinkage will be huge. – photo opposite) Power your way down, holding the steering wheel tightly to keep wheels pointing down the slope. (See p.9.11, 'Glossary', Steering feel.)

If you have to stop to await another vehicle only do so on firm sand – preferably pointing downhill: as mentioned above, drive on, swoop round the dune till you get a firm, down-pointing place to stop.

Rock-hard 'dunelets'. The photo and caption below says it all. At high noon or with the sun behind you in the late afternoon – these are the danger periods. Don't let it happen! Read the caption.

Fesh-fesh. Fesh-fesh is a thin crust of fine gravel or sand over flour-like dust with very little surface strength. Maximum flotation and instant application of power will be required to avoid getting stuck.

Damp sand. Sand that is damp – such as it might be after a rain shower or even morning dew – just makes driving easier. The water binds it together, strengthens it, gives more flotation and on tracks actually makes it compact to yield considerably more strength than the dry, churned-up sand had before the rain.

Wet sand. It becomes a matter of judgement and definition to say when damp sand gets to be wet sand. Beach sand will frequently behave as dry, cut-up, churned sand where it is dry and become considerably firmer where it is washed by the tide – though this is not an invariable rule. The warning sounded earlier refers to really wet sand of the kind encountered where a river or stream meets the sea or sometimes in a wadi with recent rain a few days previously. Here a kind of 'floating' sand is encountered. This is akin to a quicksand where motion by the person or vehicle on it just causes further sinkage. Dangerous.

Sebkha (chott or salt flat). Sometimes also marked on maps as 'chott', a sebkha

Beautiful and probably not more than 35cm high, these little 'dunelets' are rock-hard. With the sun behind you, you'll not probably see them at all and the first thing you'll know is your vehicle is airborne and heading for an axle-bending crash five metres further on. Always be on your guard. Read that again.

Clockwise from left: Sinkage on a sand-fall: powder-fine fesh-fesh; the wisdom of backing out before you get too bogged in soft sand. And (above right) the idiocy of spinning your wheels in fine sand. The locals witness the fun.

forms where salt lakes used to be and consists of a crust of dried salt-mud usually covering soft, bottomless moist salt-mud underneath. The crust is of variable and unpredictable strength but appears to have the curious characteristic of consolidating from underneath when progressively heavier vehicles run over it under certain critical conditions. Thus a track over a sebkha usually consists of wheel marks indented probably no more than a few centimetres into the surface – implying that the surrounding ground is firm. Yet, as mentioned, this is not the case and straying off the track even a tyre width or a metre can sometimes result in disastrous sinkage – see photo, previous spread. A vehicle stuck in sebkha will usually sink to the chassis and sometimes go on sinking. It is normally impossible to effect self-recovery and even assisting vehicles should have very long recovery ropes so that they themselves stay out of the soft spot.

Sand tyres

Sand vs 'desert'. In a perfect world each kind of terrain demands its own specialist tyre. And ideally that applies to the many types of sand structure and conditions that we may encounter. To that though, you must – practically – add the term 'desert' since such regions comprise a mixture of sand, small stones and rock. For many years Michelin's XS (with the ability to accept pressures as low as 0.6 bar) was the best desert tyre for its unsurpassed prowess on all types of sand – especially the delicate unbroken crusted type found on the up-wind side of dunes where you are fighting for every gramme of weight bearing strength. But the XS, though coping well with desert, had vulnerable sidewalls and was frightening on wet tarmac.

Desert tyres are particularly important in achieving optimum performance in sand. All sand has increased bearing strength if cold, dewy or rained-on.

The crown must now have passed to BFGoodrich's All Terrain (photo p.4.26). Possibly one or two percent down on the XS on crusted dune sand but exceptional for it's ability to deal with all-round desert conditions – at reduced pressure (1 bar) on soft sand, at medium pressures (1.8) on sand/track/rock mix and – fully inflated – grippy on wet tarmac.

This kind of rocky going is perfectly feasible if you have a low-range transfer box – a 1st gear crawl, with no diff-locks engaged. 'Terrain Response' (or equivalent throttle re-mapping) makes control easier. Tyre sidewalls – see next spread.

4.9 Rocks, stones, corrugations

Risks – chassis, tyres

Take every precaution against grounding the vehicle on rock. Use a marshaller when clearances are tight. Rocks 20-25 cm are about the maximum size to drive over.

Rocks – 25cm high. The sections dealing with use of the low transfer box and the methods of driving on rough tracks (pp.3.4, 4.10) will prepare you for the techniques best suited for driving over rocks and stone. The rough definition applicable here to 'rocks and stone' is that stones are taken to be anything from gravel up to fist-sized stones and rocks are taken to be over fist-sized and up to about 20–35cm high – the maximum permitted by the underbody and under-axle dimensions of most 4x4s on 16 inch wheels.

Clearances. What you have read about clearance angles and under-axle clearances at Section 3.4, 'Geometric limitations', is doubly important in the context of driving over rocks and stones. Getting it slightly wrong on clearances when traversing mud will probably scrape earth from the obstacle and take paint off the underside of the vehicle. Making the same mistake over rocks will likely bring the vehicle to a very abrupt halt and be likely to damage components as well. A separate-chassis 4x4's robustness and resistance to 'battle damage' should be regarded as accident insurance, not part of routine everyday driving. Monocoque 4x4s are even more vulnerable. Take every precaution to ensure you do not run the vehicle into contact with heavy stones or rocks. Underbody 'skid plates' should be regarded as emergency protection only (or 'audio warning'), not as something to facilitate a kind of snowboard progression over boulders.

Tyres. Tyres too are potentially very vulnerable to damage on rocky ground – especially the sidewalls of radial-ply tyres – but this and overall operating costs can be reduced by attention to:

1. Inflation. Be sure the tyres are fully inflated to road pressures before traversing rocky going – even if this means re-inflation after deflating for previous soft ground. Life is like that off road; you must get used to changing inflation pressures regularly.

2. Sidewall awareness. The most vulnerable parts of a tyre on rocks are the sidewalls. The best on/off-road tyres are radials but these, with their thinner, more flexible sidewalls, are particularly prone to 'bacon-slicer' damage, so-called because the action of the tyre sidewall against an intrusive sharp rock. Develop 'sidewall awareness' when driving over

When forced onto limiting rocks use a marshaller and great care. Grounding hard metal on rock is absolutely not an option.

rocks and use a marshaller in bad conditions.

3. Cross-ply tyres. Where operations are almost exclusively off-road on rock or stone – such as fleet operations in quarries – the more damage-resistant qualities (at full inflation pressures) of cross-ply tyres could help keep operating costs down. It is essential, however, to accommodate the following criteria:

a. Virtually all 7.50 x 16 cross-plies are 'L' speed rated (see table p.8.17), ie limited to 125kph (75mph), so should not be fitted to high powered vehicles operating on-road.

b. Cross-ply tyres have higher rolling resistance so will reduce fuel economy.

c. Cross-ply tyres have marginally less grip than radials so handling on-road would be affected.

Stony tracks and plains. Not all your rock/stone traverses will be over on-the-limits boulders. Stony tracks or vast stony plains in the desert will be very much less hazardous. Well inflated tyres and an alertness for potential further hazards, however, will be important. As with corrugations (next spread) braking will be much less efficient on loose stones.

On-foot survey, marshalling. All the points mentioned so far point to the need for looking at a difficult rocky stretch or obstacle on foot and then being marshalled across by a helper. The marshaller can see all eight sidewalls, the underside of the vehicle and axles (above right) – and this will ensure that no damage is done.

Low-range control. The relevance of low range and its ability to control the vehicle's forward motion steadily (rather than just making considerable power available) is nowhere more applicable than in traversing large rocks. First gear, low range (centre and axle diff *not* locked) clutch fully-in, low engine speed, will enable the vehicle to crawl steadily – without heaving, jerking or lurching – over the very worst rocky terrain.

On-the-limit rocky going demands 1st low range for control. Cross-ply tyres can lower costs in continuous rock/stone operations BUT note speed limitations.

(Left) Rivers usually produce rounded rocks (previous spread) but sharp-edged rocks can do terminal damage to tyre sidewalls. Only a marshaller can see all eight. (EIGHT? Yes, the inside sidewalls are just as vulnerable.)

Rocks

Semantics. It's a matter of definition, the difference between rocks and stones, but for your long-suffering tyres it hardly matters. What really matters is your mechanical sympathy. Even if you go gently – in 1st gear low range as already mentioned – tyres will still take a jaw-dropping amount of horror. Where you really have to be aware and suitably careful is with the Murphy's Law mix of soft sand and sharp rocks. You may have deflated your tyres a little for the soft ground but that is exactly what you should not use over rocks. In general err on the side of higher tyre pressures but always drive 'slow and careful'.

Transverse corrugations on track demand a 'harmonic' speed to reduce the vibration on the vehicle. Body shake is reduced but unsprung components go through hell.

Corrugations

'Harmonic' speed. A special manifestation of something between stony going and rough or unsurfaced tracks is the phenomenon of transverse corrugations across graded earth, sand or gravel tracks – regular, wave-form undulations that can stretch for tens of kilometres in front of you on remote area routes. The corrugations, also called 'washboard' in America, have a peak-to-peak distance of 0.5 to 1 metre and can be as much as 20cm deep. They are formed by the action (and harmonics) of the suspension and tyres of the track's major-user vehicles on the soil.

This latter is an important point since the technique to adopt when driving over them involves using the natural harmonics of your own vehicle's suspension to minimise the apparent roughness of the ride.

There will be a speed of driving – usually between about 40 and 65kph (25–40mph) in medium weight 4x4s like Land Rovers and Toyotas – where the effect of the corrugations *on the vehicle body* will be minimised. The italics are used as a reminder that the suspension and unsprung parts such as the axles are undergoing a raw torture over such ground, even though the passengers may be (relatively) more comfortable.

'Harmonic' speed on moderate corrugations reduces jarring on the vehicle body though the suspension still suffers. Coil springs are better than leaf here. Remember there will be dramatically reduced steering and brake effectiveness. Travel on such tracks is invariably accompanied by thick dust clouds.

Reduced brake effectiveness. An indication of the ordeal of the unsprung components will be clear when enduring the acceleration to these speeds and when decelerating from them. (If you still have any doubts about what the suspension is going through, look out of the driver's window at the front axle.)

It is vital to remember also that, since the wheels are virtually jumping from the crest of one corrugation to the next, they are in touch with the ground for a fraction of the time they would normally be. Steering and braking effectiveness will be dramatically reduced when going fast on corrugations.

Dramatic reductions in braking and steering effectiveness take place when driving on corrugated tracks.

Incompatible corrugations

Big wheels and little wheels. Most light/medium 4x4s and pickups run on 16-inch wheel rims with very roughly similar suspensions – it is this combination that forms corrugations on most tracks in the first place.

However, driving such a vehicle will be especially unpleasant on a track where the corrugations were formed by regular traffic of, say, four-ton trucks, since the suspension harmonics of the truck will not match those of your smaller 4x4 and there will be no 'harmonic speed' where the ride appears to smooth out.

4.10 Wading

With or without gumboots, check any unknown river or pool before entering. Better wet feet than an impossibly bogged or drowned vehicle.

Preparations

Think ahead. Think of wading as a wet, blind and usually cold manifestation of every other type of obstacle and hazard you may come across. This is not meant as an unduly gloomy warning so much as a reminder that the same kind of potential problems can lurk beneath the water as you may see on dry land and that advance knowledge of them is even more important.

Breathers, intakes. All internally lubricated components that can get hot will have an air vent. The reason is simple: as it heats up, the air pressure inside rises and would tend to blow lubricant out past the oil seals if there was no vent.

The same obstacles can lurk – unseen – under the water as on dry land. Plan, and recce, ahead. Be sure that breathers on gearboxes, axles etc can't ingest water.

Then comes the bad bit; as it contracts later, (often due to the cold water outside) the unit sucks water or dust back in by the same route. Engines have internal sump breathers invariably vented back into the air intake.

The same concept normally applies to gearboxes, transfer boxes and axles nowadays. Each will have a breather to allow heated expanding air out. This is usually done via long nylon tubes with the upper end of the tube safely high in the engine compartment and downward pointing or, again, venting into the engine air intake.

Know your vehicle. Know the situation in your vehicle. Very early Land Rovers, for instance, had small bell-shaped breathers on the top of each axle which could not only ingest water but the oily vapour round them caused dust and sand to adhere and in time block them up. It is not a quick job but if you are not equipped with long breather tubes and will be involved in lots of wading, then take the trouble to get them fitted, allowing enough slack in the tube for axle movement.

Wading plugs. Many older Land Rover products are also provided with drain holes in the clutch housing between the engine and gearbox and also (where such a belt is fitted) at the bottom of the camshaft belt drive housing at the front of the engine beneath the fan. They are a safety feature to ensure that, in the event of an oil leak in these regions, the oil can drain away and not get onto the clutch or cam drive-belt.

In case of deep wading, however, these holes must first be blocked off by the insertion of the screw-in wading plugs provided. It is convenient to keep these plugs (available from Land Rover dealers) and the appropriate 13mm (or 1/2"AF) spanner handy within the vehicle. It is important that the plugs be removed after wading – not necessarily at once but within a few days. If a vehicle is used for regular wading the plugs should be removed, checked for oil leakage and replaced every week or two.

Engine air intake. Far more obvious than gearbox and axle breathers is the engine's main air intake which must be kept well clear of any possibility of water ingestion. Water is incompressible and will destroy an engine if it goes down the air intake. In most vehicles the intake is high in the engine compartment but (see diagram overleaf) be sure you know

the cleared wading depth for your machine and, if in any doubt when on-the-limit wading is envisaged, fit a 'snorkel' or raised intake tube. This (often aft-pointing) helps in keeping dust out of the air filter.

A temporarily flooded national highway (albeit unpaved like this – Arak gorge, Algeria) should be OK but even so, seeing other traffic make it through first is a double check.

The on-foot recce

Walking the course. Water obstacles, large or small, should always (as mentioned at Section 3.5, 'Look before you leap', diagram page 3.13) be examined first as the photo opposite shows. Rubber boots and a long stick are the extras required for an on-foot survey before committing a vehicle. Far better to go in over your boot and get yourself wet than have your vehicle roll into an underwater pit or hollow.

Generally, stagnant water is more likely to be a hazard than a river or a stream as flowing water tends to prevent a build-up of silt. The silt in a stagnant pool or mud hollow can be several feet deep and very soft. Ensuring that the bottom of the pool or stream is firm enough along all of your proposed traverse is essential and it will inevitably take some time to do thoroughly. Markers may be necessary (such as sticks) to be sure the vehicle follows the route you have proved on foot.

Always walk through first with a stick. Better to get wet legs than have your vehicle stuck in an underwater hollow.

What to do

Wading limitations, how to proceed. The maximum advisable wading depth for most 4x4s on 16-inch wheels is about 0.5 metre – about 5-6cm (a thumb length) below the top of the wheel rim or, perhaps more memorably, 5-6cm higher than the top of the average calf-length rubber boot. Note the implications of this – your brakes will be completely immersed in water but the radiator cooling fan will be clear and so, probably, will the exhaust pipe exit. For wading at depths up to the particular vehicle's cleared normal wading depth the following precautions are advisable:

Normal wading depth limit 0.5m – just below the top of the wheel rim. It is VITAL not to let water near the engine air intake – through splash or any other cause.

1. ***Gear and speed.*** Despite the huge splashes the magazines like to show, low speed is the requirement for wading. Low range with a gear appropriate to the amount of power and control over rocks required – and enough power on tap to avoid succumbing to unforeseen sinkage. Keep enough rpm to preclude water entering the exhaust pipe if it is submerged. Speed should be low but fast enough to keep a small bow-wave ahead of the bumper, reducing the height of the water behind the bumper, to keep water away from the fan. In practice, low range 2nd gear is usually about right.
2. ***Keeping the ignition dry.*** If you are using a petrol engine-equipped vehicle it is important to keep the ignition dry. The right bow-wave will help. A sheet of plastic lowered in front of the radiator will stop water cascading straight through and onto the fan, reducing the chance of spray over the electrics; it will also prevent liquid mud from blocking the radiator matrix.

   Additionally an old blanket, sack or other heavy fabric can be draped over the engine behind the fan to keep the harness dry; remember, however, this can be a fire hazard so keep it well clear of the exhaust manifold. Do not remove the fan belt as this will stop the water pump and damage the engine.
3. ***The electronics.*** Wet ignition leads may stop the engine, then dry out and allow you to go on. Wet electronic control units (ECUs) are less tolerant and usually quit terminally. Know where they are in your vehicle (amazingly in some vehicles they are on the floor under the seats) and be sure they never get wet.
4. ***Essential – keep engine air intake clear of water.*** As already mentioned, major damage to engines can result if even

Wading depth

A typical wading depth limit of around 0.5m puts the water at about bumper height or just below the top of the wheel rim on a 16-inch wheel.

At max normal wading depth – and at the all-important moderate speed – a low bow-wave (left) produces a dip aft of bumper that keeps water away from the fan. At shallower wading depth (right) there is more latitude for slightly higher speed. Pre-attached tow rope (below) is a useful precaution when conditions could be difficult.

small amounts of water get past the air filter and into the cylinders. Never risk this happening. Choose another route where the water depth is less.

5. Don't stop the engine. Do not stop the engine whilst wading if the exhaust pipe is below water level. If you do, water will enter the exhaust system – including the catalytic converter. In rare cases water can siphon back to the engine causing catastrophic damage.

Ignore pictures you may have seen of Camel Trophy vehicles almost submerged in water; these vehicles will have been specially modified with raised air intakes for the engine; or – you may be looking at a picture of a vehicle with a destroyed engine!

Afterwards

After wading. It is essential to dry your brakes after wading, especially if your vehicle has drum brakes. Whilst still in low range, drive a short distance applying the brakes lightly; this will squeegee the discs or linings dry. Remove any plastic sheeting or other engine protection used for the operation. The wading plugs need not be removed immediately if further wading is envisaged but see previous spread about regular use. Remember the handbrake too will be wet.

Getting stuck, recovery and precautions. Covered fully under Section 5, recovery principles remain the same but are complicated by the lower part of the vehicle being under water. Anticipation is the key – such as pre-attachment of a tow rope (or pre-extension of the winch line) so that you do not have to grope with the problem under water.

Drive fast enough for a small bow-wave about 20cm high. No huge splashes. Squeegee the brakes dry after wading – low-range, against light brake.

4.11 Ice and snow

More traction, same brakes

4x4, 4x2 differences. Most readers of this book will have experience of driving on snow and ice in ordinary cars. Indeed many will have bought a four-wheel drive vehicle partly because it will give them more reliable transport in wintry conditions. Though traction in snow is best in temperatures below -20°C and less good between zero and -20°C, the basic principles of being very gentle with both the throttle and the brakes will apply in just the same way on a 4x4 as it does on a 4x2. But it is well to establish first just what the differences are between the two:

4x4s are better than 4x2s on snow and ice for traction – but remember your braking is very similar. ABS is good – but cannot change packed snow into dry tarmac.

1. Double the traction ... As we have seen, the 4x4 has double the traction of a 4x2. In snow and ice conditions this should be regarded not as a means of putting twice as much power on the road but as a means of putting the same power on the road spread between twice as many wheels. This asks less of the surface in terms of grip and so you are thus less likely to get spinning wheels.

2. ... but the same braking. What is often forgotten in the feeling of confidence that a 4x4's tractive performance in snow generates is that the method of stopping is the same as that of any normal car – four wheels on the ground, each one's rotation retarded by brakes. Indeed, 4x4s are generally a lot heavier than normal cars and have a correspondingly increased amount of kinetic energy to arrest. Beware, therefore, of letting your feeling of invincibility extend to the braking department when you are on snow or ice. A 4x4 will brake no better, and possibly less well, than a 4x2.

3. ABS – very good, but not magic. ABS anti-lock braking will give you the best braking possible under the circumstances but will not reverse the laws of physics. It will eliminate the human error of locking the wheels; it will yield the maximum retardation possible from given surface conditions – as well as enormously improving directional control – but it will not turn ice into dry tarmac. The surface conditions are still the limiting factor.

Gentle right foot – again

Driving technique. The driving techniques employed for snow and ice are generally similar to those used for slippery mud or wet grass.

1. High gear. Select the highest gear that is feasible for the conditions. ('D' with automatic transmission; some autos even have a winter setting for the gentlest step-off – see Volvo V70 photo, p.2.22)

2. 4x4 and centre diff lock. Obviously with selectable 4x4, engage four-wheel drive. If you are in a soft-roader where '4x4 lock' can be selected (eg Nissan X-Trail) then do so. Also engage the centre differential lock (if manually selectable - eg Defender) – and disengage it as soon as non-icy ground is reached.

3. Diff lock – rear. Don't engage this unless you are obviously stuck, ie stationary with one rear wheel spinning. In those circumstances, de-clutch, select neutral (in auto too) to make sure the spinning wheel is now stationary, and

It's always best if you are first out – with the right vehicle. Off-road, articulation still helps (left). Rescues (right) demand the same kind of vehicle but packed snow makes it harder to get grip. Country lanes off the gritters' routes (below) are just as challenging, but a sharply programmed Haldex (p.2.17) and winter tyres will cope.

then engage rear diff lock. Disengage it as soon as non-icy ground is reached; this is most important since an inappropriately locked rear diff will encourage slip in cornering or manoeuvring conditions.

4. Throttle, brake, steering. Use minimum throttle opening when driving away and accelerating, even if electronic traction control is fitted. Avoid violent movements of the steering wheel – especially on a BMW with xDrive since the 4x4 *disengages* when large steering angles are applied. Drive slowly and brake with great caution to avoid locking the wheels. Cadence braking will help (see pp.3.7, 9.4).

On-road – what lies beneath. As with sand, there are, of course, a dozen combinations of criteria affecting snow and ice – mainly concerned with what lies beneath the present surface of the snow. These will extend or reduce the limits of traction of your vehicle; they cannot be quantified in any book but acquire new relevance in the light of a large-wheeled 4x4:

1. First on the road? If, as if often the case, you and your 4x4 are first on the road after the first snow on untreated roads, this is the best traction you will get in snow. Bold and/or sharp treaded M+S tyres will cut through the soft snow either to the ground beneath or will make the first compressed snow 'rails' for you to travel on. These are as grippy as they will ever be. Conditions get worse from now on as subsequent vehicles pack the snow.

2. Second or later? When others have been on the roads first, their compressed tracks will make slippery going and, as you will have noticed many times, driving out of the previous tracks will get fractionally more traction. As before, four-wheel drive will give more traction but no improvement, *per se*, in braking. On long descents or hairpin bends stay in a low gear.

3. Subsequent snowfalls. Snowfall on top of previous compressed tracks which may in places have slicked-over into streaks of pure ice is the real trap but

Driving on snow and ice, the same principles apply as for slippery slopes – highest gear possible, gentle and sensitive use of brakes, throttle and steering.

another well enough known phenomenon in which a large-wheeled and heavy 4x4, delicately driven, will prove its worth in obtaining traction. Braking will be fractionally better than a car by reason of the tyre treads but only as long as it is done gently and on untrodden snow. Again, if you have no ABS, cadence braking (see p.3.7 and Glossary) will pay dividends and the big wheels' ability to steer through and towards snow having no underlying ice will prove an advantage.

Auto transmission, traction control. Vehicles fitted with automatic transmission, traction control and ABS will be at an advantage in wintry conditions but these aids to gentler traction enhance the effectiveness of the 'gentle right foot' driving philosophy; they don't replace it.

What lies under the snow? If you are the first out, it will just be road. Snowfall on top of packed snow will be very slippery. A classic case for diff lock in high box.

Snow chains for serious packed snow after a heavy fall – four sets for a 4x4. Winter tyres like the Bridgestone Blizzak have an excellent reputation and are aimed at cold/wet conditions as well as packed snow and ice on urban and country roads. Dunlop SP Sport (below) is less than ideal for snow!

Winter tyres

What's the difference? Apart from the studded Scandinavian winter-wear beneficial where there is permanent compacted snow on the roads, many may be tempted to dismiss winter tyres because they look quite similar to normal tyres. They really are different, however: tread depth, void size (the gap between tread blocks), sipe design (the 'knife cuts') and above all the softer tread compound which is optimised (high silica) for rain and low temperatures.

The benefits. Manufacturers' advice is that such tyres pay off below around 7°C while it's still wet. As if to address the doubters, Michelin quote 18% reduction in braking distance on snow / ice, 7% reduction on cold / wet and a 6% improvement in aquaplaning threshold for the '4x4 Alpin' compared to their own '4x4 XPC tyre.

Off-road, prod before you plod

Be absolutely certain of what is beneath the snow. There is rarely enough grip to let you back out of a mistake.

The Bridgestone Blizzak (US) is another well-reported and competition-winning winter tyre with similar benefits – noticeably improved snow / ice grip, softer ride.

Horses for courses. As ever with tyres, despite huge improvements and

Be prepared! Atlas Mountains (above) en route to the Sahara! Classic winter scenario (right), centre diff lock, gentle throttle ...etc!

convergence in multi-role applications (eg. the excellent BFGoodrich All Terrain – see Section 8.2) , winter tyres wear quicker in high-temperature conditions. European users usually have two sets of wheels and the winter set is stored by their local garage during the summer months.

Making it all work

Snowdrifts. Big wheels, a locked centre diff and appropriate tyres driven on all four wheels are ingredients for charging snowdrifts and getting through. Or they can be ingredients for getting it wrong and finishing up sitting on top of a vehicle's length of compressed snow and having to dig the snow out from under the vehicle.

Do not be too ambitious with what you attempt to barge through. Anything above hub depth is starting to get marginal for sustained travel; individual small drifts deeper than this can often be successfully tackled. As ever, the low box, probably in 3rd (with diff lock), will be the weapon.

Helping yourself and others. Other traffic and those inappropriately equipped having got into trouble will all too frequently be the cause, in winter conditions, of your not getting through to your destination despite your having, without them, the capability to do so. To free them and yourself from delays, carrying a long tow rope, shovels, gumboots, gloves and some kind of under-wheel traction aid (Section 5.1, 'Self-recovery') will help reduce everyone's problems. Pulling a car from a ditch with this equipment and careful use of the low range and throttle takes only minutes – see Section 5.2, 'Recovery – towing out'.

Snow chains. If you do not have a full set of four snow chains fit the first pair to the front wheels since this will give you grip as well as steering in slippery conditions. To some extent it will also prepare a path for the back wheels.

Since a 4x4 has four driven wheels a second set of chains will be beneficial. If using front snow chains off-road there is a danger, with certain types of chain, that full axle articulation and full steering lock at the same time could enable the chains to damage the front brake pipes. Check with your dealer. See also Section 5.1, 'Self-recovery'.

Snow off-road. As there is not a smooth potentially slippery surface beneath it, snow off-road is easier to cope with than snow on tarmac carriageways.

A moment's thought, however, highlights the dangers of minor drifting of the snow covering potentially destructive obstacles such as small rock outcrops or gullies on hillsides. The situation is similar to fording streams in that the dangers are hidden; the solution is the same – an on-foot recce and prodding with a stick in doubtful areas.

Tyres with bold sharp tread patterns are best. Fit only snow chains approved for your vehicle. Off-road snow is generally easier - but probe for hidden rocks or ditches.

Section 5

Recovery

5.1 Self-recovery

Traction aids

The calm approach. The brutal truth is that in most cases getting stuck is a function of driver error – misreading the ground or the obstacle, or not accurately knowing the limitations of the vehicle. Whilst we all try our best with these things and all gradually get better, equally certain is the fact that we all occasionally make mistakes – often for the best of reasons, like not wanting to overstress the vehicle.

Admitting this is at least half the battle for it enables you to go about the remedial action in the right spirit – philosophically cheerful acceptance rather than bluster, embarrassment, or the suspicion that life has just dealt you the ultimate humiliation!

Everyone gets bogged occasionally. If you've missed the chance to reverse out, smile and go on to the next stage – digging and something to go under the wheels.

Knowing the problems. It helps to know what problems may be ahead. The categories in which you may find yourself stuck are shown below. Knowing this helps you see the problems coming and avoid them.

Wheels spinning – two causes. A given amount of power plus a combination of:

- not enough grip and
- not enough weight on a wheel ... which can cause the wheel to spin without providing any motion to the vehicle. In these circumstances traction control, if fitted, will brake the spinning wheel automatically after a short pause or, again if you have one, an axle diff lock can be engaged – see p.2.6.

If grip is the problem in a static restart :

- try a higher gear and a gentle throttle
- try 'weaving' the steering wheel – from the straight ahead position move it to 11 o'clock, then 1 o'clock so the tyre sidewalls contribute to grip; it helps sometimes in mud and sand.

In the case of not enough weight on the wheel (the axle may be at an angle to the chassis and the lower wheel is spinning) see Diagonal Suspension on the next spread.

Adding grip and flotation. If these measures fail, inserting some gripping medium between the wheel and the ground is the next step – stones, brushwood, baulks of timber or items designed especially for the purpose – load spreaders, in effect (and best):

- sand ladders
- metal planking or
- recovery channels.

If you've not come across them before, these all amount to the same thing – a 'plank' of some kind to put under the wheels to stop them sinking and/or also to afford them grip. Beware (see sub para 2 below) of anything that can flick up beneath the vehicle and cause damage.

1. ***Sand ladders*** can of course be used in any medium – sand, mud, snow. They are specially-made aluminium ladders about 1.5 metres long, 35cm wide and with rungs only about 15cm apart (gripping edges outermost). They are thrust under the front – or rear – of the wheels (see diagram and far-right picture opposite) and the vehicle will find grip and flotation on the ladders.
If necessary, as the vehicle moves, the ladders are moved round to the front (or rear, if you are going out in reverse) of the vehicle a second, third or fourth time to provide further traction in the direction of travel. Sand ladders of the right type – side members 6-7cm deep – can be used for minor bridging of dips..
2. ***Steel planking*** (PSP – the perforated lengths of interlocking steel planking originally made for WW2 bush airfields) is used in the same way as sand ladders. PSP is heavier and more difficult to use than aluminium sand ladders; it is too flexible to be used for bridging (and can bend upward to snag the underside of the vehicle) but is excellent for laying over logs or branches to provide a vehicle trackway. PSP is also available in aluminium – see photo and p.7.13.
3. ***Recovery channels*** cover a multitude of variants of the above, often combining the best aspects of sand ladders with less bulk. An articulated version is shown above (centre picture) and in the photos on pp.5.5, 7.13. The articulation afforded by the rope links makes them easier to

Recovery channels – for grip and load-spreading.

1. Sand ladders – may kick up, 2. Barong articulated alloy grip plates – light, won't kick up, easy to pack; very good. 3. Australian MaxTrax purpose-designed nylon units, light, tough, easy to handle, available world-wide. 4. Alloy PSP – bendy, kicks up, awkward.

push in front of the wheels without – as is the case with ladders or PSP – the danger of the unit kicking up and fouling the vehicle chassis, exhaust or plumbing. When you have finished with them, the three sections can be folded up, bagged and stowed within the vehicle.

Flotation – sinking in soft ground. Although technically there is a difference between a lack of traction and a lack of flotation, in practice the two usually strike together and a joint solution – use of reduced tyre pressures (see Section 8.2, 'Tyres') and/or load spreaders such as sand ladders etc mentioned above – will be the answer. If no load spreaders are carried, branches or brushwood are an unsatisfactory alternative. If sinkage is considerable so that the vehicle is hung up digging to remove the obstacle or jacking to permit the channels to be put under the wheels will be necessary (see methods next page).

Use shovels early to save a wheelspinning bogging getting worse. Invest an extra few minutes' digging and get out first time.

Use of sand ladders

Always dig away in front of a wheel before inserting the sand tracks. This helps ensure first-time grip.

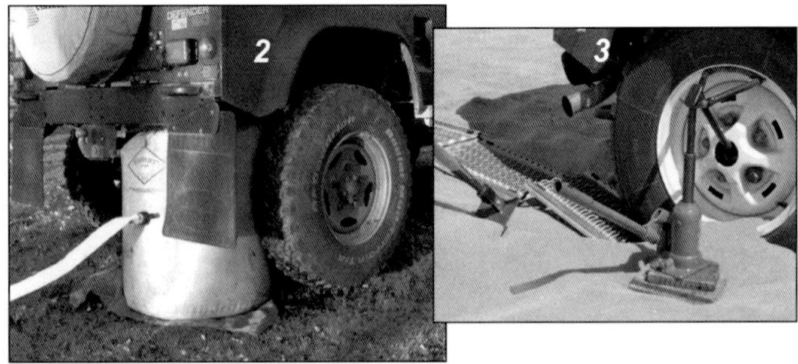

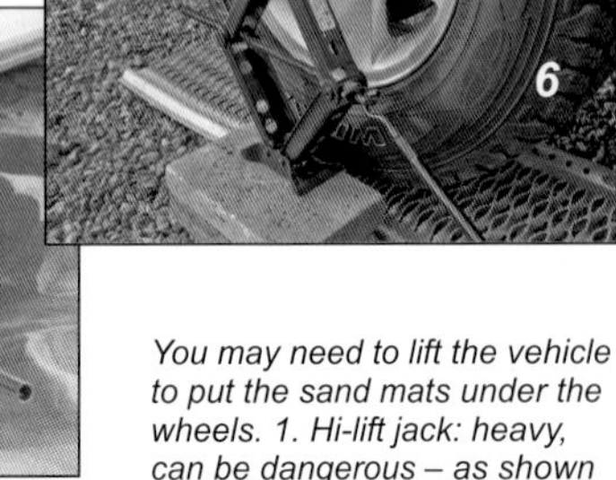

You may need to lift the vehicle to put the sand mats under the wheels. 1. Hi-lift jack: heavy, can be dangerous – as shown here. 2. Easilift exhaust-inflated airbag; suffers similar suspension drop. Be sure under-belly area can take jacking load. 3,4,5,6. Raising the axle at the wheel with custom wheel-claw obviates suspension drop or grovelling under axle. Uses standard on-board jack.

There will be times when it is necessary to lift the wheels to insert the sand channels beneath rather than risk further wheelspin and a deeper bogging. Lifting the axle is more efficient than lifting the vehicle.

Inserting the sand channels

Lifting the wheels. Pushing the sand ladder or channel against the wheels, even after digging as in the diagram overleaf, may not be enough for the wheel to grip and pull the vehicle out. Rather than risk even a small amount of additional wheelspin and the resultant sinkage it is often better to lift the wheels to insert the channels by hand. Lifting the axle is better than jacking the chassis; in the latter case you have to accommodate full suspension drop as the chassis rises.

Hi-lift jack. The hi-lift jack is a mechanical bumper jack capable of a lift of a metre or more. A vehicle that has been run into deep ruts and is unable to get out could have the front end physically lifted out of the ruts and, by then pushing the jack over sideways, could be 'pole-vaulted' onto more suitable ground. Equally, the front end could also be lifted to insert ladders under the wheels. Hi-lift jacks are effective but very heavy. As bumper jacks they require a special bumper or modifications to accept the jack spigot. You will also likely need to make modifications to enable it to be carried in an external rack.

Hi-lift jack – safety. Pay special attention to safety when using a hi-lift jack. As a 'mono-pod' it is inherently unstable – see above. It must be used with strict adherence to safety instructions; do not leave it unless the operating handle is vertical.

Wheel jack. The normal wheel jack with a specially made wheel-claw adapter can lift the axle for insertion of sand mats (above, 3, 4, 5 and 6) and is far easier than digging to put a jack under the axle casing.

Winch. Unless required for operating in particular conditions (eg, jungle), a winch is expensive and heavy to have as a 'just-in-case' recovery aid. When trying to co-ordinate it with power from driven wheels it is slow in operation, but provided there is something to winch onto it can work wonders in certain situations. A capstan winch is best for continuous use; (p.5.13).

Use a marshaller to prevent this. Chassis hang-up is one of the most awkward situations from which to recover. Having to dig the ground from under a vehicle provides good motivation for not letting it ever happen again.

Digging, recovery tools

Under-vehicle obstacles – bellied on ridges or rocks. Least forgivable of driver-inflicted situations, especially if you have a passenger with you who could have got out and marshalled you over the obstacle, is getting the chassis hung up on ridges or rocks – photo right. It is also potentially the most damaging. The price will be paid, however, since the only way out of this predicament unless you have a high-lift bumper jack (see photo opposite), is actually to dig the obstacle away from under the vehicle with a shovel.

It will be difficult using the shovel at full arm's length under the vehicle and in addition the vehicle will be tending initially to collapse down onto the shovel as it is used. Knowing what is involved and having the patience to do it slowly-but-surely will get you out of this situation but you will vow not to let it happen again. If it is immovable rock that you are hung up on the situation is more serious but jacking front or rear to put packing under the wheels will achieve a recovery just as reliably.

Diagonal suspension – wheels in the air. As we have seen (Section 4.3, 'Ridges and ditches') it is possible to get a vehicle immobilised by misjudging the amount of axle articulation involved in crossing a ridge or ditch diagonally. (An axle is on full articulation when one wheel is pushed up into the wheel arch as far as it will go and the other wheel is hanging down as far as it will go.) A very common manifestation is 'the diagonal tightrope' in which, say, the rear offside wheel and front nearside wheel are both on full bump and the complementary wheels are hanging down – with the axle differentials allowing the hanging wheels to spin when you apply power (see pics pp.2.8,.4.15).

If you have no locking differentials or traction control this situation will stop you but has a very straightforward solution – either pack up beneath the spinning wheels or dig away beneath the full bump wheels as shown on the diagram, page 4.14. It is difficult to get earth packed in tightly enough under the hanging wheels (though inserting a sand ladder, levering up and packing with rocks can work) so almost invariably digging under the hung-up wheels is the solution. As with the case above, the vehicle is trying to collapse on your shovel as you dig but, again, patience will invariably win the day.

Under-belly hang-up on ridges can be damaging and recovery very awkward. Exceeding articulation limits is a common way of becoming stuck. Diagram p.4.14.

Recovery tools. If you are planning a journey in which off-roading and the risk of getting stuck exists (see also Section 7.4), the following equipment is worth taking:

- Rubber boots, gloves, overalls.
- Electric tyre pump for re-inflation of tyres; accurate pressure gauge.
- Two shovels (pointed blades, not square ends like spades).
- Two tow ropes (totalling 25 metres) and shackles (photo next spread) for towing and/or joining the tow ropes
- Articulated sand channels or sand ladders – see previous page.
- Hi-lift jack – if appropriate to the vehicle bumper (see opposite).
- Wood block(s) about 30 x 20 x 5cm to prevent jack sinkage.

5.2 Towing out

Ropes and attachments

Second-vehicle safety; long ropes. Where conditions are likely to be close to the limits of your 4x4's capabilities, you are strongly advised not to go off-roading without a second vehicle. As this and the next spread will show, the potential for recovery where one vehicle is able to help another is a considerable improvement on the situation of a solo vehicle trying self-recovery. Firstly, always use a long towing rope – better still a combination of two. A short rope is easy to stow without tangling but, shackled to another one, will make a long rope to ensure the towing vehicle is not in the same bog or soft sand that has stopped the first one.

Tow rope attachment – vehicle. Tow rope attachment to the towing vehicle should naturally be at the towing hitch if one is fitted. This uses the longitudinal chassis members and the rear cross member to provide a load-spreading attachment point. At the front and rear of most vehicles, beneath the chassis, lashing points are fitted (two front and two rear), principally for securing vehicles on trailers. If a tow hitch is not fitted these can be used (as pairs, not singly) for towing. Better still, and designed to cope with far higher loads, extra-strong lashing / towing rings can be fitted in lieu of the normal lashing rings at the same chassis points on some vehicles. On Defenders, ask for military 'JATE' rings. Many modern vehicles have substantial screw-in towing eyes (pic opposite).

Take a second vehicle for safety and to assist recovery if you are going off-roading. Use – and prepare – a long tow rope. Never loop tow rope round the axles: risk of brake-pipe damage.

Use of towing bridle

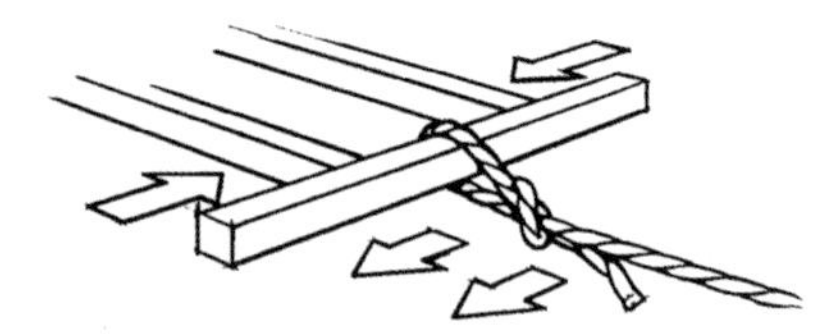

Attached at mid point, tow rope will bend a weak bumper, drawing chassis members together. Move rope close to bumper attachment points.

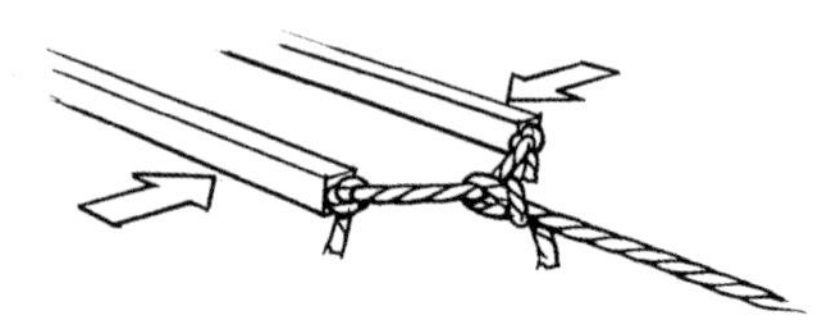

Too short a towing bridle will have same effect – also putting extreme strain on bridle rope.

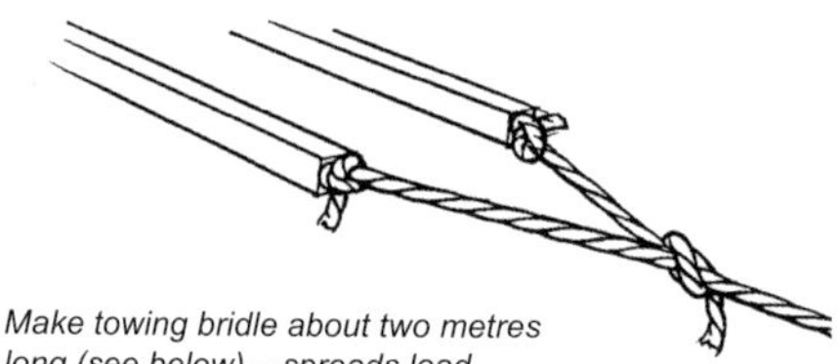

Make towing bridle about two metres long (see below) – spreads load without any 'pinching' component.

Standard ball hitch (centre of vehicle) is cleared for 3500kg pull. If not fitted use a long bridle on the tie-down lashing rings under the chassis. Here these have been replaced by military-spec JATE-rings.

Bridle and two attachment points. The standard vehicle tie-down lashing points are designed for loads less than maximum towing loads but can be used for normal recovery towing (NOT snatch towing – see next section) if both eyes are used with a long bridle. A bridle is a rope attached to both lashing eyes and joined to the main tow rope two or three metres away of the vehicle.

(Do not make this bridle less than two metres in length and do make it of a rope to each lashing ring rather than a single loop through both rings. This way you will minimise rope tension and also eliminate any tendency to draw the chassis members together – see diagram, left.) Never put a tow rope round a metal bumper since this will lead to the rope being cut by the bumper's sharp edge. Nor should a rope be put round an axle since this involves the strong likelihood of damaging brake pipes.

Tow rope ends. Ensuring that your tow ropes have properly prepared ends is a very worthwhile precaution. Few things can add so effectively to the problems of having to extract a bogged vehicle than finding that tow ropes have to be knotted round tow points and then need a marlin spike in order to undo the knot afterwards. Spliced-in metal eyes and the use of U-bolts and shackle pins

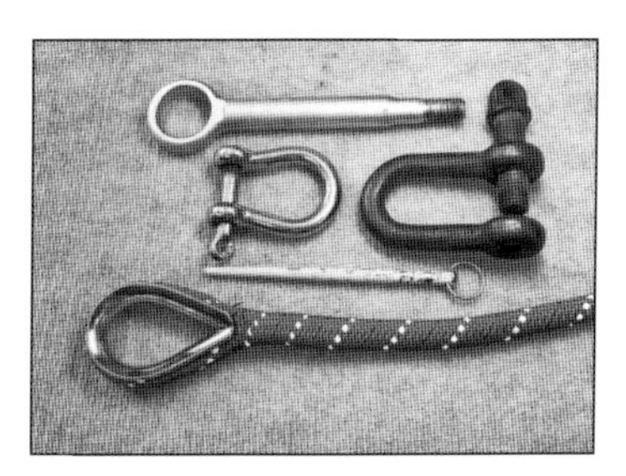

Screw-in vehicle towing eye (top), U-bolt shackles and spliced-in tow-rope eye – a reliable way of attaching and detaching a tow-rope without the hassle of trying to untie immovable knots.

(photo above) on properly prepared ropes makes the exercise extremely simple and quick. If you do not have a tow hitch at both ends of the vehicle, prepare a suitable length of rope with U-bolts at each end to pick up on the chassis lashing eyes and act as a two-metre bridle onto which the main tow rope can be attached. The main tow rope should be similarly prepared for your particular vehicle.

Ideally don't use bumpers for towing; most bumpers' sharp edges cut tow ropes. In emergency pad with sacking, move rope close to the bumper attachment bolts.

Towing autos. If recovering automatics and then towing them home some distance, remember, if there is no neutral on the transfer gears, there is often a tow limit of 30 miles and 30mph due to lubrication requirements in the auto gearbox (see p.2.47). Over that, the propeller shafts have to be removed or a trailered recovery done.

A separate marshaller is invaluable to take up slack, signal the clutches of both vehicles to be engaged at the same time and give the 'Stop' sign – but see p.5.10 if solo. If the stuck vehicle is being towed out backwards its driver is looking the wrong way so a relay man is needed – see photo overleaf.

Co-ordinate power output from the tug and the stuck vehicle. Where the latter is being towed out backwards, its driver cannot see the marshaller so a 'relay' marshaller is needed – distant to left of vehicle here.

Use a long tow rope and a marshaller to control the operation. Take your time. Marshaller should use only visual signals, not voice, to co-ordinate both vehicles' power

Co-ordinated recovery

Meaning, procedure. A co-ordinated recovery is one in which the power and traction of both vehicles – even though one of them, being stuck, has a limited capability – are used together at the moment when the tow is undertaken. This is a common sense point but all too often, in the stress of a vehicle becoming bogged, the point is forgotten and spinning wheels and slack, then jerking tow ropes become the ingredients of minor confusion – or worse. A helpful sequence aide-memoir for a normal assisted recovery would be as follows:

1. Marshaller, co-ordinator. Ingredients of a co-ordinated recovery: one stuck vehicle, one recovery (towing) vehicle, appropriate (long) tow ropes, two drivers, a third person visible to both drivers to act as marshaller / co-ordinator.

2. Take your time. If the stuck vehicle is hung up on an obstacle invest ten minutes spade work to ensure the first extraction attempt is the one that works. Even if there is no digging, still take your time.

3. Backwards best? Towing out backwards is sometimes a more reliable option. At least the stuck vehicle has wheel tracks leading to its present position. In this case, with the vehicles back-to-back during recovery, a second marshaller standing in 'front' of the stuck vehicle is useful to keep that driver in the picture by relaying the hand signals of the principal marshaller ahead of the tug – see photograph. As with reversing back down a hill (p.4.18), the driver of the stuck vehicle should keep both hands on the steering wheel to preclude steering 'runaway' in reverse.

4. Towing vehicle well clear. Position the towing vehicle so that it is well clear of the conditions that bogged the first vehicle. A long rope is almost invariably more use than a short one for this reason. Attach the rope to both vehicles, position the third person so that both drivers can easily see him and have him marshal the tug forward until any slack is taken up and the rope is tight.

5. Visual signals, simultaneous clutches. Decide on the gear to be used – not necessarily 1st low range; 2nd could well be better. Have both vehicles start engines, engage gear and wait for the signal from the marshaller for both drivers to engage the clutch. As with all marshalling (Section 3.5 'Marshalling'),

Tandem tow

If the stuck vehicle is heavy or badly mired, a tandem two, carefully co-ordinated, will usually achieve first-time results

Classic tandem-tow (right and above) has two smaller vehicles towing a low power-weight ratio truck up a difficult sand slope. In the photo visibility problems necessitate the marshaller standing beside rather than in front of the lead vehicle for all drivers to see him.

this should be a visual not a spoken signal:

- A raised arm to instruct both drivers to be ready and in gear,
- Raised arm describing small circles to instruct them to rev the engines,
- Then drop the raised arm to instruct them to engage the clutches.

6. Marshaller in control. The marshaller should move backwards as the vehicles move towards him, still controlling the operation and being ready to give an immediate STOP signal if he sees any problems. He is the only one who can properly judge how the recovery is going. He too can judge when it is done; he can signal the lead vehicle to stop and the now mobile towed one to come forward slightly to slacken off the rope before disconnecting.

Safety – the danger of breaking ropes

Keep clear. A tow rope breaking whilst under strain can be lethal or inflict serious injury to bystanders in a multi-person co-ordinated recovery. No bystanders or crew should be allowed near a tow rope during the actual tow. Four to five metres is usually a safe distance but the danger area varies with the length of rope and the techniques used – see overleaf, 'Snatch towing'. A breaking rope recoils with whiplash violence. Adequately strong tow ropes are essential as well as rigidly enforced safety procedures in their use.

Use a tow rope with a breaking strain about equal to the weight of the vehicle. WARNING. When tow starts, NO-ONE should be near the tow rope. Breakage can be lethal.

Pull required. As a guide, the pull required to move a vehicle (as a proportion of its total weight – ie including payload) assuming level ground, is given below (overleaf):

White knight! No, not a tow for the 42-tonne artic which was destined to have time to enjoy the scenery, but the procedure in the diagram was used to recover a number of the 4-7 tonners also in the queue behind at this flood washout.

- Hard metalled road – about 5% of total vehicle weight.
- Grass – about 15%.
- Hard wet sand, gravel, soft wet sand – about 15-20%.
- Sand – soft, dry, loose – about 25-30%.
- Shallow mud – about 33%.
- Bog, marsh, clinging clay – about 50%.

Rule-of-thumb. It makes sense that the rope to keep in the back of your off-roader is the worst-case rope – the one for marsh/bog/clay. Allowing a safety margin to account for unseen damage to the rope and other exigencies, it should have a quoted breaking strain about equal to the laden weight of your vehicle. For example, when new and undamaged, a 14mm 3-strand polypropylene rope has a breaking strain of 2.79 tonnes (quoted breaking strains are governed by British Standards in the UK) which would be an appropriate minimum for most medium off-roaders except perhaps a laden dual-cab pickup.

If it's just you rescuing a fellow traveller, the recovery can still be coordinated and controlled. The briefing can even be done in sign language!

And if it's just you?

Solo rescue. If you are alone and coming to the rescue of someone needing help you can still effect a safe co-ordinated tow-out without a marshaller if you are methodical and brief the other driver. (Diagram, below)

- Lay out the tow rope with a kink in it that you can see with your door mirror.
- Edge forward till the kink moves in behind you and out of your view (see diagram, item 1).
- Continue to edge forward very slowly to take up the final slack, then stop.
- Having earlier briefed the other driver, put your hand out of the window and describe small circles to indicate "In gear, rev up, prepare to engage clutch".
- Drop hand to indicate "Engage clutch" on both vehicles.

Solo tow recovery

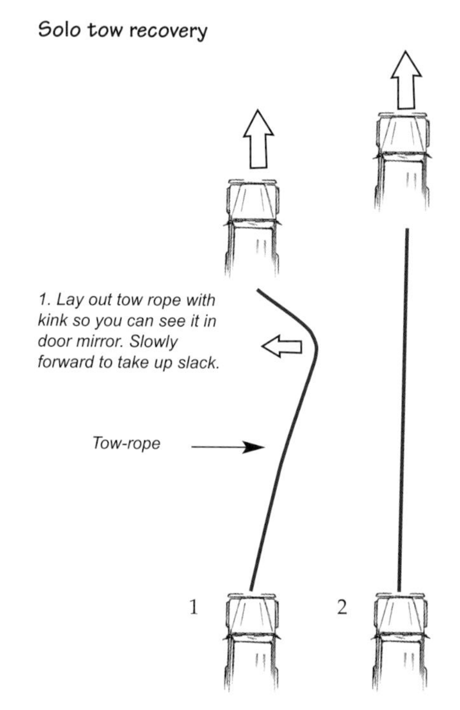

5.3 Snatch towing

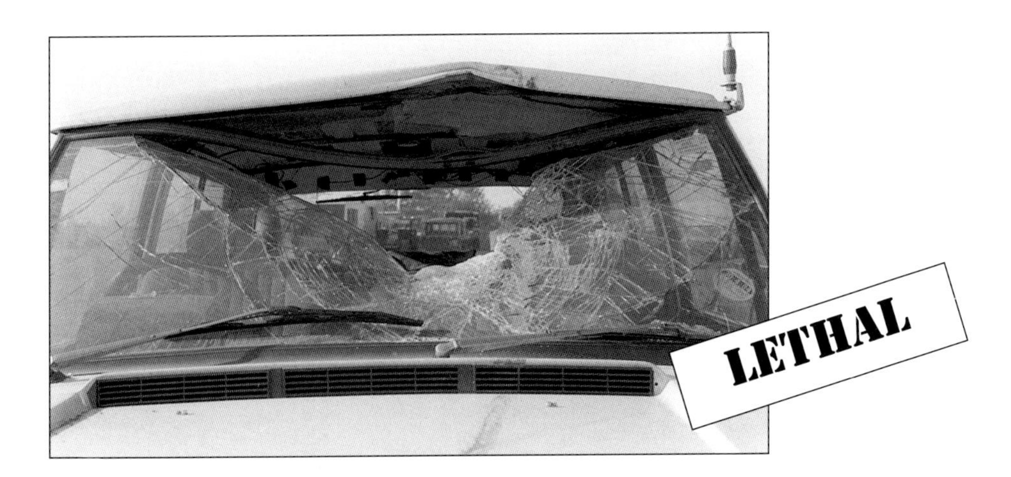

Snatch towing is only safe when carried out within very closely defined limits in terms of materials, vehicle integrity, speeds, length of rope, stretch maxima and procedures – in effect R&D conditions. This picture shows what can happen when it goes wrong. The tow vehicle had a chassis that was rusty on the inside. The tow hook was attached to the rusty chassis. When the 'snatch' took place, the complete tow hook and pintle was torn from the tug's rear cross member and, using the energy in the stretched rope, ***recoiled through front and rear windscreens*** *of this Range Rover. Miraculously no-one was killed.*

What is snatch towing?

The rough concept. First of all, using:

- a very specific type of rope (long) and
- suitably strong tow attachments

the rope is attached to the stuck vehicle and then to the tug. The tug moves forward to take out all the slack. It then reverses towards the stuck vehicle (the 'step-back') for a short distance (about a metre and a half), putting a predetermined slack in the rope and giving a predetermined acceleration distance before it again goes taut. With the stuck vehicle in gear and using power, the tug then accelerates in a low gear – 2nd gear, low range. Rope breakage can be almost as dangerous as a towing fixture coming loose.

Lethal? Oh yes. After advice in the last edition against snatch towing, I am indebted to Joe Risser of Atascadero, California for forwarding the following:

"...I was just reporting for my shift patrolling the Pismo Dunes on holiday weekend with the local Sheriff's Search and Rescue Unit. Some of the guys were just coming back from a first aid call to a spot down the beach (in the dunes). Seems a guy with a Jeep had hooked on to a stuck vehicle with a strap and chain and attempted to "snatch 'em" out of the sand where they were mired. Whether the chain hook had slipped or the chain broken, the result was pretty much the same – the strap recoiled back to the Jeep bringing a length of chain with it. With the open topped Jeep, there was no protection for the back of the driver's head. The ambulance went by a few minutes later – no lights or siren needed."

The only appropriate recommendation is that snatch towing should not be carried out at all.

5.4 Winching

Winch types – drum and capstan

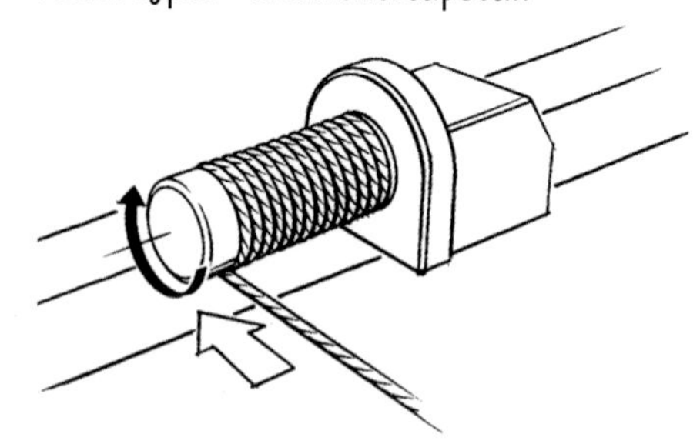

Drum winch (above). *Electrical (or mechanical/hydraulic). Geared, heavy duty electric motor, uses around 350amps. 8–9.5mm wire rope, probably 30 metres.*
Capstan winch (below). *Mechanical drive direct from crankshaft or power take-off shaft. Low geared, operates from idling engine. 20mm Terylene or polyester rope of limitless length.*

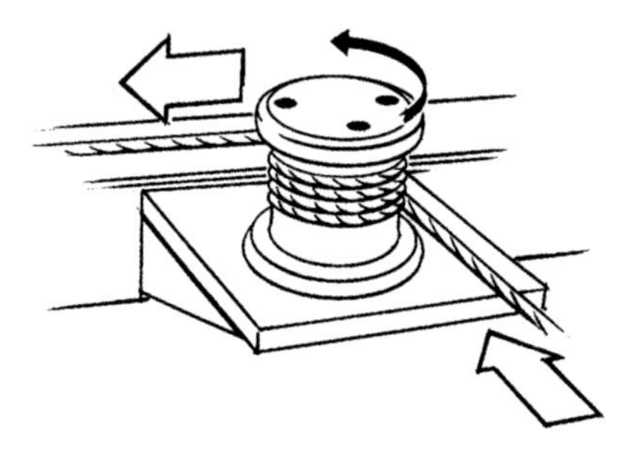

Concepts, winch types

Weighty decision; safety vital. The subject of winching requires a book on its own – in fact there are many – so cannot be covered fully in this Section. A broad overview can be provided, however, which will enable you to make your choice and get a feel for some of the principles of operation. Give careful thought to the implications of a winch before buying – it is more than an add-on accessory. In general, winches are expensive and heavy, sometimes requiring heavy duty front springs for the vehicle and special chassis reinforcement.

Do you really need a winch? Electric drum winches are not the best for continuous use. Opt for mechanical drum or capstan winches for continuous heavy duty work.

Electrical and mechanical add-ons. Depending on the type of winch, mechanical and electrical additions will have to be made to the vehicle as well – power-take-off shaft drives, hydraulic pumps or fitment of an uprated alternator and/or second battery where an electric winch is involved, further increasing weight. Winches require special care in operation since enormous mechanical forces are involved. Children, animals, under-informed adults – and that includes spectators – should be kept well away from the vicinity of cables under tension.

Slow operation – can be good. Winches are slow but immensely powerful and usually amenable to precise control. This will be what you want a winch for in most cases. There are many applications for this low speed alone – the slow controlled pull of a boat from the water or of heavy tree trunks. If your business includes recovering defunct passenger cars from ditches or the like, the slow speed and precise controllability of a winch will be exactly what you need.

Slow operation – can be bad. Where a towed extraction is difficult due to poor grip for the tug on slippery ground, extreme boggings can be handled well by a winch – provided the tug can be anchored properly. Such anchors can be ground anchors (see page 5.16) or a strop from the back of the tug to a tree or further vehicle. But for recovering other (still functioning) vehicles off-road you will find many occasions are better catered for by a vehicle tow with a long rope (see Section 5.2) and power employed by both the tug and the stuck vehicle.

Using a winch to recover a stuck vehicle makes it hard to coordinate the slow speed of the winch with power from the stuck vehicle's own engine and this is where the winch's slowness is a major disadvantage. When you do use this 'drive and winch' technique, care should be taken not to overrun the cable when the towed vehicle begins to grip.

Approved winches. Fitting a winch and ensuring that the stresses involved in winching are properly channelled into the structure is a specialised skill. Not all 4x4s make satisfactory bases for winches. It is essential to consult your vehicle supplier when buying a winch and to buy only winches that have been approved for your machine. The fitting kit will have been specifically engineered for it with safety in mind and so as not to overload the structure. Winches may be ordered factory-fitted by some manufacturers with some models – the Land Rover Defender being a classic example. Additionally there will be a small Handbook of Winching Techniques issued with the winch which will summarise how to prepare and operate the unit. The following few pages cannot deal with the subject comprehensively.

Winch types. There are two generic classifications of winch:

1. *Drum winches* comprise a drum rotating about a horizontal axis parallel to the bumper and use 8–9.5mm wire rope stored on, and spooled onto, that drum. They can be driven electrically (occasional short-term use) or there can be mechanical or hydraulic drive for continuous heavy duty operation.

2. *Capstan winches* consist of a bollard – like a giant cotton reel – rotating about a vertical axis. Such winches do not store any rope; they function by moving appropriate ropes – usually 20mm Terylene/polyester or polypropylene – which have been wound two or three times round the bollard and manually tensioned on the out-feed side. Capstan winches are mechanically or hydraulically driven and are ideal for continuous heavy duty work with the vehicle engine at idle or fast idle.

Pros and cons. Relative advantages and disadvantages of generic and particular types are dealt with in the table on the next spread.

Know your proposed needs for a winch. Of prime concern is whether your work is intermittent – 'casual' – or continuous heavy duty winching. See next spread.

Capstan winch (above) powers rope – of any length – looped round capstan. 10000 lb Superwinch E10 (above far right) is among most powerful electrically powered winches and is designed for intermittent heavy duty use; cable is stored on the drum. Mechanical H14 (right) is designed for continuous heavy duty work.

Match the winch to the job

Be aware of the different generic types of winch and the very broad spectrum of applications. A winch ideal for one kind of usage can be quite unsuitable for another.

Casual or heavy duty. Winching can be 'casual' – towing a boat out of the water or the occasional use for self-recovery – or 'heavy duty' which implies regular continuous use, usually for professional purposes such as logging or cable laying. Electric winches are not normally suitable for continuous heavy duty use. Very high amperages are involved, considerable heat is generated and a very high charge rate from the alternator is required.

A capstan or drum winch that is mechanically driven is an altogether more relaxed concept which operates directly from the engine at tick-over or very low rpm. It can thus be used all day without mechanical stress.

Assess your requirement. Assess your needs very carefully and accept the fact that installation of a heavy duty winch will be necessary where use is continuous and that such an installation will be heavy and relatively expensive since either mechanical shafting from a power take-off (PTO) or installation of a PTO-mounted hydraulic pump will be required.

Airbag-equipped vehicles. Modern vehicles with airbags will have triggering devices for the airbag Secondary Restraint

Table 1. Winch types and general characteristics

Type	*Applications*	*For*	*Against*
Electric drum winch	Intermittent light, medium or heavy duty use according to specification.	Low cost, simple installation, relatively low weight 54-87kg. Wide range from light to medium/heavy duty. Easy to use. Minimal maintenance. Cable is stored on the drum.	Electric motor will overheat if used for long periods. Very high amperage draw from battery necessitates high engine rpm and alternator output to recharge. Installation may need second battery.
Hydraulic drum winch	Continuous heavy duty industrial use.	Can operate for long continuous periods of industrial use with engine at low output or tick-over. Automatic rpm control. Vehicle has capability for other hydraulic tools/applications.	High initial cost for winch and PTO hydraulic pump installation. Needs specialised maintenance for precision components. Engine must be running. Heavy – up to around 115kg.
Mechanical drum winch	Continuous heavy duty industrial use.	Can operate for long continuous periods of industrial use with engine at low output or tick-over.	High initial cost for PTO gear and drive shafts to winch position. Two-man operation – one controls engine, one controls winch. Engine must be running. Heavy – up to around 112kg.
Mechanical or hydraulic capstan winch	Continuous heavy duty industrial use.	Can operate for long continuous periods of industrial use with engine at low output or tick-over. Constant pulling power due to rope being constant distance from drum axis all the time. Easy to operate. No limit to length of rope used. Around 63kg.	High cost plus specialist maintenance if hydraulic drive. Not all vehicles can accommodate this type of winch. Rope not contained on winch. Engine must be running.

Table 2. Snapshot data on some Land Rover approved winch types (Superwinch)

Type	*Name*	*Max line pull*	*Gearbox type*	*Brake type*	*Free spool*	*Elec/hydraulic power requirements*
Electric drum	1. X6 2. X9 3. Husky 4. E10	6000 lb 9000 lb 8500 lb 10000 lb	Planetary Planetary Worm/wheel Planetary	Dynamic In drum Irreversible Disc, wet	Lever Lever Lever Plunger	12v, 390amps 12v, 435amps 12v, 360amps 12v, 360amps
Hydraulic drum	1. H8 2. H14W	8000 lb 8000 lb	Planetary Worm/wheel	Disc, wet Irreversible	Plunger Plunger	32 litre pump, 2500psi 32 litre pump, 2500psi
Mechanical drum	1. H14W	8000 lb	Worm/wheel	Irreversible	Plunger	Power take-off shafts
Mech/hydr'ic capstan		4000 lb	Worm/wheel	Irreversible	N/A	Power take-off shafts or PTO hydraulic pump

In considering choice of winch, relate your proposed work to existence/type of brake, power requirements and amount of use at a given session.

Terminology
1. Gearbox type. This is an indication of the kind of reduction gear used in the winch. Worm and wheel can be arranged (and is here) to be irreversible hence there is no need for a brake.
2. Free-spool. Free-spooling is the process of disengaging the winch in order to reel out the cable to the item being winched. 'Lever' or 'plunger' indicates the method of activating winch cable release.
3. Brake. Braking is provided for the mid-pull power failure case. Knowledge of brake principle is needed. 'Dynamic' brake is only the running of the winch motor in high-geared reverse as a generator so is a retarder rather than a stop brake. (X6CD has centre drum brake.) Drum and disc brakes activate automatically via one-way clutch in the event of power being lost in mid pull. Worm and wheel gearing is itself irreversible so runaway after power failure is just not possible.

Discovery with Superwinch X6 winch low-profile fitting. Bumper protrusions are 'crush cans' to set deformation rate for airbag deployment. Only approved winch fitments should be used on these vehicles.

System (SRS) that are sensitive to specific crush rates encountered in front-end collisions. These crush-rates could be affected by an inappropriate winch installation – another reason (see previous spread) for consultation with the vehicle manufacturer before fitting a winch. Factory-fitted installations will take account of this but an incorrect installation could well result in premature triggering of the airbag system. In the case of Land Rover, for example, only approved winches, mounts and crush units are factory-fitted to vehicles with airbags. Being front-mounted, the mountings of these winches will have been engineered for the correct crush-rates compatible with the SRS.

Where a braked wheel would simply slide across slippery earth, ground anchors of this kind will give the winch something to pull against. Weight of the vehicle contributes to bite. Ground anchors like these are very heavy and need proper stowage. Aluminium units are available.

Techniques overview

Accessories. Paradoxically, it is wise to consider the accessories you will need before going firm on your choice of winch since you must envisage the entire operating regime and method of use before you have a clear picture of what is involved. The number of operating crew is a fundamental first consideration since if you are always going to be solo then a mechanical drum winch may not be suitable despite its conceptual appeal.

Protect trees, by using a strap. Protect people by observing safety rules and keeping clear of ropes and cables. Unless self-recovering, anchor the winch vehicle with ground anchors or back-anchor.

Length of cable is a consideration too. Most drum winches are supplied with 30 metres (100 feet) of cable and, whilst this can be attached to extensions, there may be times when a continuous long pull is required and thus a capstan winch would be the best equipment. If this is the case then thought must be given to storage of the rope within the vehicle. It will be bulky and must be kept in good condition. For any winch you are going to need some or all of the following additional ancillary equipment:

• ***D-shackles*** – see photo page 5.7. For winching, where line pulls will be higher than for normal vehicle-to-vehicle tow-outs, stronger D-shackles will be needed. A 3/4-inch pin diameter is a good guide.
• ***Tree strap.*** Usually available from the winch manufacturer, an 8-foot by 4-inch tree strap should be acquired to put round trees to protect them from bark damage that would occur when using a tree as a winching anchor with a bare steel cable. Always use a tree strap – and as low as possible on the tree.
• ***Split pulley block.*** Where direction of pull is likely to be off vehicle axis or where a double-line pull is required, a pulley block will be needed to direct or increase the line pull. See photo opposite and diagrams/photo next spread.
• **Ground anchors.** Where high line-pulls are envisaged, possibly on slippery ground, a pair of ground anchors (photo, left) will prevent forward movement of the vehicle during the pull. The right ones will be heavy and cumbersome and take up space and payload in the vehicle.
• ***Back-anchor rope.*** Where ground anchors are not available or where additional security is required, the winching vehicle can be anchored with rope and tree strap to a tree behind it.
• ***Gloves.*** Steel cables can have small broken strands along their length; use thick winching gloves to protect your hands. Do not let a steel winch cable slip through your hands even when using gloves. Always pay it in or out hand-over-hand. The same gloves will be useful for the handling of capstan winch ropes too.

The extent of your proposed winching activity will dictate how much of the above you need. It will vary from very little if you are going only to pull a boat out of the water once per weekend, to virtually the whole kit if you are going to be a recovery marshal on an off-road trial or are carrying out logging operations in a forest area. It will all figure in and be part of your eventual choice of winch – if you decide your really need one.

Slope and line pull. Knowledge of your required line pull in various conditions is necessary as the final consideration before choosing a winch.

1. Level ground. For recovering vehicles – or any wheeled object with reasonably large wheels – the pull required to move it varies according to the surface on which it is standing. The pull, as an approximate proportion of its weight, is:

Hard road – 5%
Grass – 15%
Hard/soft wet sand, gravel – 15-20%
Soft dry sand – 25-30%
Shallow mud – 33%
Bog, marsh, clay – 50%.

Thus if the vehicle to be winched is a part-laden Discovery with a total weight of 2300kg (5060 lb), the line pull to get it out of shallow mud will be just under 759kg (1700 lb).

2. Sloping ground. If the ground you are winching up is sloping you must add an increment to account for this. This is very simply calculated as the slope in degrees, divided by 60, times the total load of the vehicle being towed. Thus going up a 15° slope with the Discovery above would add 15/60 = 1/4 of its 2300kg total weight to the line pull. So in this example we have:

Terrain component = 759kg
Slope – 1/4 of 2300 = 575kg
So total pull is 1334kg (2935 lb).

Note that the slope component is surprisingly high – and this is assuming an even slope. In real life, of course, ground is uneven and a small local obstacle like a rock or a tree root can put the immediate local slope up to 30 or 40°. Note also that it is the heaviest ground, eg clay, that is likely to get you stuck and in this case the terrain component goes up to 1150 kg and the whole total to 1725 kg.

Margins. Comfortable margins and, probably even more important, a knowledge of how the winch works and whether your usage is to be intermittent or continuous should then be applied in establishing your choice of equipment. Electric winches being hard-working, high revving, hot-running devices that also require the vehicle engine to be running fast are obviously less suited to continuous work than, say a capstan winch running at engine idle speed. Their relative lightness and cheapness, however, would win the day where the occasional winching of a boat or caravan is concerned.

Always use thick leather gloves when handling winch cables. A split pulley is an invaluable 'carry always' accessory to double or direct pull.

Winch cable (above) looped through a split pulley block (right) and back to vehicle bumper doubles effective pull of the winch – 8500 lb Husky is shown in this mode above (see diagram next spread). Pulley can also be used for indirect pull – photo next page.

Photo shows indirect pull electrical winching with cable through a split pulley block – see facing page. Although itself winch-equipped, the stuck vehicle (left) is being winched up a slippery slope by a recovery vehicle (right). Note use of strap to preclude damage to tree bark and that the winching vehicle is square-on to the direction of initial pull.

Winching is a potentially dangerous procedure. But the danger can be eliminated by care and operator knowledge. Take your time. Take your time.

Safety first. Whilst a clichéd paragraph heading like this will not always do its job, the reminder is nonetheless very necessary since winching is laden with the possibility of accidents if real care is not taken. The good news, however, is that you, as operator, are in charge and there is seldom if ever any rush. Rest assured that thinking ahead, thinking things through, keeping people away from tow ropes and winch ropes, observing the few rules outlined here and reading the instruction book thoroughly WILL result in safe winching.

Breaking cables. Breaking cables and ropes are extremely hazardous. Never step over or get near to a cable under tension and ensure no-one is close to it when winching is in progress. Wire cables as used on drum winches flail laterally when they break so are particularly dangerous.

Control cable safety. Be particularly careful that electrical cables going to the control unit handset are kept well clear of the winch wire. Caught up in the winch, a short circuit could make the winch unstoppable without disconnecting the wire.

Radio control. Control cable safety is taken care of if a radio control is used. It also enables the user to get closer to the job when precision is required.

Directing – or doubling – the pull. Unlike the bulk and weight of ground anchors, split pulley blocks (photo, previous spread) are light and small and worth carrying at all times with extra straps and ropes. Be sure its rating is compatible with your winch. They are invaluable as a means of producing an indirect pull (facing photo) and for producing a given pull with half the strain on the winch at half speed (diagram below).

Maintenance, care of cables and ropes. Drum-winch cables should spool onto the drum evenly and will do so if the pull is at the correct angle. This is very important since the spooled cable is under enormous pressure as the winching cable is laid over it. If there are signs of it not spooling-on evenly, stop the winching, pay out the cable and spool back onto the drum guiding it by (gloved) hands. Inspect and clean cables and ropes regularly. Excessive mud will get into the strands or fibres and cause damage. Extend the cable to full length and check in detail for damage. Check gearbox oil levels and check for the presence of hydraulic leaks regularly.

Towing attachments – vehicle recovery. As with towed recovery, the towing attachments on vehicles being recovered must be sound and purpose-built. Attach cables using D-shackles tightened and then backed-off half a turn. NEVER attach cables to axles or steering rods.

Training and practice. Fully absorb the winch instructions, be familiar with the equipment and take time to train and practise before real-life use.

Practise to gain complete familiarity with your equipment before using it on real situations.

Pulley doubles winch max pull for moving obstacles: vehicle stationary, object dragged

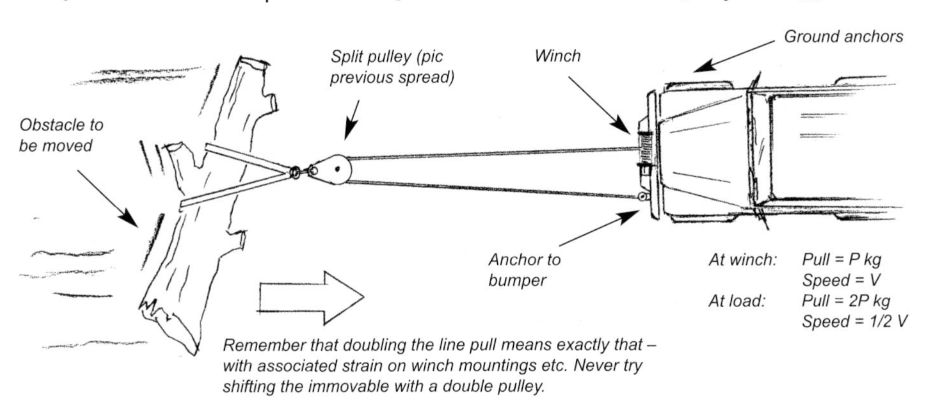

Pulley increases the pull in self-recovery; object stays, vehicle moves

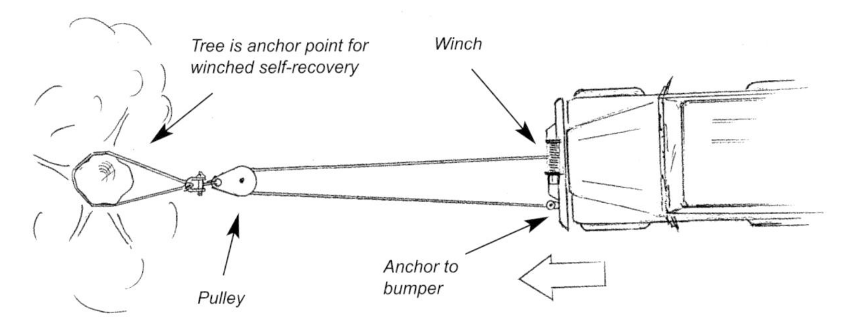

Section 6

Advanced driving

6.1 Non-synchro gearboxes

Main gearbox

Synchromesh? Er ... what?R umbling into the twenty-first century you could be forgiven for taking synchromesh for granted so please don't feel that you would lose credibility by reading what synchro actually does and why it hasn't always been there. If you drive a Series 1 or 2 Land Rover, an old 4x4 truck or any number of other older or commercial vehicles, you may have a gearbox that is not all-synchromesh.

Obviously a gearbox contains wheels and shafts going at different speeds. 'Changing gear' entails, in effect, sliding one gear or shaft into mesh with another. Unless they are going at compatible speeds there will be a 'grinding of the gears' or a huge and solid 'clonk' when the move is made.

Synchromesh is now so widespread you may have to check what it means! Classic outback vehicles – Series 2 Land Rovers, Bedfords have some non-synchro gears.

What it is. The frictional drag created by the outside of a male cone on one shaft engaging with the inside of a female cone on another co-axial shaft is a means of synchronising their speeds. That is what synchromesh does to one shaft or 'gear' before it actually engages with another.

Although the idea is decades old, synchro was once only fitted to passenger car gearboxes and then usually only the upper two or three gears. So first gear, and maybe second too, was non-synchro and virtually all trucks or working vehicles had no synchro on any gear. Cost was the main reason for keeping synchro out of a lot of gearboxes but all cars now have all-synchro on manual gearboxes and most trucks do too.

No synchro; what to do. If there is no synchro on a gear (or any gear) in a gearbox you should change gear into that ratio in a different way. To most people who took their driving test on a modern car, changing gear consists of dipping the clutch and moving the gear lever from one position to another. What actually happens (in the gearbox) is that as you move the lever the 'synchro cones' touch, synchronise the speed of the approaching gear wheels or dog-clutches, and then, with the last part of the gear lever movement, the gears are engaged. As you may have already found, even on a synchro box, you can often get a smoother take-up of power by adjusting the throttle a little bit as you engage the next gear to 'cushion the change'.

If you are going down from 3rd to 2nd, for example, blip the throttle slightly to raise the revs while the gear lever is passing neutral. Going up, make sure the engine revs do die off a bit going from 2nd to 3rd. That way, when you let the clutch in again the engine speed will better match the road speed and you will avoid the lurch and transmission snatch that otherwise occurs.

No problem these days. Synchromesh is brilliantly effective in modern manual transmissions that lightning-quick gear changes can normally be made with no danger of crunching the gears.

Double de-clutching. In a non-synchro box, without the speed synchronisation of the gear wheels going on, there is still quite a bit we can do with the throttle and clutch to ensure a smooth gear change. It is called 'double de-clutching' and, as its name indicates, it involves de-clutching twice with some rpm adjustment in between with the throttle. It will sound complicated to describe but, like riding a bicycle, after some initial concentration it becomes far easier to do than to describe.

It can be summarised as spending a fraction of a second in neutral with the clutch up (ie engaged), before dipping the clutch again and moving the gear lever on to the gear you are about to select. So, specifically:

- ***Double de-clutch – down-change.*** This is the procedure for a down-change on a no-synchro gearbox, say 3rd to 2nd:

Clutch	Throttle	Gear lever
Dip –	M	ove to neutral
Up B	OOST REVS –	
Dip –	M	ove, 3rd to 2nd
Up R	esume drive –	

You will get to know the amount by which the throttle needs to be boosted but, if you think about it, you must select the kind of engine revs that would apply at that road speed in the gear you are about to select. Going from 2nd to 1st at any but the very slowest road speed you will find you have to boost the throttle a surprising amount; only do this at about walking speed.

If you don't double de-clutch on a down-change into a non-synchro gear you will often get a dreadful grinding of gears and the gear may not engage at all. There have been examples of unskilled off-road drivers being so put off by this that they will stall in 2nd gear rather than face trying to engage 1st gear on the move.

• ***Double de-clutch – up-change.*** This is the procedure for an up-change on a gearbox with no synchro, say 1st to 2nd:

Clutch	Throttle	Gear lever
Dip	–	Move to neutral
Up	FOOT OFF	–
Dip	–	Move, 1st to 2nd
Up	Resume drive	–

If you don't double de-clutch on an up-change you will 'just' get a heavy clonk when the gear goes in. This equates to a small sledge-hammer being applied to the transmission; don't let it happen!

Practise – off-road too. Practise the procedure first with the vehicle stationary in your driveway without the engine even running, just to get familiar with the sequence. Then practise on quiet roads so that you get to know the best speeds and engine rpm boosts suited to change-downs.

Change-ups will be easier. Practise up- and down-changes until a smooth silent change can be made into all gears – including first. The whole thing is tied up with road and engine speeds and vehicle-speed decay during the time spent in neutral. This latter, and therefore the whole feel of the gear change, will thus differ on-road compared to when on grass, rough terrain or off-road.

The sort of on-road to off-road adjustments to technique to expect would be:

• Down-changes – a little less rev boost.
• Up-changes – a little less rev drop.

Touching third ... . A trick worth knowing, applicable, for example to old Series 2 Land Rovers, is how to avoid that dreadful grinding of gears when engaging a gear to move off from stationary. When moving off get into the habit of 'touching third' before engaging first or reverse. Dip the clutch in the normal way, touch the gear lever into third gear (the synchro cones on that gear will calm things in the gearbox) and then, when you engage first or reverse the gear will go in quietly without any noise.

Ex-military trucks like this one, a natural choice for expeditions, are remarkably agile. But two or more non-synchromesh gears in the gearbox calls for driver agility too. It is well worth getting it right.

This is a particularly valuable tip when doing any backing and filling – three- or four-point turns getting out of tight spaces. Each time you go from 1st to reverse, or vice versa, touch third gear to still the shafts.

The procedure will apply to any vehicle where you have synchro on an upper gear ratio like third or top and no synchromesh on first or reverse.

Double de-clutching is hard to describe, far easier to do. Remember revs adjustments take place with gear lever in neutral and clutch pedal up. Practise static, with dead engine, first.

Transfer gearbox

As we have seen (p.2.42) although one or two manufacturers are at last addressing the issue, it is rare to get synchro on a transfer box so range changes, in normal 'handbook conditions', have to be made with the vehicle stationary. But see next two spreads.

6.2 Range change on the move – manual gearbox

On-the-move range change – the need

Low to high change – when you need it. There are times when it is very useful – essential even – to be able to start in low range and, while still moving, continue in high – typically, towing a heavy trailer on hard roads (Section 4.1), towing a trailer off-road (Section 6.5) or just starting the vehicle in marginal traction conditions such as soft sand or mud where it would be risky, once moving, to stop in order to re-select high range – photo opposite.

The problems. Few manufacturers have designed their drivelines to enable an on-the-move range changes to be executed easily – or at all. Push-button range change selection often has an electronic lockout built in to actually prevent – unhelpfully – an on-the-move change. Where the change is by lever, synchro in the transfer box would make life a lot easier but is provided on few. The procedure opposite, however, can – with a sensitive driver – work without synchro in the transfer gearbox.

Low range is not just extra-low gearing. It overlaps high range letting you choose best gearbox span. Changing from low to high on the move is well worth learning.

Speeds in the gears. If you study your gear ratios data – and the diagram below – you will see that there is inevitably an overlap between low range and high range – for example 4th or 5th gear low is roughly equivalent to 2nd gear high so that a given piece of ground could be covered equally well in either and at roughly the same engine rpm. Often, where there is a choice, being in low range rather than the high will give you the ability to tackle sudden track deteriorations such as road washouts or obstacles, without having to carry out a range change. So being in low range – and wanting the capability to move to high easily – is a fairly normal scenario. (See also 'Low range – when and how', Section 3.2.)

On-the-move range change – manual

Low/high change – what gear, speed? A change across from low to high is usually possible on vehicles having a lever range change with or without synchro in the transfer box. In practice it is best to get the vehicle properly moving first – say 25-30mph in low range. That way, momentum will keep you going whilst you execute the change. Before contemplating a change from low range to high you should also be sure that conditions are suitable for sustained travel in high range since to change back again from high to low range you'll usually have to stop.

No clunks or grinding gears please. The procedure outlined here should only be done if you can *execute it without heavy clonks or grinding gears in the transmission.* It is a way of getting round the absence of synchro on most

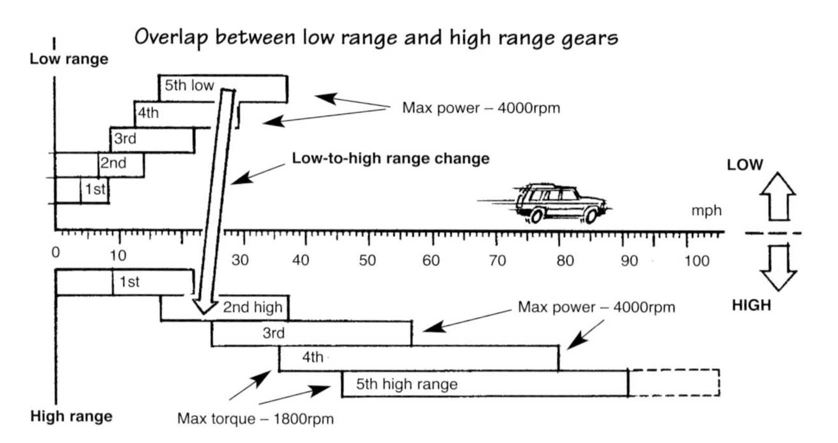

Bars represent speed in that gear between max torque (c.1800rpm) and max power (c. 4000rpm). Land Rover Tdi diesel engine shown but values for many engines are similar. Best change point for low to high on the move is 25-30mph – 5th low to 2nd high. Don't just move the transfer lever on its own.

transfer boxes. Currently, the Mercedes G-Wagen and one or two of the more recent Land Rovers (Discovery and Range Rover) are some of the few cleared by the manufacturer for on-the-move (synchro) transfer ratio change.

Procedure: manual gearbox – 5th low to 2nd high on the move. With no transfer box synchro, try this (diagram right):

1. In low range, accelerate through the gears to 25-30mph.

2. With the main gear lever still in 5th, depress the clutch and move the transfer lever into neutral. (Note, this will need a short, sharp action with a definite halt at the neutral position; don't let it go through to high yet.) Keep the clutch depressed. Then move the main gear lever from 5th into 2nd gear. Main gearbox synchro will make this quiet.

3. Clutch foot up then down again – performing a kind of double-de-clutch operation – *then* move the transfer lever from neutral to 'H'.

4. As the engine was losing rpm whilst you moved the transfer lever, you will need a blip of throttle to raise engine revs to the right level for 2nd gear, high range at 25mph. (since vehicle speed will have dropped to that from the 25-30mph at 1.) Gently up with the clutch pedal and accelerate away.

Push-button range change ... ?. With one or two exceptions – see Discovery next spread – none of the above is usually possible with a push-button range change since there are often electrical inhibits and no neutral position between low and high is selectable.

High to low on the move ... ? This can be done under certain conditions to demonstrate driving skill but there is little practical application. Deteriorating heavy going is when you might need this change and here the time taken to execute it will be enough for the vehicle's speed to have decayed to nothing. Make life easy; change to low range when stationary. Discovery and Range Rover however, have a synchro transfer box and are cleared for hi-to-lo changes on manual.

Low to high range on the move – manual

Set up: *Manual transmission, no transfer-box synchro, lever range change, with neutral.*

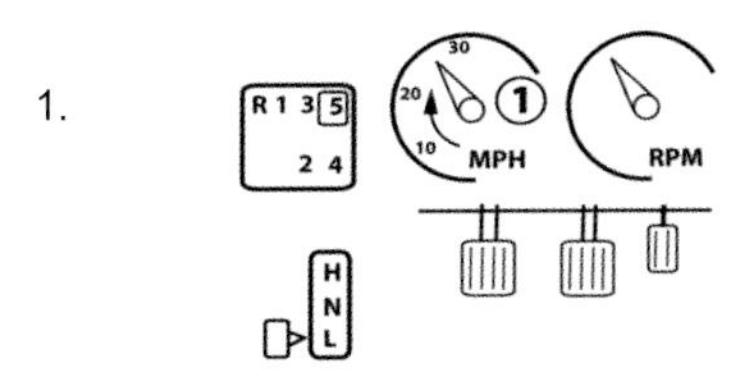

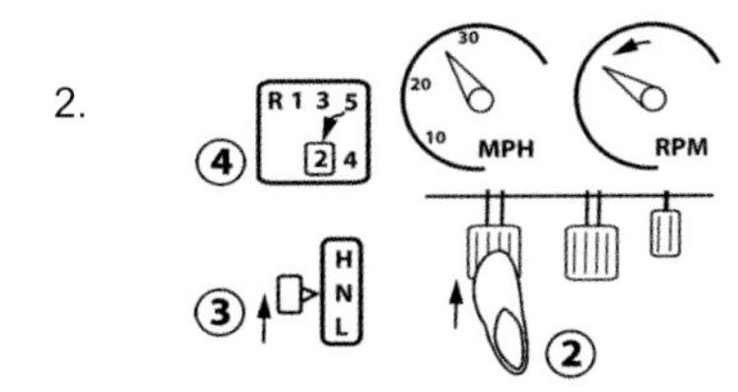

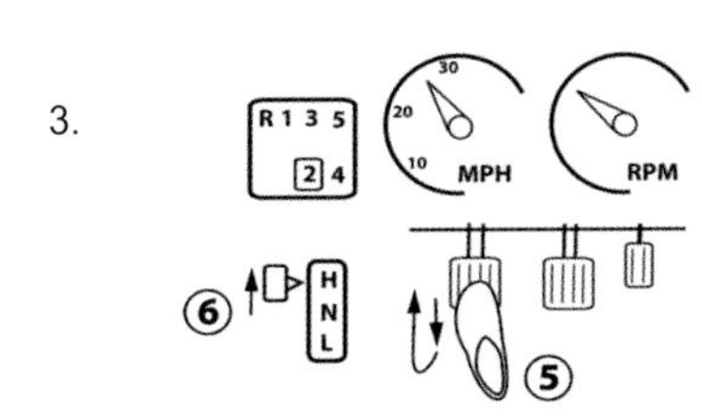

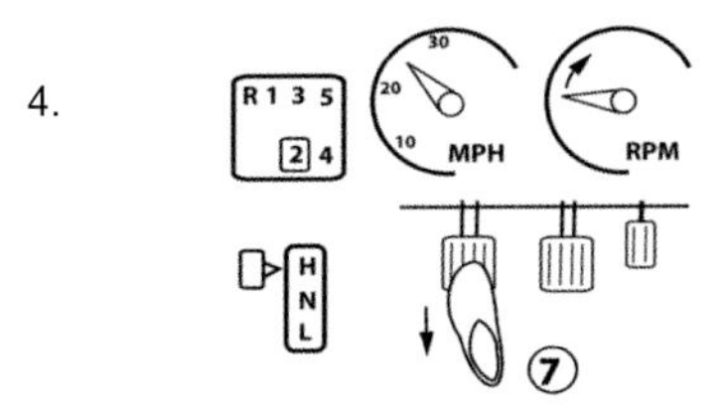

Low to high – do it from 30 mph in 4th/5th low. Complex to read but simple to do. Practise it first on hard roads, then off-road where speed decay will be different.

Classic situation needing a low-to-high range change on the move – softish sand, hard to start in but which, once moving, you can take in high range. More usual example is heavy trailer towing – hill starts or moving off from traffic lights. Get it going in low range, then change to high.

6.3 Range change on the move – automatic gearbox

A large-throw transfer box lever makes an on-the-move range change easier since the all-important neutral is easier to locate. Sadly, Jeep's Grand Cherokee now has switch selection with a neutral only available (but usefully) for towing.

Do use low range in auto

Don't overheat the transmission. First a reminder. Just because it will often work, don't be tempted to use high range in auto transmissions in conditions that demand low range (see p 2.45). Excessive torque converter slip can cause serious overheating of the transmission fluid. Once in low range, you will need to go back to high range eventually, and doing it on the move can be very useful – at times essential. So ...

Low to high – moving (auto)

Just because automatic transmission is so accommodating, don't omit to use the low range gears. Using high range inappropriately will overheat transmission.

Generic method. Using the procedures shown here this is possible – but check, if necessary, with the vehicle manufacturer that there are not special design features making it inadvisable with your particular vehicle.

Where an electric button/switch selection is involved, speed sensors may prevent range change unless the vehicle is stationary and the main gear selector is in neutral. However, since there are a number of different techniques that can effect an on-the-move range change with an automatic transmission, first some general principles:

- Get up to 25-30mph in the low range.
- Get the main transmission lever into 'N' before moving the transfer lever/button.
- With or without synchro on the transfer box, match the rpm to the road speed and gear before the final move.

Lever range change, with a neutral. So, following the diagram (below):

1. Accelerate to 25-30mph in low.
2. Main lever to 'N', then range to 'N'.
3. Allow rpm to drop.
4. Match rpm to road speed. Range lever to 'H', then main lever to 'D'. Drive on.

Low to high range on the move – auto

Set up: *Automatic transmission, lever range change, with a neutral position*

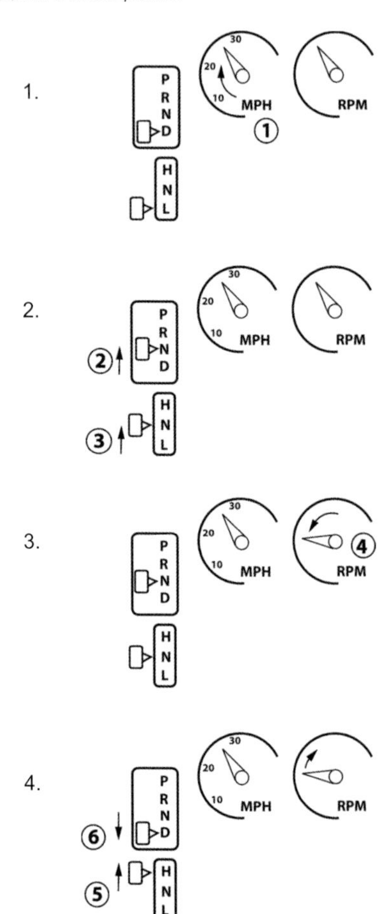

Button/switch range change, no neutral. When the range change of the transfer gears is selected electrically via a button or switch there is often an inhibit built into the system that precludes execution until the vehicle is stationary.

But the value of an on-the-move change is at last being recognised by some manufacturers – Land Rover were among the first, on the Discovery 3 and Range Rover in 2005, to follow the Mercedes G-Wagen's 25 year lead in providing synchro on the transfer gearbox.

Manufacturer's OK. The procedure for the Discovery 3, for example, is shown on the right.

1. Accelerate to 25-30mph in low range though the system will allow changes at up to nearly 40 mph.

2. Main transmission lever to 'N'.

3. Allow rpm to drop. Match rpm, move transfer gear lever to 'H'.

4. Move main transmission lever to 'D'. Drive on in high range.

Refreshingly, this procedure is not only approved by the manufacturer but covered in detail in the driver's handbook for both the automatic and manual transmission.

High to low on the move. Less frequently required but still useful – and applicable to the case when difficult terrain ahead looms – the drivelines on the G-Wagen, Discovery and Range Rover enable a change from high to low range gears to be made without stopping.

This is less often needed in day to day off-road operation – since in deteriorating going the vehicle's speed will decay so quickly while the change sequence is undertaken that a stationary engagement is rarely that much of an inconvenience. It is nevertheless a valuable facility to have at the driver's disposal.

High to low, no synchro. Without synchro on the transfer gears this high to low change has usually to be made at under five mph – main gear selector to neutral first, boost engine rpm, then move the range change lever or switch (in the absence of an electric lockout) to low.

Low to high range on the move – auto

Set up: *Automatic transmission, transfer-box synchro, button range change, no neutral.*

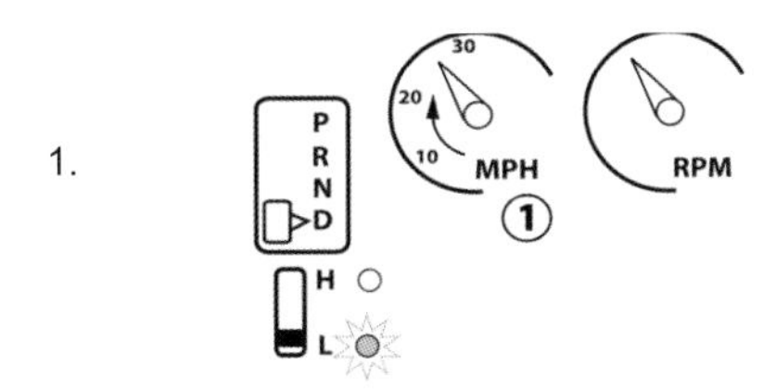

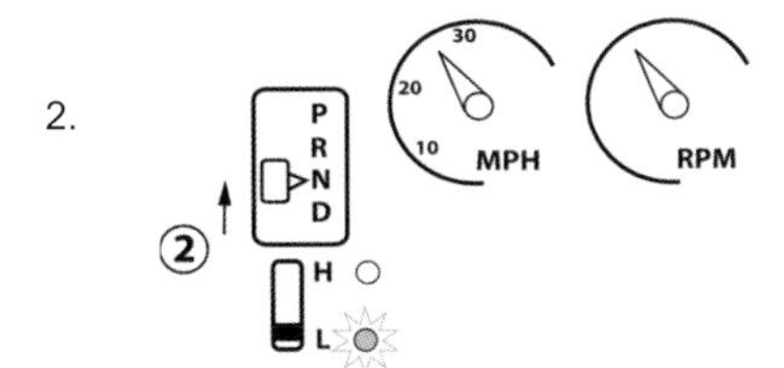

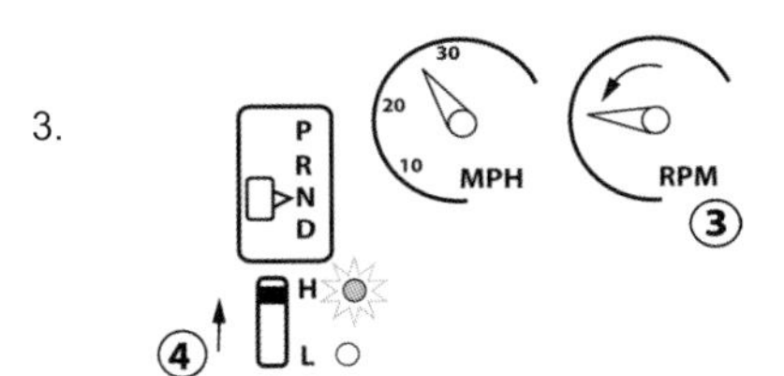

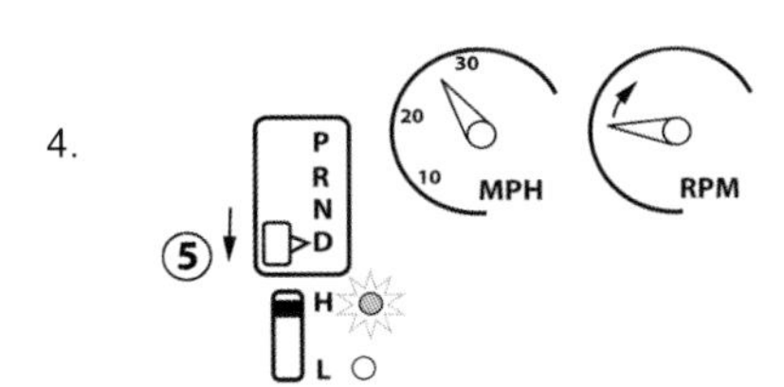

Unlike manual transmission, high to low with auto can – occasionally – be a useful technique in certain cases.

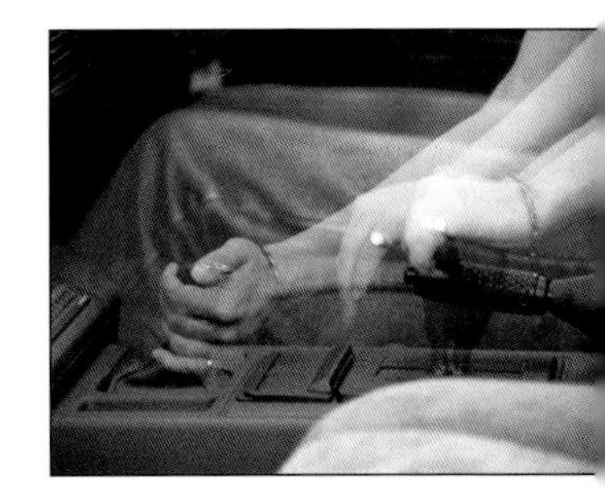

Range change, mobile. It is definitely worth practise before using this capability in real conditions – confidence is all! Where a transfer lever, as opposed to a switch or button is involved, a short, crisp movement is usually required and the tendency to overshoot without stopping in neutral must be avoided.

6.4 Down-slopes

Engine braking

Engine braking recommended...but. Read this section after reading Section 4.5. Engine braking is the safe way to keep speed in check – especially on steep off-road slopes. On long hills – classically, on-road Alpine pass descents – use engine braking to avoid overheating the brakes. Even today's disc brakes can suffer from a degree of 'fade' (reduced efficiency) when they get very hot. All this is a well accepted part of our armoury of safe driving techniques.

Old wives' tales and delicate braking. But it is also something of a relic of the days of poor brakes. Indeed, on a two-wheel drive car, engine braking derives retardation through only one pair of wheels on the driven axle whilst sensitive and delicate use of the foot brake uses all four – clearly better. The same retardation spread between four wheels instead of two reduces the risk of wheel locking. (ABS? Read on … .)

Just as excessive braking can cause wheel slide, so can excessive engine braking – 1st gear low range on a very steep, long, slippery slope. Remember cadence braking.

There is thus a place for sensitive and delicate braking in many situations, certainly the short off-road ones, in which we have learned to leave the brakes alone. ABS and cadence braking (see Section 3.3, 'Gentle right foot') are especially relevant here. What we are really trying to avoid is sliding wheels – whatever their cause (that diagram, p.3.6).

Bedrock tenets. Engine braking (especially on a 4x4) and readiness to use cadence braking are bedrock tenets of safe descent of steep slippery off-road slopes and must never be forgotten.

ABS, HDC, DAC, etc, etc. But now there is more. There is ABS to do the cadence braking for you should it be required – but be certain whether your system is cleared for off-road use. And we are starting to see ingenious, logic-controlled systems emerge that will automate it further. If you have one of the iterations of automated steep-down-slope auto pilots such as Land Rover's Hill Descent Control (HDC) or Toyota's Downhill Assist Control (DAC) or Joe Blogg's lookalike three-letter-acronym system, then these will get you safely down extreme descents. Land Rover pioneered the concept with HDC which keeps the vehicle at or below a target slow descent speed by use of various sensors and the ABS braking.

Emergency down-slope sequence

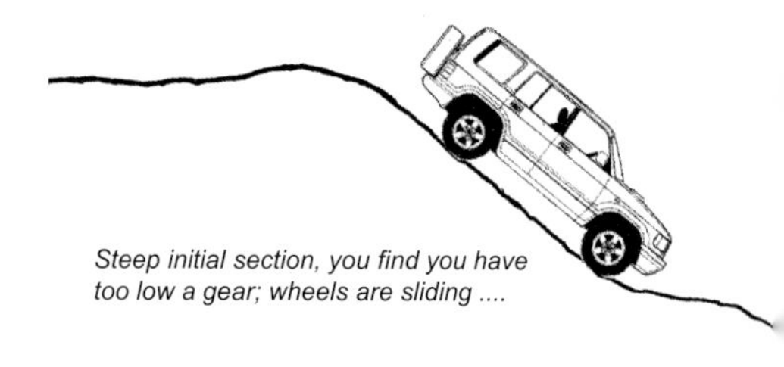

Some may say, though, that if you're smart enough to recognise a situation demanding descent control then you'll not need it anyway: just use cadence-braking.

But there will be an experience level where knowing is one thing and doing is another and an automated, flexible concept like HDC could be a comforting fall-back.

Beware, however, of over-cautious systems like the recent Jeep Grand Cherokee which selects an absurdly slow downhill speed that could itself provoke sliding on a slippery down-slope.

Manual procedures

Beware sliding wheels. If you have selectable four-wheel drive ('Type 1' on page 2.11) then you must, of course, be in 4x4 before tackling any really steep down-slopes. With or without automated descent control, however, you must still be aware of the risk of selecting too low a gear on steep and slippery slopes. Just as excessive use of the brakes can cause lock-up and discontinuity of rolling contact between the wheels and the ground (diagram p.3.6), so tackling a really steep slippery slope using 1st gear low range can sometimes amount to excessive engine braking and also result in wheel slide.

Accelerate. Be ready to use the accelerator. Or it will likely be better to use a higher gear such as 2nd – even 3rd

... add throttle. Delicate application of brake; quit at the first suspicion of lock-up.

If, in gear, wheels just cannot keep up with speed increase, de-clutch and use cadence braking. Keep front wheels pointing straight down slope.

Select a higher gear once the problem is over, boost the revs as you engage clutch and resume engine braking.

A matter of judgement. If it is this steep – and this long – you want retardation but too low a gear when it is slippery or loose will give you slide. 2nd low, rather than 1st, would be best if it were muddy earth. In the special case of this high sand dune you need to go higher still – 3rd or 4th low or even 1st high range – to prevent the vehicle nosing into the sand. (In this context see also Glossary 'Castor angle', and 'Steering feel', Section 9.1.)

sometimes. (See photo opposite.)

What to do. Firstly remember that some ABS systems do not work properly off-road or the system may have auto-disabled when you select 4x4. There are two classic cases of extreme down-slope slide to consider – (which off-road-capable ABS brakes will make very much simpler):

1. Almost the right gear, brake assist. Take the case of an initially steep, long slippery down-slope with a loose surface. You judge that 1st low would result in slide and that 2nd low is appropriate. But the initial section is so steep that the vehicle gains speed faster than you anticipated. Clearly it is inadvisable to attempt to change down at this critical stage (even an automatic will not always change down to 1st in these conditions), so a gentle and intermittent use of the brake pedal – gentle cadence braking (or ABS) – can be used to slow to the limits of the available grip. Don't let the wheels lock; and if they do, release the brakes altogether, immediately.

2. Wrong gear, braking takeover. Take the same steep, long, slippery down-slope. Starting down it in 1st gear low box may result in wheel slide because in such a low gear – even with the engine revving hard – the wheels will not be able to turn fast enough to maintain rolling contact with the ground. You realise too late that you have got the wrong gear so, after using all the throttle you can, you must undertake a rescue operation. De-clutch so that the wheels can regain rolling contact with the ground, then with great sensitivity carry out cadence braking – rapid gentle jabs at the brake pedal that never permit the wheels to lock but which give you the best retardation the circumstances allow. This is a rare scenario but keep it in the back of your mind rather than slide out of control, throttle wide, in 1st.

Emergency procedure: really sensitive use of the brakes, releasing them the instant they lock the wheels – or cadence braking.

6.5 Off-road towing

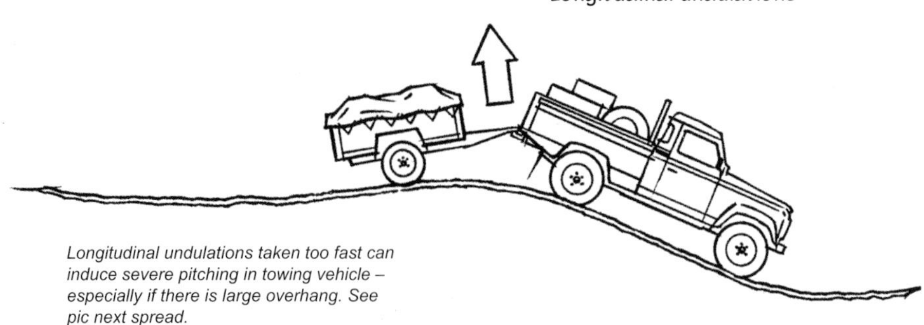

Longitudinal undulations taken too fast can induce severe pitching in towing vehicle – especially if there is large overhang. See pic next spread.

Potential problems

Heavy trailer off-road – or light trailer driven briskly – will feed back considerable inertia loads to tug.

Greater trailer feedback. (Read Section 4.1, 'Towing – on-road', first, noting the typical maximum off-road towing weights shown in the table.) Using trailers off-road requires even greater anticipation and care. Feedback effect to the towing vehicle is much more noticeable than on hard road. Inertia fed into the trailer by the tug has to be arrested at every change in direction. For example, traversing track undulations too fast can cause interactive responses between vehicle and trailer. Specifically, the trailer can cause considerable pitch in the towing vehicle as it swoops into and out of a dip. This can be bad enough in extreme cases to lift the rear end of the vehicle momentarily off the ground, especially if there is a long tail overhang in the towing vehicle (see picture, next spread. p.6.13).

Trailer inertia – drag and push. Off-road trailer drag over uneven ground and 'trailer-push' down steep slopes will be more pronounced – with braking correspondingly

Gently does it. Bulky body, light construction, small wheels and minimal underbody clearance make this trailer far less capable off-road than the tug.

High-density industrial plant trailers need treating with more than expected care off-road – mainly due to very high inertia, feedback to the tug and limitations of trailer suspension. Often wheels are small and the unit is designed for simple site mobility, not for extended off-road towing.

more difficult and liable, in extreme cases, to provoke the trailer to try to overtake the vehicle in a form of jack-knifing.

Lateral roll. Off-road there is also a surprising susceptibility to lateral roll by the trailer. Trailer suspension is seldom damped sufficiently in the laden condition compared to that of the towing vehicle, often compounded by a degree of roll-steer due to crude axle location geometry on the trailer. Lateral roll over an uneven track which the tug suspension will cope with easily can result in alarming roll angles on the trailer – sometimes resulting in capsizing. (See next spread, revolving tow hooks.)

Centre of gravity position vital. This background and the aspects of trailer dynamics, covered at Section 4.1, emphasise the vital importance of low, and forward centre of gravity (giving appropriate nose-weight) when off-road towing. Remember to take twice the trailer nose-weight out of the available vehicle payload.

Beware especially of under-damped lateral roll of trailer on poor tracks.

Trailer push under braking

Trailer influence is especially noticeable on steep slippery down-slopes – adversely affected rear wheel adhesion and, under braking, promoting a tendency to jack-knife. Accelerate out of it.

Keep trailer light compared to the tug – well done here, albeit trailer load of luggage and camping gear will be high density. Small wheels and tyres at high pressure on trailer will put it at disadvantage on softer going and the prodigious traction of the Unimog may be needed. Compare this with the desert optimised combination shown opposite. Unimog's short rear overhang is good. Its long wheelbase compared with the trailer towing arm length will make reversing difficult.

Checks and procedures

Trailers can obviate vehicle overload in expeditions. Large tyres enhance flotation. Manpower is needed when trailer bogs; solo trips with heavy trailers (opposite) not recommended.

Overload solution: provisos. For overlanding expeditions, use of a really robust trailer can be quite an elegant solution to the problem of having a payload requirement in excess of that shown as the maximum for your vehicle on its own. Spreading the load over six wheels is better than the unacceptable alternative of overloading the vehicle's four. The prolonged stress of an overland trip is perhaps an extreme case but it encapsulates the potential problems of all off-road towing so is worth examining. Four provisos should be remembered for sustained off-road trailer operation:

1. Weight. Minimise the weight of the trailer and vehicle load to give the vehicle the best working conditions off-road – see photo caption page 4.2. An ex-military 750kg trailer with overrun brakes, loaded to no more than 500kg gross provides a sensible margin of strength and is in roughly the right category for a medium 4x4 towing vehicle – photo facing page.

2. Tyres. The same rationale mentioned earlier about big wheels applies to trailers and is arguably even more important since the trailer wheels are following in ground already cut up by the towing vehicle. Trailer axle loads of the order indicated above will enable trailer tyre pressures to be lower (see Section 8.2) than those of the tug, enhancing flotation in the wake of the towing vehicle. Note that off-road a trailer needs the best combination of low rolling resistance and flotation (mainly the latter), not traction, so in absolute terms its tyre requirements will be unique.

However, in practice it is sensible to use the same wheels and tyres on the trailer as you have fitted to the towing vehicle; this is right functionally and has the additional advantage that the same spare wheel will fit trailer and towing vehicle. – see upper picture on facing page

3. Personnel. There will be times, off-road and overlanding, when the trailer has to be detached and manhandled. It will be necessary to have at least two people to do this; three or four will be better still.

4. Towing hitch. Every manufacturer will have their own approach to towing problems and accessories. The standard 50 mm ball hitch is widely used in the UK and Europe but on Land Rover products, for example, it is suitable for a maximum gross trailer weight of 1000kg off-road. The European specification ball hitch (Part no RTC9565) is stronger than the standard UK item. Note also the ratings of the 2-bolt and 4-bolt Land Rover Parts combined ball/pin hitches shown at p.4.6. Because of problems of trailer lateral stability in extreme off-road conditions as noted on the previous spread, be sure your trailer has an EC-standard hitch that can rotate at the trailer since a trailer that has rolled would not then tip the towing vehicle.

Low range start. As with heavy trailers on hard roads (see Section 4.1) there will be many occasions off-road when it will make for a smoother start to move off in low range 2nd gear, continue up the low ratio gears and change into high range on the move using the techniques outlined in Sections 6.2 and 6.3. For off-road towing, low range is sometimes the better choice to stay in.

Pay meticulous attention to condition of towing hitch, bolts and attachment areas. Starting in low range with an on-the-move change to high ratio is useful off-road.

Classic demonstrations. The film sequence of the dune descent (above) showed the (very heavy) fuel trailer pitching forward over the dune edge, compressing the tug springs and then the rebound lifted the tug back wheels almost off the ground.

Note (right) the tug is bogged and on sand ladders.The picture shows the benefits of trailer tyres being larger than those of the towing vehicle and thus able to run on lower pressures; better flotation, less sinkage, less drag. Caution, however: low trailer tyre pressures can cause weaving at speed. Trailer here is deliberately and beneficially running at well under rated payload.

Section 7

Expedition basics

7.1 The call of the wild

Freeing the spirit

Examining the operating envelope. The pace of everyday life often constrains us to under-utilise what we have – be it our own skills, the potential of our hobbies or the potential of our four-wheel drive vehicle. Our early plans, made at the time of purchase, may not have been realised and we may be left with a gnawing urge to use more of the latent capability of our 4x4, to use it for some of the more adventurous projects for which we bought it.

With a machine of such potential in your possession it would perhaps be the more unusual not to want to stretch its operating envelope. Without any doubt at all, there is little to compare with the feeling of being in the world's wilder places with a well-equipped and well-trained expedition savouring the space, the beauty, the feeling of being self-sufficient.

'Expeditions' – a day in the hills or a major overseas project – hugely enhance enjoyment of your vehicle. But you have just stepped into careful-planning territory.

Entrepreneurs too. Whilst this Section is inevitably aimed, primarily, at private recreational use it is hoped that it will also be of interest to commercial operators, perhaps in tourist-related or leisure pursuits, where operation of a vehicle in complete safety away from its home territory may form part of a package or proposal.

Basics only. Note, right from the start, however, that the whole of Section 7 is entitled 'Expedition basics' and it claims to be no more than that. An 'expedition' can be a half-day trip to the hills or a major three-month overseas project. They will have in common the importance of infallible preparation – an examination of all the 'what-if?' situations – but there will be in the major projects less margin for error and the need for very precise logistic control.

This Section is an introduction to the subject and aims to help you prepare to broaden your enjoyment of your off-roader in relatively short trips. More demanding projects including the planning of overseas expeditions that may include a scientific project are covered in depth in the book *Vehicle-dependent Expedition Guide*, also published by Desert Winds. The book also contains considerable extra detail on vehicle preparation, modifications, navigation, equipment, communications, clothing and emergency procedures.

One step at a time. Start with off-road tuition, then practise on your own. Get completely comfortable with your own and your vehicle's limitations.

Day trip or major expedition?

The methodical approach – again. We are not all able to respond unquestioningly to the call of the wild since time, cost and other responsibilities will influence where we are able to go. What is certain, however, is the importance of how we tackle what we propose to do, however 'big' or 'small' it may be. As has been observed about that most unforgiving of all environments, the Sahara desert, you can die pinned under a capsized motorcycle behind a knoll a kilometre from the track just as easily as if you did the same thing 500 kilometres farther out in the desert.

A sombre example that nevertheless makes the point well regarding the differences between everyday on-road operations where the swish of passing traffic is your assurance of some help, and being only a few miles up a mountain track with an escalating problem on your hands.

One step at a time equals confidence. Although a gentle progression up the scale of challenge is the natural way to do things, the importance of taking things a step at a time cannot too strongly be emphasised here. Going hand in hand with this – importantly and almost inevitably – will be the growth in your confidence. Confidence begets early

Safely operated, a 4x4 epitomises – and realises – the need to seek the earth's wild places. Allow time. Never be in a hurry, Enjoyable as a 4x4 is to drive, don't turn your journey into a mile-eating marathon.

recognition of, thus avoidance of, and measured response to ... problems. Confidence – well-founded confidence, not over-confidence or cockiness – further begets the ability, comfortably, to say 'no' and turn back before getting into trouble.

Savour but beware the feeling of amazement and invincibility you may have experienced on your first competent off-road demonstration of your (or your dealer's) off-roader. The feeling of unstoppability is very strong but, as has been emphasised throughout this book, all vehicles have their limitations and in most demonstrations you will have been shown what can be done, not what happens when you get it wrong or the no-go limits. A significant omission.

So, assuming you are just making a start, the answer to the 'day-trip-or-major-expedition' question is clearly 'day-trip' – and then only after planning and training. If you are already thinking that actually it was release you were after and not another career development project, be of good cheer; the training and practice is great fun – putting into effect what you have read in the other Sections of this book. And during training there is someone to help when you get into trouble. You have a mobile phone and there is a hot shower to go home to afterwards.

Planning

The aim. Paradoxically, despite the emphasis on planning, it will not be easy to plan in a 'capability vacuum'. In other words, until you know a little of what you can do individually with your vehicle it will be hard to make a realistic plan for an expedition. It is likely, however, that you may want to explore some unsurfaced tracks you have seen on the map as part of a weekend break you may be taking in the hills. The aim can be as general as this for the time being.

Maps, research – the UK example. Small, 'white-roads' trailing off into areas of close contours or wide-open space on the map, together with a ford or two and linking up – still in the context of UK Ordnance Survey maps – with another 'white' or 'yellow' road away from all the traffic, can have an irresistible appeal. It is worth, at this stage, re-reading the 'Fundamentals' (p.0.12) to remind yourself that ownership of a 4x4 brings considerable responsibilities in regard to environmental care, the obligation to set an example and accept the often complex matter of rights of access. This will be different in all countries and must be individually checked.

Take your projects a step at a time. Confidence and competence will then build on a sound foundation.

The yahoos. The rising population of 4x4 vehicles has regrettably brought with it a small element of irresponsible users and a corresponding tightening of access rules. Awareness of these rules is thus essential.

The UK scenario. Quoting a summary of those rules applicable in the UK will give an idea of what to expect in 'developed' countries – countries with relatively high populations and a legislature steeped in historical evolution. The UK situation is at once knocked slightly off-balance by the fact that a new system of classification was recently introduced which will not be reflected on older copies of maps. The maps to use are the excellent 1:50,000 Ordnance Survey Land Ranger maps, backed where possible, by the 1:25,000 Explorer series.

Know first what you and your vehicle can do – train; see Section 7.2. Be sure about rights of land access for off-road vehicles – sensitive in developed countries.

You will find:

• ***Public footpaths*** – foot only, no vehicles.

• ***Public bridleways*** – foot, cycle & horse, no vehicles.

• ***Byways Open to All Traffic*** (BOATs) – motorised vehicles are permitted.

• ***Road Used as a Public Path*** (RUPPs) – this category ceased to exist when the new category of Right of Way; Restricted Byways, came into being. The change was part of the Countryside and Rights of Way Act 2000, section 47.

• ***Restricted Byways*** – carry a right of way for those on foot, cycle, horse and horse & carriage drivers, but not for mechanically propelled vehicles. They replaced all RUPPs recorded on the Definitive Map & Statement (DM&S). Private vehicles allowed only if access required to premises.

• ***Unclassified County Roads*** (UCRs) – minor roads or lanes, with a sealed surface, others comprising only rough stone. These may be driven by vehicles and are not shown on the DM&S but on the 'List of Streets' also held by the County Council or local Highway authority.

Thus the indication of a road on a map does not automatically confer a right of way. At the Council offices you'll find the Definitive Map & Statement, which will indicate the current legal access status of every recorded public Right of Way in the authority's area. Asking permission from the local landowner, if you can ascertain who it is, will always be a safe alternative. A catch-all and usually temporary TRO (Traffic Regulation Order) can, however, be issued at the discretion of the Highway Authority on given routes in relation to given types of vehicles to cover the case, for example, of local overuse causing damage – a reasonable enough concept despite the further confusion factor.

Navigation. It goes without saying that close attention must be paid to map-reading and navigation in order that you may, at any time, be able to pinpoint your position on the map and know where the next track-junction or other waypoint may be.

Ascertaining heading in a vehicle with a magnetic compass is virtually impossible since the magnetic field in a wagon is strong, variable and virtually uncorrectable for a normally mounted magnetic compass. Use a hand-held compass outside the vehicle and about five metres from it.

'Sat-nav'. Nowhere is satellite navigation more useful than on vehicle expeditions – local or major. GPS (Global Positioning System – a constellation of 24 satellites from which 3D position, speed and heading may be derived) is invariably at the core of all satnavs. Though GPS is central to them, all satnavs are not the same. GPS is just that: a system (albeit amazing) that gives position on a conceptual grid – latitude and longitude or national grid covering the earth. GPS is thus only as good as the maps (also grid-based) it is used with. 'Consumer' satnavs as fitted to many cars are already internally integrated with an on-board digital map. At the other end of the scale, basic marine units may just give lat/long position and leave the user to apply that to his own map.

'Consumer' satnavs, external maps. Most consumer car satnavs do a staggeringly impressive job navigating, turn-by-turn to street destinations or post codes in the country for which they are designed, but are

GPS, the 'satnav' systems utilising it, and satellite imagery such as GoogleEarth are unquestionably the greatest gifts and advances ever to navigation on the planet. Consumer satnavs used in developed countries have built-in maps. In truly remote areas marine units giving latitude and longitude and the ability to establish and navigate to waypoints are needed. But they are only as good as the 'maps' they are used on – usually a combination of existing mapping and GoogleEarth images with a fine-detailed lat/long overlay. The Lowrance 3500 unit shown (right) is exceptionally reliable. In wild regions there is still much manual work with maps, images and instruments.

seldom programmed to give lat/long positions, create lat/long or grid waypoints or operate independent of their own mapping. As an exception, Land Rover's Discovery has a factory-fit satnav that can cope with street nav and also switch to off-road navigation for use with external maps.

This latter is a facility that will be essential if you are operating overseas or in remote areas so be sure to fit a satnav with this capability. Lowrance in the US (lowrance.com) make an exceptionally wide range of equipments categorised as marine, aviation, automotive or 'outdoor'. This latter category , usually also capable of accepting an MMC card digital map suite, will be best for expeditions – up to and including the most demanding off-piste African exploration using such paper maps as exist. Large-display units, hard-wired, possibly needing an external antenna, will be best for serious expeditions but smaller, hand-held 'outdoor' satnavs are obtainable that will cover much of the same function (including card-sourced mapping). These, of course are invaluable to take with you when hill walking, for instance, so you can locate your vehicle should the weather turn bad, but the disadvantage is a smaller display, less practical for driving, and an internal antenna. Antennae, however, are getting smarter.

Second vehicle, safety message. Two vehicles driven in not-too-close convoy is a wise precaution on most routes off the tarmac and certainly when off-tracks. If one vehicle gets stuck in mud the other (long tow-rope – see Section 5) will be able to tow it free, or go for help if mechanical damage has occurred. It is well appreciated, however, that the whole point of some trips will be to 'get away' in a single vehicle. It behoves you for such excursions to take a mobile phone, recovery equipment and inform people where you are going. Train (next spread) with schools organising safaris to understand the terrain and safety requirements.

As with all expedition projects, develop your navigation skills a step at a time. Take a second vehicle for safety unless you are certain about a particular route.

Getting the feel of your vehicle off-road before an expedition is important. Professionally-run group safaris and dealer demo days make an excellent introduction.

7.2 Training for the trip

Developing the skills

Learn first. 'Training for the trip' may initially sound a forbidding concept when many 'expeditions' are no more than recreational excursions. But you would not go rock climbing without knowing how to do it and having the equipment; and you would not go canoeing without being instructed on how to control the canoe and observe the correct safety precautions. To do any of these things without proper preparation would be foolhardy; and that applies to vehicle-based expeditions – in spades, as it were.

Learn the full spectrum of your vehicle's and your own capabilities before planning a trip.

Off-road training. Use one of the many off-road driving schools to become familiar with your vehicle away from tarmac and in the low-range transfer gears. Many 4x4 dealers run off-road demonstration days. Start with these; they will be invaluable and are often free. Initially it may be no more than a sedate trundle round without the need even for gear changes but you will find it easy and that, at first, is the important bit. You will start to see what the vehicle can do as the performance envelope opens up.

If you have read this book you will have the advantage of having absorbed the theory – and the written practice – but it is essential that you try it yourself and become completely comfortable with your own and your vehicle's behaviour in demanding conditions before going out on an expedition, however minor. Taking on board the message is a very significant first step.

Practise on your own

Consolidation. Going to a dealer demonstration you will have experienced the dynamics of off-road driving and the significance of the gentle right foot but you will need a lot more practice and for this you should go to a local school for consolidating tuition and, most important of all, a day-pass access to their off-road site which will enable you to 'play' in your own time and practise the techniques you have been taught. Take your time, read this book, know and analyse what you are doing. Being on a driving school site you will do so in the knowledge that should you get stuck, help will be on hand to tow you free.

Crucially, though you'll learn when to say 'No' and back off. That way you won't want towing out of anything.

Such sites, additionally, are designated for off-road practice and you will not have the worry of seeking special permission for where you go. A considerable number of such schools advertise in the off-road magazines; go for the ones that emphasise thorough briefing and care for the vehicle. Do not be rushed into precipitate driving methods; you are paying the bill and it is your vehicle.

Safari. A number of schools also organise 'safaris' lasting one to three days in which a small group of owner-driven-vehicles is led along pre-chosen routes which incorporate a variety of demanding driving conditions – and usually some exhilarating scenery.

The experience is enjoyable in itself and valuable in a hundred ways for learning driving techniques. Choose, if you possibly can, a safari school that operates under similar terrain conditions to those you wish to travel later.

Fitness. Your off-road driver training and the physical effort required to push, jack, lay sand channels or dig out a stuck vehicle will be a reminder that your own fitness is no less important than that of your vehicle. In a perfect world your training will have conferred such skill and judgement that you never get your vehicle into a condition warranting the undignified description of 'being stuck'. Few will need reminding of the world's imperfections and from the fitness point of view it is prudent to be prepared ... !

Initial impressions of your vehicle's off-road performance will be dazzling; but learn the demarcation between what it can and cannot do. Then practise on your own.

Mechanic?

Skill with the spanners. This far into the book the importance of mechanical sympathy and not damaging the vehicle in off-road jaunts hardly needs further emphasis. Modern vehicles are very reliable but overseas, and really far from the beaten track, pre-trip training must have included a thorough knowledge of the vehicle and – within feasible limits applicable to electro-fest 21st century vehicles – how to maintain it. Read that again.

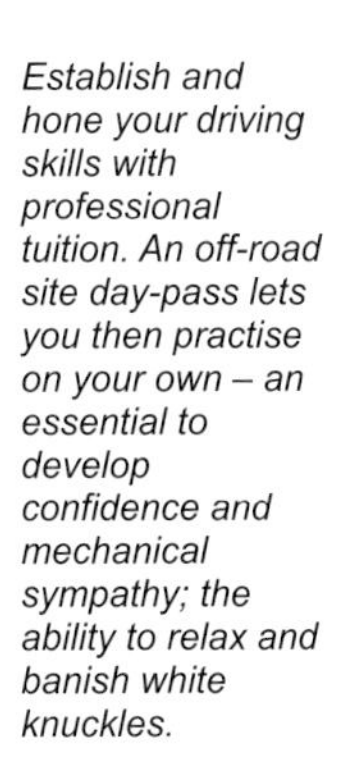

Establish and hone your driving skills with professional tuition. An off-road site day-pass lets you then practise on your own – an essential to develop confidence and mechanical sympathy; the ability to relax and banish white knuckles.

7.3 Vehicle preparation

What preparation?

Off-road requirements. Just a few 4x4s can be driven straight from the showroom and turn in a competent off-road performance. Most vehicles, however will need further preparation for an expedition. Tyres are usually the most obvious item requiring attention – see below. On-road accessories and equipment like front spoilers, side step-cum-running boards and low-set towhooks, however, all affect real-life off-road agility. You will have to accept the limitations they incur or, as part of your off-road preparation, opt for their removal.

Payload, securing the load (p.8.2), recovery equipment, mobile phones or other rescue aids are further aspects to bear in mind. Naturally you must ensure that your vehicle has been properly maintained, at least to manufacturer's servicing schedules, and is thus on the top line mechanically. 'Up there' on the hills is no place to be breaking down for the want of proper servicing.

Vehicle knowledge. Earlier sections of this book and your training sessions should have refreshed your knowledge of the traction features such as low range and the applicability for your vehicle of differential locks, stability control systems, ABS brakes, traction control. Some vehicles – like the Touareg, later Discovery and Range Rover – have extra under-belly clearance available where air suspension has been specified.

Initial preparation will be mundane – simple things like knowing the driver's manual, jacking. Tyres are fundamental to defining your expedition capability.

Tyres

Compromises. Tyres can usually only be optimised for one set of conditions. Used in other environments, there will be a degree of performance compromise. Quiet-running tyres with treads designed for on-road wet grip need a measured objective assessment if you are going off tracks – the point has already been made that particular tyres perform best in one set of conditions only. This applies to wheels also. Following fashion rather than (as you might hope in a business-like 4x4) function, some vehicles are bought with large diameter rims fitted with low profile tyres. Both are fundamentally unsuitable for any off-tarmac activity (And even on-road bring significant disadvantages – ride comfort, rim damage). Go for smaller wheels and deeper tyres.

Tyres for the job. BFGoodrich Mud-Terrain (235/85 left) and All-Terrain (265/75 right) on 16" rims for a Mercedes G-Wagen.

Types. Study the detail on tyre types, axle loads and pressures, pressure reductions for tracks and emergency conditions, Load Index and Speed Symbol (see p.8.17). You will likely find your 4x4 fitted with road-oriented or M+S (mud and snow) tyres when you buy it and you would be wise to adjust the route of your first expeditions to be within their still considerable capabilities before going to the expense of buying others.

As if to invalidate the mantra of tyres having to be selected for defined conditions, some 'all terrain' tyres – specifically the BFGoodrich All-Terrain (right in pic above) – do live up to their name: grippy on wet tarmac, robust and very versatile in desert. In temperate zones such as Europe you will find the main compromise with these tyres is reduced performance in mud (due to the treads filling up) compared to such tyres as the Michelin XZL or BFG Mud-Terrain.

Remember that one aspect of a mud tyre's effectiveness derives from a carefully judged width – or narrowness – that enables it, together with an equally deliberate tread design, to cut through slippery upper layers of soft mud and into the grippier ground beneath – see page 4.26.

Fat tyres not always best. Thus the extra-wide after-market tyres frequently seen on recreational vehicles may well yield poorer traction on wet grass and mud than will standard items. Certainly they will be less effective than the mud tyres mentioned above.

Jacking. Tyre reliability these days is such that few of us get experience even in fitting the spare wheel, much less repairing a flat. An off-road expedition may result in sidewall damage and a flat if you are not sufficiently vigilant – see Section 3.5 on Marshalling.

Check the handbook procedures; practise choc-ing the wheels, positioning and operating the jack (take the main tightness off the wheel nuts with the wheel still in contact with the ground). You will find it quite a stretch positioning the jack under a rear axle. Keep a set of overalls for this job. Be sure you can undo and properly tighten the wheel nuts – and that includes, of course, having the key nut for the locking wheelnuts!

If you have to jack on soft ground you will need a small wood baulk as a load spreader – about 45-50mm thick and a little bigger than this book. Keep it in the vehicle. A second jack and extra wood block is useful where the ground is really soft and you may have to jack up a stage at a time.

Tidiness – inside and out

Ground clearance. The obvious hang-downs that affect front-end, rear end and side clearance have already been mentioned. But it is worth re-familiarising yourself with the under-belly clearance of your vehicle and the 'what will touch first' parameter. Whilst many off-roaders do have vulnerable items like silencers, neatly tucked away underneath, getting down on your hands and knees before a trip may show that others do not! There will be items underneath that should definitely not be run into rocks. Check page 3.8 for a refresher.

Tie-downs, internal stowage. Similarly, aim to keep the inside tidy too by ensuring the cargo stays where it is put. As mentioned in Section 8.1, there is much to recommend the fitting of tie-downs in your vehicle if it is to operate over rough ground.

Keep it tidy. Lidded boxes, lashed-down. No lost kit, no rattling and sliding on bumps and corners. A calm, beatific smile on your face!

Vehicle manufacturers are at last waking up to the uses of tie-downs and fitting them as standard. Used for really heavy items such as jacks and with modular containers like lidded plastic storage boxes, equipment such as wet-weather gear, camping equipment, recovery items, and refreshments can be strapped-down so that they do not slide around the vehicle on corners, uneven tracks or off-road.

Think ground clearance. Does spoiler or tow-hook have to be removed to enhance approach and departure angle? Plan, containerise and secure the load.

This is part of the basic philosophy of eliminating loose articles so that not only does equipment avoid damage but the vehicle itself, as a result, is free from rattles and other internal noise. Few aspects of off-road driving can be so nerve-jangling as boxes and loose items sliding about in the back of a vehicle. It is a curious but repeatedly observed fact but you will find that vehicles that are tight and rattle-free are driven better and more sympathetically than those full of randomly noisy avalanches of equipment.

Modifications. Further vehicle modifications for more demanding trips are covered on page 7.18.

A Goretex array (above) with bullet-proof nylon reinforcement where needed, For driving, a boot with a low-rise aft support (left item) allows ankle flex.

7.4 Equipment

Influencing criteria

What if ... ? Television news bulletins continually remind us of how easily a short recreational excursion can turn into a life-threatening drama. Common to many of these news items is how simple were the precautions that could have avoided trouble. Occasionally, this is proven when someone, well prepared, has survived cheerfully by digging a snow-hole or taking appropriate action that has enabled them to ride out the storm or assist rescue teams to find them when things have gone wrong.

A second vehicle and a long tow-rope (pic above) is a good start. Simple problems can develop into emergencies. Don't be self-conscious about taking sensible safety measures.

European weather systems, especially in the regions attractive to outdoor or adventurous people are notorious for their changeability and the suddenness with which conditions can become threatening.

Some of the 'what-if' questions that must be asked in deciding what equipment to take on even a minor, 'day-trip', expedition are:

- ***Weather.*** If the weather turns from today's 'fine-and-sunny' to zero visibility, a downpour or 'snow-on-high-ground', am I appropriately equipped?
- ***Track condition.*** Can I self-recover a vehicle brought to a wheelspinning halt in mud?
- ***Off-road.*** If my vehicle bellies-out on a ridge can I recover it?
- ***Overnighting.*** If my recovery problems take so long that we are overtaken by darkness or sudden bad weather, have we food, drinks and warmth enough to overnight in the vehicle and resume operations in the morning?
- ***Going for help.*** If I get myself into such deep trouble off-road that I am unable to recover, how far is it to help? Can I walk it with the equipment I have?
- ***Emergency equipment.*** Do I have any means of attracting attention or calling for help?

(These are questions that will also influence your taking along a second vehicle and that all-important long tow-rope.)

Protective clothing

Plan for the worst. Most often you will be protecting against cold and wet. On any expedition, even a short drive on mountain tracks, you will not wish to – and certainly not be able to – remain in the vehicle with the

Congo or Wales at -8°C, be sure you have appropriate clothing – wickable, breathable, layered insulation. insect-repellent, rainproof, washable, quick-dry ... check the catalogues.

heater on all the time. Assume, as a matter of course and whatever the weather at the start of your trip, that it will rain, get cold and blow a gale. Assume also that you will find it necessary to wade up to your knees in mud or water and/or walk a number of kilometres on rough ground. Equip yourself with appropriate clothing and add overalls and a groundsheet to lie on when you have to dig under your vehicle or change a wheel.

Consult one of the many outdoor centres or camping gear shops for advice on the latest clothing. Cotswold Outdoor branches, for example, (UK), are staffed by young 'do-ers' who actually use the gear they are selling. Blacks likewise. Cotswold issue comprehensive catalogues containing full information on equipment as well as fielding sensible on-line videos on choosing and using equipment.

Standards of design and materials technology have never been higher. Goretex and many other breathable water and wind-proof membranes, windproof fleeces and Thinsulate insulation have made considerable impact on the design and effectiveness of outdoor clothing. Do your own study, adopt the layering principle – several layers of garments rather than a single very thick/warm one. The following will act as a guide:

• ***Footwear.*** Versatile, new-generation, Goretex-lined boots from Clarks high-street shops, low at the heel for ankle-flexing driving are a comfortable and practical multi-role proposition. Hill-walking boots will be a little more robust but, high on the Achilles tendon, aren't always good for driving. Gumboots are for wading emergencies – you would not wish to walk far in gumboots nor carry out a reconnaissance wade-through of a stream in walking boots. Stow them in a boot-bag or plastic sack to keep the inside of the vehicle clean.

• ***Outer layer.*** Take fabric-and-Goretex overtrousers and a roomy-fit hooded anorak of similar material with draw-cords at hood, waist and hem. Waxed cotton, which (like large alloys with low-profile tyres) has an inexplicable following, is a disaster. Its stickiness holds dirt, spoils seats, cannot be machine-washed, does not breathe and needs regular re-proofing. Woolly hat or similar to prevent heat-loss from the head. Two pairs of gloves – thin leather for driving, another grippy set for mucky outside work or walking.

• ***Inner layers.*** As experience demands. Merino wool long-johns-and-top base layer for real cold (eg Icebreaker), fleece

Most problems are climatic – too cold or too hot. Be properly equipped. Breakdown or bad bogging involve prolonged work or walking; plan for it.

The satisfaction of being properly clad against the elements is complementary to that of being the master of difficult terrain in a 4x4.

Don't hazard your enjoyment of scenery like this by cutting down on safety equipment. The same applies in 'green and pleasant lands' as in harsher climates.

(Polartec *et al*) or fibre-pile jackets are excellent for warmth and wicking of perspiration vapour; use as an either (or additional to) a warm zip-in liner to your anorak. Often a boiler-suit or overalls of generous cut can make a very practical layer over your day clothes when not wearing the wind/water-proof outer layers.

• ***Other.*** Groundsheet, as mentioned above, for under-vehicle access or digging.

• ***Emergency.*** Take a sleeping bag for emergency use in case you are overtaken by night or storm when stuck. It seems to be a rule of nature that all serious boggings take place just as the sun is going down.

• ***Head torch.*** How did the human species survive before Petzl-type LED head torches? Take one.

• ***Vehicle heater.*** Remember, if you run the engine to keep the vehicle heater effective in snow, to be sure the exhaust pipe is clear of drifting snow that could prevent escape of poisonous exhaust fumes.

Recovery gear

Causes. Getting stuck with a greater or lesser degree of permanence will the be result of a temporary mismatch of your driving skills, assessment of the ground, capability of the vehicle and what the ground is actually like. More direct and specific causes will be:

- Soft ground.
- Slippery ground.
- Limit of vehicle's articulation.

Commonly a combination of all three is what will halt you. Note the exclusion of gradient as a cause of getting stuck. A 4x4 vehicle capable of a nearly one-in-one climb on dry concrete is unlikely to be halted by any reasonable gradient.

What to take, what to do. Getting close to the specifics like this will again emphasise the value of a second vehicle in the convoy. Re-read Section 5 (and 4!) and take:

- ***Two shovels*** (pointed ends, not spades); fold-away type will do.
- ***Long towrope,*** 4-tonne breaking strain minimum, not less than 25 metres long, with soft spliced-in eyes and U-bolt shackles (see p.5.7). (Two tow ropes, one short, totalling 25m is even better.)
- ***Standard hydraulic axle jack*** as supplied, wood baulk load spreader as above, plus second jack and baulk.
- ***Aluminium sand ladder.*** PSP, MaxTrax, Barong or other grip/load spreaders to put under the wheels.

Rescue aids

Use the technology. Though you may be on your trip to get some peace and quiet, the potential of the dreaded mobile phone as a safety life-line in areas served by appropriate networks makes it essential emergency equipment. Used with GPS (p.7.5) to also transmit your actual position in Ordnance Survey grid or latitude/longitude, it would be invaluable. A simple and sensible set of rescue aids would thus be:

- ***Mobile phone and GPS***. The Iridium satellite-phone network will work from anywhere on the planet. Thuraya covers Europe, Middle East, Gulf and also works in-country GSM networks.
- ***Mini-flares***. Commonly carried by boat people, a pack of six or eight is not much bigger than a spectacles case.
- ***EPIRB beacon.*** For major expeditions overseas a satellite emergency beacon (such as yachtsmen use and registered with the UK Coastguard) triggering a transmission on 121.5 Mhz or 406 Mhz is a life saver. Quiz the yacht chandlers.

Selection of recovery gear – all good but PSP planks (lower left) are clunky, weak, awkward to stow. Awesome foursome (right) rescue aids – satellite EPIRB, Thuraya sat-phone, standby GPS and voice recorder for nav log.

Sound recovery gear need not be complex. Shovels, long tow ropes with shackles, jacks and load spreaders – reread Section 5.

7.5 Logistics, vehicle choice

Strategic thinking

The broad view. Sections 7.1 to 7.4 have assumed introductory expeditions probably carried out with your own existing vehicle. If you are planning something a little more ambitious – going to the full extent of your 4x4's capabilities or considering a team of vehicles that could fulfil a particular expedition project – then it is well to have a feel for the kind of strategic thinking involved. This concerns, mainly:

- ***Payload/range*** – how far you can go with what payload. The two parameters are interdependent: the more payload you carry, the less capability you have to carry fuel, water and supplies. The more fuel and water you take, the less capacity you have for payload. The unbreakable rule here is the maximum gross vehicle weight – GVW: *never exceed it.*
- ***Specials?*** If the sums don't come out right and you need special vehicles for a project, what are the criteria?

Preliminary criteria, payload/range

Preliminary criteria. If you are already wondering why there is so much talk about weight, the philosophy of sound expedition planning revolves around taking care of the life-blood of the trip – the vehicle. It will already have enough to cope with on a demanding expedition and these are the very conditions in which a breakdown is unacceptable. So preliminary criteria before even thinking about an expedition are:

- Vehicle in top class condition.
- Thorough overhaul and service.
- Impeccable driving.
- Vehicle operating *within design limits.*

And this latter includes the most often abused aspect of vehicle operation on expeditions – the weight of the payload. It is the most often abused because it seems to be the item that most often catches people out.

For long range trips, know your available payload and break it down into fuel and cargo (supplies) – the payload/range see-saw. But stop (well) short of your GVW.

Gross weight, kerb weight. Never, ever, overload a vehicle on a trip. It is easy enough to avoid. The diagram on the right shows a typical expedition vehicle and how its kerb weight (its 'empty weight') and its gross weight are made up.

Long-range trips. Since most expeditions involve going long distances and subsisting there on supplies brought with you, it is instructive to look at the interplay of payload and range quantitatively. The diagram opposite (top) and its caption show how the further you have to go, the less payload (for kit, passengers etc) is available. Again, a typical expedition vehicle is used, albeit here it is fitted with an inappropriate and thirsty engine to emphasise the effect of fuel supply weight. Diesels are usually the best for expeditions (but see p.7.22).

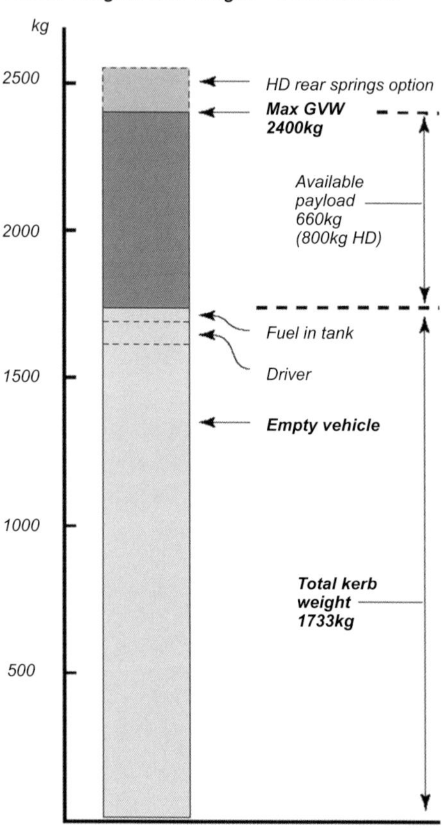

Logistics – spare payload dwindles with range – V8 Defender 90 example

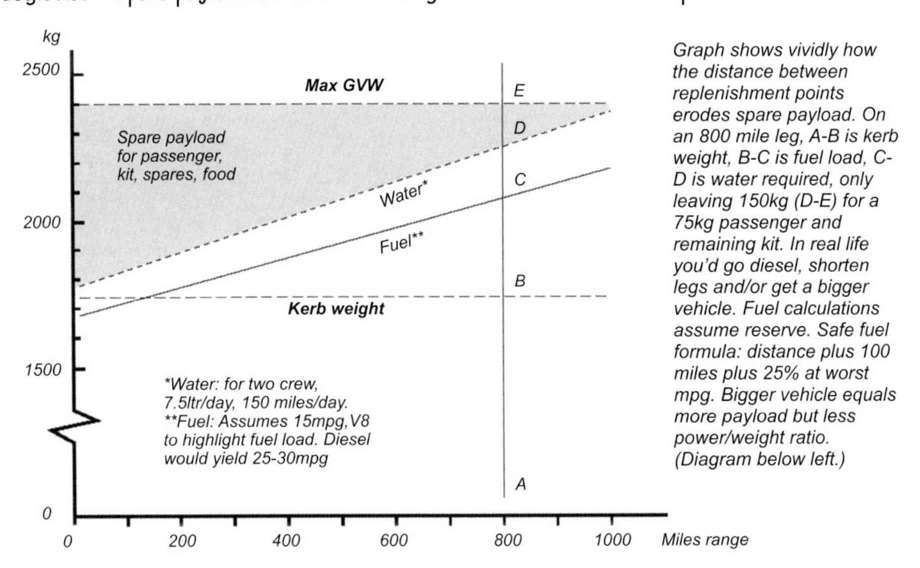

Graph shows vividly how the distance between replenishment points erodes spare payload. On an 800 mile leg, A-B is kerb weight, B-C is fuel load, C-D is water required, only leaving 150kg (D-E) for a 75kg passenger and remaining kit. In real life you'd go diesel, shorten legs and/or get a bigger vehicle. Fuel calculations assume reserve. Safe fuel formula: distance plus 100 miles plus 25% at worst mpg. Bigger vehicle equals more payload but less power/weight ratio. (Diagram below left.)

Jimny or Unimog. All off-roaders will have weight maxima that beget graphs of the kind shown here. In general, bigger ones, all the way up to medium or heavy trucks, can carry more and go further than little ones – but at the expense of agility and power-to-weight ratio (see pic right). The size trade-offs diagram (below) shows the trend. Luxury vehicles tend to have low spare payload (in order that springs can give a better ride – see unsprung weight, p.1.6). 'Working' vehicles carry a lot more – classic examples are pickups, hard-tops (van bodies) and light-bodied vehicles like the Land Rover Defender.

Power-weight ratio vs payload .... Range Rover has agility but little payload. Bedford has huge payload but struggles in dunes. Long wheelbase Land Rovers sit between.

The size trade-offs

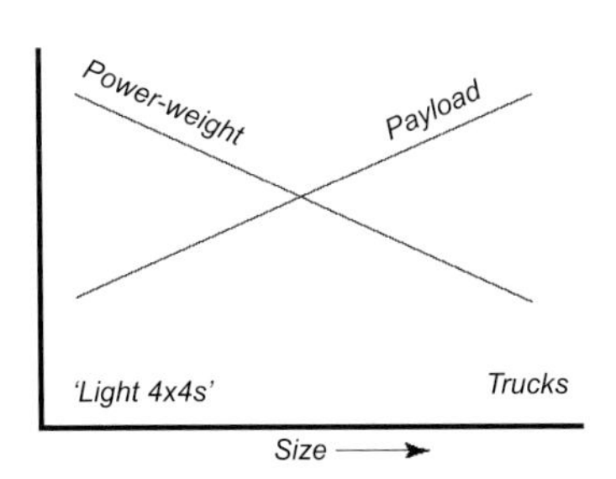

For its kit list the Toyota 78 'Troopie' is probably the ultimate expedition vehicle. 1000kg payload, long range tanks, centre and (optional) factory front/rear diff locks, simple, lazy 4.2 litre diesel, worldwide dealerships. 110 Defender a close second but still no in-house axle diff-locks: crazy.

The criteria

Ingredients. How is an expedition vehicle made up? How is any 4x4 made up? If you are wondering what vehicle to buy next and want more incisive criteria than the average brochure-writer's obsession with cup-holders, Bluetooth, MP3 docks and large alloy wheels then look slowly at the list opposite (and also p.2.38).

Legislation-driven vehicle design leads to complexity, acceptable on short trips within reach of assistance but needs careful thought for long trips in remote areas.

The evolutionary chain. These are criteria that chart a vehicle's growth from a basic two-wheel drive pickup through to an exceptionally capable off-roader. Beware the trap of equating all upmarket vehicles with flabby, dilettante incompetence. Some. certainly, are like that. Others, even in deluxe trim – the Range Rover, Discovery, Land Cruiser, G-Wagen and Touareg of course jump to mind – are very capable even though their payload may not be as high as a stripped-out pickup.

Under-axle clearance – portal axle (Unimog)

See also p.3.9 for beam axles and independent suspension clearances

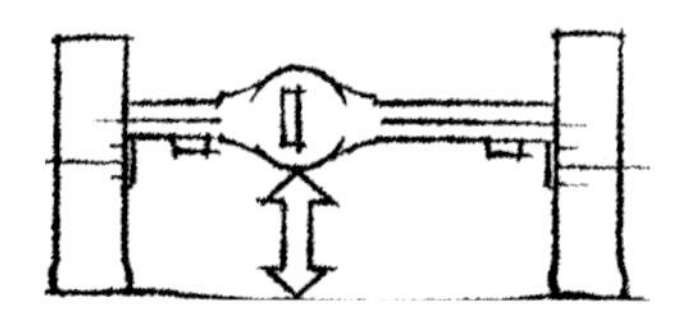

High ground clearance but high CG and cost

New-fangled stuff

Simplicity, reliability? What cannot be covered here is individual brand reliability. Whilst in general an expedition vehicle should be a simple one, easy to service in the field and less likely to go wrong anyway, designers and engineers entering the 21st century are confronted with wholly laudable emissions regulations which nevertheless force them to use electronic solutions and thus the need for complex and expensive test gear for checking systems. If you are going to truly remote areas you have to face this problem head-on.

- Can I be absolutely certain that this complex vehicle will be 100% reliable?
- Have I the knowledge, special tools and equipment to fix if it is not?
- If not, is there a sufficiently simple vehicle maintainable in the field by me or by local mechanics? Toyota, catering to a world market, address this by offering 'non-electronic' simple-spec vehicles for distant markets – not available in the EU.

Luddite reaction? In comparison to vehicles even 20 years ago, present-day cars are – despite the increased complexity that regulations demand – enormously reliable. But failures on a Spanish mountain track can be bad news. Even worse in the Sahara.

EXPEDITION VEHICLE ATTRIBUTES – IN ORDER OF PROGRESSION FROM SIMPLE 4X2 PICKUP*

Feature	Benefits	Disadvantages
Leaf-springs	Low cost, simplicity, easy replacement. Springs act as means of locating axles.	Inter-leaf friction gives stiff ride, poor traction; limited wheel movement. Long springs are best.
Large diameter wheels (ie 16" not 15" or 14")	Improved under-axle ground clearance. Goes *over* pot-holes rather than into them.	No functional disadvantage, provided low profile tyres not fitted on eg, 18-22" rims.
Torsion-bar front springs	Smoother ride than leaf-springs. Better traction and braking. More wheel movement?	Usually associated with independent front suspension so less ground clearance.
Beam axles	Good under-axle clearance, wheels always perpendicular to ground.	Clearance above axle needed for wheel movement makes vehicle tall. High unsprung weight difficult to damp.
Coil springs all round	Smoother ride than leaf-springs. Better traction and braking. On beam axles more wheel movement than leaf springs so best traction on uneven ground.	More expensive than leaf-springs due to need for alternative axle location links. If too short and stiff (Lada Niva), ride is still poor.
No anti-roll bars (See pic p.1.6)	Permits full axle articulation – twist relative to body – off-road wheel movement enhanced.	Body roll. Designer's nightmare to balance on- and off-road performance.
Short wheelbase	Improved off-road capability but only noticeable in extreme conditions.	Lower max payload than long wheelbase versions. Pitching, lumpy ride.
Large approach, departure, ramp angles, 'high stance' (See p 3.8)	Off-road agility without danger of grounding body parts. Short tail overhang specially valuable exiting ditches.	High centre of gravity can cause body roll.
High payload	Obvious advantage when there are long distances between provisioning points.	Less pliant ride, lower power/weight ratio. Classic division between luxury/working.
Automatic transmission (See p 2.44 and 6.6)	Helps driver. Smoothest gear changes safeguard driveshafts, precludes lost traction through jerkiness. Very good, reliable.	Cost mainly, some weight. In some cases if it breaks down, prop shaft removal for towing. Minor fuel consumption penalty.
Auto-engage 4x4. (See p 2.11)	Very smart these days. No driver input. Some have 4x4 select override (eg X-Trail), Most auto-select 4x4 on start-off.	Not suitable for sustained off-roading. Front/rear speed axle differences have to be sensed before 4x4 is engaged.
Selectable 4x4 (See p 2.11)	Huge improvement over two-wheel drive (4x2) in all off-road conditions. Simplicity, in effect 'centre diff locked' drive. Low cost.	Compared with 4x2, cost. Must be selected when needed and de-selected on hard surfaces. Permanent 4x4 (+ centre diff) better.
2-speed transfer box (See pp.2.13 and 3.4)	In effect a 2nd set of extra-low gears for off-road use. Essential for expeditions.	Cost and complexity but a must-have for any serious expedition.
On-the-move range change (Lo to Hi range) (See pp.6.4-6.7)	Invaluable if you start in Lo and need to change to Hi without stopping. Can't be done with most 'electronic' range changes.	No real disadvantage except some skill / technique required to do it on most vehicles
Permanent ('full time') 4x4 with centre differential (See p.2.11)	The best. Better than part-time 4x4 or auto-engage 4x4 because it is there all the time. Best kind has lockable centre differential.	Compared with part-time 4x4, more cost since a centre differential is needed.
Traction control (See pp.2.3, 2.6, 2.19)	Foolproof way round wheelspin. Automatic.	Electronic, brake heat,wear. Slow to react. Auto/manual diff-locks far better.
Locking axle differentials (See pp.2.3 and 2.6)	Precludes those 'one spinning wheel' situations superbly to preclude getting stuck.	Cost. Risk to half-shafts if not properly engineered. Must remember to de-select.
Portal axles (See diagram opposite)	Dramatic increase in under-axle clearance for rough ground and deep ruts. Used in Hummer H1 and the unstoppable Mercedes-Benz Unimog.	Very expensive to produce, high centre of gravity, higher unsprung weight.

Know the progression of features that take a vehicle from a boulvardier to an expedition star. All the time try to match this to known terrain and requirements.

See also p.2.38 – Pre-purchase Checks

Demands of an ultra-long-range, solo trip exemplify fuel and water needs/stowage. Note: lashed securely, weight (p.8.4) at mid-wheelbase, NOTHING on roof. Fold-down shelf on rear door (with light provision and handy fire extinguisher) serves as 'kitchen'.

Modifications?

Why modify? There is a blur between preparation (p.7.8) and modification. Many vehicles can lope through a dozen outings of a fairly routine nature just as they left the showroom. Anything more focused – say, overseas, with a lot of cargo and a lot of camping covering demanding off-road terrain may call for some 'optimisation'.

Moths and insects attracted by the interior light in the evenings can be kept out and your sanity saved by simple slip-over window nets with Velcro and elastics at the bottom – windows still down for air.

The hazards ahead. Cargo tie-downs, compartments, racks, and a bit more interior light are the usual starting points for modifications. Think in any depth and you quickly come up with a list of issues that may need to be addressed:

Dust
Extreme heat
Extreme cold
Getting stuck
Tracks with deep ruts
Cargo bumping around
Deep wading
Animals, insects

Modifications – the spectrum

The categories. Having regard to what is designed-in already, most modifications fall into three categories. Not all of the following are 'do' mods; some are 'don't do' or 'think very hard first' headings.

1. Vehicle function – engine, electrics.
• ***Engine and fuel system:***
Fuel filler extension for jerry-can top-ups
High level air intake (dust, wading)
Tachometer (old vehicles not so equipped)
Long-range fuel tank – but see p 8.6
Fuel sedimenter / filter
Fuel system and / or block heaters
Electronic contact breakers (old vehicles)
Oil temp gauge, oil cooler (old vehicles)
(NB Most modern vehicles are type-tested in ambients up to 50°C so extra oil cooling will not be necessary. Axle and gearbox oils often get hotter anyway.)
• ***Electrical system:***
HD or 2nd battery, split charge system
Battery master switches
Extra interior lighting (fluorescent / LED)
Accessory power points, front / rear
Courtesy lights – deactivate / switchable
Battery warmer (mains powered)

2. General and expedition function.
Special fitments related to the role of the expedition:.
Tyres – mud, desert, winter (Sec 4)
GPS installation (see p.7.5)

Security alarm (old vehicles)
Reflective film on rear windows
Rear seats out for cargo space
Internal tie-downs
Fire extinguisher
'Kitchen' arrangements
Sand ladder and shovel racks
Tow hooks and rings
Roof tent
Belly protection
Sockets for hi-lift jack (see p.5.5)
Winch (see p.5.14)
Rollover cage

3. Crew function. *Mods – crew comfort:*
Insect nets for windows (facing page)
Seat upholstery – cloth best, not leather
Extra ventilation ducts
Roof, body-side, floor insulation
Side window in 'van' bodies
Audio, MP3/iPod plug-in facility

Priorities

Fit for purpose. Every proposed modification should be carefully considered before being undertaken but the most common need is beefed-up electrics – the ability to run lighting and accessories and still be sure of starting the engine in the morning. (Don't fit those six extra spotlights!)

A second battery, with a split-charge system and accessories coming off that battery often applies. Rechargeable LED lights can be a lightweight solution – see pic.

Next in importance, as already hinted in Section 7.3, is organising the load, not only to strap it down but to render things more accessible and easy to locate. Secure location of heavy items like fuel and water cans is extremely important (pic facing page); when tied down they should be all but impossible to budge by hand. Force yourself to consider the consequences of such heavy items, loose, in the event of an accident or roll-over.

No roof rack. Roof racks and the explorer image seem, alas, to go hand in hand, but, as covered in Section 8.1, avoid roof racks in off-road vehicles if at all possible. If you do have a major storage problem, use roofracks only for featherweight items like sleeping bags, tents and the like; definitely not for heavy items like fuel cans. Limit the roof load to a max of 75-100 kilos (see p.8.4).

Above: In-cab meals, snacks and evening work usually demand a 'place to put things'. Home-made clip-on table stows behind driver's seat when dismantled.
Below: Camp lights often require a split-charge auxiliary battery. Here, rechargeable 160-LED (Vango) light-wands clip to roof-bar, yield 2-3 hours' light and can re-charge during day run. Solar heating in the cab is minimised by rear-window reflective film, a white roof exterior and, for this thin-roofed Wrangler, Insuliner roof panels.

7.6 Fuels

Fuels – petrol engines

Octanes, unleaded fuel. Using the right fuel for your engine, or, in some cases, matching your vehicle and engine to what fuel is available, is important. Running an engine on fuel it is not designed for can shorten its life dramatically – or cause terminal damage. Engine specifications in vehicles destined for developed countries are generally high compression (9.5:1 or higher) and thus require high octane fuels to run on – the graph opposite gives a guide. If you are going, with a petrol engine, to an area where only low octane fuel is available a low compression engine should be used. If your engine is old and simple enough, richening the mixture (if possible), retarding the ignition, and/or fitting low compression pistons accommodates lower octane fuels.

Sustained knock kills petrol engines. Modern engines are less easy to tune for low octane fuels so be sure you know the fuel available where you are going.

All this requires expert knowledge. Most modern engines aren't amenable to such tweaks and combustion is controlled by an ECU. The parameters for this are not easy to change. Modern engines will also have been designed to run on unleaded fuels for emissions reasons and recent ones will have a catalytic converter in the exhaust system – a very expensive item that can be ruined ('poisoned' is the term used) by using leaded fuel. And running a much older engine on unleaded fuel can damage the valve seats.

Study this carefully. The table below gives a broad indication of petrol engine fuel requirements. Electronic ignition control via an ECU and/or the provision of variable valve timing (VVT) broadens the spectrum of fuels a gasoline engine can operate on. In general, fuel quality – unleaded at higher octanes – has improved worldwide. Check with the in-country oil companies if you can before your overseas trip. Your vehicle manufacturer's Customer Service department should be able to help.

Go diesel. The only sensible solution to expeditioning abroad used to be: Go diesel – better mpg, greater flexibility, usually greater durability and simplicity. It's not that simple now: see pp 7.21-7.25

Caution: not gospel. The fuels overview here will be mainly of interest to those taking their vehicles to less developed countries overseas on expedition or civil aid or engineering projects.

Read this section – all of Section 7.6 – but treat it with caution: the fuels scenario is changing all the time. It does, however, give you the broad picture and a clear indication of how and where to probe before deciding on your expedition and/or vehicle. The oil update on p 7.26-27 – galloping on in the same way – applies wherever you are. Oils get smarter and more supportive of longer engine life, longer oil change intervals and, rightly, lower emissions.

GASOLINE ENGINES: HIGH OCTANE, LOW OCTANE, LOW GRADE LEADED FUELS

Engine type (CR = compression ratio)	Run on high octane petrol? *('4-star', 'premium', 'super', RON 95-97)*	Run on low octane petrol? *('2-star', 'regular', 'normal', RON 91-92)*	Run on low grade petrol? *(RON below 90, down to 80 or lower)*
1. Low compression engine (CR = around 8.5 or less)	Yes but needless expense. No damage.	Yes	Often yes, but if knocking retard ignition. See para above.
2. High compression engine (CR = 8.5 to around 10)	Yes	Rarely. If knocking, retard ignition. See para above.	Almost certainly no.

Note:
Retarding ignition alone can only accommodate lower grade fuels to a certain extent. Fitting low compression pistons would be the next step – a major job that can be very expensive. Don't do this randomly or lightly; manufacturer's advice and approval should be sought first, then that of specialist engineers. JE Engineering Ltd of Coventry, tel 02476 30518 well known for extra-power tuning of Rover engines is one company that could undertake such work in the UK.

Compression ratio vs minimum required fuel octane – conceptual guidance only

Examples:
1. Engine with 8:1 CR (A) in normal tune requires 88 RON fuel (B). With retarded ignition it can make do on 84 RON (C). If mixture can be richened it will run on 83 RON (D).

2. Or, if your engine has 9.5:1 CR (E), and you'll only have 90 RON fuel, then low compression pistons to achieve 8.4:1 CR (F) will be needed – or max retard and richening.

Note: This is conceptual only. Take the manufacturer's advice. Engines vary a lot and CRs of 10:1 or 11:1 routinely use 95 RON. At the lower end, however, poorer fuels do demand lower compression ratios.

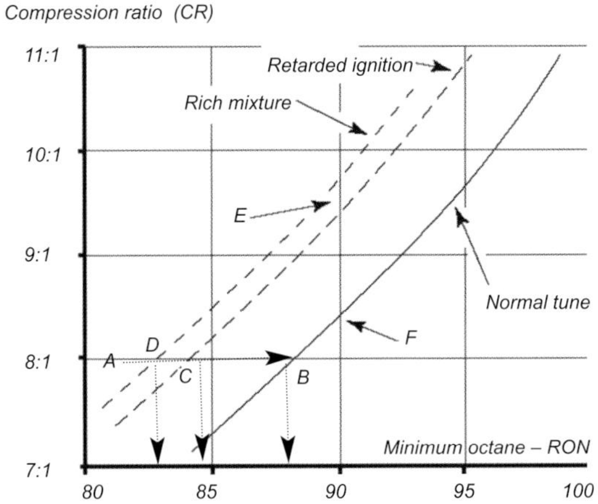

Expeditions: petrol or diesel?

The price of low emissions. It used to be a simple choice and a simple decision. Diesels were more tolerant of the varying fuel quality you might encounter on an expedition; plus diesel fuel, rather than high octane gasolines, was what was most readily available in outback regions of the world. So 'Go diesel' were the watchwords for long-distance travellers. The reduced accidental fire risk was a peripheral benefit in an expedition cooking-stove environment.

Know more. It helps to go into a little detail. (No-one reading a Desert Winds book will be unfamiliar with the phrase 'Life is about detail.'!)

Progress in the field of exhaust emissions regulation has had some unfortunate side-effects when it comes to buying a vehicle with the aim of driving to distant lands; lands where such regulation is notional, non-existent or even then probably not adhered to. What is the relevance of that?

Kyoto, Doha-2012. 'Brussels', often said with a disparaging grunt in Western Europe, has done an unenviable but thorough job crystal-balling and balancing the desirable with the possible in terms of legislation on emissions, post-Kyoto – and Doha 2012. Engine designers have bravely tagged along with the challenge – albeit often holding on by their very fingernails and not averse to a bit of skulduggery to achieve the targets set up by the new rules.

Euro standards. Nevertheless we had (and have), in Europe, standards over the years with the familiar overview titles Euro 1, 2 and 3 (1992, 1996, 2000), Euro 4 in 2005/6, Euro 5 2009/10 and, soon, Euro 6 scheduled for 2014/15. (Eleven vehicle categories – petrol or diesel, passenger cars, light commercials and heavies, plus variations according to gross weight – each have their own quantified set of parameters. Carbon monoxide, unburnt hydrocarbons, NOx and 'particulate matter' – soot, etc – are what have to be nailed – a process that generates almost equally undesirable CO_2.) Other regions of 'the developed world' have their own regulations and manufacturers have to comply if they want to sell vehicles there.

Petrol engines are designed exclusively for leaded or for unleaded petrol with only a small overlap. Know the table opposite or expect damage.

It's about money – again. Meeting these emissions limits required input from the oil companies. Producing compatible fuels – lowering sulphur content, including certain additives, excluding others – puts fuel costs up. Countries with struggling economies that had not got around to imposing emissions regulation were just as uninterested in buying fancy fuels to keep rickety transport systems mobile. There, rock-bottom fuels at the cheapest rates are on offer. But so what?

High sulphur diesel also causes engine lubricant contamination. Use an oil formulated to minimise exhaust after-treatment hardware – eg Mobil 1 ESP (see p.7.27).

ECUs rule. In an age where the combustion process is controlled and tuned by an ECU (electronic control unit), vehicle manufacturers go to enormous lengths to make vehicles' specifications accord with the region in which they will operate. Economy, emissions compliance and available fuels dictate the outcome. Chrysler, for example, carried out tests over vast regions of China to establish common-denominator fuel specifications before deciding on a suitable engine-tune setting for Jeeps.

The technology to achieve appropriate settings and controls for the target territory is challenging and expensive – catalytic converters ('cats') and diesel particulate filters (DPFs) are part of the solution, very costly and must be tuned for the region.

Upstream – and immediately downstream – of the engine combustion event, sensors and the engine ECU monitor or control knock, ambient air pressure and temperature, intake gas flow and oxygen content, turbocharger (if fitted) pressure and volume, exhaust gas recirculation (if fitted) and a host of other parameters.

Fuel quality matters. Low quality fuels (and engine oils that can generate sulphated ash unless carefully specified) can have an adverse effect on both engine life and the functioning and durability of exhaust after-treatment systems – specifically the expensive catalytic converters and, on diesels, the DPFs. These can be 'poisoned' by sulphur and metallic particulates which can cling to the filters and clog them, This can lead to excessive auto-regeneration in the cat and DPF (the process of burning-off accumulations of particulates) which in turn could lead to temperature overload and cracking of the ceramic filter cage.

Low octane petrol can cause 'knocking' – a hard metallic noise from a gasoline engine – especially when the throttle is opened suddenly or when you are in too high a gear for the torque you are demanding.

If your engine is a modern one with an ECU, knock sensors will sense this and retard the ignition as far as it can to alleviate the problem. If you have variable valve timing (VVT) that too will come to the rescue. Many modern petrol engines can cope with a surprisingly low octane fuel. Jeep's new 3.6 litre V6 is cleared down to 87 octane (plus, they say without being drawn on figures, a 'small cushion' slightly below that!)

Diesels can be fussy. Modern diesels, especially if fitted with a DPF (a requirement for Euro 5 and 6), are less accommodating than they used to be. Cetane – not the same as octane in gasolines but still related to starting performance and response characteristics – around 50 is the usual fuel requirement and, more often than not, is met satisfactorily. Sulphur content, though, is very important and there were (and still are) huge worldwide variations in available fuels – see opposite. Too high and it can causeacidic contamination of the engine lubricating oil as well as soot and sulphated ash accumulation on the DPF if there is one.

Sulphur again. Too little sulphur and there can be lubricity problems for fuel injector pumps; these rely on the fuel itself for lubrication of the mechanism. This was an initially serious problem when low-sulphur fuels were first introduced but formulation has been adjusted. (The surreptitious addition of an eggcup full of lube oil into the fuel is no longer necessary!)

DPF damage is the more immediate risk for a Euro 5 diesel on high-sulphur fuel. (The danger of diesel fuel waxing in, and clogging, the fuel lines when summer fuel is used in extreme cold conditions also exists.)

The emissions deal. To sum up the whole emissions scenario, carbon monoxide, unburnt fuel remnants, nitrogen oxides and particulate matter are the targets that legislation aims to reduce. In general terms the first three are addressed by the catalytic converter; the particulates are filtered out by the DPF which clogs and unclogs itself automatically thanks to 'regeneration burn-offs' – follow the story on the next spread!

Chemical scrubbing. NOx is more of a problem and (Euro 6 here we come!) requires – on current technology – 'chemical scrubbing'. The diagram with all the arrows overleaf attempts to walk you through what

WORLD-WIDE DIESEL SULPHUR CONTENT (ppm = parts per million) – OVERVIEW mid-2012

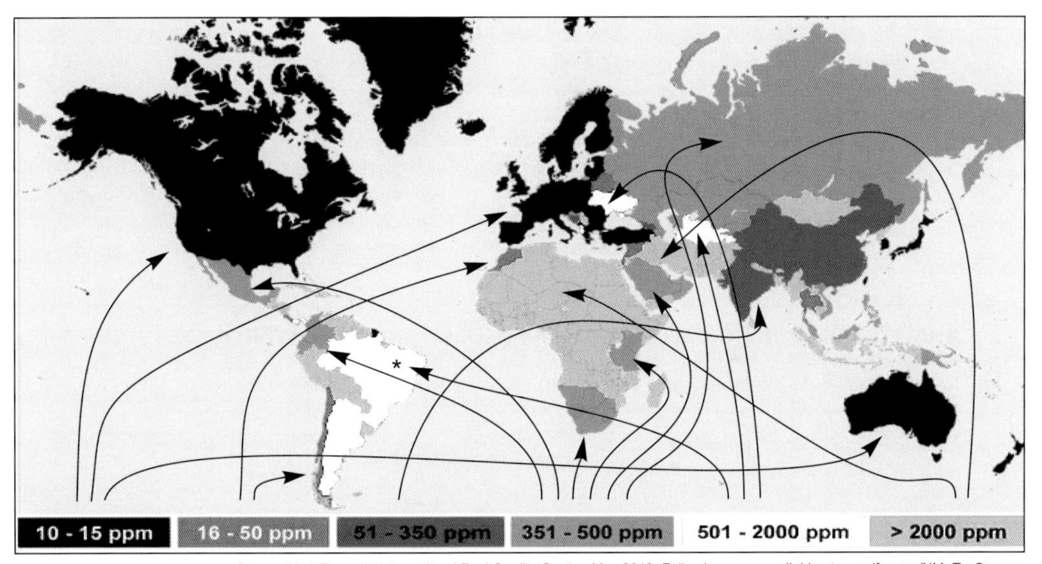

Source: Hart Energy's International Fuel Quality Center, May 2012. Full colour map available at www.ifqc.org/NM_Top5.aspx

* *As in India, Brazilian diesel specifications vary between metropolitan and 'interior' (ie up-country) areas to minimise urban pollution. Sources indicate rising biodiesel content has been legislated and many municipalities prescribe 50ppm and even 10ppm diesel from Jan 2013. By Jan 2014 interior regions are scheduled to sell diesel not exceeding 500ppm. Updates at www.dieselnet.com/standards/br/fuel.php*

World fuels data

As explained, producing high quality fuel, low in sulphur and other harmful constituents, is expensive. Such formulation is necessary in regions where stringent emissions regulations apply - see next spread.

Where there are no such regulatory imperatives, the default is cheaper fuel of lower quality.

If you are an aid agency, NGO (non-governmental organisation) or just an expeditioner planning a long trip, an overview of the fuels you will be using along your route or in your area of operation will be necessary so that you can ensure your vehicles are compatible.

Obtaining such information is not always easy. Theoretically, contacting the national fuel importers and distributors should yield the data - often easier said than done.

There are efficient organisations that hold data on the complete spectrum of world-wide fuels. Their clients are international oil companies, vehicle and engine manufacturers operating on a membership basis; obtaining, analysing, updating and collating such information is expensive too but it is worth making contact as an individual.

One such organisation is IFQC - the International Fuel Quality Center run by Hart Energy in Houston, Texas. Website: www.ifqc.org. e-mail: ifqc@hartenergy.com. Tel: (+1)713.981.9320.

In Europe, Brussels-based CONCAWE may also be ale to help. Website www.concawe.be. Tel: (+32).2.566.91.60

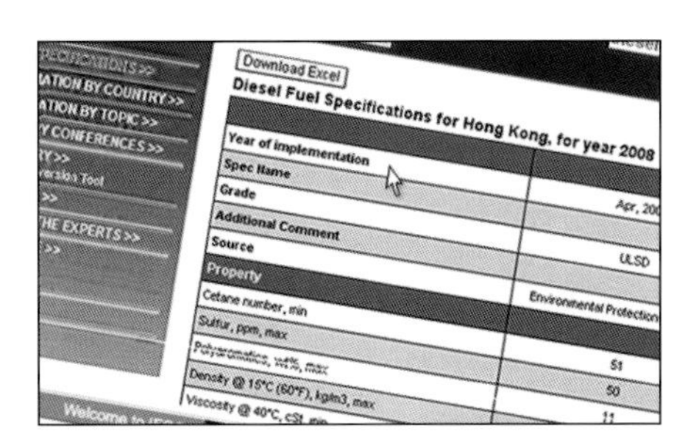

Top and above: ifqc map gives invaluable overview of diesel fuel quality world-wide. Membership yields detailed regional data. Right: Asking the attendant – if you can find one – is unlikely to yield fuel specification! Get information from the oil companies and vehicle manufacturer way in advance so that any tweaking of the engine can be done. Probably not feasible on modern petrol engines.

is going on. (It's not as complex as it looks; start on the left side and follow the pointers!)

'Chemical scrubbing', in terms of fancy hardware, is, usually, a continuous spray (quoted as about 2% of the fuel consumption in terms of volume) of an aqueous urea fluid into the exhaust gases which turns the NOx into pure nitrogen and water. If you've heard of 'BlueTEC' or 'AdBlue', that is Mercedes jumping the gun to Euro 6 compatibility. A 'BlueTEC' Merc will have a small tank at the back of the wagon into which AdBlue is decanted at every service interval.

So what to do? A morsel of good news: as the application of emissions standards spreads, so fuel standards are on the whole rising worldwide. In India, for example, legislated sulphur content has gone from a staggering 10,000 parts per million in 1995 to 350ppm, nationwide (Euro3) – and 50ppm in selected areas – in 2010. (Sulphur content is just one of 19 parameters making up the fuel

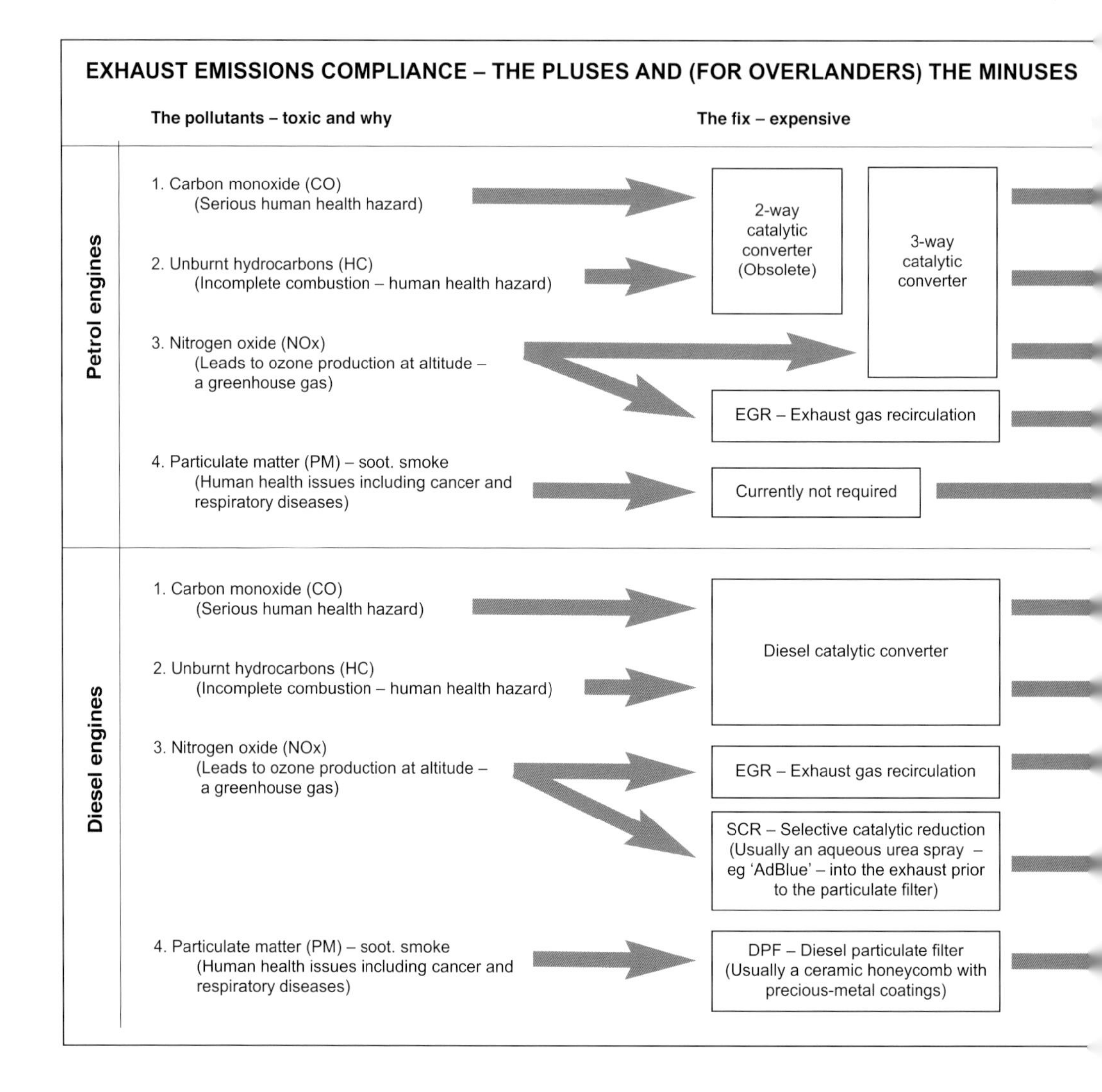

specification!)

But in very remote regions fuel identification is often achieved by removing the bung of a dented barrel and taking a sniff. So what can an expeditioner do? Sadly, not much. Buying a Euro 4 vehicle will help. Stoically accepting the reduced life of your cat and DPF is good training! And, after the last five pages, a bit of a let-down!

Looking aft towards the right-hand rear wheel, the DPF (diesel particulate filter) on a 2012 Jeep Wrangler CRD (2.8 litre VM diesel) is clear to see. The catalytic converter sits upstream of it (top left in the photograph, just out of sight) close to the exhaust manifold so that it warms quickly on startup.

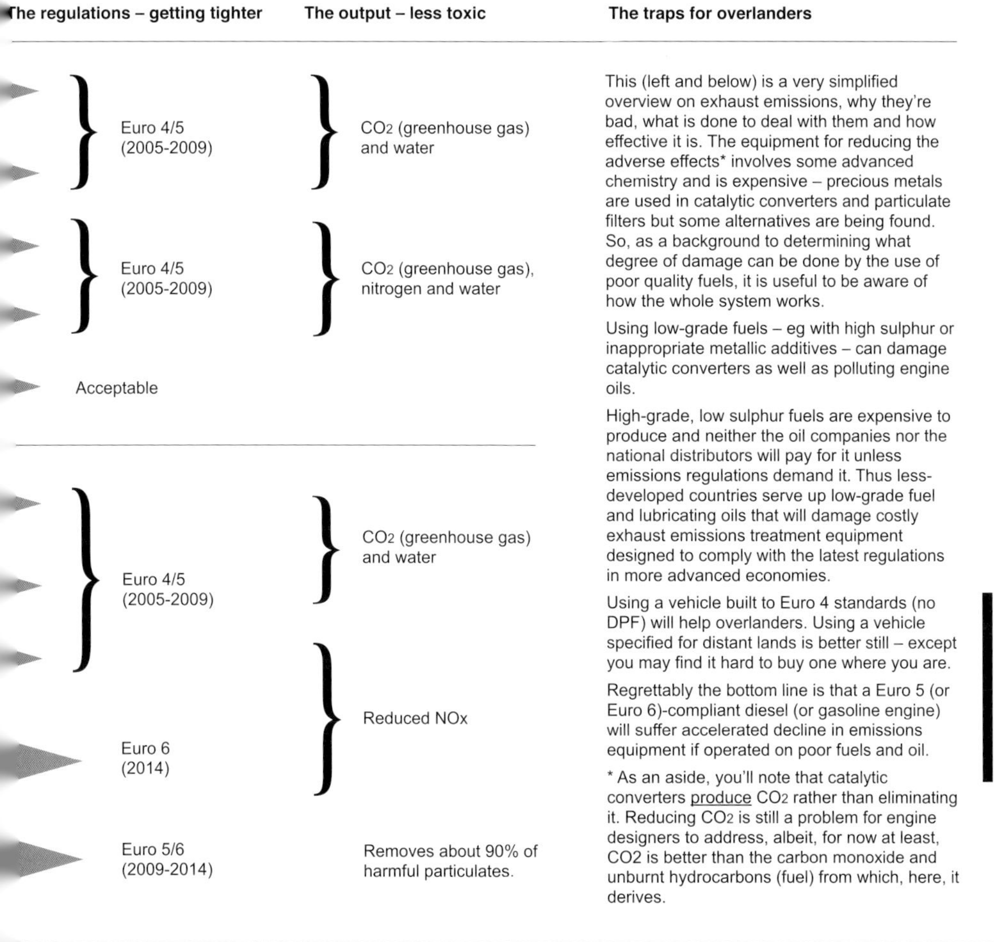

This (left and below) is a very simplified overview on exhaust emissions, why they're bad, what is done to deal with them and how effective it is. The equipment for reducing the adverse effects* involves some advanced chemistry and is expensive – precious metals are used in catalytic converters and particulate filters but some alternatives are being found. So, as a background to determining what degree of damage can be done by the use of poor quality fuels, it is useful to be aware of how the whole system works.

Using low-grade fuels – eg with high sulphur or inappropriate metallic additives – can damage catalytic converters as well as polluting engine oils.

High-grade, low sulphur fuels are expensive to produce and neither the oil companies nor the national distributors will pay for it unless emissions regulations demand it. Thus less-developed countries serve up low-grade fuel and lubricating oils that will damage costly exhaust emissions treatment equipment designed to comply with the latest regulations in more advanced economies.

Using a vehicle built to Euro 4 standards (no DPF) will help overlanders. Using a vehicle specified for distant lands is better still – except you may find it hard to buy one where you are.

Regrettably the bottom line is that a Euro 5 (or Euro 6)-compliant diesel (or gasoline engine) will suffer accelerated decline in emissions equipment if operated on poor fuels and oil.

* As an aside, you'll note that catalytic converters <u>produce</u> CO_2 rather than eliminating it. Reducing CO_2 is still a problem for engine designers to address, albeit, for now at least, CO_2 is better than the carbon monoxide and unburnt hydrocarbons (fuel) from which, here, it derives.

7.7 Engine oils

Preliminaries: types and specifications

Hold on. Don't let the technology get away from you. Even the people in overalls with makers' logos admit that oil specifications can be a bit complex. But it's important, especially in the light of emissions regulations. And, you'll be pleased to know that though it is also important to know what is going on, the final answer is simple.

Get what you pay for. As elsewhere in life, the best is more expensive. Luckily, with engine oils, there are set criteria for defining – or at least getting a feel for – 'best': base oils and Service Categories. This is separate from simple viscosity categories such as SAE 40 which only describes how 'thick' the oil is. (Virtually all engine oils now are multigrade, eg 5W-30. 'Multigrade'? See paragraph opposite under 'API'.)

Expedition usage is niche in the oil market. Seek the most advanced grades capable of also dealing with the worst climates, stress and fuels. Look first at the Service Category.

Oil type – base oils. This is the type of oil from which the product is made – in ascending order of longevity and general benefit: straight mineral oil, part-synthetic, full synthetic. Synthetics give better protection – for longer – against wear, friction, chemical degradation, sludge and evaporative losses. There are also additives to tailor an oil for a particular operating regime.

Service Categories. A Service Category is the internationally-recognised pigeon-hole into which a particular oil fits, defined here in very general terms by the uses to which the oil will be put, eg light diesel (car), petrol engine, heavy duty diesel in trucks. Don't let it confuse matters but there are (wouldn't you know it!) two or three overlapping sets of Service Categories, further explained in the page opposite – the US API, the European ACEA, the Japanese ILSAC. Etc.

Engine oils – the broad picture

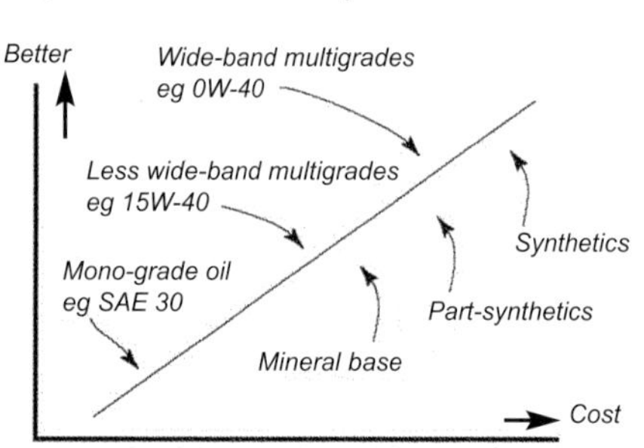

Lubrizol spidergraph oil spec comparison

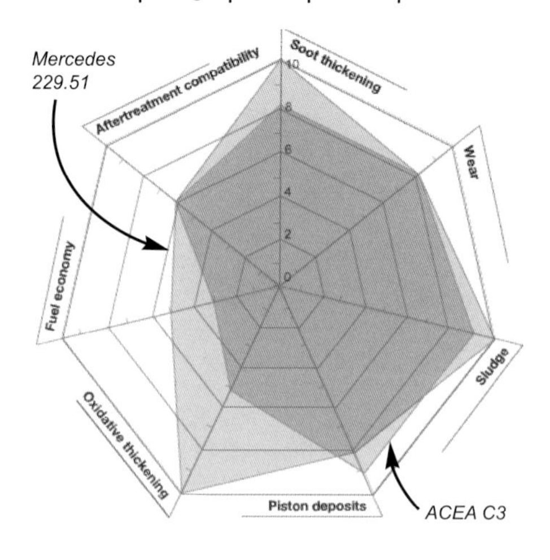

To be awarded a Service Category, an oil must meet certain criteria established by particular defined tests on given representative test engines. These tests, and the categories awarded, got more demanding as the years went by. Beware, however. In recent years different, apparently ascending, categories represent defined usage rather than one being 'better' than the other.

Manufacturers' specifications. As particular engine designs have advanced in the quest for performance, long life and efficiency, some manufacturers have laid down their own oil specifications that are invariably more demanding than the internationally set categories. Take a look at the 'spidergraph' above generated by Lubrizol that, with admirable (qualitative) clarity, here compares the six-parameter demands of ACEA C3 Service Category with those of Mercedes spec 229.51.

Both Mercedes and Volkswagen were early protagonists of 'in-house' oil specifications. Camshaft wear, extreme fuel-injection mechanism demands and meeting up-coming emissions regulations were the driving forces in most cases.

WHAT THE LABEL SAYS – AND DOESN'T SAY: SERVICE CATEGORIES – ENGINE OILS

No manufacturer will say 'This is not our top product' or 'This is our cheapest'. Here, **'Mobil 1, ESP'** – one of their best in the UK – is proudly presented as Fully Synthetic (that 'ESP' is also very important – see p.7.29). There are more than *eight* versions of 'Mobil Super 3000' and the data sheets are coy about exactly what the base oil is. A lubricant's base oil should be indicated on the label but seldom is unless it is a full synthetic. Technical information is available on the Mobil website if you dig. Castrol's 2012 website is cringingly dumbed-down to look like a movie trailer and hardly mentions base oil at all. Look for the all-important Service Categories (the 'API' and 'ACEA' letters and numbers), on the back of the container – and the even more important engine manufacturer's oil specification. Below is an example of typical packaging and what it means.

GB IRL M Designed for modern Diesel and Gasoline vehicles fitted with emission reduction systems. Formulated to be fully compatible with latest Diesel Particulate Filters (DPF) and Gasoline Catalytic Converters (CAT). Reduces deposits and sludge build-up to enable long and

Meets requirements of/Répond aux exigences de/Καλύπτεις τις απαιτήσεις του:
ACEA C2, C3; API SN/SM Engine Tests; JASO DL-1
Approved/Approuvé/Εγκεκριμένο: **MB-Approval 229.51/229.31; VW 504 00/507 00; BMW Longlife-04; Porsche C30; Peugeot/Citroën Automobiles B71 2290/B71 2297**
ExxonMobil Quality Level/Niveau de qualité/Επίπεδο ποιότητας: **API CF**

'5W-30' – viscosity (multigrade): Description of the oil.Irrelevant to how 'good' it is.
'Fully synthetic' – the base oil: Full synthetic is best so it is trumpeted on the label. Only rarely (plaudits for Halfords) will the package clearly indicate when it is part-synthetic or straight mineral oil.

Manufacturers' specifications. Mobil clearly covered all the manufacturers' spec tests they could here; and this is an abbreviated list. An expensive exercise. But they have come out with a high grade lubricant for those who want the best. Note the numbers carefully; they represent very different specifications.

Read the label – all of it, not just the '5W-30' viscosity. Wide-band multigrades are best. Be very particular where manufacturers' specifications are concerned. Stick to them.

ACEA *(Association des Constructeurs Europeéns d'Automobiles)* oil performance standards – engine type (letter) and number. Prefix 'A' applies to petrol engines, 'B' to 'light' diesels; now usually combined as 'A/B', 'E' refers to 'heavy duty' diesels. The all-important 'C' prefix indicates a 'Catalyst compatible' oil (see next page) that will minimise contamination of expensive catalysts and DPFs (see previous spread) on low-emissions vehicles. Beware: ascending ACEA numbers usually define *type* of oil rather than quality. See table next spread for fuller ACEA categories list.

ILSAC *(International Lubricants Standardisation and Approval Committee*) oil performance ratings (not shown here) appear more often in the US in conjunction with API standards and imply ECII fuel economy – see below – (and other) benefits over the standard API rating. ILSAC GF-5 includes and meets GF-1 to 4 categories. Formulated for pre-2010 engines and accommodates ethanol-laced fuels to E85.

Fuel economy – **EC** (energy conserving) indicates a +1.5% fuel economy over a standard Reference Oil. **EC II** indicates +2.7%. Economy seekers often opt for ACEA A1 or B1 oils (next spread). EC or ECII is sometimes shown on its own but more often implied when an ILSAC category (above) such as GF-3 or GF-4 (both ECII) featured.

Global DHD, DLD etc. Projected new classification system applicable world-wide. Applicable to heavy trucks mainly..

API (*American Petroleum Institute*) oil performance standards for spark ignition engines (**S + letter suffix – SM**) or diesels – compression ignition – **C + letter suffix – CF**, not shown here but listed on the Mobil data sheet). Suffix *usually* denotes ascending standards: control of deposits, oxidation, wear, corrosion. Table next spread. Note: The **SAE** (*US Society of Automotive Engineers*) system, accepted world-wide, indicates viscosity – how 'thick' the oil is. 'SAE' as in "SAE 0W-40'. High numbers mean thick oil, low numbers thin, free-flowing. Two together as here is a **multigrade** – virtually standard now in all engine oils. When cold the 0W-40 behaves like an SAE 0W, when hot like an SAE 40.

Motorcycle oils. Motorcycles are different in that in the majority of cases the gearbox uses the engine's lubricating oil. Most importantly there is also a 'wet' clutch – ie it operates in the engine oil. Excess friction-modifiers – as found in oils of API SH category and above would normally give rise to the risk of clutch slip on a motorcycle. Thus only oils specifically for motorcycles API SG (or SH, SJ or SL *but with* JASO MA) should be used in motorcycles..

Beware those marketing people – again! As with the fanciful names for simple 4x4 concepts (p.2.10), so with oils. Flashy packaging, glossy tell-you-nothing leaflets, wowee websites, the compulsion to portray every product as 40% better than something else (usually ill defined) and associate full synthetics only with 'racing' or 'max power' ... . The marketeers do a major disservice to their own research departments, obscuring the basic information you need to make a mature decision on what engine oil to use. Does it matter? Yes, it matters if you value your engine.

Oil Service Categories overlap – API and ACEA cover the same ground in different ways – the latter is a smarter system. ILSAC (US/Japan) is an API add-on

API SERVICE CATEGORIES – US System

Gasoline engine oil categories – prefix 'S'

Prefix 'S' = spark ignition, ie petrol engines. Suffixes run from 'SA' to (mid 2011) 'SN'. Categories SA to SH are now obsolete (but see SG regarding motorcycles, previous spread). For petrol engines the latest engine oil Service Category includes the performance properties of each earlier category. List starts with the latest.

SN For 2011 and older vehicles. Improved high temperature deposit protection for pistons, more stringent sludge control, and seal compatibility. Combines this with improved fuel economy, turbocharger protection, emission control system compatibility, and protection of engines operating on ethanol-containing fuels up to E85.

SM Current for 2010 and older petrol engines.

SL Current for 2004 and older petrol engines.

SJ Current for 2001 and older petrol engines.

SA-SH These categories are all obsolete. API issue ***specific cautions*** against using engine oils with Service Categories SA to SE in any engine built after 1979: ' ... may cause poor performance or equipment harm.'

Diesel engine oil categories – prefix 'C'

Prefix 'C' = compression ignition, ie diesel engines. Categories from 'CA' to (mid 2011) 'CJ-4'. CA to CG-4 are now obsolete. Latest categories address fuel sulphur content, the preservation of emission-control devices such as catalytic converters and diesel particulate filters (DPFs). List starts with the latest.

CJ-4 For 2009-2010 emission standards. For fuels up to 500 ppm sulphur (0.05% by weight). Controls catalyst poisoning, DPF blocking, engine wear, piston deposits, soot handling properties, oxidative thickening, foaming, and viscosity loss due to shear. But use with greater than 15 ppm (0.0015%) sulphur fuel may impact exhaust after-treatment system durability and/or drain interval.CJ-4 oils exceed performance criteria of API CI-4 with CI-4 PLUS, CI-4, CH-4, CG-4 and CF-4. When using CJ-4 oil with higher than 15 ppm sulphur fuel, consult the engine manufacturer for service interval.

CI-4 (2002) Accommodates emissions regulations involving EGR (exhaust gas recirculation). For high speed, 4-stroke diesels using fuels with sulphur content up to 0.5%. Can be used in place of CD, CE, CF-4, CG-4 and CH-4 oils.

CH-4 Introduced 1998. For high speed, 4-stroke engines using fuels with sulphur content below 0.5%. Can be used in place of CD, CE, CF-4, CG-4 oils.

ACEA CATEGORIES – European system

Gasoline and 'light' diesel engine oil categories

ACEA 2010 categories address subtly different parameters compared with API – mainly in the emissions area. Categories:
'A' for gasoline engines,'B' for light duty diesels, 'C' specifically for both types *with exhaust after-treatment devices* (catalysts and DPFs - see pp 7.22-24); and 'E' for heavy duty diesel engines. Sub-categories reflect different performance requirements, the suffix number (1.. 5 etc) *may* reflect the performance tests – highest number = highest performance; but this is not always the case. 'C' categories reflect more tailored-for-type specifications.

A1/B1 Low viscosity, fuel economy oils for moderately stressed engines. May not suit all engines.

A3/B3 Stable, 'stay-in-grade' (reduced tendency for thickening by contaminants) for higher performance engines and/or longer drain if specified by maker.

A3/B4 As A3/B3 but high performance engines and including direct injection diesels.

A5/B5 In effect a stable, 'stay-in-grade', long-life, version of the low viscosity oils at A1/B1. Due to the low viscosity, may not suit all units.

Catalyst compatibility oils (see note above)

Certain 'good' qualities of lubricating oils – like coping with high-sulphur fuels – generate sulphated ash. Sulphated ash shortens the life of the exhaust after-treatment devices like catalysts and particulate filters. 'Low SAPS' oils (sulphated ash, phosphorous and sulphur) are formulated to be catalyst-friendly by preserving diesel particulate filter (DPF) functionality. Though in the context of expedition use the C1-C4 categories are similar, these are very specific categories to be applied only to engines cleared for their use; check owner's handbook.

Catalyst and DPF (diesel particulate filter) compatible oils

C1 'Low SAPS' (see above), stable, stay-in-grade, low viscosity oil formulated to reduce catalyst and DPF degradation and enhance fuel economy.

C2 As C1 above for engines not *dependent* on low friction, low viscosity oils but capable of using them.

C3 As C2 above for engines requiring slightly higher high-temperature viscosity and not compatible with low viscosity oils.

C4 As C3 with refinements aimed at fuel economy, reduced sulphur, and certain Mercedes spec requirements.

Engine oil – what to actually do

Owner's manual? Before we go on, what is wrong with just following the driver's handbook? Right: that, more than ever, is the place to start (and probably finish) – so long as it is precisely specific about what oil to use. They aren't always, and certainly have not been in the past – often some very general viscosity vs ambient temperature table with no mention of base oil or service category. It's a lot clearer now.

Jeep nails down all the corners for the 2012 Wrangler 2.8 diesel equipped with a catalytic converter and DPF: 'Use only oil conforming to ACEA C3 requirements. ... and .. a 5W-30 ESP fully synthetic, low ash oil that meets Chrysler Material Standard MS-11106 must be used.' Any questions?

Expeditions are different. We are considering exceptional conditions here – expeditions, aid work, probably poor fuels. no dealership to do your oil change and possibly extended oil drain intervals. Why bother with all that detail on the facing page? Here's why: if you can't get your regular oil in some distant land you can check that what you are offered is right or the closest to what is required. It really does matter. OK?

Categories vs manufacturer specs. The oils Service Categories are important. However, engine manufacturers' own oil specifications have overtaken, and are more demanding than, the 'national' Service Categories in terms of defining what is best for the engine and exhaust after-treatment equipment in use and the oil companies are coming up with the right product.

High sulphur diesel: drain intervals. High sulphur in diesel is the enemy of just about everything. It will pollute engine lubricating oil as well as (if fitted) clogging the cat and DPF and triggering repeat DPF re-generation burn-offs.. If you are aware (see table on p.7-23) of having to use high-sulphur diesel then reducing oil change intervals will benefit your engine – with or without any exhaust after-treatment.

The US diesel doyens Cummins have an elegant formula for quantifying the problem and what to do about it which, reduced to expedition terms , amounts to:

- Diesel fuel sulphur content 0.05%-0.50% – reduce drain intervals to 75% of
the usual mileage.
- Diesel fuel sulphur content over 0.5% –reduce drain intervals to 50%.

'Older engines'. As we have seen, emission controls bring yet another problem area in their wake. Phosphorous is an important anti-wear additive to traditional engine oils .. but it also 'poisons' catalytic converters. Thus modern oils (for modern engines with cats and DPFs) need oils formulated not only to reduce sulphated ash but also low in phosphorous.

So beware the natural inclination to give your trusted old, non-cat, non-DPF, engine the 'best' and most up to date oils. Such engines often have 'sliding contact' valve gear that is dependent on the phosphorous content of an oil to minimise cam-lobe wear and could well suffer if operated on a 'low-SAPS' oil.

Ascending numbers and letters used to be a 'better oil' guide. But you have to read it carefully now. Global categories (DHD, DLD etc) is an attempt at a common system.

Whilst the oil companies' write-ups about an 'oil for older engines' may sound patronising it usually has this problem in mind – as well as, of course, the fact that older engine may be more worn and require a thicker oil. Old engines need phosphorous.

And finally. Use the vehicle manufacturer's precisely designated oil. Take extra for top-ups. If there is inadequate detail in the owner's manual, consult the oil manufacturer for their recommendation. Know from the information here and websites, what the acceptable alternatives are en route.

Total mechanical reliability is even more important in remote areas. Use the best lubricants you can.

7.8 Water

When to carry it and how much

Quick overview. As with the coverage on fuels and oils for the engine, space here permits only an overview of the subject, covered in greater detail in *Vehicle-dependent Expedition Guide.*

Constant need. Even in normal day-to-day business driving, most drivers will be champing for a cup of tea or coffee by the end of three or four hours. Any excursion that could remotely qualify for the term expedition, right down to a half day in the hills, is certainly going to call for water to be included in the planning.

Fluid intake can increase by up to 400% in hot climate, high-workload conditions compared with sedentary use. Plan water requirements carefully and add reserves.

How much. Ranging between sedentary, no work to vigorous work in ambients of 42°C the span of consumption will be 2.5 to 10 litres per day . Much dependent on workload; safe planning figures:

- Temperate climate: 2.5-5.0 litres per head per day.
- Night/day temperatures 5°/35°C: 5-8 litres per head per day.
- Night/day temp 20°/45°C: 6-10 litres per head per day.

Warm climate, moderate workload can be accommodated with a planning figure of about 4-7 litres per day usually. This is a minimum and is to take care of drinking, cooking and very small amounts for personal hygiene. Body mass is hugely important: not surprisingly, overweight people use more; skinny ones use quite a lot less.

Even on a demanding trip, well managed reserves can yield an occasional 3-4 litre hoard – enough for a de-luxe shower like this (above)! Military 20-litre hard plastic water can is the best for storage. Plastic squeezy-siphon (here with extended pipe to reach bottom of can) permits filling of water bottles, kettles, with can still lashed in place. Doubles as dip-stick.

Temperature. Once ambients exceed about (37°C), consumption rises sharply.

Not like home. Our profligate use of water at home has to be abandoned on an expedition where, as already seen, weight is of major importance. You soon get adept at washing in a single half-mug of water on a long-duration overseas trip. The above are minima and assume constraints on weight which invariably apply on long trips. A day trip or weekend of camping, of course, does not have to be a session of ascetic self-denial.

Reserves. Carry a sensible reserve to cover possible breakdown on a long trip. In very remote areas with very little traffic this should be two or three days' supply.

Carrying it, dispensing it

Beyond the cup-holders. Supermarket plastic bottles are not the way to carry water for any trip longer than a few hours. Really robust hard-plastic jerry cans, pre-disinfected with a strong bleach solution and then rinsed, are the only practical method of carrying expedition water. Military 20 litre cans have found their way onto the normal market and are ideal. As with fuel cans, padded racks and tie-downs for water cans should be arranged.

Robust personal water bottles are a necessity so that each crew member has their own supply and fill-ups can all take place at the same time.

Dispensing it. It is tedious having to unlash the can every time you need to dispense water so a dip-in squeezy pump is a lightweight, simple way to get over the problem. They can usually be found in caravanning and camping shops.

Using it. If you are not pushing the payload limits there is nothing to stop you taking more than minimum drinking needs and, as it were, splashing out. When Honda brought out the CRV in the UK they made a camp shower accessory available, a solidly-made electrical pump that could be dipped into a can. Three litres for a shower is possible – bliss at the end of a long hot day! If you can't spare that and hate dirt in your hair, a hair-wash alone, using a cup and a bucket, catching and re-using the rinse, can be done with 0.75 - 1.0 litre.

Water for drinking

Know the enemy. Surprisingly, most tap supplies are – after reassurance from locals – safe to drink. Equally surprising is the fact that virtually all streams, no matter how clear and sparkling, are not. Either way it is not worth risking illness on your trip. Knowing what you are up against and what to do is half the battle. Keeping it simple, the main hazard classifications are:

- ***Big bugs – protozoa, parasites.*** Unpredictable distribution worldwide. Carried in human and animal faeces, resistant to chlorine and iodine but UV (Steripen) and chlorine dioxide work.
- ***Small bugs – bacteria.*** Prolific. Main causes of stomach upsets. Can be filtered by the finest filters, chemicals and UV.
- ***Very small bugs – viruses.*** Too small to filter except when they clump (and you don't know when they're doing that.). Viruses succumb to chemicals and UV.

Know the bug sizes rather than their names. Know what zaps what. Giardia and crypto are immune to chemicals so micro-filters are needed.

The weapons. Whilst smells and tastes can also be removed with activated carbon, for the bugs you can use:

- Filters and purifiers
- Chemicals
- Heat and boiling (see page 7.33)

'BUG' SIZES AND WHAT YOU CAN DO ABOUT THEM

	Big bugs (parasites, protozoa) eg: giardia, cryptosporidia, schistosoma, amoebic dysentery, worms	Small bugs (bacteria) eg: E Coli, bacillary dysentery, cholera, typhoid, leptospirosis	Very small bugs (viruses) eg: Polio, hepatitis, rotavirus	Tastes and smells eg: Residual iodine, and chlorine, pesticides, 'bad eggs', chemicals
Size: (1 μm is a micron: 1/1000th of one millimetre)	4 - 12μm ie, well over 1μm	0.5 - 3.0μm ie, around 1μm	0.02 - 0.08μm ie, less than 1μm	Dissolved
Can be filtered out by:	Virtually all micro-filters (see over)	The finest micro-filters	Too small to filter but may attach to larger impurities	Activated carbon granules or resin
Can be killed by:	Hot / boiling water. Resistant to chorine but UV (ultra violet light) and chlorine dioxide are effective.	Iodine, chlorine. silver in most cases. UV and chlorine dioxide kill everything.	Iodine, chlorine. silver in most cases. UV and chlorine dioxide kill everything.	n/a

Chemical treatment

Three options. Chemical treatment for water is of three (four?) types:

- Chlorine (Puritabs etc). In some developing countries needs to be used at up to five times 'normal' strength.
- Chlorine dioxide (no after-taste) kills everything (see table last page.)
- Silver-based (eg, Micropur). Now considered safe for long-term use after doubts in the late '80s. No after-taste.
- Iodine (eg, Potable Aqua). Should not be used for period longer than 3 to 6 months. After-taste.

Note that these chemical treatments leave some parasites virtually untouched.

Three-pronged attack on water impurities is best – micro-filtration, chemical attack on smallest bacteria and viruses and a charcoal de-taster. Then relax.

Selecting your hardware

Three-pronged problem. A slow look around the table on the previous page and the conclusion on expedition water treatment soon becomes clear. Three facts present themselves:

- Parasites like giardia and cryptosporidia are less numerous than bacteria but very bad news (they lay you low and are then difficult to get rid of). They are immune to iodine and simple chlorine but large enough to filter easily.
- Bacteria are the main risk and respond to chemicals as well as being filterable.
- Chemicals like iodine and chlorine leave a taste – albeit silver does not.

Three-pronged attack. Clearly your water filtration equipment to take care of all of these problems must address each one in turn and will have:

- A micro-filter with a pore size of 1μm (1 micron) or smaller.
- A chemical element to be sure about the bacteria and take out viruses.
- A de-tasting element to remove tastes and smells from the chemical purifiers and any others in the water.

These stages can be arranged separately by the user but filters are available that combine all three. Micro-filter pore size will be quoted in catalogue literature. A favourite way of incorporating chemical disinfection is to incorporate an iodine resin element into the filter. This will have a finite life which you should check on. And finally many filters have an optional activated charcoal final stage to take out tastes and smells from water. Use of silver obviates the need for charcoal de-tasting (see Katadyn opposite).

Go shopping. The above and the table on the previous page will equip you sufficiently to be able to go shopping for a suitable filter for your needs. The only characteristic not mentioned is flow rate which could be relevant to large group expeditions. Flow rates will vary from 0.5 litres per minute for the very small rucsac units weighing under half a kilo, to 4.5 litres/min for stirrup-pump types weighing over 5.0kg.

Check filter capacity too which varies from 380 to 7000 litres before a change of filter element is due.

Names of manufacturers that jump to mind are Katadyn, First Need, MSR and, for large remote-group use, Pre-Mac (UK).

Getting fuel and water quantities right is bedrock fundamental. Stowage, lashing-down and getting the high-density loads mid-point of the wheel-base is also important. Strapped down, and braced against a can-height bulkhead for the heavy containers to rest against, the setup here is close to ideal – especially for a large load like this.

Katadyn Pocket ceramic/silver filter/purifier (1): 2μm pores, 1.0 litre/min, 50,000 litre capacity. Chlorine dioxide (2), unlike straight chlorine tablets, kills the whole spectrum of bugs (p.7.31): de-tasting not needed. SteriPen (3) inserted for 90 sec into 1-litre water-bottle radiates ultra-violet light, kills all organisms. In all cases, let the water settle, pre-filter to remove detritus before filtration. No filter will improve brackish water like that from some desert wells (4).

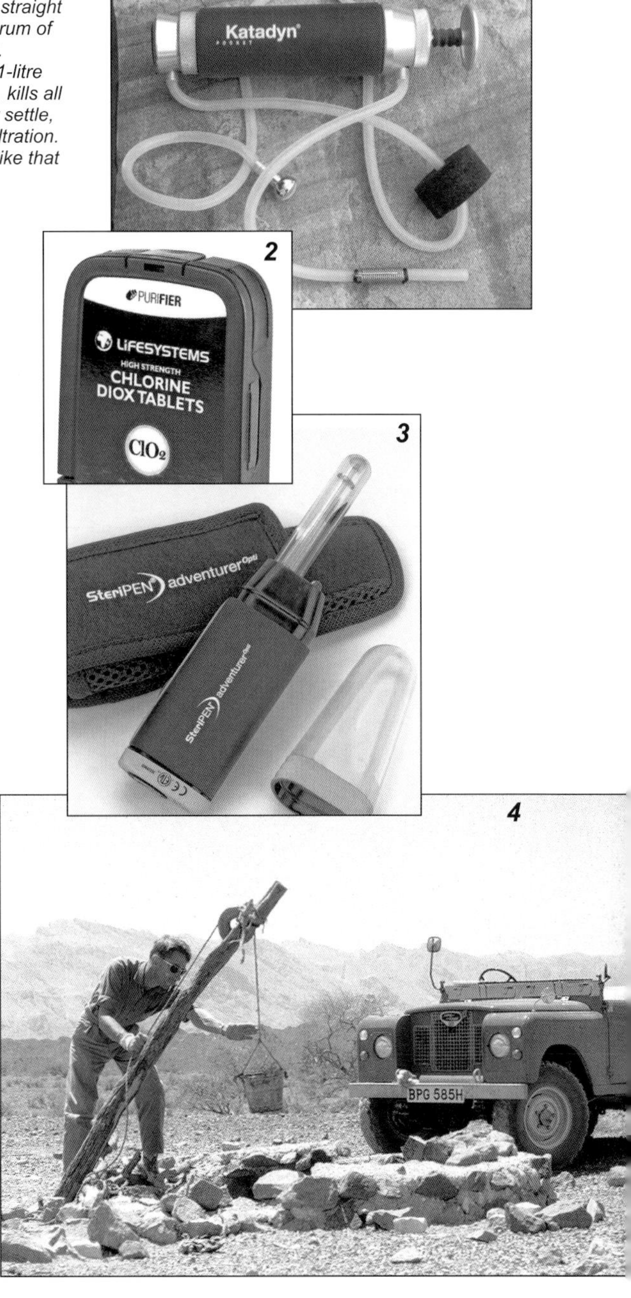

Heat and boiling

The old standby. Tedious, fuel-hungry and productive of warm, flat-tasting water, heat is a good standby method of purifying water. Old standbys often accumulate old wives' tales too and a study of research on the subject carried out over the past 25 years shows that it is not necessary to 'boil for 10 minutes' – or anything like that. The table shows that in fact many bugs begin to lose interest at temperatures as low as 45-50°C.

As you might expect, lower temperatures for a relatively long time equals higher temperatures for a short time and the table shows this too.

You will probably have a small digital thermometer with you in the field and if you take the photographic type with a separate probe you can save a lot of time and fuel if you have to purify water using heat. What it all amounts to is:

1. Almost any heat is better than no heat.
2. The real baddies, like giardia and cryptosporidia, start to keel over at 55°C.
3. In emergencies, heat to 60-65°C and hold for 10-15 minutes.
4. Just bringing to the boil will kill everything. No need to hold it there.

Lethal temperature-x-time combinations:

Worm eggs	50-55°C
Cryptosporidium	45°C x 5-20min
	55°C x 20min
	64°C x 2min
Giardia	60°C x 10min
Salmonella	65°C x 1min
Cholera	62°C x 10min
Viruses	60°C x 20-40min
	70°C x 1min
Hepatitis A (waterborne)	98°C x 1min
	60°C x 19min

Section 8

Loading and tyres

King Cab or Double Cab – solutions for work or expeditions where there's a mix of people and cargo. Beware (see next spread) of too much weight over or behind the rear axle. Low-density kit only here.

8.1 Loading

Margins of durability, strength, handling and braking will be eroded if you overload. Remember also load density. Max GVW may arrive with space still spare.

Off-roaders move things

Off-roaders' work. Probably as many off-roaders are bought for their ability to move things as for their ability to go off-road. As already discussed on p.7.15, a manufacturer will, according to the market, make his vehicle an all-payload workhorse on stiff springs (to take the weight) or a luxurious five-seater with softer springing for a smooth ride and a very much lower payload capability. Neither is 'better' than the other; they are just each made for a specific job.

Same rules apply in loading. To the surprise of some, the same rules apply to loading of both vehicle types and concern:

- Size of load
- Weight distribution
- Packing method
- Securing the load

Capacity – weight and bulk

Never overload. The prime rule in operating any vehicle is not to overload. Despite their toughness, it applies to off-roaders as well. Every engineered object has strength criteria to which it is designed – with margins that are adequate or generous according to design philosophy. Overloading eats into strength and durability margins, (see above!) adversely affecting handling and performance – as well as safety.

Max payload? EEC kerb weight includes a 75kg driver and a tank of fuel. 'Payload' is the remaining weight you can carry before hitting max GVW – gross vehicle weight. Salesmen and handbooks are equally shy of stating these figures clearly. Knowing them, though, you can come up with some simple guidelines for your useable payload:

- 4 passengers plus x kilos cargo
- 2 passengers plus xx kilos cargo
- Driver plus xxx kilos ... etc.

Belt-and-braces strap further binds cross-bar rack to wheel

Cross-bar rack claws to top of wheel and is held down by threaded bar to A-bracket hooked to wheel spokes

Bracket rubber-clamped to wheel spoke steadies cycle down-tube with tube-clamp

Custom cycle rack optimised for off-road – only 15kg including bike. Keep back-end add-ons to absolute minimum

Overloaded and overworked (above): a broken rear diff in the desert. Brave load (high centre of gravity) en route to Sudan (left) but well-secured.

Beware load density. A cubic foot of lead vs a cubic foot of compressed straw is an analogy of weight vs bulk that would immediately catch our attention. With high density loads the availability of spare space will often obscure the fact that the payload limit has been reached. Equally, with sacks of feathers you'll run out of space before you run out of payload. This kind of problem often sidles up, uninvited, if you are running a vehicle commercially or planning an overland journey in it.

Margins, off-road weights. If you are coming at the problem from the other direction – What vehicles do I need for this job? – choose a vehicle specification which will comfortably cope with the weight involved – with margins – rather than be on the limits. This is especially important off-road where you need to give the vehicle the widest margins you can.

Bicycles. Your trip may include carrying bicycles. Some commercial cycle racks claim to carry four bikes and are frighteningly flimsy even for on-road use. Trust your common-sense when buying and check practicalities. Item on facing page is exceptionally firm and permits rear-door opening with bike still in position. Note rear lights are still visible through bike wheels

All 4x4s have a max payload. Know the figure you can add to the driver + fuel-inclusive kerb weight. X people plus Y kg of cargo. Affects handling, safety.

Mid-wheelbase is right for a load like this but a higher bulkhead (with the straps) would give safer load restraint in the event of an accident. Keep loads like this off the roof.

Weight distribution

What it can take. As the sample axle load table at p.8.10 shows, all off-roaders are designed, when fully laden, to take a greater load on their springs and axles at the rear because that is the inevitable nature of a normal bonneted design.

Mid-wheelbase, low down. But you have seen them; running around, tail-down, headlights pointed skywards ... . Control over weight distribution lies with the operator. On-road, where speeds are higher it is important from a handling point of view; off-road and where conditions are on the limits, especially regarding flotation, the nearer a vehicle can get to a 50/50 fore and aft axle-load condition the better it will be. The overloaded end is the end that sinks first in the mud or soft sand. Keeping the main load ahead of the rear axle and as *low down* as possible (see pics below!) will enhance both handling and flotation.

Weight distribution would be better termed weight concentration. Keep it low down and at the front of the load bed. Aim for 50/50 front/rear.

Distribution within the load. Thus even within a given load which may get close to your vehicle's maximum GVW it is sensible to place high-density items at the front of the load bed and as close to the floor as possible (eg. jerry cans, see pics pp.8.3 and 7.32).

Check weights for best tyre pressures. Users regularly operating in limiting flotation conditions at less than maximum payload where rear axle load is low, can benefit from a calculated assessment of how low rear tyre pressures can go. Where standard loads or load kits are involved it would pay, as suggested at p.8.10, to have a vehicle weighed front and rear to determine what axle loads really are.

Eliminate roof racks, external bolt-ons. A natural corollary of this attention to weight distribution is the elimination of roof racks or other external bolt-on paraphernalia. These items increase a vehicle's moment of inertia in pitch and roll and can be a safety hazard when misused. Many expedition vehicles have been grossly overloaded on the roof rack – and some, unsurprisingly, have paid the price by tipping. That is if fatigue cracks have not taken their toll beforehand.

Oh, alright then. There are many operators, however, for whom a roof rack is essential and in these cases remember that the maximum roof load recommended for most vehicles is seldom much above 75kg. This is enough to accommodate light bulky items such as ladders, small-section timber, canoes and the like.

Whatever you do, and however many

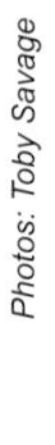

Overladen roof-rack, unseen dune edge. Good loading and driving could have avoided roll.

times you may have seen pictures of the misguided doing so, do not be tempted to put rows of fuel cans on the roof. It will overstress the vehicle and is a handling-related accident waiting to happen.

Effect of trailers. Remember that a trailer, with its appropriate trailer nose load on the towing hook (see Section 4.1 and 6.5), will, for a given actual nose load, exert a disproportionately high download on the rear axle because the tow hitch is well aft of the axle line. If this sounds unlikely, check the diagram below. This is another reason to keep cargo mass as far forward as possible. If you still don't believe then, *reductio ad absurdum,* imagine the load so far aft that the front wheels are off the ground. What is the rear axle load then?

The camel seems to be drawing the owner's attention to a Case B situation in the diagram below. Experienced Toyota pickups like this are not designed to bulk-out with high-density cargo, especially with that much rear overhang. (See previous spread.)

Axle load vs load position – 250kg load

Note how in position B, with the 250kg 40 inches aft of the axle, the rear axle load increases by more than the added payload. Front axle load is less than at kerb weight.

Defender 110 HCPU Tdi at kerb weight

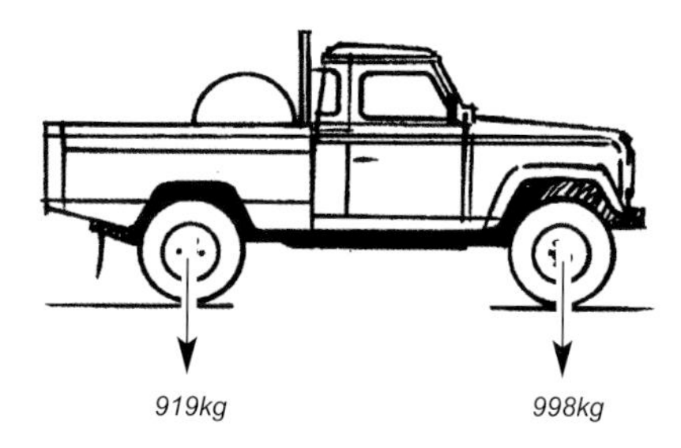

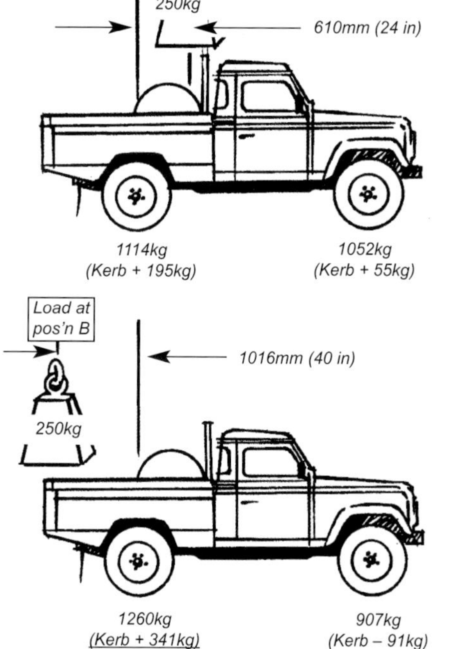

Concentrate load mid-wheelbase. Avoid roof racks or anything that will increase vehicle's moment of inertia. If you really do need one, put only light loads on it.

NB. Danger of exceeding axle weights. *A 638kg load positioned aft at B would increase rear axle load to the top limit of 1850kg. Front axle load in this case would be 250kg lighter than at kerb weight.*

Packing

Serious work. For other than day-to-day errands, regard packing and securing the load in an off-roader as a separate and discrete task. For recreational, commercial or public utility work it is essential:

- **Packing**. Aim for a methodical modular system so that it is easy to load and unload (in a severe bogging say) and so that you know where everything is. Put a list of contents in each box and also in a folder.
- **Lashing**. Ensure the load is lashed down (use ratchet-tensioner straps) to prevent it sliding around and causing damage to the vehicle.

Gravity keeps things tidy but not in a moving 4x4 off-road. Box, stack and strap-down regular loads. Modular boxes for random loads bring order and accessibility.

Spare fuel. Built-in fuel tanks cannot be off-loaded to lighten the vehicle when it is badly bogged but they do offer compact storage low-down (ie low centre of gravity) when underfloor tanks are fitted. Metal jerry cans for extra fuel, however, can hardly be bettered for safety and ease of handling. For large quantities, 205 litre (45 gallon) steel drums are effective and very robust but the drums themselves are very heavy and, being round, are not space-efficient within a vehicle. Drums are more appropriate to carriage of fuel on trucks.

Water. Beware the thin flimsy caravan-shop type containers.Hard plastic jerry cans (p.7.30) are the best way to carry spare water: moveable, demountable and easy to lash.

Modular storage. Methodically organised modular storage within the vehicle(s) is essential if you are to keep track of and prevent damage to the equipment you take. Professional expedition organisations such as British Antarctic Survey have for many years used plastic-lidded boxes that locate one above the other without slipping sideways. Storage boxes similar in concept are now available from most DIY superstores.

It is useful to indicate broad contents on the side and the lid of each box, put a detailed list inside and also in a folder.

Securing

Tie-downs. Secure your load to avoid damage to the vehicle and the load itself. Not all vehicles have the right number of (or any) tie-downs – cleats to which you can attach straps or ropes – so positioning and installing these will be part of your modifications programme (see p.7.19.) The driver of a quiet, rattle-free vehicle becomes subject to the 'Rolls-Royce syndrome' and drives more confidently and more smoothly than when his nerves are a-jangle with repetitive internal noise.

Typical generic payload span*	
Ford Explorer	440kg
Toyota Colorado TF 5-dr	585kg
Defender 90	654–923kg
Shogun 2.5TD 3-dr	700kg
Defender 110	1020–1245kg

**Depending on engine, body type, suspension and transmission.*

Typical unit weights	
205 litre (45 Imp gal) barrel, empty	20kg
205 litre barrel full of petrol, kerosene	185kg
" " diesel, lube oil	200kg
" " water	225kg
20 litre (4.5 Imp gal) steel jerry can, empty	4kg
20 litre steel jerry can full of petrol, kerosene	20kg
" " diesel, lube oil	22kg
" " water	24kg

Standard 205 litre (45 Imp gal) barrel, metal jerry can. Dimensions in mm (inches)

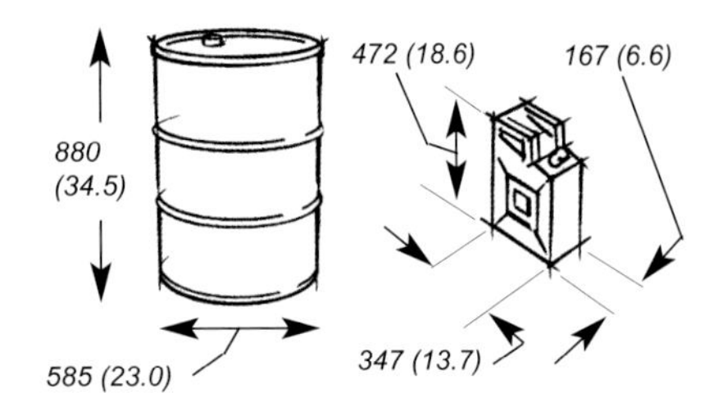

Packing and security of the load is important in an off-roader. Start with a modular, lidded, interlocking boxes. Use, or make, flush tie-downs (above) if you can, plus ratchet-tensioning straps. Rattle-free vehicles get driven well: expedition food tins need careful packing to keep them quiet.

Straps and nets. Grip-buckle luggage straps or quick-release tensioning straps are the only reliable ways of securing a load against the provocation of a vehicle ride over a bad track. You will learn too that often the use of a soft item between the box and the strap will enable it to be cinched tighter.

Storage boxes are strapped-down in ones and twos but when soft baggage such as personal kit is then put on top, that too has to be secured, especially in a soft-top vehicle. In this case a groundsheet or other dustproof fabric sheet should be used first with a cargo net on top – it has the additional advantage of denying to thieves a view of the vehicle contents. Grip-buckle and tensioner straps are usually available in DIY stores and outdoor shops. Ratchet-tensioner strapping can often be bought in motorcycle outlets – they are used for securing bikes to trailers and invaluable on 4x4s.

Install internal lashing cleats to suit your most-used cargo format and for special heavy items that slide about on corners. Well worth the trouble – and essential off-road.

Typical working vehicle load criteria – Defender 110 HCPU example

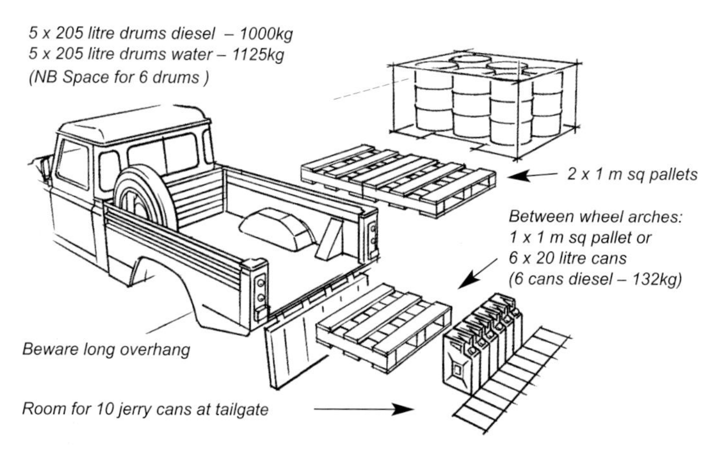

8.2 Tyres

Tyre types

Specialisation vs compromise. It's a swings-and-roundabouts world full of conflicting alternatives and nowhere more so than when equipping 4x4s (especially off-roaders) with tyres. The diagram, devised by a leading manufacturer, right, says it neatly. There's a special tyre for every condition and the converse is usually true: whatever tyres you have fitted will have disadvantages in conditions other than those for which they were designed. This is a simple fact of life – and the laws of physics. Any attempt to produce a multi-purpose, compromise tyre results in exactly that – a compromise. Tyre 'A' above is optimised for off-road conditions so is probably noisy and jolty on highways. Tyre 'B' tries to encompass it all, grips well on wet tarmac, is quiet but doesn't do so well off-road as 'A'. Having said that, there are now some very impressive 'all-terrain' tyres.

Specialist tyres exist for every use. The converse of that is that for any variation in vehicle use all tyres are a compromise.

Tyres – what to look for. The table opposite gives more detail. Seek:

1. ***Tread suitable*** to your main terrain type without too much sacrifice on others you will encounter – see table.
2. ***Flexible sidewalls*** to permit lower inflation pressures where needed. A higher-than-needed load index (p 8.17) means thicker, stiffer sidewalls – albeit they may better resist rock damage.
3. ***Speed rating*** appropriate to your vehicle – table page 8.17.
4. ***Low-inflation capability*** appropriate to emergency conditions you may encounter – especially soft sand.

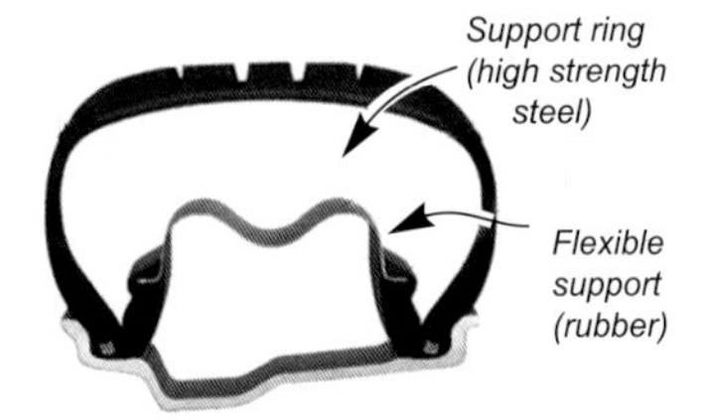

The shape of things to come? Bridgestone run-flat as fitted to T180 Toyota RAV4. Like Michelin's Pax, conventional sidewalls permit normal ride and handling. 100 miles at 50 mph deflated. Just as well; specialist fitting needed.

Tyres – the either/or options

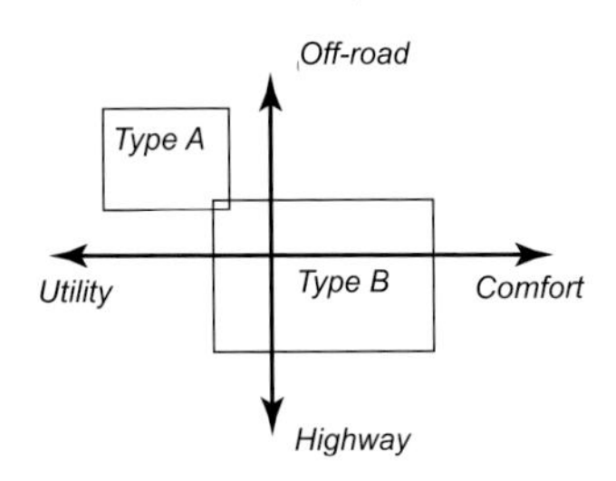

5. ***Remember the on-road case*** is also a special case. Most off-road-biased tyres are noisy on-road and may have poor – or bad – wet-tarmac grip.

Makers know best. Know what you want but listen to the tyre makers too. Many will have worked closely with the vehicle manufacturers and will give a technically informed final OK to your choice.

Choosing your tyre. Because an even-handed multi-brand appraisal would take volumes, the well-deserved reputation of Michelin and affiliate BFGoodrich have been singled-out as examples here for their wide range and especially their combined skills with on- and off-road tyres.

Tyres – wider, thinner, less functional

Visual extravagance, cornering and ... ?. If the sidewall of your tyre has '265/30R22' written on it, the '30' means the distance between the rim seat and the tread is only 30% of the tyre width of 265 mm – very thin indeed. The 30 is the aspect ratio. On most sensible tyres it is around 75-85%. Such low profile tyres, invariably purchased with large diameter alloy wheels (22" here) keep stylists and accountants happy and many owners regard them as 'cool'. They usually offer extra cornering grip, high speed capability – and poor ride on any but the smoothest roads. Minimalist sidewalls allow little flex. They're inappropriate for off-tarmac use.

Lo-pro – limited choice. With the hitherto virtually standard 15- and 16-inch rims for 4x4s, tyre makers offered tyres for a wide range of needs on these rims – road, heavy mud, snow, sand, 'all-terrain'. With

TABLE 1 – TYRE TYPES FOR 4x4s

Road oriented A car tyre only bigger.	Optimised for tarmac. Close tread, relatively smooth, often with sipes ('knife cuts') for wet-tarmac grip. Michelin Diamaris shown.	**For:** Fairly hard 'summer' compound gives long life, quiet, smooth running, good braking. **Against:** Close tread susceptible to quickly filling in mud off-tarmac, reducing traction. Pretty useless off-road in wet conditions.	
Winter tyre Optimised for conditions of rain, snow or ice below 7°C.	'Softer', high silica rubber, quantifiably better at low temperatures. Close, small bold tread. Multiple sipes help wet grip and on-tarmac cornering. Bridgestone LM25.4x4 Blizzak shown.	**For:** Reduced braking distances,better cornering grip on snow and ice or even at low temperatures in the wet. **Against:** Faster wear in summer conditions. Close tread susceptible to filling in mud, reducing traction.	
Mud tyre General purpose off-road, mud and stony tracks tyre.	Bold, open tread pattern, sharp right-angle edges. Quite narrow, some have 'swept-back' tread pattern designed for particular direction of rotation. The larger the blocks and bigger the spaces between them (voids) the better the mud performance – and the worse the noise and, on wet tarmac, grip. BFGoodrich Mud Terrain (top) – well respected. Below is Michelin 4x4.O/R, chunkier, noisier.	**For:** Very good in all types of mud and clay. **Against:** Grip on wet tarmac not as good as road tyres or 'all-terrains' (below). Some 'heel and toe' wear on large tread blocks shortens life. May be noisy or have limited speed rating. (Note: This is the worst tyre for dry unbroken 'piecrust' sand – dunes – though where sand is already churned and the crust broken, mud tyres can be surprisingly effective.)	
Multi purpose Usually called 'all terrain'	Milder tread than mud tyre. BFGoodrich All Terrain here – an established classic. Very good in sand/rock desert. Accepts low pressures (at low speeds). Sipes enhance wet road grip.	**For:** Excellent compromise for frequent on/off road use, eg farming. Very good at handling the demands of mixed sand/stone desert terrain. Grip on wet tarmac very good. **Against:** Outclassed in bad mud by the above.	
Sand tyres Michelin XS shown is benchmark for sand. Tread design brazenly pirated.	XS has subtle tread with shouldered blocks to compress sand in inverted 'cups' (enhancing flotation and traction) rather than cutting through it. Circumferentially grooved tyres look good but are ineffective in sand.	**For:** XS excels in all types of sand. Robust enough for all desert terrain. **Against:** Very poor grip on wet tarmac. 'Heel and toe' wear on tread blocks, noisy.Takes ultra low pressures but sidewall bulge vulnerable to damage on rock; take care. (Note: In mud, good flotation, poor traction .)	

Every optimised tyre has its pros and cons; best off-road performance is often at cost of on-road grip in wet conditions. Best sand and best mud tyres are opposites.

low-profile tyres , choice is usually limited to road treads only. Just as well.

Deflation pressures? The off-road scenario for low profile tyres is not good since a softer tyre here puts the rim even closer to the ground risking rim and tyre damage. But Michelin OK off-road deflation to 80% of road pressures for tracks (but not below 1.5 bar, max speed 40mph) and 70% for mud and sand (1.5 bar min, 12mph max).

Many owners are irrationally besotted by the so-called 'style' of wheels and tyres such as this 325/30R21W on 11" 'cotton reel' rims on a BMW X5 (the W = 168mph max which should liven up the school run.) With a reputation for tramlining and poor ride, though, these tyres are absurdly inappropriate for an all-round 4x4. They also increase the likelihood of rim damage on kerbs.

Axle loads and tyre pressures off-road

Off-road tyre pressures – axle loads. For 'best' off-road tyre pressures you need to know axle load. The sequence:

- Know front/rear axle load – see below. Go to a weighbridge, weigh front and rear axles separately, pic next spread.
- From this determine tyre pressure for a chosen maximum speed – Table 3. (Ask for a similar table for your tyres.)

The figures in your vehicle handbook assume maximum load and a vehicle free to go to its maximum speed; in other words, foolproof day-to-day on-road conditions.

There are also handling considerations. Off-road you'll sometimes get better performance – flotation and traction – with tyres at lower pressures. Going too low – or too fast at these low pressures – can damage the tyres (or produce handling problems) so you have to do some checks.

Simple checking first. Tyres give their optimum performance – the best combination of grip, handling response, operating temperature (important for structural reasons) and a degree of shock absorption – when their elements (tread, beads and sidewalls) are optimally disposed to one another. The main criterion in

Tyre pressures and axle loads are interdependent – both affect sidewall deflection, a critical criterion.

TABLE 2 – SAMPLE VEHICLES: ACTUAL FRONT / REAR AXLE LOADS

Vehicle type *Maximum weights:* *GVW and maximum individual axle loads.* *See notes 1 and 2.* *GVW / front / rear max*	*Body type and/or manual/auto*	*Axle loads at kerb weight – 2.5 petrol engine Front/rear Kg*	*Axle loads at kerb weight – V8 petrol engine Front/rear Kg*	*Axle loads at kerb weight – 2.5D or VM engine Front/rear Kg*	*Axle loads at kerb weight – Tdi engine Front/rear Kg*
Defender 90	Soft top	922/714	908/719	946/710	971/724
Std: 2400/1200/1380	Pick up	919/717	905/722	943/722	967/727
Hi-load suspension:	Hard top	916/767	902/770	940/763	960/786
2550/1200/1500	Station wagon	911/790	897/793	935/786	959/834
New Range Rover			*4.0 V8*	*4.6 V8*	*2.5 diesel*
All versions:	manual		1171/1081	1171/1081	1187/1072
2780/1320/1840	auto		1176/1086	1176/1086	-

NOTE 1 – Using the figures. *Example, ringed above:*

Defender 90
Std: 2400/1200/1380

This means the Defender with standard suspension (ie not fitted with the hi-load heavy duty springs) has a maximum loaded weight of 2400 kg. *Individual* axles can take a max of up to 1200 kg at front, 1380 kg at rear – but not at the same time (since 1200 +1380 = 2580 which would exceed the 2400kg GVW maximum for standard suspension).

NOTE 2 – Using the figures. *Example, ringed above:*

Defender 90. Station wagon, Tdi engine, axle loads at kerb weight: 959/834

This means an *empty* Tdi Defender 90 Station Wagon has axle loads of 959kg front and 834 kg rear. If you aim to carry a **300kg payload in the rear** (assume exactly over the rear axle), the rear axle load will be 1134kg. So **959/1134** are the figures you would enter into the tyre pressures table on the next page.

NOTE 3: Gross vehicle weight (GVW), ie weight fully laden, is the maximum weight for which the suspension was designed so is constant for a given vehicle type. Only where the suspension itself has an alternative specification, as in the Defender 90 , or where heavier diesel engines are fitted, are different GVWs or GVW axle loads shown.

NOTE 4: Because it is not always easy to get weight distribution front/rear precisely correct, individual axles may be loaded to the 'max' figures shown so long as the *overall* GVW is not exceeded. Note that in most cases the sum of the front and rear 'max' figures would exceed the GVW so do not load both axles to max. The Defender 110 has max and actual axle loads at GVW that are the same.

NOTE 5: Kerb weight (sometimes 'EEC kerb'), is defined as unladen weight plus full fuel plus a 75kg driver.

determining this is sidewall deflection and this is established by the load on the tyre and its internal pressure. There is thus a theoretically optimum tyre pressure for every change in axle load or payload within the vehicle – and then for every speed. This is why front and rear tyre pressures are different. In practice, and to ensure you do not spend your whole life changing tyre pressures, there is some latitude and usually just two sets of pressures (ie front and rear) are quoted for vehicles – one for the unladen and one for the fully laden condition. These, of course, are based on individual front and rear axle loads – the weight each axle carries – and they assume freedom to use all the performance the vehicle offers in terms of speed.

Desperate for traction and flotation? But you can get more from your tyres if you know the loads and can stick to strict speed limits. Michelin are mature enough to quote these for the sensible user. Examples of axle loads, and an indication of what affects them, are given in Table 2 opposite. If you apply these to Table 3 below – use the Note – you will get the minimum pressures that you may use for a given load and speed. If all this seems a bit academic sitting reading this book, in practice you will find it a pillar of common sense and harmony between tyre makers who know their stuff and an off-road operator who needs all the help he or she can get in difficult conditions.

If this sounds as if it is written from the heart, it is! Sometimes off-road flotation is very poor indeed. You don't want to run your tyres so soft as to risk damaging them but you do need to know the most deflation you can safely use, accept the associated speed and load limits – and keep moving.

If you want the best tyre performance or want to save the time wasted in recovery in your fleet, check axle loads and tyre pressures.

NOTE – Using the figures. *Example: Take the Tdi Defender 90 Station Wagon on the previous page (Note 2) with front/rear axle loads 959 and 1134kg.*
*• **On-road.** Reading from the axle load column below, for a 120kph road speed (interpolating or using next highest pressure), the vehicle should run at 1.5 bar front and 1.9 bar rear minimum.*
*• **Off-road.** Similarly the off-road figures that may be used, where you want the lowest pressures for reasons of flotation or ride, are 1.0 bar front and 1.3 bar rear on tracks at a speed not exceeding 65kph. If you got bogged in soft sand, the emergency soft would be 0.6 bar front and rear at a speed not over 20kph (12mph). (NB Here, for handling reasons, 0.6 bar not advised; Table 4.)*

TABLE 3 – EXAMPLE: 7.50x16 MICHELIN XS – PRESSURES vs WHEEL LOAD/ SPEED

Axle load kg	Wheel load kg	On-road tyre pressures – bar (Speed km/hr) 120	110	100	90	80	65	50	40	30	20	Off-road pressures – bar: Track 65 kph	Sand/ mud 20 kph
2000	1000	3.75	3.8	3.8	3.5	3.4	3.4	3.4	3.3	3.3	3.1	2.6	1.3
1880	940	3.5	3.4	3.3	3.2	3.2	3.1	3.1	3.1	3.0	2.8	2.4	1.2
1800	900	3.3	3.2	3.1	3.0	3.0	3.0	3.0	2.9	2.8.	2.7	2.2	1.1
1600	800	2.8	2.7	2.7	2.6	2.6	2.6	2.5	2.5	2.4	2.3	1.9	0.9
1400	700	2.4	2.3	2.3	2.2	2.2	2.2	2.1	2.1	2.1	1.9	1.6	0.7
1200	600	1.9	1.9	1.8	1.8	1.8	1.8	1.7	1.7	1.7	1.6	1.3	0.6
1000	500	1.5	1.5	1.5	1.4	1.4	1.4	1.4	1.3	1.3	1.2	1.0	0.6
800	400	1.1	1.1	1.1	1.0	1.0	1.0	1.0	1.0	0.9	0.9	0.8	0.6

So axle loads really matter? If you are wondering how you got by all these years without knowing axle loads to work out tyre pressures, it is because vehicle manufacturers usually quote catch-all figures that assume max payload, on-road driving up to max speed – and play safe. The axle load calculations apply when, off-road, you are trying for the lowest a tyre pressure you can safely use to get best flotation and traction.

The span of the figures is surprising. An unladen Defender 90 rear axle carries only 38% of the load that the rear axle of a laden Defender 110 does. Axle load is greatly (and just as surprisingly) affected by load distribution – that diagram on page 8.5 gives the well-I'll-be-darned facts. Get those facts on a real live weighbridge (pic left).

What to actually do. Having chosen your tyre type from Table 1, and ascertained your axle load from Table 2 (or from a weighbridge – left) you would apply it to a manufacturer's data sheet like Table 3 to get the operating pressures on- and off-road.

NOTE – Table 4

Michelin off-road tyres. *Although low speeds are involved, using the example in Table 5, Land Rover have imposed their own lower limits of tyre pressures for handling reasons and to reduce the possibility of dislodging a tyre.*

Certain of Michelin's off-road tyres are, however, cleared by Michelin structurally and operationally to function at and benefit from exceptionally low pressures – down to 0.60 bar (9 psi) – where the absolute limit of flotation must be combined with the tyres' other unique features. Michelin stipulate only that 'track' and 'emergency flotation' speed limits (right-hand columns, Table 4) are observed and that, in sand, tubes should be used in case sand gets between bead and seat.

These tyres will perform magnificently but you must still treat them with care; beware of damaging sidewalls, beware of lateral stress like sharp steering inputs that could roll them off the rims. Observe the speed limits scrupulously, re-inflate when clear. Pressures, listed against axle load, for the various tyres are shown right. Sample axle loads are show at Table 2 (page 8.10). If not available, check yours on a weighbridge.

Other manufacturers. If you use another brand of tyres, information like this should be available. Don't go down to these kinds of pressures without specific clearance from the manufacturer's Technical Department.

TABLE 4 – MICHELIN OFF-ROAD TYRES

Tyre type/size	*Axle load kg*	*Tracks 40 mph max*	*Sand/mud 12 mph max*
7.00 R16 XCL	1000	1.20	0.60
	1400	1.90	1.00
	1600	2.30	1.20
	1800	2.70	1.40
7.00 R16 XZL	1200	1.30	0.60
	1400	1.50	0.80
	1600	1.80	0.90
	1800	2.70	1.30
7.50 R16 XCL	1000	1.10	0.70
	1400	1.80	0.90
	1600	2.20	1.10
	1800	2.50	1.30
	2240	3.30	1.80
7.50 R16 XS	1200	1.30	0.60
	1600	1.90	0.90
	1800	2.20	1.10
	2000	2.60	1.30
7.50 R16 XZL (Also known as '4x4 O/R')	1200	1.40	0.70
	1400	1.70	0.90
	1600	2.00	1.10
	1800	2.40	1.30
	2240	3.10	1.80

What deflation does

Tyre footprint of Michelin XS at (left to right) road pressures, track pressure and emergency flotation pressure. Percentage increases in area are considerable.

Tyre pressures – three conditions

Optimum pressures. So to recap and re-establish perspective on a subject you may not have considered quantitatively before, to get the best out of your tyres and vehicle on:

- roads
- on tracks and poor roads and
- emergency flotation conditions

you need three sets of tyre pressures. As we have seen (Sections 4.7, 4.8 and in the diagram above), lowering tyre pressures increases the size of the tyre 'footprint' and thus lowers the pressure per unit area on the ground. The ground is thus less stressed and will yield better traction and flotation, so assisting a vehicle in traversing difficult terrain or in self-recovery if it is stuck.

The on-road constraints. Having the best soft sand flotation in the world isn't much use to you if are hustling down a winding tarmac road late for an appointment. The on-road handling requirements of the vehicle have to override possible off-road demands when the vehicle is in everyday use. Low off-road pressures bring problems on-road:

- Overheating of the tyres
- Danger of rolling the tyre off the rim
- Sluggish, soggy steering response.

These are symptoms that range from the inconvenient to the downright dangerous. Hence there are optimum pressures and concomitant speed limits – which must be observed – for roads, tracks and emergency flotation conditions. Re-inflate for on-road.

What you finish up with. What you need, as a result of all these deliberations, then, is a table like the one below. Do it on a piece of card, laminate it and keep it in the vehicle with your inflator and pressure gauges – see overleaf.

TABLE 5 – SAMPLE VEHICLE – DEFENDER 90: MANUFACTURER'S TYRE PRESSURES

Single, all-loads, all-speeds handbook pressures underlined. Track/emergency pressures are higher than those at Table 4 for handling reasons. Drive very carefully and Table 4's lower figures could be used.

Tyre no	*Tyre name and size*	*Load index / speed symbol (See table on page 8.17)*	*Vehicle weight*	*Hard-road pressures (to max speed) Front / rear*	*Tracks and poor roads. 40 mph max Front / rear*	*Off-road emergency flotation. 12 mph max Front / rear*
1.	Michelin 205 R 16 X M+S	99Q	Kerb	1.9 / 2.1	1.6 / 1.9	1.2 / 1.2
			GVW	1.9 / 2.4	1.7 / 2.1	1.2 / 1.4
2.	Michelin 7.50 R 16 X 4x4	108N	Kerb	1.8 / 2.0	1.4 / 1.6	1.1 / 1.2
	Michelin 7.50 R 16 X-CL	112L	GVW	1.9 / 2.9	1.5 / 2.2	1.1 / 1.7
	Michelin 7.50 R 16 XS	108N				
	Michelin 7.50 R 16 XZL	108N				
3.	Goodyear 7.50 R 16 G90	116N	Kerb	1.8 / 2.0	1.4 /1.6	1.1 / 1.2
			GVW	1.9 / 2.9	1.5 / 2.2	1.1 / 1.7
4.	BFGoodrich 265/75R16 MudTerrain	120Q	Kerb	1.7 / 1.9	1.4 / 1.4	0.8 / 0.8
and....	BFGoodrich 265/75R16 AllTerrain	120Q	GVW	1.9 / 2.4	1.4 / 1.6	1.0 / 1.4

Inflation, pressures, tubeless, repairs

Tyre pressures – speed warning. It is important to emphasise, again, the speed limitations when driving with tyres at reduced off-road pressures shown in the columns on the previous spread. Never exceed the speed limits shown there. Driving too fast on under-inflated tyres will cause structural damage to your tyres through overheating and possible delamination of the carcass. It will usually produce unacceptable handling and the possibility of rolling the tyres off the rims on corners. Be sure always to be equipped with an accurate tyre pressure gauge and a re-inflation pump (see below) if you are going off-roading.

WARNING. A repeat warning about not exceeding speed and load limitations on tyres at reduced pressures. Get, and take care of, an accurate tyre pressure gauge.

Pressure gauges. Care of tyres can be set at nought by that weakest of weak links the tyre pressure gauge. The pen-type gauge is often inaccurate and some dial gauges are not necessarily much of an improvement. Even the good ones should still be checked against one or more air hoses at service stations which in the UK have to be checked by law . Alas these too cannot always be trusted. Keep your proven tyre gauge in a dust-proof plastic bag in the vehicle at all times.

High-flow, fan-cooled (that's important), 12v inflators are essential for 4x4s anywhere, eg TruckAir (left), Michelin's recent 12262 (below, on the ground) is quick, compact and has LED lights for night work. Their digital and mechanical gauges: 10/10.

Always take a back-up pump: a high-quality cycle floor-pump like this is surprisingly quick on 4x4 tyres.

Re-inflation. After pressure reduction for off-road work tyres must be re-inflated before road speeds are resumed. A half-hearted resolve to 're-inflate at the next garage' is not good enough and is dangerous.

Re-inflation is best done by an electric pump carried with you. That way it can be done as and when needed. Again you should be circumspect about the standard of unit you buy. Tyres fitted to off-roaders need a lot of air compared to car tyres so get a pump that is large, robust, fan-cooled and can stand up to long periods of use without overheating. The Michelin 12262 (pic bottom left) permits desired pressure to be pre-set.

Tubeless tyres – no. When prolonged severe off-road conditions are likely – an expedition or an aid project, for example – it is in most cases sensible to fit tubes in your tyres. In extreme conditions when inflation has been reduced to emergency soft, unseating of a tubeless tyre from the rim and total loss of pressure could occur. Secondly, changing or repairing a tyre by hand in the field is possible with a tubed tyre: the same thing would not normally be possible with a tubeless tyre. For those you need a lot of air at a high pressure – but see below.

Tubes from? Tubes are increasingly hard to locate but Soopa Toobs Ltd (www.soopatoobs.co.uk) is one reliable UK importer and supplier.

Tubeless tyres – yes? An on-board compressor and air reservoir, however, would make re-mounting tubeless tyres in the field feasible. It would provide a large volume of fast-moving air to blow a tubeless tyre back onto its rim. BOAB, originating in ever-practical Australia, (www.boab.biz) have devised exactly that – amongst other sensible, down-to-earth equipment for tyre related problems in the outback such as bead-breakers, and a repair kit for properly fixing punctures and

BOAB stow-and-forget, all-types repair kit includes subtly-shaped tyre levers and ingenious 'Tyre-plier' (far right and lower right) for shifting tyre beads. Repair kit box (below) is comprehensive and includes all-important step-by-step booklet to refresh your memory in the stress of the moment. Needs only paintbrush and jar of tyre lubricant – makes a big difference.

damage to outer covers (above).

New wheels? Wheels designed with an internal AH rim (asymmetric hump) profile to enhance bead retention of tubeless tyres at very low pressures are, by some, not recommended for use with tubes. Low pressure flexing of the tyre is said to cause chafing of the tubes on the internal rim humps. This is seldom the case in fact but check with your tyre manufacturer when fitting tubes to tubeless tyres.

'Cold' tyre pressures. Tyre pressure should always be checked 'cold', ie after the vehicle has been standing for an hour or more, nominal 17°C. Pressures should be varied (up or down) by 5% for every 10°C. So a 'book' figure of 2.0 bar at 17°C should be set at 2.2 on a cool vehicle at an ambient of 37°C. Don't 'bleed' air from a warm tyre.

Tyre repairs in the field. For prolonged operation in the field in remote areas you should acquire the ability to remove and repair tyres and tubes. It will take time but is surprisingly easy to do once you have had a demonstration from your local tyre-fitting establishment. Be sure they show you the all-manual way, not using a rotary bead breaker. Long tyre levers, tyre lubricant and technique are the ingredients. Exclusion of grit or sand from the tyre during the process is vital; use a clean ground sheet. Your driving should preclude the possibility of serious damage to the tyre carcase so there is no need for the carriage of heavy extra spare wheels. If you do not have the 'Tyre-plier' shown here, placing the wheel under the chassis and jacking between the chassis and the tyre will shift the reluctant bead.

Tyre pressure transmitters are standard on some modern 4x4s and will give an alert when you deflate for special conditions (p.8.13). You shouldn't need them to tell you to re-inflate when back on firm ground.

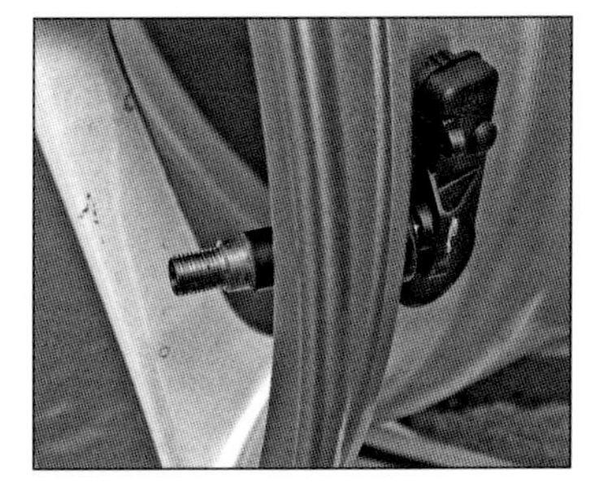

Data on load and speed ratings, tyre construction and build are inscribed on the sidewall – see diagram opposite for full data and tables below right for de-coding load index and speed symbol. Thus the Michelin X M+S 244 in the photographs, having a 99T load/speed rating is (from the tables opposite) cleared to a maximum load per tyre of 775kg up to 118mph – at appropriate pressures based on axle load.

Tyre nomenclature

If you have to buy an unfamiliar tyre, everything you need to know about it will be written on the sidewall. If it isn't, don't buy it.

The small print. A considerable amount of information is inscribed on the sidewall (and tread) of tyres, all of which is relevant to its specification – despite the assurances of those who would try to sell you tyres that are 'the same' as the one you specifically seek.

Old style ... . The principal dimensions of a tyre in old parlance are its width (not the depth between tread and bead) and the wheel diameter to which it is fitted. Thus a '7.50 x 16' is a tyre designed for a 16-inch diameter wheel and having a normal inflated width (ie the external nominal width of the inflated, unladen tyre) of 7.50 inches; it is not necessarily the width of the tread itself. This width data can also be shown in millimetres (still, oddly, allied to a rim size in inches) as in the 205x16.

New style. Modern tyres are more often designated, eg 265/75 R16. This means a tyre with a width of 265mm, and aspect ratio of 75% (ie the distance between the rim and the tread is 75% of the width – see also pp.8.8 and 8.9); the 'R' means it's a radial-ply tyre and fitting on a 16 inch rim a glorious mixture of metric and Imperial measures!

Tyre specification inscriptions

Manufacturer's generic name such as Michelin 'X'
Manufacturer's type number or name, eg XCL, Rangemaster, Wrangler
Nominal section width in mm, eg 205, 235 (ie, max width of tyre, not tread, on normal rim)
Aspect ratio (cross section height divided by width – shown as a percentage) – follows metric width when shown (so a 235/70 would be nominally 235mm wide with a tyre sidewall height approx 70% of the width, ie 164.5mm)
'R' for radial
Overall tyre diameter (usually given in the US, not Europe)
Load index/speed symbol – see tables opposite
Maximum load and pressure – in lb and psi in addition to load index (US requirement)
Sidewall and tread construction – plies, material: eg steel, polyester (US requirement)
Ply rating – (equivalent) sidewall plies in a cross-ply tyre
Wear indicators
Country of manufacture
Direction of rotation – sometimes shown when relevant
ECE and US Dept of Transport type approval mark

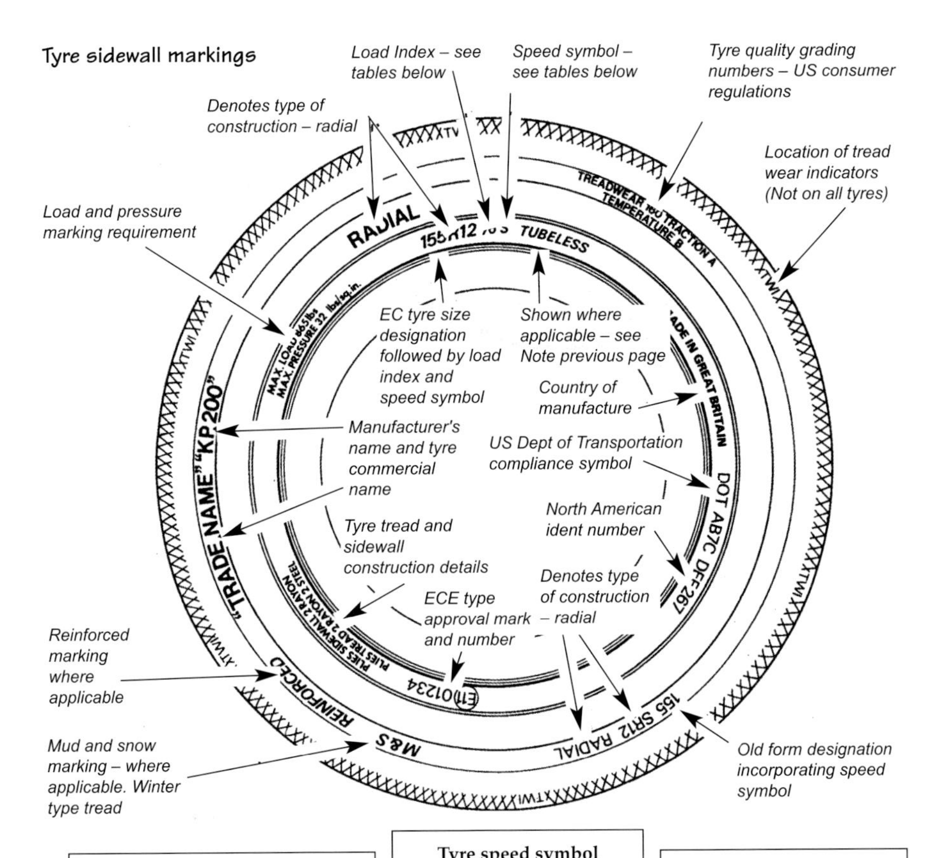

Tyre load index (NB Max load *per tyre* at full road pressures at speed shown by accompanying speed symbol)			
Index	kg	Index	kg
97	730	111	1090
98	750	112	1120
99	775	113	1150
100	800	114	1180
101	825	115	1215
102	850	116	1250
103	875	117	1285
104	900	118	1320
105	925	119	1360
106	950	120	1400
107	975	121	1450
108	1000	122	1500
109	1030	123	1550
110	1060	124	1600

Tyre speed symbol (NB Max speed at full road pressures at per-tyre load shown by load index		
Symbol	kph	mph
J	100	62
K	110	68
L	120	75
M	130	81
N	140	87
P	150	93
Q	160	100
R	170	105
S	180	113
T	190	118
U	200	124
H	210	130
V	240	149
VR	>210	>130
W	270	168
Y	300	186
ZR	>240	>149

Tyre pressures – bars to (nearest whole) psi			
Bars	psi	Bars	psi
1.1	16	2.7	39
1.2	17	2.8	41
1.3	19	2.9	42
1.4	20	3.0	44
1.5	22	3.1	45
1.6	23	3.2	46
1.7	25	3.3	48
1.8	26	3.4	49
1.9	28	3.5	51
2.0	29	3.6	52
2.1	30		
2.2	32	4.3	62
2.3	33	4.4	64
2.4	35	4.5	65
2.5	36	4.6	67
2.6	38	4.7	68

Using the figures: A load/speed index of 108N defines ultimate capability: max load of 1000kg per tyre; max speed 87mph. Having selected your tyre, then apply tyre pressures according to actual loads and speeds in the tables 1 to 5 on pages 8.9-8.13.

Section 9

Reference

9.1 Glossary

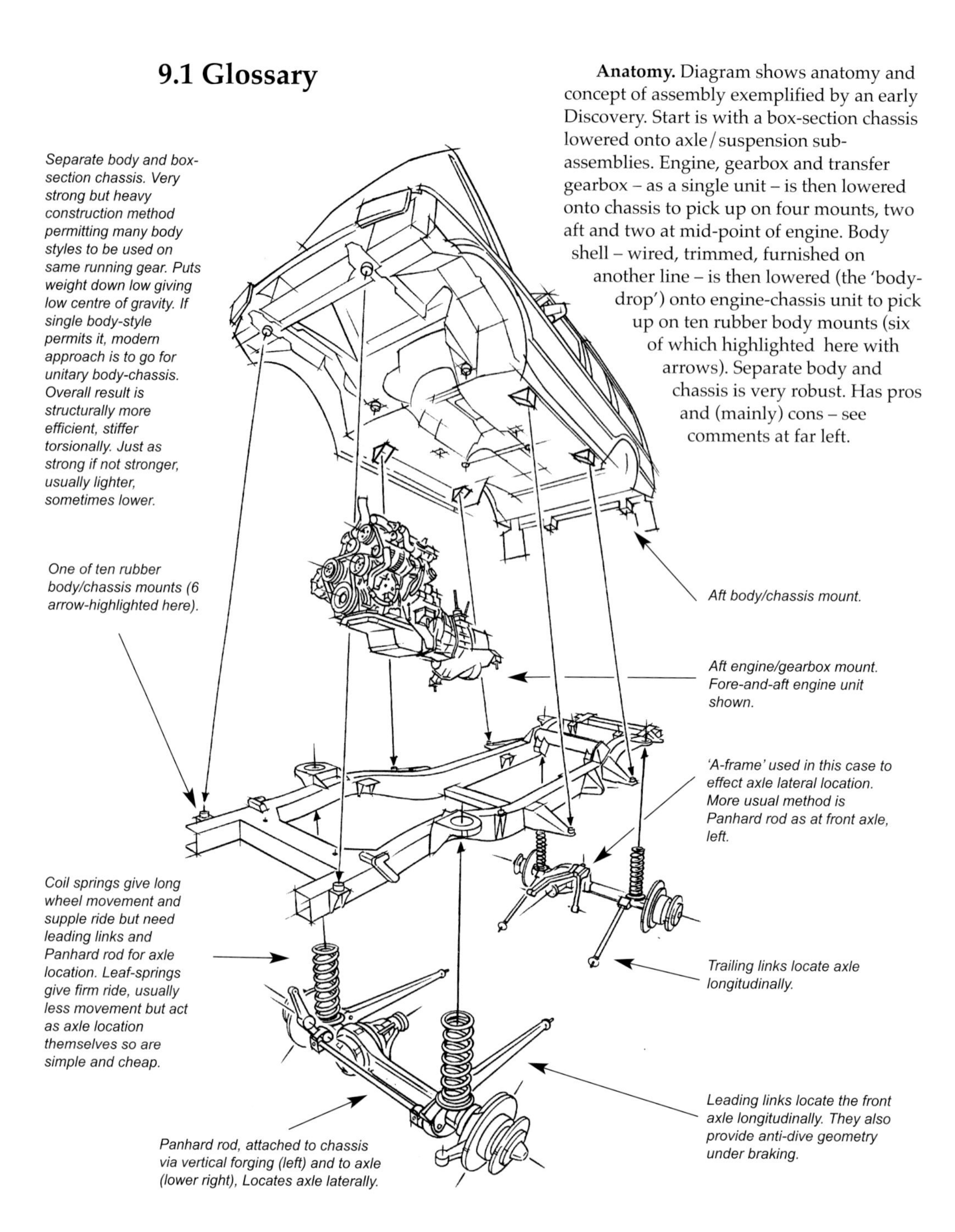

Anatomy. Diagram shows anatomy and concept of assembly exemplified by an early Discovery. Start is with a box-section chassis lowered onto axle/suspension sub-assemblies. Engine, gearbox and transfer gearbox – as a single unit – is then lowered onto chassis to pick up on four mounts, two aft and two at mid-point of engine. Body shell – wired, trimmed, furnished on another line – is then lowered (the 'body-drop') onto engine-chassis unit to pick up on ten rubber body mounts (six of which highlighted here with arrows). Separate body and chassis is very robust. Has pros and (mainly) cons – see comments at far left.

ABS. Anti-lock braking system; prevents wheels locking under maximum braking. Works on the principle of braking a wheel until it just begins to skid (this is the point where braking efficiency would drop off dramatically) and then releasing the brake pressure and re-applying the brakes. Wheel speed sensors identify the skid point and trigger a release in brake pressure. The cycle is repeated many times a second – with appropriate 'cobblestone' feedback on the brake pedal to indicate you are in ABS mode. See also Cadence braking.

A-frame. Means of effecting lateral location of the rear axle in some vehicles. Also controls axle rotation. See diagram left. Axle lateral location usually by Panhard rod.

Air suspension. Rear (and sometimes front and rear) springing effected by inflatable airbags as in buses and commercial vehicles. Supple ride. Easy to engineer self-levelling and variable suspension heights into the system. Used by Land Rover, Porsche, Volkswagen and Toyota 4x4s.

Anti-lock brakes. See ABS above.

Anti-roll bar (ARB). A U-shaped bar of steel (about 25mm diameter) anchored at the bottom of the U to each side of the chassis in pivoting rubber mounts. The free ends of the U are attached to each end of a front and/or rear axle to limit roll of the body relative to that axle. If the chassis/body is called on to move up and down parallel to the axle the ARB offers no interference; if, however body roll forces are induced by cornering, the twisting moments on the ARB tend to inhibit roll. For off-roaders an ARB must be carefully designed not to limit axle articulation excessively and affect off-road performance. Some 4x4s have disconnectable ARBs (eg Jeep Wrangler, Nissan Patrol).

Approach angle. In side-view, the angle between the ground and a line, ahead of the vehicle, joining the periphery of the front wheel and (typically) the front bumper or other low component. It represents the size or steepness of a slope or obstacle that can be approached or climbed without striking bodywork. See p.3.8.

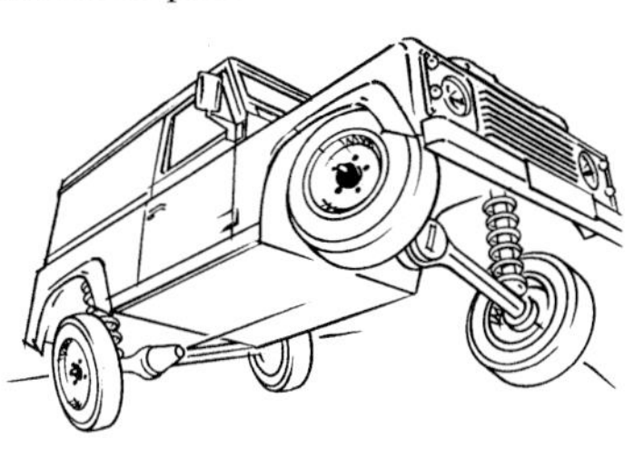

Articulation. The ability of one axle to move – left wheel up, right wheel down or vice versa – relative to the chassis or its fellow axle. It is a measure of the ease with which wheels can stay in contact with the ground – and thus retain traction – on very 'twisty' off-road terrain. See pp.3.10, 5.4. Diagonal suspension.

Axle location. Axles and wheels move vertically relative to a chassis/body but must be located accurately longitudinally and laterally. Semi-elliptic leaf-springs fulfilled the suspension and location function at the same time in the old days and on many current pickups at the rear. Diagram facing page shows how the function is achieved with coil springs favoured for better ride and longer wheel movement.

Axles, live, one-piece. Also referred to as rigid or (incorrectly as) beam axles, in which the drive shafts to the wheels run within rigid casings as in the diagram above and opposite. Live axles permit large wheel movement and give better ground clearance for a given wheel diameter compared with independent suspension (see p 3.9) but unsprung weight is higher so ride quality can suffer. Early Toyota Landcruiser was available with live or independent front axle.

Battery designation. Three figures define battery designation by encapsulating performance in relation to standard criteria. A '380/120/90' battery thus has a maximum rapid-discharge current at -18°C of 380amp; it can maintain a discharge of 25 amp at 25°C for 120 minutes before reaching a terminal voltage of 10.2 volts. Its rate of voltage drop at the max rapid-discharge of 380amp (at minus 18°C) will be such that 5-7 seconds after commencement of discharge, voltage will have dropped to 9.0 volts. This is multiplied by 10 to give 90.

Bridle. A rope or cable attached to two points – typically the right and left chassis members – of a vehicle and converging to a point of tow rope attachment (see p 5.6).

Cadence braking. A method of manual braking with the foot brake to simulate the action of ABS brakes – see above. Very effective in slippery conditions where brake locking has occurred or might otherwise occur. The driver applies the footbrake in a series of very rapid jabs at the pedal taking the wheels up to the point of brake locking and then releasing them before the inevitable fall-off in braking efficiency takes place. Effects improved braking in any extremely slippery conditions such as ice, snow, wet mud, or rain. See pp.3.7, 6.9.

Front axle

Camber angle

Camber. The angle at which, when viewed from the front, the front wheels of a vehicle splay out (positive camber) from the vertical – as shown in diagram. In some layouts it varies with position of suspension. Camber affects lateral control and ideally should be zero at all times. On an off-roader with live ('beam') axles, camber angle is always zero.

Capstan winch. A winch, generally mounted on or just behind the front bumper, usually run from an engagable extension to the engine crankshaft. The active component is usually a slowly revolving drum, about 15cm in diameter, round which a rope may be wound to effect a winching operation. Has the advantage of being powered by the engine at idling speed and being a very low-stress unit that may be used all day without overheating or high (any) electrical load. See p.5.12.

Castor (or caster) angle. When the front wheels are moved right or left to steer the vehicle they each move about a steering axis. The aft inclination of this steering axis from the vertical (when viewed from the side) – about 3° in the case of some off-roaders – is the castor angle. Like castors on a tea trolley or office chair, this puts the ground contact point of the wheels behind the pivot axis and the result is a self-centring action tending to keep the front wheels pointing forward when in forward motion. Note that in deep sand, with a 'bow-wave' build-up of sand ahead of the wheels, the effective ground contact point moves ahead of the steering axis and can give the effect of negative castor with 'runaway' steering. The same thing happens when vehicle is travelling in reverse – the ground contact point being 'ahead' of the steering axis and again tending to make the front wheels 'runaway' to full lock – see p.4.18, (failed climbing of steep off-road inclines). Also see Steering feel, p.9.11.

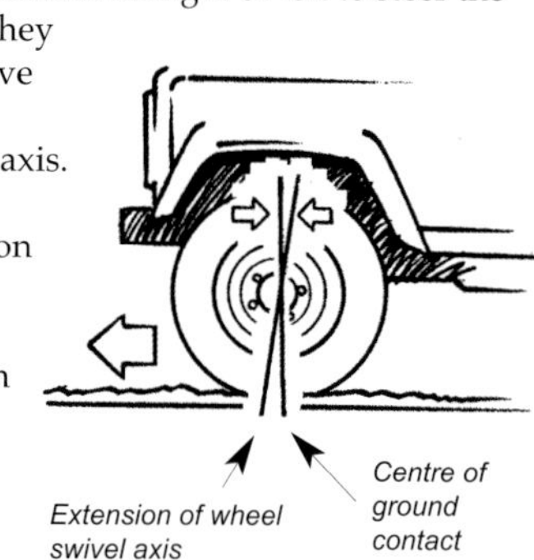

Distance between the two is 'trail'. Angle between the two lines is castor angle.

Centre differential. A differential gear device – diagram p.2.5 – between front and rear propeller shafts, installed at the point where the drive from the engine splits power between the front and rear propshafts. Working in the same way as the conventional rear axle differential on a two-wheel drive car, it allows front and rear shafts to accommodate the small front/rear rotational differences encountered in normal running, going round sharp corners etc. Such a device is essential in a vehicle having full-time or permanent 4x4. Vehicles with selectable 4x4 are not fitted with centre differentials and thus cannot be used in four wheel drive on hard roads. See pp.2.3, 2.11.

Chott. Local name for salt flat or sebkha in Tunisia, Algeria and Morocco.

Constant velocity (CV) joints. Another battleground for the accountants vs the engineers. It's CV joints vs Hooke's joints; the latter being the well-known type found as universal joints on prop shafts – cheaper but less able to cope with large angles between input and output shafts. With Hooke's joints at high angles the output drive is jerky – variable velocity rather than constant velocity. For front-wheel drive cars or 4x4s with permanent four-wheel drive, CV joints at the ends of the front axle are virtually essential. (This is between the front drive shafts and the stub axles that the front wheels are mounted on). Without CV joints there is driveline vibration and unacceptable steering feedback on full lock – the steering wheel tending to jerk one way then the other as you go round a steady full-lock turn. Quite a few selectable-4x4 vehicles have Hooke's joints at the front stub axles. Even one or two permanent-4x4 vehicles (see p.2.11) have appeared in this format where bought-in axles were involved. Your showroom salesman will almost certainly not know, but it is worth checking you have CV joints at the front axle ends when you buy a vehicle.

Continuous rolling contact. Description of a wheel in steady rolling contact with the ground without slip, wheelspin or slide (as with locked brakes). Should be the aim at all times both on- and off-road under drive or braking conditions. See p.3.6. Also see Discontinuity of rolling contact, below.

Co-ordinated tow. When recovering a stuck vehicle, the process by which the engine power of both the tug and the stuck vehicle are co-ordinated – usually by a signal from an external marshaller – and the clutches of both vehicles are engaged at the same time. See pp.5.8, 5.9.

Corrugations. Deformation of an unsurfaced track taking the form of transverse, close-pitch undulations at right angles to the direction of the track. Often referred to as 'washboard'. See p.4.34.

Coupled brakes. Brake system installed with certain large trailers whereby the trailer brakes get to be applied at the same time as the brakes of the towing vehicle. Vehicles must be specifically modified to operate this system – with appropriate trailers. See p.4.8.

Cross-axled. See Diagonal suspension.

Cross-ply tyre. Old-design tyre in which the sidewall reinforcement plies run diagonally from the bead towards the tread – each layer of textile at a different angle to its adjacent layer (below left). Generally superseded by radial-ply tyres (right) whose

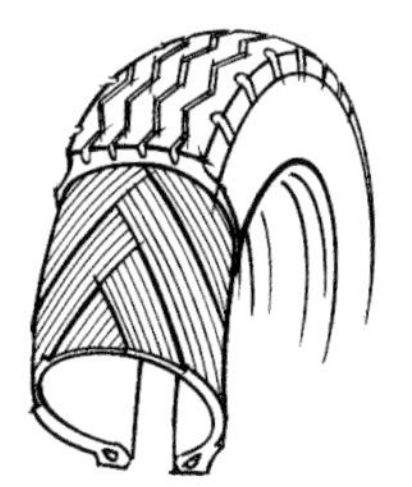

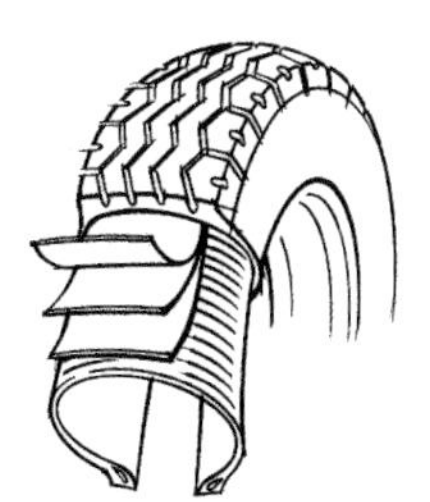

thinner, more flexible sidewalls and braced tread yield better grip and lower rolling resistance. Cross-ply tyres usually have thicker, multi-ply sidewalls, not so flexible as those on radials, hence yield less surface grip on tarmac and return slightly higher fuel consumption. More tolerant of sidewall damage than radials and – see p.4.33 – can have low-cost applications when operating continuously on rock. They are intolerant of reduced pressures in soft going which due to the thick sidewalls, causes overheating and possibly delamination of the tyre.

DAC – Downhill Assist Control. Toyota's version of Land Rover's Hill Descent Control enabling slow, controlled descents to be made on very steep slippery off-road hills. See p.6.8, and HDC next page.

Departure angle. In side view, the angle between the ground and a line, aft of the vehicle, joining the periphery of the rear wheel and (typically) the rear chassis member or other low component. It represents the size or obstacle that can be approached or climbed in reverse without striking bodywork. See p.3.8.

Diagonal suspension. A condition occurring off-road when a vehicle is, for example, diagonally crossing a small but well-defined ridge. When the ridge is so severe that, say, the right front wheel and the rear left wheels are on full 'bump' (ie fully up in the wheel arches) and the other wheels are hanging down to the full extent of wheel travel (see p.2.8), the vehicle may be described as being diagonally suspended or on diagonal suspension. Some also refer to this state as being 'cross-axled'. The hanging wheels are usually spinning unless a cross-axle diff-lock is in use. What to do is dealt with at p.4.14..

Diagonal wheelspin. The wheelspin that can take place on the fully extended (or off-loaded) wheels in a condition of diagonal suspension as described on the previous paragraph. Can occur crossing ditches or ridges diagonally (see Section 4.3) but, in the presence of weak ground under these wheels is usually the basis of every lost-traction situation – hence the importance of cross-axle diff-locks (see p.2.6 *et seq*).

Differential. See p.2.5.

Diff-lock. See first 'Centre differential' above and, for a light summary, the 'Leonardo' system, Phase 3 on p.2.3. Differentials permit power delivered to an axle or pair of prop shafts to be split in any ratio from 100% to 0%, usually self-adjusting according to the load that is at each wheel. If you off-load one wheel completely (eg let it spin on ice) it will spin happily while its companion wheel stays still. To prevent this, a differential lock is provided – for the centre diff almost invariably, less often for the axles.

The diff-lock locks the centre differential, thus locking front and rear prop shafts together (or, in the case of an axle, the left and right half-shafts). This ensures they revolve at the same speed and traction is regained. Diff-lock is usually engaged for difficult off-road conditions but should never remain engaged on hard grippy roads.

Differential casing. Not to be confused with the centre differential. Each axle, of course, has a normal cross-axle differential at the point where the propeller shaft from the transfer gearbox meets the axle. The size of the crown wheel and pinion plus differential demands a bulge in the axle casing – referred to as the diff casing. It has special significance in off-road vehicles because it is the lowest point of the axle and thus the point of least ground clearance – diagram, p.3.9.

Direct injection. See Indirect injection!

Discontinuity of rolling contact. Generic term for wheelspin and wheel slide – as on locked brakes. See Continuous rolling contact, above.

Divergent. A dynamic condition that 'gets worse of its own accord' – eg an oscillation of ever-increasing amplitude or a turn that, once initiated, tightens up on its own. See also Oversteer, divergent.

DPF. Diesel particulate filter. An exhaust after-treatment to trap small particles of soot – see pp.7.22-25.

Electric parkbrake. Electrically actuated parking brakes found on some recent 4x4s. Beware flat battery etc.

Electric range change. Method of shifting transfer gears by pressing a button or turning a switch instead of by manual lever.

ETC – Electronic traction control. See 'Traction control'.

Emergency flotation (tyre pressure). Very low tyre pressure (50-60% of normal road pressures), always associated with a low maximum permitted speed (20kph or 12mph) used for traversing or recovery from very soft ground. Such low pressures cause extreme tyre sidewall flexing, hence the speed limitation. See p.4.27 and pp.8.10-13.

Emergency soft. Another name for emergency flotation tyre pressure – above.

Engine braking. Vehicle retardation derived from engaging a low gear and taking your foot off the throttle. See also pp.4.20, 6.8.

Fesh-fesh. Desert terrain: a thin crust of fine gravel or windblown sand laid over deep very fine dust of powder consistency – usually gypsum – often found in hollows around chalky outcrops.. Can be bad enough to bog a vehicle. Hard to spot due to overlay of normal-looking sand. See p.4.31.

Flotation. Characteristic of a vehicle, by reason of large softly inflated tyres, not to sink on soft going such as mud or sand. See pp.4.24-27, 8.13.

Four-wheel drive (4x4). Vehicle transmission system in which engine power is applied to all four wheels. The term '4x4' (four by four) has the specific connotation that it is a four (wheeled vehicle driven) by four (wheels). See p.1.4

Full-time 4x4. A transmission system on a four-wheeled vehicle in which all four wheels are driven by the engine all the time. (As opposed to a vehicle that is normally in two-wheel drive with four-wheel drive selected by a separate lever or button when required.) See p.2.11.

Gerotor. Hydraulically engaged multi-plate clutch used in diff locks in Jeep's earlier versions of Quadra-Drive 2. See also Haldex coupling, p 2.17.

Geometric limitations. A term coined for this book to describe the limitations and extent of approach and departure angles, ramp angle, steering lock, articulation. See p.3.8

GDI. See Indirect injection, next page.

Ground clearance. Space between the ground and a given mechanical part of the vehicle. Usually, when quoted for a vehicle, taken as the least for any component on the vehicle – the space under the differential casing. But note difference between under-axle and under-belly clearance – see diagram p.3.9.

Ground offset. Sometimes also called 'steering offset' and concerns what is happening at the point the front tyres touch the ground. Ground offset is the lateral distance, when viewed from the front, between the centre line of the front wheel at ground level and the point where the extension of the steering swivel pin (or king pin) axis touches the ground. Ground offset influences the amount of 'drag' present at each front wheel tending to splay the front wheels outward from each other. When ground offset is positive (the norm) these forces cancel out, side-to-side, in normal straight, hard-road driving. But if, say, the left wheel hits a bump or soft patch the offset drag on that wheel will exceed the drag on the right wheel and cause the steering to also pull to the left. Off-road, the condition is greatly magnified. If one wheel goes through thick 'draggy' mud off-road, or hits a large bump, steering feel and the feedback of shock is considerable, hence the need for a steering damper. Zero offset is the ideal but very hard to achieve with the complexities of all-wheel drive and brakes to cram into the relatively small space of a front wheel. Designers are getting better at it. Land Rover products used to have ground offset approaching three inches but the 'P38' Range Rover reduced ground offset to 17mm, enabling use of recirculating ball steering system instead of the feedback-absorbing worm and roller of yesteryear. Some light 4x4s with very small ground offset use high-feedback rack and pinion steering.

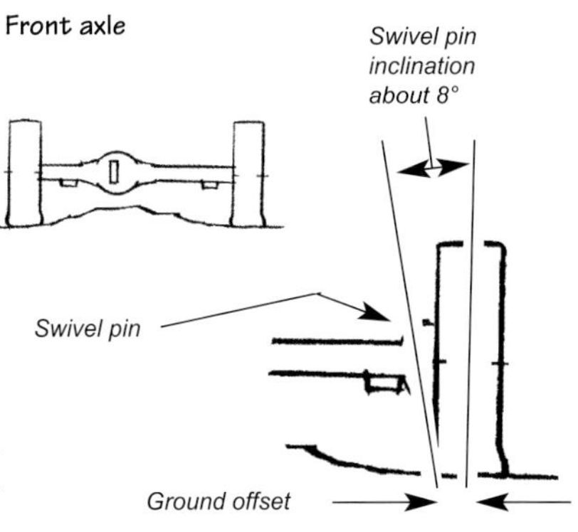

Ground stress. Term coined for this book to indicate how much strength is being asked of a particular piece of ground in terms of flotation or lateral shear to accommodate traction, braking or acceleration. See p.4.24.

GVW. Gross Vehicle Weight – the maximum permitted laden weight of a vehicle including payload, fuel and driver. This is the figure for which the entire vehicle is designed and stressed. To exceed it is to endanger its durability and safety.

Haldex. An auto-engage 4x4 driveline system. See p.2.17.

Half-shaft. The shafts taking drive from the axle differential to each wheel.

Handbrake. What it sounds like, usually implemented by small drum brakes on the rear wheels, even if disc brakes are standard. See also Transmission brake, p.9.13. See also 'Electric parkbrake'.

Harmonics. Here taken as relating to the natural frequency of a vehicle's suspension system that can influence the formation of transverse surface corrugations on unsurfaced tracks. See p.4.34.

HDC – Hill Descent Control. A method, pioneered by Land Rover, using ABS and throttle control, for keeping a vehicle at or below a target speed enabling slow, controlled descents to be made on very steep slippery off-road hills.

Heel and toe wear. Jargon for the uneven front to rear wear on individual blocks of a chunky off-road tyre tread when used for extended periods on roads. Affects on-road grip; see p.8.9, 'Mud tyre' and 'Sand tyre'.

Hi-lift jack. Versatile lever-operated mechanical bumper jack capable of a lift of about a metre. See p.5.5.

Hi-lo lever. Term sometimes used to describe the transfer gearbox range change lever.See p.2.13.

High box. Transmission status when the two-speed transfer gearbox lever is in the high ratio position – for normal, on-road, day-to-day use. See p.2.13.

High load suspension. An option on some vehicles (stronger, dual-rate rear springs) enabling GVW and payload to be raised.

High ratio, high range. Term to describe the transmission when the transfer gearbox lever is in the high position – high box above.

Hydraulic tappets. Method of operating the engine cylinder valves incorporating what is in effect an oil-filled section of the operating rod. Method is 'self-adjusting', eliminates need for. and noise emanating from. 'valve clearances' associated with normal actuation method.

Hydraulic winch. Winch with rotational function actuated by a hydraulic motor. Power source is hydraulic pump mounted on power take off at rear of gearbox. See p.5.14. Some add-on winches work using the vehicle's own power-steering pump.

Independent suspension. Suspension system in which each wheel is separately sprung rather than being attached to a common beam axle. See diagram p.3.9.

Indirect injection. Diesel fuel injection system in which fuel is injected into a pre-combustion chamber separate from the cylinder. With direct injection, the fuel is sprayed directly into the top of the cylinder – more power, more economical, noisier. GDI – gasoline direct injection – has now come to petrol engines offering very lean burn, good economy.

Kerb weight. As defined by EEC, empty vehicle plus full fuel tank plus 75kg driver.

King pin. See Swivel pin.

Leading link. Axle locating component. See Trailing/leading link.

Leaf-springs. Suspension system that combines a springing medium with axle location both longitudinally and laterally. Semi-elliptic 'cart springs' anchored at the front, attached to a swivelling link at the rear end. Usually used as rear suspension (front too, sometimes) in pickups and a number of US 4x4s. See Table,p.7.17.

Levelled suspension. A means of eliminating the squat of the rear suspension under load using a hydraulic self-levelling unit or air in air suspension. In the latter case, some vehicles (eg Discovery, Range Rover and – p.2.34 – Land Cruiser) offer extreme high position for off-road use, or squat to ease the attachment of a caravan for towing.

Low box. Low range; when the transfer gearbox lever (or button) is in the low position – used for difficult off-road conditions demanding greater traction or low speed control. See p.2.13.

Low ratio, low range. Term to describe the transmission when transfer gearbox lever is in the low position. See Low box above.

Low-SAPS oil. Engine oil formulated to be low in sulphated ash, and phosphorous and thus less likely to damage exhaust diesel particulate filters (DPFs) on Euro 5 emissions-compliant engines. Mobil calls this an 'ESP' (exhaust system protection) oil. See also DPF and pp.7.22-25.

M+S tyres. 'Mud and snow' tyres. A generic term for 4x4 tyres with a road-oriented, not especially bold, tread pattern suitable for mild snow and mud conditions. Now rather superseded by the 'All terrain' description. See Section 8.2, Tyres.

Marshalling. ('Marshaller' derived from ground-crew who marshal aircraft at airports.) In the context of off-road operations, the detailed direction of a vehicle by a marshaller outside the vehicle who is able to see all four wheels and also the difficult ground being traversed. Marshalling should be undertaken when there is the danger of damaging tyre sidewalls or the underside of the vehicle on rocks or other obstacles. See Look before you leap, Section 3.5.

Mechanical sympathy. In the context of this book, concern for and empathy with the structural stress, durability of, and possible damage to mechanical components of your vehicle. In a phrase, caring about your 4x4. See Mind-set, p.3.2.

Mud tyres. Bold, open-tread tyres optimised for mud with noise and grip disadvantages on hard roads. Seep.8.9, Tyres.

Multigrade oil. Lubricating oil exhibiting characteristics of a thin oil at low temperatures and a thick oil at high temperatures. See pp.7.24-29.

NATO towing hook. Large, robust, four-bolt attachment, towing pintle with top-closure originally specified for NATO 7.5 tonne military vehicles. Suitable for off-road towing ; noisy, due to trailer towing eye not being a close fit over the hook. See p.4.6.

Nose load. Trailers should be nose heavy in order to avoid weaving instability; the nose load is the amount of nose-heaviness measured at the tow-hitch and must be considered part of the towing vehicle's payload. See p.4.7.

NVH. Abbreviation for 'noise, vibration and harshness', an affliction the engineers try very hard to eliminate by the likes of carefully tuned power train mounts, suspension isolation pads, air suspension etc.

OEM or OE. Abbreviation for 'original equipment manufacturer', usually referring to tyres as supplied on a vehicle when bought from the factory.

On-foot recce. Inspecting a difficult off-road obstacle on foot before committing your vehicle to it. See p.3.12.

Overrun brakes. Trailer brakes activated by the tendency of the trailer to overtake – or overrun – the towing vehicle when the vehicle brakes or slows down. See p.4.9.

Oversteer, divergent. Tendency for an initiated steering command to 'run away' toward full lock (p.4.18) or for an extremely nose-heavy trailer to cause this condition on a fast, sharp bend (p.4.9) . See Steering feel.

Over-torque. Used in this book to convey the concept of applying too much torque (or power) to the wheels so that they break their grip with the ground and spin.

Panhard rod. A suspension component, a rod of the order of 30 mm diameter and about a metre long, that laterally locates a front or rear axle relative to the chassis. One end is attached and pivoted to the (say, right hand) chassis member and the other end to the (in this case, left hand) end of the axle. The arrangement permits vertical movement of the axle, and articulation, whilst constraining lateral movement relative to the chassis. See 'Anatomy', p.9.2.

Part-time 4x4. See Selectable four-wheel drive, facing page and p.2.11.

Permanent four-wheel drive. See Full-time 4x4, above and p.2.11 *et seq*.

Power take-off. Attachment to rear of gearbox for running accessories such as hydraulic pumps or shaft drives to winches and saws.

PTO. See Power take-off above.

Radial ply tyre. (See diagram p.9.5 under heading 'Cross-ply tyres'.) A type of tyre construction originated by Michelin in the 1950's and now almost universally adopted by all makers, in which sidewall structural plies run radially (ie. as if from the centre of the wheel) out towards the tread instead of criss-cross diagonally. With their thinner, more flexible sidewalls, radial tyres have lower rolling resistance than cross-ply tyres (yielding better fuel consumption) as well as giving longer tread life. They can accommodate the use of low inflation pressures off-road without overheating, again due to their flexible sidewalls, but are sometimes more prone to sidewall damage when operating in rocky or stony conditions. Because radial tyres invariably also have a braced tread area of great dimensional stability, they 'track-lay' the tread (like a tank), do not suffer from 'tread shuffle' and so achieve more traction in limiting off-road conditions.

Ramp angle. A measure of vehicle under-belly clearance or the ability to drive over a sharp ridge or ramp without touching the underside of the vehicle on the obstacle. A short wheelbase vehicle with large wheels will have the smallest ramp angle and best under-belly clearance. See diagram and text p.3.8.

Ramp breakover angle. The fuller title of Ramp angle, above.

Range change. Term sometimes used for the transfer gearbox lever. See p-.2.40.

Rolling contact – see Continuous rolling contact.

Salt flat. Salt marsh (also known as 'chott' or 'sebkha' – see p.4.28) of very unreliable consistency and bearing strength found in desert regions – inland as well as near coasts – and characterised by a top crust of varying thickness and strength with soft salt mud of great depth beneath it. Very dangerous to drive over.

Sand ladders. A pair of aluminium ladders, about 170cm long, specially made with rungs closer than normal, to lay beneath the vehicle wheels in soft sand to give grip and flotation. See p.5.3.

Sand tracks, sand channels. Generic name often given to any item fulfilling the role of a sand ladder, eg PSP (pierced steel planking), articulated grips. See p.5.3.

Sand tyres. Term often used to mean *desert* tyre – which implies an ability to cope with desert rock and stones as well as sand. These tyres are characterised by tread blocks of a gentle, shouldered profile with no bold, right-angled edges such as a mud tyre would have. Radial construction is far more suited to the low inflation pressures sometimes used in sand. Despite their appearance, smooth 'balloon' or 'aircraft' tyres with circumferential groove treads are far less effective in sand than a radial such as the Michelin XS. See pp.4.31, 8.9,

Sebkha. See Salt flat above.

Selectable four-wheel drive. Also known as 'part-time 4x4', a four-wheeled vehicle which proceeds normally in two-wheel drive but on which, by means of a lever or button control, four-wheel drive may be selected. It is important to remember that such vehicles in four-wheel drive seldom have the benefit of a centre differential so should not be used on hard roads or firm grippy surfaces in this mode. See p.2.11.

Self-centring. The characteristic of steered wheels to resume the straight-ahead position due to castor angle (see Castor angle, p.9.4) when the steering wheel is released. This characteristic can be utilised to enhance safety when driving in deep wheel ruts on slippery ground. See pp.4.11 and Steering feel, this page.

Self-levelling suspension. See Levelled suspension.

Sidewall. The external 'walls' of a tyre between the tread and the bead or wheel rim. This area is particularly vulnerable on radial ply tyres to damage in off-road operations from side-swiping sharp rocks. Driver awareness essential. See p.4.34..

Sidewall deflection. Outward movement of the tyre sidewall in the region of the ground contact patch. This is a normal phenomenon but can also be caused by inflation pressures being too low or hitting a sharp

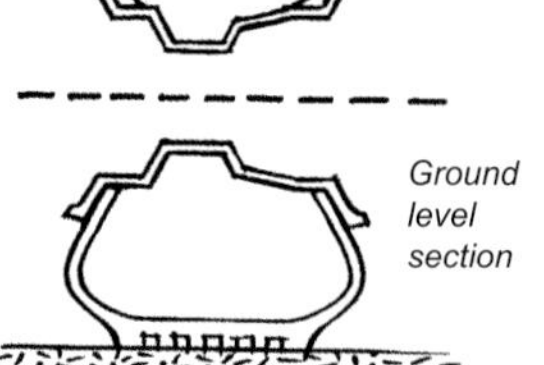

bump with excess speed. It is fundamentally important not to run tyres at less than the recommended inflation pressures for given maximum speeds and loads (see table p.8.13). If these limitations are not observed you will exceed the manufacturer's specified limits for sidewall deflection and thus cause overheating and serious damage to the tyre.

Shock loading. In the context of this book, taken to mean the arrest of mechanical motion in an excessively abrupt way or the application of sharp load reversals in such a way as to risk structural failure. For example, the application of a transmission handbrake whilst the vehicle is in motion, the sharp arrest of a spinning wheel on a rock or the forced engagement of low ratio transfer gears can cause unacceptable shock loading of the axle half-shafts. (See Transmission brake, next page.) Engaging diff lock whilst one or more wheel is spinning could also result in severe and damaging shock load to the transmission (See also Mechanical sympathy, pp.3.2, 9.9.)

Small gear lever. Don't be embarrassed if you can't remember the name for the transfer gear lever..! See p.2.40.

Snatch tow. A method of recovering a stuck vehicle in which the towing vehicle is in motion before taking up the slack in the tow rope. A potentially very dangerous and extremely specialised procedure demanding special-purpose stretch ropes and precise methods. The chief, and likely, hazards derive from broken ropes or attachments breaking away from the vehicle to hazard bystanders or the vehicles involved. See Recovery – snatch towing, See p.5.11.

'Soft-roader'. Common usage term to describe a 4x4 vehicle not designed for arduous off-road use and thus not equipped with a two-speed transfer gearbox providing low-range gears - see 'Transfer gearbox', next spread. 'Soft roaders' are also usually equipped with auto-engaged 4x4 systems – see page 2.14

Steering feel. Steering feel is a vital and safety-relevant ingredient of the feedback between vehicle and driver. The communication is achieved almost entirely by assimilating the amount of self-centring or castor action present and how it compares with normal on-road conditions. (See first Castor action and Castor angle above – p.9.4.) It is important for drivers always to be alert to variations in steering feel and to know what may cause them. A very brief summary follows:

1. Power steering. On most off-roaders steering is power assisted so feel is retained at all times. In most Land Rovers, for instance, the centre 6°, ie 3° either side of straight ahead, is not power assisted and this aids straight-ahead feel. Be alert to the possibility of inexperienced mechanics having adjusted this out. Electric power steering is more energy efficient in that a hydraulic pump does not have to be running all the time. After an initially poor reception from the pundits, it is now an effective and accepted innovation.

2. In slippery ruts accurate feel – the correlation between steering command, resistance at the wheel and the behaviour of the vehicle – will be lost because the wheels will not grip the sides of the ruts. Because of this you will find it hard to know exactly which way your wheels are pointing. It is essential to check visually until back on normal ground – see photos p.4.11.

3. In soft sand, as noted above, the effective ground contact point may well be ahead of, rather than behind, the swivel pin axis (see diagram p.9.4) and this can give 'negative castor action' effect – ie a tendency for the wheels to run away to full lock. This will be particularly – and dangerously – apparent when descending the slip face of a sand dune. Grip the steering wheel firmly with both hands and, down a sand-fall, have a marshaller guide you. Watch the marshaller – he is the only one who can tell which way your front wheels are pointing.

4. Rock or rough ground. Whilst the steering design and power assistance of most 4x4s is optimised for on- and off-road driving, be aware of the potential for serious kickback when traversing rough ground, rocks and boulders. If the vehicle's steering geometry includes large ground offset (eg early Land Rovers, see Ground offset, p.9.7), one wheel sidewalling an obstructive rock will cause excessive sharp kickback to that side. Grip the steering wheel firmly and keep your thumbs outside the rim so that sudden, unexpected kickback does not cause injury.

5. Ice, snow, slippery conditions – on road. This will be well-enough known to experienced 4x2 drivers but is still worth mentioning here since the same laws of physics apply to 4x4s. When grip is at a premium obviously the self-centring of the front wheels will be dramatically diminished – ie castor action will be all but absent – and that heart-sinking 'lightness' of the steering wheel will be experienced. As in a surprising number of off-road situations, really delicate 'finger-tip' steering and 'the midwife's touch' are the order of the day. Plug in the sensory amplifiers.

Steering lock. Extent to which the steering wheel may be moved to the right or left. 'Full lock' implies movement of the steering wheel as far as it will go, right or left.

Steering offset. See Ground offset, p.9.7.

Survey on foot. Inspect before you drive. See On-foot recce, above and p.3.12.

Swivel pin. Sometimes known as king pin. The axis about which a front wheel pivots in order to effect steering. Swivel pin axes are invariably inclined aft to achieve a castor angle or trail thus providing self-centring – see p.9.4, Castor angle. When viewed from the front, the swivel pin lower end is further outboard than the top end. This inclination helps reduce ground offset and improves steering in other respects. See diagram at p.9.7, Ground offset.

Swivel pin inclination. Relates to steering geometry. See above.

Synthetic oils. Advanced lubricating oils for engines and transmissions demonstrating exceptional stability, film strength and less volatility (so less tendency to 'boil off'). Traditionally, engines should not be run-in using these oils but once carefully bedded-in (2000-3000 miles) on mineral oils, wear will be dramatically reduced by use of synthetics. However, many modern engines come factory-filled with a semi-synthetic from new. It'll usually be difficult to find anyone at your dealership who can advise but it's worth finding our the situation with your new vehicle. Often blended with mineral or special oils and sold as 'Semi-synthetic' or 'Part-synthetic' – usually with around 30% full-synthetic content.

TBN. (Total base number). A characteristic of engine lubricants indicative of the its ability to neutralise the corrosive acid contamination of that oil by high-sulphur diesel fuels encountered overseas. For an indirect-injection diesel aim for 20x the sulphur content, for a direct-injection, 10x. For example, a high sulphur fuel (Turkey, say) at 0.70% demands a TBN of 20x0.7 = 14 for an indirect-injection engine. See pp.7.23, 7.26 re fuels and the TBN of typical oils.

'Terrain Response'. A trade name and concept, peculiar to Land Rover vehicles, for tuning automatic transmission change points, throttle response and diff lock settings according to the off-road terrain being negotiated – eg ice and snow, mud and ruts, sand, rocks. Terrain response mode is selectable on a rotary switch. See pp.2.36, 3.6.

Toe-in / toe-out. Amount by which front wheels, in plan view, are not parallel to each other. This is a designed-in feature that affects handling and steering feel and there are defined limits for each vehicle.

Traction. In the context of this book the concept of achieving grip between the wheels and the ground without slip, skid or sinkage.

Traction control. This inhibits wheelspin by applying brake to a spinning front or rear wheel and thus enhances traction on ice, snow or in severe off-road conditions. It is usually an automatic function though may be switchable. It utilises ABS sensors for wheel speed determination and brakes the spinning wheel and thus applies, through the axle differential, torque to the stationary wheel. Like ABS, it is especially effective in maintaining control when one side of the vehicle is on a more slippery surface than the other – a so-called 'split-μ' surface (pron: 'split-mu'). Often a dashboard light illuminates when the system is operating. The function is usually inhibited above a certain speed to preclude overheating Can be a good day-to-day aid to off-road traction if the cut-in time is not too extended but in serious, continuous, on-the-limit off-road driving a solid mechanical – and mechanically engaged – diff-lock is better. See pp.2.19, 3.6.

Tractive effort. The amount of 'pull' exerted by a vehicle as a result of traction.

Trailer nose load. See Nose load, p.9.9 above and p.4.7.

Trailer preponderance. Term sometimes used to denote down-load on the vehicle towing hitch – see Nose load, p.9.9 above and Towing – on-road, p.4.2.

Trailing link / leading link. These are suspension components (see large diagram, p.9.2) that locate a coil- or air-sprung axle fore and aft relative to the chassis, allowing it to rise and fall as required whilst also transmitting braking loads and thrust from the wheels. Used in conjunction with a laterally locating Panhard rod (or an A-frame) to locate an axle totally and associated with what is often termed 'five-link' suspension.

Transfer gear lever. The 'small gear lever', in the cab next to the main gear lever. It controls whether the transmission is in 'high range' or 'low range' in the transfer box – and in selectable 4x4 vehicles, whether 4x2 or 4x4 is in use. The same lever often controls the engagement of the centre diff lock. Many 4x4s now have an electrically operated, switch-controlled range change

Transfer gearbox. Originally the name implied the transfer of power from the main gearbox to the front axle as well as the rear axle on a four-wheel drive vehicle. In many off-roaders a two-speed transfer box is fitted, thus providing low range gears as well as high range. Here the transfer gearbox has the additional role of permitting power from the main gearbox to go to the axles at normal 1:1 gearing (high range) or geared down, usually by around 2:1 (low range). So-called 'soft-roaders' usually do not have a two-speed transfer gearbox. See diagram p.2.12.

Transmission brake. The handbrake on Land Rover Defenders and other early models, traditionally, operates through a single large brake drum on the rear propeller shaft at the point where it leaves the transfer gearbox and is thus called a transmission brake. By doing this, when the vehicle is in four-wheel drive it was in effect a handbrake on all four wheels. (Except for certain Freelander and Evoque models, current Land Rover products have permanent 4x4, but early models did not)

To be safe using the transmission brake on a slope off-road, the centre diff lock should be engaged. Even then, there are conditions of near-limits articulation where the axle differentials will permit the handbrake to fail in its primary function; be sure all four wheels are firmly on the ground. The same transmission brake principle is used on 4x4 Bedford trucks. On any vehicle it should be used as a parking brake only and should *never be operated whilst the vehicle is in motion* except in emergency.

Transmission wind-up. Read first 'Centre differential', p.9.4. A 4x4 with no centre differential (ie a 'Type 1', selectable 4x4 – see p.2.11) or one driven with the centre diff locked (ie in both cases the front and rear propeller shafts are locked together) is unable to accommodate the small differences in distance normally travelled by the front wheels compared to the rear wheels.

The diff-lock ensures both propeller shafts rotate exactly the same amount despite the small differences in distance actually travelled. This results in some wheel slip and scuff which, on loose ground, can take place without any harm. On hard roads, however, the superior wheel grip makes it difficult for the wheels to slip much and in the process of trying to do so considerable torsional stress builds up in the transmission.

This is known as transmission wind-up and can sometimes exert so much stress that the diff-lock gears (or the selectors for engaging 4x4 from 4x2) will not disengage when so selected. You will also sense very heavy steering.

If this occurs due to your forgetting to de-select diff-lock (or four-wheel drive) on hard ground and the diff lock or 4x4 lever will not disengage, the solution is to reverse the vehicle some distance until the selectors are free (depress the clutch and give the lever a sharp thump) and/or the diff-lock warning light extinguishes. (Note, despite there being no centre diff there either, none of this applies to a 'Type 2' (p 2.11 diagram) auto-engage, 'soft roader' since the front-rear prop shafts can accommodate some slip.)

Tyre sidewall markings. Details of all information inscribed on the sidewalls of tyres is indicated at p.8.17.

Unladen. Vehicle carrying full fuel tank, driver but no payload or other load – see Kerb weight, p.9.8.

Viscous coupling unit (VCU). Imagine two shafts facing each other end-to end. On the end of one shaft is, conceptually, a jam jar, internally splined – which overlaps the second shaft so that one shaft (externally splined) is inside the hollow end of the other. A classic viscous coupling (VC) between two shafts is a bit like that. It consists of interleaved vanes, alternate vanes being splined to each shaft. So vane 1 is splined to the 'jam jar'; and vane 2 is splined to the shaft inside the 'jam jar'. Special silicone fluid takes up the space between the vanes.

A VC has the paradoxical characteristic that when one shaft moves at a markedly different speed to its neighbour, the viscous fluid is 'stirred' and very soon locks the vanes together, inhibiting relative movement and causing both shafts to move as one. You have the makings of an automatic diff-lock.

A typical application for a VC is to engage 4x4 on a basically front-wheel drive vehicle when the front wheels spin due to poor traction conditions. The difference in rotational speed between front prop shaft and the rear prop shaft causes the VC to lock-up and transfer drive to the rear axle as well. However the lock is not 100% and there is a time delay before it does what it does.

Viscous coupling pre-load. In Land Rover's first generation Freelanders (and Fiat's Ducato van before that) with a VC between front and rear prop shaft, slightly different front and rear axle ratios caused the prop shafts to turn at slightly different speeds even without obvious front wheel spin.

Thus the VC is in a part-locked condition all the time and transferring some power – about 10% – to the rear axle. A neat idea.

Wading plugs. Applicable to older Land Rovers. Insert before fording streams of deeper water. See p.4.36.

Wheel movement. The phrase generally used in the context of maximum available vertical suspension movement at each wheel. This is of major importance to an off-roader in the pursuit of maximum axle articulation (see Articulation, p.9.3 et al). Long-travel coil springs are the classic solution to this pioneered by early Range Rovers.

But associated body roll displeased mainly on-road users and roll-inhibiting devices like anti-roll bars are now limiting axle movement relative to the body. Manufacturers are using traction control in the off-road case to deal with any wheelspin resulting from more limited wheel movement on very uneven ground.

Wheel-slide. See above Discontinuity of rolling contact, p.9.6 and diagram, p.3.6. A condition in which one or more wheels slide over a slippery surface rather than rolling over it. Wheel slide can be provoked by brake lock-up or excessive engine braking – for which also see Section 6.4.

Wheelspin. See Discontinuity of rolling contact, p.9.6 and diagram, p.3.6. A condition in which a stationary or moving vehicle has power applied to the transmission in conditions of poor grip and one or more wheels spins without associated forward motion (or rearward if in reverse). See Gentle right foot, p.3.6, dealing with control of throttle and brake.

Zero offset. Refers to steering geometry – see 'Ground offset' p.9.7 diagram.

Published by

Desert Winds Publishing, 44 Salusbury Lane, SG5 3EG, England

Written, illustrated, designed and produced by Tom Sheppard, MBE

 British Library Cataloguing in Publication Data: A catalogue record for this book available from British Library.

First published as *Off-roader driving,* Edn 1, 1999; Edn 1.2 2005. *Four-by-four driving,* Edn 1, 2006,

Four-by-four driving, Edition 2, 2011

This book, third edition, published 2013

ISBN 978-0-9532324-9-9

Graphics – 282 photographs, 100 drawings

Grateful thanks and acknowledgement for corporate PR, or purchased, photography ...

Including: Autocar, Roger Crathorne, Nick Dimbleby, Mike Hallett, Simon Herd, Toby Savage,

Remaining c.200 photographs: Tom Sheppard.

Author's acknowledgments

This book has evolved from – way back – the first two editions of *The Land Rover Experience*, and two editions of *Off-roader driving*. Plus some influence from the three years' work on (and subsequent three new editions of) *Vehicle-dependent Expedition Guide.* For their invaluable assistance with those books – and with bits of this one – I would like to express grateful thanks to:

BMW Group UK (Alan Goodchild), Fiat-Jeep UK (Steve Rose, Barry Stallard, Tom Johnston, Steve Mirfin), BP-Castrol (Elspeth Barley), ExxonMobil (Dr Mike Wharton and Robin Gregory), Devil's Pit (Simon and Kathleen Smith), Fortune Promoseven, Dubai (Matt Jones and family), Fresh Tracks (Daniel Collins), Haldex AB, Sweden (Sebastian Quick), Hertfordshire County Council, Rights of Way Dept (Richard Cuthbert), Michelin Tyres (Steve Dolby, Alan Baxter, Jeremy Wheeler), Nissan UK (Terry Steeden), John Nowell (Dubai), Paul O'Connor, Geoff Renner, Superwinch (Terry Mason), Suzuki GB (Alun Parry, John Brambley), Toyota GB (David Crouch, Richard Seymour), Volkswagen UK (Nicki Finlayson)

At Land Rover: John Carter, Bob Dillon, Neil Doswell, Colin Hill, Phil Jones, Tony Northway (Dubai), Tim Pettit, Karl Richards. And of course, Roger Crathorne.

The pre-distillation analysis for Section 4.1 (On-road towing) was particularly demanding and special thanks go to Brian Bevan (The Motor Industry Research Association and IMechE paper C132/83), Professor Robin Sharp (Cranfield University), and Malcolm Burgess (Land Rover) for their help.

It's hard to know who to thank for the inspiration and breathtaking beauty of the remote regions of Algeria, Botswana, Libya, Mali, Namibia, Oman, South Africa, the United Arab Emirates and Zimbabwe portrayed here photographically.

And there would be no book at all without the typically unsung designers and digital technorati at Apple, Epson, QuarkXpress, Adobe computer software (Photoshop, Acrobat and Illustrator) and the wizards at Canon and Ricoh cameras. Heroes all; may they prosper, sup wine and peel grapes to a contented old age.